P9-CCY-142

Chapter In Review Cards at the back of the Student Edition provide students a portable study tool containing all of the pertinent information for class preparation.

THE

COMM
Are you in?

SOLUTION

ONLINE RESOURCES INCLUDED!

CourseMate   **Engaging. Trackable. Affordable.**

CourseMate brings course concepts to life with extra problem sets, and interactive learning, study, and exam preparation tools that support COMM2.

FOR INSTRUCTORS:
- Custom Options through 4LTR+ Program
- Instructor's Manual
- Test Bank
- PowerPoint® Slides
- Instructor Prep Cards
- Engagement Tracker

FOR STUDENTS:
- Interactive eBook
- Auto-Graded Quizzes
- Flashcards
- Games: Crossword Puzzles and more
- PowerPoint® Slides
- Speech Builder Express
- Videos
- Simulations
- Student Review Cards
- Web links

Students sign in at
www.cengagebrain.com

WADSWORTH
CENGAGE Learning™

COMM2
Rudolph F. Verderber
Kathleen S. Verderber
Deanna D. Sellnow

Editor-in-Chief: PJ Boardman

Sr. Publisher: Lyn Uhl

Executive Editor: Monica Eckman

Sr. Developmental Editor: Greer Lleuad

Developmental Editor: John Choi, B-books, Ltd.

Assistant Editor: Rebekah Matthews

Editorial Assistant: Colin Solan

Executive Brand Marketing Manager,
    4LTR Press: Robin Lucas

Project Manager, 4LTR Press: Kelli Strieby

Marketing Director: Jason Sakos

Marketing Manager: Amy Whitaker

Marketing Coordinator: Gurpreet S. Saran

Sr. Marketing Communications Manager:
    Tami Strang

Rights Acquisitions Specialist: Mandy Groszko

Production Director: Amy McGuire,
    B-books, Ltd.

Content Project Manager: Corinna Dibble

Media Editor: Jessica Badiner

Manufacturing Manager: Denise Powers

Production Service: B-books, Ltd.

Art Director: Linda Helcher

Internal Designer: Beckmeyer Design

Cover Designer: Lisa Kuhn

Cover Image: Jupiterimages/Comstock Images/
    © Getty Images

Photo Researcher: Sam Marshall

© 2012, 2009 Wadsworth, Cengage Learning

ALL RIGHTS RESERVED. No part of this work covered by the copyright herein may be reproduced, transmitted, stored or used in any form or by any means graphic, electronic, or mechanical, including but not limited to photocopying, recording, scanning, digitizing, taping, Web distribution, information networks, or information storage and retrieval systems, except as permitted under Section 107 or 108 of the 1976 United States Copyright Act, without the prior written permission of the publisher.

For product information and technology assistance, contact us at
Cengage Learning Customer & Sales Support, 1-800-354-9706

For permission to use material from this text or product,
submit all requests online at **www.cengage.com/permissions.**
Further permissions questions can be e-mailed to
permissionrequest@cengage.com

Library of Congress Control Number: 2010934182

ISBN-13: 978-0-495-91448-8
ISBN-10: 0-495-91448-7

Wadsworth
20 Channel Center Street
Boston, MA 02210
USA

Cengage Learning is a leading provider of customized learning solutions with office locations around the globe, including Singapore, the United Kingdom, Australia, Mexico, Brazil and Japan. Locate your local office at **international.cengage.com/region**

For your course and learning solutions, visit **www.cengage.com**
Purchase any of our products at your local college store or at our preferred online store **www.cengagebrain.com**

Printed in the United States of America
5 6 7 13 12

COMM2
Brief Contents

Learning Your Way

89% of students surveyed found the interactive online quizzes valuable.

We know that no two students are alike. **COMM** was developed to help you learn communication in a way that works for you.

Not only is the format fresh and contemporary, it's also concise and focused. And, **COMM** is loaded with a variety of supplements, like chapter review cards, printable flash cards, and more.

At **www.cengagebrain.com**, you'll find Speech Builder Express 3.0™, Interactive Quizzing, Downloads, Games and Simulations, and Interactive Video Activities to test your knowledge of key concepts, and plenty of resources to help you study no matter what learning style you like best!

COMM2 Contents

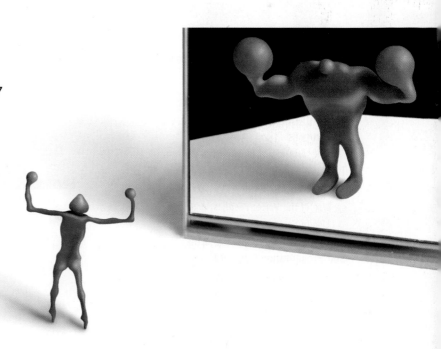

PART **2**   **Interpersonal Communication 62**

Online Tools

Check out all the study tools at
www.cengagebrain.com

- Interactive Videos
- Audio Study Tools
- InfoTrac
- Speech Builder Express
- Student Workbook
- Chapter Notepads
- Flashcards
- Interactive Quizzing

- Skill Learning Activities
- Action Step Activities
- Beat the Clock
- Quizbowl
- Crossword Puzzles
- Critical Thinking Activities
- Test Bank
- Power Point slides

www.cengagebrain.com

1

Communication
Perspectives

Learning Outcomes

LO[1]   Define the communication process and the settings in which communication takes place

LO[2]   Identify communication principles

LO[3]   Discover how to increase communication competence

> ## **"** *How effectively you communicate with others is important not only to your career but also to your personal relationships.* **"**

Numerous studies done over the years have shown that for almost any job, employers seek oral communication skills, teamwork skills, and interpersonal abilities (College learning for the new global century, 2008; Hansen & Hansen, 2007; Young, 2003). For example, an article on the role of communication in the workplace reported that in engineering, a highly technical field, speaking skills were very important for 72 percent of the employers surveyed (Darling & Dannels, 2003, p. 12). A survey by the National Association of Colleges and Employers (Koncz, 2008) reported the top 10 personal qualities and skills that employers seek from college graduates. The number one skill was communication, including face-to-face speaking, presentational speaking, and writing. Other skills ranked in the top 10 that you will learn about and practice in this course include teamwork skills (number three), analytical skills (number five), interpersonal skills (number eight), and problem-solving skills (number nine). The employers also said that these very skills are, unfortunately, the ones many new graduates lack. So this course can significantly increase your ability to get a job and be successful in your chosen career.

> **communication**
> the process of creating or sharing meaning in informal conversation, group interaction, or public speaking

What do you think?

I prefer to share my ideas in a group setting.

Strongly Disagree									*Strongly Agree*
1	2	3	4	5	6	7	8	9	10

How effectively you communicate with others is important not only to your career but also to your personal relationships. Your ability to make and keep friends, to be a good family member, to have satisfying intimate relationships, to participate in or lead groups, and to prepare and present speeches depends on your communication skills. During this course, you will learn about the communication process and have an opportunity to practice basic communication skills that will help you improve your relationships.

In this chapter, we begin by explaining the process of communication. Next, we describe several communication settings and how we'll address improving communication skills for them in this book. From there, we describe several fundamental principles of communication. Finally, we discuss communication competence, the role that managing communication apprehension plays in achieving it, and a strategy for improving your communication skills.

LO¹ The Communication Process

Communication is the process of creating or sharing meaning in informal conversation, group interaction, or public speaking. To understand how this process works, we begin by describing its essential elements: participants (who), messages (what), context (where), channels (how), interference (distractions), and feedback (reaction).

© WOJTEK KRYCZKA/ISTOCKPHOTO.COM

participants
individuals who assume the roles of senders and receivers during an interaction

messages
verbal utterances, visual images, and non-verbal behaviors to which meaning is attributed during communication

meanings
thoughts in our minds and interpretations of others' messages

symbols
words, sounds, and actions that are generally understood to represent ideas and feelings

encoding
the process of putting our thoughts and feelings into words and non-verbal cues

decoding
the process of interpreting another's message

Participants

Participants are the individuals who assume the roles of senders and receivers during an interaction. As senders, participants form and transmit messages using verbal symbols, visual images, and non-verbal behavior. As receivers, they interpret the messages that have been transmitted to them.

Messages

Messages are the verbal utterances, visual images, and non-verbal behaviors to which meaning is attributed during communication. To understand how messages are created and received, we need to understand meanings, symbols, encoding and decoding, and form (organization).

Meanings

Meanings include the thoughts in your mind as well as the interpretations you make of another's message. Meanings are the ways participants make sense of messages. It is important to realize that meanings are not transferred from one person to another, but are created together in an exchange. Some communication settings enable participants to verify that they have shared meanings; in other settings this is more difficult. For instance, if Sarah says to Tiffany that many female celebrities are unhealthily underweight, through the exchange of verbal messages they can together come to some degree of understanding of what that means. But if Sarah is giving a speech on the subject to an audience of 200 people, Tiffany's ability to question Sarah and negotiate a mutual meaning is limited. If Sarah shows a slideshow of before-and-after photographs of some of the celebrities she is referring to, she can make the meaning clear even for a large audience.

Symbols

To express yourself, you form messages made of verbal symbols (words), non-verbal cues (behaviors), and visual images. Symbols are words, sounds, and actions that represent specific ideas and feelings. As you speak, you choose word symbols to express your meaning. At the same time, you also use facial expressions, eye contact, gestures, and tone of voice—all symbolic, non-verbal cues—in an attempt to express your meaning. Your listeners make interpretations or attribute meaning to the messages they receive. When you offer your messages through a variety of symbols, the meaning you are trying to convey becomes clearer.

Encoding and Decoding

Encoding is the process of putting your thoughts and feelings into words, non-verbal cues, and images. Decoding is the process of interpreting another's message. Ordinarily, you do not consciously think about either the encoding or the decoding process. Only when there is a difficulty, such as speaking in a second language or having to use an easier vocabulary with children, do you become aware of encoding. You may not think about decoding until someone seems to speak in circles or uses unfamiliar technical words and you have difficulty interpreting or understanding what is being said. Have you ever taken a course where the instructor used lots of unfamiliar technical words? If so, how did that affect the decoding process for you?

Form (Organization)

When the meaning we wish to share is complex, we may need to organize it in sections or in a certain order. Message form is especially important when one person talks without interruption for a relatively long time, such as in a public speech or when reporting an event to a colleague at work. Visual images also need to be organized and in good form if they are to aid understanding.

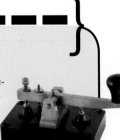

© ADRIO COMMUNICATIONS LTD/SHUTTERSTOCK

{ C ■ ● ■ ● O ■ ■ ■ M ■ ■ M ■ ■ 2 ● ● ■ ■ ■ }

Dot Dot Dot Dash Dash Dash

In 1836, Samuel Morse developed the telegraph. Using a key, an operator would tap a sequence of short and long elements, each one representing a letter, number, or punctuation mark. This revolutionized the world, since it allowed for near-instantaneous communication at a time when mail service could take weeks and months. In the modern age, Morse code continues to be used by pilots, air traffic controllers, and the military.

Context

Context is composed of the (1) physical, (2) social, (3) historical, (4) psychological, and (5) cultural situations in which a communication encounter occurs, including what precedes and follows what is said. According to noted German philosopher Jürgen Habermas, the ideal speech situation is impossible to achieve, but considering its contexts as we communicate with others can move us closer to that goal (Littlejohn & Foss, 2007, p. 335). The context affects the expectations of the participants, the meaning these participants derive, and their subsequent behavior.

Physical Context

The physical context includes the location, the environmental conditions (temperature, lighting, and noise level), the distance between communicators, and the time of day. Each of these factors can affect the communication. For instance, the meaning shared in a conversation may be affected by whether it is held in a crowded company cafeteria, an elegant candlelit restaurant, over the telephone, or on the Internet.

Today, more and more of our communication exchanges occur in technologically mediated spaces. When you call someone on your cell phone, for instance, you are in different physical places and your conversation will be influenced by the physical contexts each of you occupy as well as by the quality of your phone connection. Moreover, the messages and meaning are affected by whether the technology used is synchronous or asynchronous. Synchronous technologies allow us to exchange messages in real time, and asynchronous technologies allow delays between sending, receiving, and responding to messages. Telephone calls are synchronous, and voice mail messages and e-mail are asynchronous. Instant messages (IMs) and text messages may be either synchronous or asynchronous.

Social Context

The social context is the nature of the relationship between the participants. Whether communication takes place among family members, friends, acquaintances, work associates, or strangers influences what and how messages are formed, shared, and interpreted. For instance, most people change how they interact when talking with their parents or siblings as compared to how they interact when talking with their friends.

© ROBERTO A SANCHEZ/ISTOCKPHOTO.COM

How might this person's mood affect your conversation with him?

Historical Context

The historical context is the background provided by previous communication episodes between the participants. It influences understandings in the current encounter. For instance, suppose one morning Chad tells Shelby that he will pick up the rough draft of a paper they had given to their professor for feedback to help prepare the final manuscript. When Shelby joins Chad for lunch in the cafeteria, she says, "Did you get it?" Another person listening to the conversation would have no idea what the *it* is. Yet Chad may well reply, "It's on my desk." Shelby and Chad would understand each other because of the content of their earlier exchange.

Psychological Context

The psychological context includes the moods and feelings each person brings to the interpersonal encounter. For instance, suppose Corinne is under a lot of stress. While she is studying for an exam, a friend stops by and pleads with her to take a break and go to the gym with her. Corinne, who is normally good-natured, may explode with an angry tirade. Why? Because her stress level provides the psychological context within which she hears this message, and it affects how she responds.

Cultural Context

The cultural context includes the values, attitudes, beliefs, orientations, and underlying assumptions prevalent among people in a society (Samovar, Porter, & McDaniel, 2007, p. 20). Culture penetrates into every aspect of our lives, affecting how we think, talk, and behave. Each of us belongs to many cultural groups, though we may differ in how much we identify with each group. Mina, for example, was born in Taiwan

---

context the settings in which communication occurs, including what precedes and follows what is said

physical context the location, the environmental conditions (temperature, lighting, noise level), the distance between communicators, seating arrangements, and time of day

social context the nature of the relationship that exists between the participants

historical context the background provided by previous communication episodes between the participants that influence understandings in the current encounter

psychological context the mood and feelings each person brings to the conversation

cultural context the values, attitudes, beliefs, orientations, and underlying assumptions prevalent among people in a society

channel
both the route traveled by the message and the means of transportation

interference (noise)
any stimulus that interferes with the process of sharing meaning

physical interference
sights, sounds, and other stimuli in the environment that draw people's attention away from intended meaning

psychological interference
internal distractions based on thoughts, feelings, or emotional reactions to symbols

internal noise
thoughts and feelings that compete for attention and interfere with the communication process

semantic interference
distractions aroused by certain symbols that take our attention away from the main message

but was raised in Boston, where she attended Chinese elementary school. She is also a college student and a Democrat. Each of these groups helps characterize her cultural setting. When two people from different cultures interact, misunderstandings may occur because of the cultural variations between them. For example, the role of a "good student" in many Asian cultures typically means being quiet, respectful, and never challenging others' views, but the good-student role in U.S. classrooms often includes being talkative, being assertive, and debating the views expressed by others.

Channels

Channels are both the route traveled by the message and the means of transportation. Messages are transmitted through sensory channels. Face-to-face communication has three basic channels: verbal symbols, non-verbal cues, and visual images. Technologically mediated communication uses these same channels, though non-verbal cues such as movements, touch, and gestures are represented by visual symbols like emoticons (textual images that symbolize the sender's mood, emotion, or facial expressions) and acronyms (abbreviations that stand in for common phrases). For example, in a face-to-face interaction, Barry might express his frustration about a poor grade on an assignment by verbally noting why he thought the grade was unfair, by visually showing the assignment along with the grading criteria for

it, and by non-verbally raising his voice and shaking his fist. In an online interaction, he might insert a frowning-face emoticon (☹) or type "po'ed" to represent those non-verbal behaviors.

Interference (Noise)

Interference (noise) is any stimulus that hinders the process of sharing meaning. Interference can be physical (based on external sounds or images), psychological (based on internal distractions), or semantic (based on our emotional reaction to certain symbols).

Physical interference includes the sights, sounds, and other stimuli in the environment that draw people's attention away from intended meaning. For instance, while a friend is giving you instructions on how to work the new MP3 player, your attention may be drawn away by the external noise of your favorite TV show, which is on in the next room. External noise does not have to be a sound, however. Perhaps, while your friend is giving instructions, your attention is drawn momentarily to an attractive man or woman. Such visual distractions are also physical interference.

Psychological interference includes internal distractions based on thoughts, feelings, or emotional reactions to symbols and can fall into two categories: internal noise and semantic noise. Internal noise refers to the thoughts and feelings that compete for attention and interfere with the communication process. If you have ever tuned out the lecture your professor is giving and tuned into a daydream or a past conversation, then you have experienced internal noise.

Semantic interference refers to the distractions aroused by certain symbols that take our attention away from the main message. If a friend describes a 40-year-old secretary as "the girl in the office," and you think *girl* is an odd and condescending term for a 40-year-old woman, you might not even hear the rest of what your friend has to say. Whenever we react emotionally to a word or a behavior, we are experiencing semantic interference.

© PHIL MORLEY/ISTOCKPHOTO.COM

Anything that hinders the process of sharing meaning is **NOISE.**

Feedback

Feedback is the reactions and responses to a message that indicate to the sender whether and how that message was heard, seen, and interpreted. In face-to-face communication, we can express feedback verbally through words or non-verbally through body language. In online interactions, we can express feedback verbally through words or non-verbally through emoticons and acronyms. We continuously give feedback when we are listening to another, if only by paying attention, giving a confused look, or showing signs of boredom. Or we may give direct verbal feedback by saying, "I don't understand the point you are making" or "That's a great comment you just made." In online interactions, we might use an acronym like CC (I understand) or WDYM (What do you mean?).

A Model of the Basic Communication Process

Figure 1.1 illustrates the communication process between two people. In the minds of these people are meanings, thoughts, and feelings that they intend to share. These thoughts and feelings are created and shaped by the people's values, culture, environment, experiences, occupation, sex, interests, knowledge, and attitudes. To communicate a message, the sender encodes thoughts and feelings into messages that are sent using one or more channels.

The receiver decodes or interprets the symbols in an attempt to understand the speaker's mean-

ing. This decoding process is affected by the receiver's total field of experience—that is, by all the same factors that shape the encoding process. Feedback completes the process so that the sender and receiver can arrive at a similar understanding of the message.

feedback
reactions and responses
to messages

The model depicts the context as the area around the participants. This may include the physical, social, historical, psychological, and cultural contexts that permeate all parts of the process. Similarly, the model shows that during conversation, physical and psychological interference (noise)—including internal and semantic distractions—may interfere at various points and therefore affect the people's ability to arrive at similar meanings. As you might imagine, the process becomes more complex when more than two people are conversing or when someone is speaking to a large and diverse audience.

Communication Settings

Although the basic communication process describes how meanings are shared, you can learn some important skills that will help you communicate effectively across a variety of communication settings. Communication settings, also identified more formally as *communication contexts* by some scholars, describe the different environments within which we communicate (Littlejohn & Foss, 2008, pp. 52–53). In this book, we focus on intrapersonal, interpersonal, small group, and public communication settings.

Intrapersonal communication is essentially communicating with yourself. Usually we don't do this orally but rather by thinking through choices and possible consequences. When you sit in class and think about what you'll do later that day, you are communicating intrapersonally. Similarly, when you send yourself a reminder note as an e-mail or text message, you are communicating intrapersonally. Much of our intrapersonal communication occurs subconsciously

Figure 1.1

A Model of Communication between Two Individuals

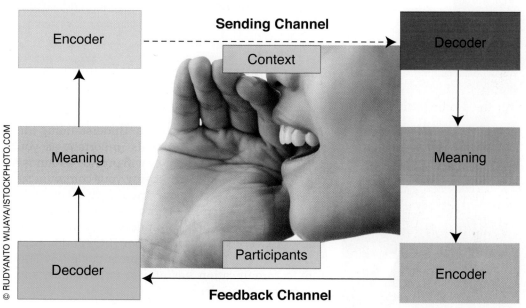

Encoder

Sending Channel

Decoder

Context

Meaning

Meaning

Participants

Decoder

Encoder

Feedback Channel

© RUDYANTO WIJAYA/ISTOCKPHOTO.COM

interpersonal
communication
interactions among a
small number of people
who have relationships
with each other

small group
communication
participants who come
together for the specific
purpose of solving a
problem or arriving at a
decision

public
communication
one participant, the
speaker, delivers a
prepared message to a
group or audience that
has assembled to hear
the speaker

(Kellerman, 1992). When we drive into the driveway "without thinking," we are communicating intrapersonally on a subconscious level. The study of intrapersonal communication often focuses on its role in shaping self-perceptions and in managing communication apprehension—that is, the fear associated with communicating with others (McCroskey, 1977). Our study of intrapersonal communication will focus on self-talk as a means to improve your self-concept and self-esteem and, ultimately, your communication competence in a variety of situations.

Interpersonal communication is characterized by informal interaction between two people who have an identifiable relationship with each other (Knapp & Daly, 2002). Talking to a friend between classes, visiting on the phone with your mother, texting or chatting online with your brother, and comforting someone who has suffered a loss are all examples of interpersonal communication. In Part II, our study of interpersonal communication includes the exploration of how we develop, maintain, improve, or end our relationships with others. We will also focus on listening and responding to others with empathy and on sharing personal information.

Small group communication typically involves three to 20 people who come together to communicate with one another (Beebe & Masterson, 2006; Hirokawa, Cathcart, Samovar, & Henman, 2003). There are many kinds of small groups; examples include a family, a group of friends, a group of classmates working on a project, and a management team in the workplace. Small group communication can occur in face-to-face settings as well as online through electronic mailing lists, discussion boards, and blogs. In Part III, our study of small groups focuses on the characteristics of effective groups, ethical and effective communication in groups, leadership, problem solving, conflict, and group presentations.

Public communication is communication delivered to audiences of more than 20 people. Public communication includes public speeches and other types of mass communication that you may experience in person, or on a delayed or mediated basis. For example, when President Barack Obama delivered his inaugural address, some people were there, others watched on TV or the Internet at the time he spoke, and still others experienced his speech after Inaugural Day by viewing it in the form of televised snippets or via a Web site such as YouTube. The Internet is also becoming the medium of choice for posting job ads and résumés, for advertising and buying products, and for political activism. In Part IV, our study of public communication will focus on preparing, practicing, and delivering effective oral presentations in both face-to-face and virtual environments.

LO² Communication Principles

Principles are general truths. Understanding the principles of communication is important as you begin your study because they will provide a foundation for practicing and improving your communication skills. In this section, we discuss seven generally agreed-upon principles: communication has purpose, communication is continuous, communication messages vary in conscious thought, communication is relational, communication is guided by culture, communication has ethical implications, and communication is learned.

© R. GINO SANTA MARIA/SHUTTERSTOCK

Communication Has Purpose

When people communicate with each other, they have a purpose for doing so. The purpose may be serious or trivial, and they may or may not be aware of it at the time. Here we list five basic purposes for communicating that we'll be addressing throughout the book.

- **We communicate to develop and maintain our sense of self.** Through our interactions, we learn who we are, what we are good at, and how people react to how we behave.

- **We communicate to meet our social needs.** Just as we need food, water, and shelter, so too do we, as social animals, need contact with other people. Two people may converse happily for hours, chatting about inconsequential matters that neither remembers afterward. Still, their communication has functioned to meet the important need simply to talk with another human being.

- **We communicate to develop and maintain relationships.** Not only do we get to know others through our communication with them but, more importantly, we develop relationships with them—relationships that grow and deepen or stagnate and wither away. For example, when Beth calls Leah to ask whether she'd like to join her for lunch to discuss a project they are working on, her purpose actually may be to resolve a misunderstanding they've had because she wants to maintain a positive relationship with Leah.

- **We communicate to exchange information.** We get some information through observation, some through reading, some through media, and a great deal through direct communication with others, whether face-to-face, via text messaging, or online through e-mail and social networking sites such as Facebook and MySpace. Whether we are trying to decide how warmly to dress or whom to vote for in the next election, all of us have countless exchanges that involve sending and receiving information.

- **We communicate to influence others.** It is doubtful that a day goes by in which you don't engage in behavior such as trying to convince your friends to go to a particular restaurant or see a certain movie, to persuade your supervisor to alter your schedule, or to convince an instructor to change a grade.

Communication Is Continuous

Because communication is non-verbal and visual as well as verbal, we are always sending behavioral messages from which others draw inferences or meaning. Even silence communicates if another person infers meaning from it. Why? Because your non-verbal behavior represents reactions to your environment and to the people around you. If you are cold, you shiver; if you are hot or nervous, you perspire; if you are bored, happy, or confused, your face or body language probably will show it. Not only that, we are continuously sending and receiving multiple messages when we communicate with others. For example, as you talk with your friend about where to go

on spring break, you are both simultaneously sending and receiving multiple verbal and non-verbal messages to each other. As skilled communicators, we need to be aware of the explicit and implicit messages we are constantly sending to others.

Communication Messages Vary in Conscious Thought

Recall that sharing meaning with another person involves encoding and decoding verbal messages, non-verbal cues, and even visual images. Our messages may (1) occur spontaneously, (2) be based on a "script" we have learned or rehearsed, or (3) be carefully constructed based on our understanding of the unique situation in which we find ourselves.

Many of our messages are **spontaneous expressions**, spoken without much conscious thought. For example, when you burn your finger, you may blurt out "Ouch." When something goes right, you may break into a broad smile.

At other times, our messages are **scripted**. Scripted messages are phrasings that we have learned from our past encounters and judge to be appropriate to the present situation. Many of these scripts are learned in childhood. For example, when you want the sugar bowl but cannot reach it, you may say, "Please pass the sugar," followed by "Thank you" when someone complies. This conversational sequence comes from your "table manners script," which may have been drilled into you at home. Scripts enable us to use messages that are appropriate to the situation and are likely to increase the effectiveness of our communication. One goal of this text is to acquaint you with general scripts (or skills) that can be adapted for use in your communication encounters across a variety of relationships, situations, and cultures.

Finally, our messages may be carefully constructed to meet the unique requirements of a particular situation. **Constructed messages** are those that we put together with careful thought when we recognize that our known scripts are inadequate for the situation.

Communication Is Relational

In any communication setting, in addition to sharing content meaning, our messages also reflect two

spontaneous expressions spoken without much conscious thought

scripted messages phrasings learned from past encounters that we judge to be appropriate to the present situation

constructed messages messages put together with careful thought when we recognize that our known scripts are inadequate for the situation

immediacy
the degree of liking or attractiveness in a relationship

control
the degree to which one participant is perceived to be more dominant or powerful

culture
systems of knowledge shared by a relatively large group of people

important aspects of our relationships: immediacy and control.

Immediacy is the degree of liking or attractiveness in a relationship. For instance, when José passes Josh on campus he may say, "Josh, good to see you" (a verbal expression of friendliness); the nonverbal behavior that accompanies the words may show Josh whether José is genuinely happy to see him or is only expressing recognition. For instance, if José smiles, has a sincere sound to his voice, looks Josh in the eye, and perhaps pats him on the back or shakes hands firmly, then Josh will recognize these signs of friendliness. If, however, José speaks quickly with no vocal inflection and with a deadpan facial expression, Josh will probably perceive the comment as impersonal communication offered merely to meet some social expectation.

Control is the degree to which one participant is perceived to be more dominant or powerful. Thus, when Tom says to Sue, "I know you're concerned about the budget, but I'll see to it that we have money to cover everything," his words and the sound of his voice may be saying that he is "in charge" of finances—that he is in control. How Sue responds to Tom determines whether, on this issue, she submits to his perception of control. If Sue says, "Thanks, I know you have a better handle on finances than I do," then she accepts that on this issue, she is willing to submit to Tom at this time. A few days later, if Tom says to Sue, "I think we need to cut back on credit card expenses for a couple of months," and Sue responds, "No way! I need a new suit for work, the car needs new tires, and you promised we could replace the couch," then the nature of the relationship will require further discussion.

Communication Is Guided by Culture

Culture may be defined as systems of knowledge shared by a relatively large group of people. It includes a system of shared beliefs, values, symbols, and behaviors. How messages are formed and interpreted depends on the cultural background of the participants. We need to look carefully at ourselves and our communication behavior; as we interact with others whose cultural backgrounds differ from

our own, we may unintentionally communicate in ways that are culturally inappropriate or insensitive and thereby undermine our relationships.

We must also be sensitive to how differences among people based on sex, age, class, physical characteristics, and sexual orientation affect communication. Failure to take those differences into account when we interact can also lead us to behave insensitively.

Throughout the history of the United States, we've experienced huge migrations of people from different parts of the world. According to the *New York Times Almanac* (Wright, 2002), at the turn of the 21st century people of Latin and Asian descent constituted 12.5 percent and 3.8 percent, respectively, of the total U.S. population. About 2.4 percent of the population regards itself as multiracial. Combined with the approximately 13 percent of our population that is of African descent, these four groups account for nearly 32 percent of the total population. According to the U.S. Census Bureau, this figure is predicted to rise to nearly 50 percent by 2050.

According to Samovar, Porter, & McDaniel (2007), "a number of cultural components are particularly relevant to the student of intercultural communication. These include (1) perception, (2) patterns of cognition, (3) verbal behaviors, (4) non-verbal behaviors, and the influence of context" (p. 13). Because cultural concerns permeate all of communication, in each chapter of this book we will point out when

> " We need to look carefully at ourselves and our communication behavior . . . and be sensitive to how differences among people affect communication. "

© OLIVIER BLONDEAU/ISTOCKPHOTO.COM /
© ANDRESR/SHUTTERSTOCK

the concepts and skills you are learning are viewed differently by cultural groups other than the dominant American one.

Communication Has Ethical Implications

In any encounter, we choose whether or not to communicate ethically. Ethics is a set of moral principles that may be held by a society, a group, or an individual. Although what is considered ethical is a matter of personal judgment, various groups still expect members to uphold certain standards. These standards influence the personal decisions we make. When we choose to violate the standards that are expected, we are viewed to be unethical. Here are five ethical standards that influence our communication and guide our behavior.

Truthfulness and Honesty

Truthfulness and honesty mean refraining from lying, cheating, stealing, or deception. "An honest person is widely regarded as a moral person, and honesty is a central concept to ethics as the foundation for a moral life" (Terkel & Duval, 1999, p. 122). Although most people accept truthfulness and honesty as a standard, they still confess to lying on occasion. We are most likely to lie when we are caught in a moral dilemma, a choice involving an unsatisfactory alternative. An example of a moral dilemma would be a boss asking us if our coworker arrived to work late today and knowing that telling the truth would get the coworker fired.

Integrity

Integrity means maintaining a consistency of belief and action (keeping promises). Terkel and Duval (1999) say, "A person who has integrity is someone who has strong moral principles and will successfully resist the temptation to compromise those principles" (p. 135). Integrity, then, is the opposite of hypocrisy. A person who had promised to help a friend study for the upcoming exam would live up to this promise even when another friend offered a free ticket to a sold-out concert for the same night.

ethics
a set of moral principles that may be held by a society, a group, or an individual

truthfulness and honesty
refraining from lying, cheating, stealing, or deception

moral dilemma
a choice involving an unsatisfactory alternative

integrity
maintaining a consistency of belief and action (keeping promises)

fairness
achieving the right balance of interests without regard to one's own feelings and without showing favor to any side in a conflict

respect
showing regard or consideration for others and their ideas even if we don't agree with them

responsibility
being accountable for one's actions and what one says

Fairness

Fairness means achieving the right balance of interests without regard to one's own feelings and without showing favor to any side in a conflict. Fairness implies impartiality or lack of bias. To be fair to someone is to listen with an open mind, to gather all the relevant facts, consider only circumstances relevant to the decision at hand, and not let prejudice or irrelevancies affect how you treat others. For example, if two of her children are fighting, a mom is exercising fairness if she listens openly as the children explain "their side" before she decides what to do.

Respect

Respect means showing regard or consideration for others and their ideas even if we don't agree with them. Respect is not based on someone's affluence, job status, or ethnic background. In a classroom, students show respect for others by attentively listening to another student's speech with a main point that violates their political or religious position.

Responsibility

Responsibility means being accountable for one's actions and what one says. Responsible communicators

Ethical communication requires:

1. truthfulness and honesty
2. integrity
3. fairness
4. respect
5. responsibility

© GAVIN DUNT/ISTOCKPHOTO.COM

communication competence
the impression that communicative behavior is both appropriate and effective in a given situation

skills
goal-oriented actions or action sequences that we can master and repeat in appropriate situations

credibility
a perception of a speaker's knowledge, trustworthiness, and warmth

social ease
communicating without anxiety or nervousness

communication apprehension
the fear or anxiety associated with real or anticipated communication with others

recognize the power of words. Messages can hurt and messages can soothe. Information is accurate or it may be faulty. A responsible communicator would not spread a false rumor about another friend.

In our daily lives, we often face ethical dilemmas and must sort out what is more or less right or wrong. In making these decisions, we usually reveal our ethical standards.

Communication Is Learned

Just as you learned to walk, so too you learned to communicate. But talking is a complex undertaking. You may not yet have learned all of the skills you will need to develop healthy relationships. Because communication is learned, you can improve your ability. Throughout this text, we identify communication skills that can help you become a more competent communicator.

LO³ Increasing Competence in Communication

Communication competence is the impression that communicative behavior is both appropriate and effective in a given situation (Spitzberg, 2000, p. 375). Communication is *effective* when it achieves its goals; it is *appropriate* when it conforms to what is expected in a situation. We create the perception that we are competent communicators through the verbal messages we send as well as the non-verbal behaviors and visual images that accompany them. Competence is an impression or judgment that people make about others. Because communication is at the heart of how we relate to each other, one of your goals in this course will be to learn strategies to increase the likelihood that others will view you as competent. Perceptions of competence depend, in part, on personal motivation, knowledge, and skills (Spitzberg, 2000, p. 377).

Motivation is important because we will only be able to improve our communication if we are *motivated*—that is, if we want to. People are likely to

> COMMUNICATION IS *EFFECTIVE* WHEN IT ACHIEVES ITS GOALS; IT IS *APPROPRIATE* WHEN IT CONFORMS TO WHAT IS EXPECTED IN A SITUATION.

be more motivated if they are confident and if they see potential rewards.

Knowledge is important because we must know what is involved in increasing competence. The more knowledge people have about how to behave in a given situation, the more likely they are to be able to develop competence.

Skill is important because we must know how to act in ways that are consistent with our communication knowledge. Skills are goal-oriented actions or action sequences that we can master and repeat in appropriate situations. The more skills you have, the more likely you are to be able to structure your messages effectively and appropriately.

In addition to motivation, knowledge, and skills, credibility and social ease are important components of communication competence. Credibility is a perception of a speaker's knowledge, trustworthiness, and warmth. Listeners are more likely to be attentive to and influenced by speakers they see as credible. Social ease means managing communication apprehension so you do not appear nervous or anxious. To be seen as a competent communicator, it is important that you can speak in a style that conveys confidence and poise. Communicators who appear apprehensive are not likely to be regarded as competent, despite their motivation or knowledge.

Although most people think of public speaking anxiety when they hear the term *communication apprehension* (CA), there are actually four different forms of CA. Generally speaking, communication apprehension is "the fear or anxiety associated with real or anticipated communication with others" (McCroskey, 1977, p. 78). The four specific types are traitlike CA, audience-based CA, situational CA, and context-based CA. If you experience *traitlike communication apprehension*, you feel anxious in most speaking situations. About 20 percent of all people experience traitlike CA (Richmond & McCroskey, 2000). If you experience *audience-based communication apprehension*, you feel anxious about speaking only with a certain person or group of people. *Situational communication apprehension* is a short-lived feeling of anxiety that occurs during a specific encounter—for example, during a job interview. Finally, *context-based communication apprehension* is anxiety only in a particular situation, for example, when speaking to a large group of people. All these forms of communication anxiety can be managed effectively in ways that help you convey social ease when communicating with others. Throughout this book, we will offer strategies for managing communication apprehension in various settings.

The combination of our motivation, knowledge, skills, credibility, and social ease leads us to perform effectively in our encounters with others. The rest of this book is aimed at helping you increase the likelihood that you will be perceived as competent. In the pages that follow, you will learn about theories of interpersonal, group, and public speaking that can increase your knowledge and your motivation. You will also learn how to perform specific skills, and you will be provided with opportunities to practice them. Through this practice, you can increase the likelihood that you will be able to perform these skills when needed.

Develop Goals to Improve Communication Skills

To get the most from this course, we suggest that you write personal goals to improve specific skills in your own interpersonal, group, and public communication repertoire.

Before you can write a goal statement, you must first analyze your current communication skills repertoire. After you read each chapter and practice the skills described, select one or two skills to work on. Then write down your goal statement in four parts.

State the problem. Start by stating a communication problem that you have. For example: "*Problem:* Even though some of my group members in a team-based class project have not produced the work they promised, I haven't spoken up because I'm not very good at describing my feelings."

State the specific goal. A goal is specific if it is measurable and you know when you have achieved it. For example, to deal with the problem stated above, you might write: "*Goal:* To describe my disappointment to other group members about their failure to meet deadlines."

Outline a specific procedure for reaching the goal. To develop a plan for reaching your goal, first consult the chapter that covers the skill you wish to hone. Then translate the general steps recommended in the chapter to your specific situation. For example: "*Procedure:* I will practice the steps of describing feelings. (1) I will identify the specific feeling I am experiencing. (2) I will encode the emotion I am feeling accurately. (3) I will include what has triggered the

feeling. (4) I will own the feeling as mine. (5) I will then put that procedure into operation when I am talking with my group members."

Devise a method of determining when the goal has been reached. A good goal is measurable, and the fourth part of your goal-setting effort is to determine your minimum requirements for knowing when you have achieved a given goal. For example: "*Test for Achieving Goal:* This goal will be considered achieved when I have described my disappointment to my group members about missed deadlines."

Figure 1.2 provides another example of a communication improvement plan, this one relating to a public speaking problem.

Figure 1.2

Communication Improvement Plan

Problem: When I speak in class or in the student senate, I often find myself burying my head in my notes or looking at the ceiling or walls.

Goal: Look at people directly when I'm giving a speech.

There are even MORE Study Tools for Chapter 1 at www.cengagebrain.com

☑ Speech Builder Express
☑ Printable Flash Cards
☑ Interactive Games
☑ Interactive Video Activities
☑ Chapter Review Cards
☑ Online Quizzes with Feedback
☑ Audio Downloads

2

Perception of Self and Others

Learning Outcomes

LO **1** Discuss the perception process

LO **2** Examine self-perceptions and how they affect communication

3 Describe how self-esteem is developed and maintained

4 Discuss how we present ourselves to others

LO **5** Discuss how we perceive others

> ❝Our self-concept is essentially our identity—that is, who we think we really are. We develop our self-concept based on our experiences and others' reactions and responses to us.❞

Have you ever had an argument with a friend where the two of you had totally different views on the same thing? How do we come to have different takes on the same event? Much of this is because we have different perceptions. Because much of the meaning we share with others is based on our perceptions, this chapter begins with a discussion of the perception process before moving into perceptions of self, perceptions of others, and how these perceptions influence and are influenced by our communication with others. We end by offering suggestions for improving the accuracy of your perceptions.

perception
the process of selectively attending to information and assigning meaning to it

LO¹ The Perception Process

Perception is the process of selectively attending to information and assigning meaning to it (Gibson, 1966). At times, our perceptions of the world, other people, and ourselves agree with the perceptions of others. At other times, our perceptions are significantly different from the perceptions of other people. For each person, perception becomes reality. What one person sees, hears, and interprets is real and considered true to that person. Another person who may see, hear, and interpret something entirely different from the same situation will regard that different perception as real and true. When your perceptions are different from those with whom you interact, sharing meaning becomes more challenging. So how does perception work? Essentially, your brain selects some of the information it receives from your senses (sensory stimuli), organizes the information, and then interprets it.

What do you think?

My self-perception usually matches other people's descriptions of me.

Strongly Disagree   Strongly Agree
1   2   3   4   5   6   7   8   9   10

Attention and Selection

Although we are subject to a constant barrage of sensory stimuli, we focus attention on relatively little of it. To help clarify, consider how many television channels you watch regularly compared to the number of channels offered. Why? Your choices of sensory stimuli depend in part on your needs, interests, and expectations.

Needs

We are likely to pay attention to information that meets our biological and psychological needs. When you go to class, how well you focus on what is being discussed is likely to depend on whether you believe the information is relevant to you. Your brain

© ANTHONY BROWN/ISTOCKPHOTO.COM

pattern
a set of characteristics used to differentiate some things from others

interpret
assigning meaning to information

communicates intrapersonally by asking such questions as, will what I learn here help me in school, in the work world, in my personal life?

Interests

We are likely to pay attention to information that pertains to our interests. For instance, you may not even recognize that music is playing in the background until you suddenly find yourself listening to some old favorite. Similarly, when you are really attracted to a person, you are more likely to pay attention to what that person is saying. Likewise, when you get an e-mail from someone you don't like, don't recognize, or that appears to be spam, you might simply delete it.

Expectations

Finally, we are likely to see what we expect to see and to miss information that violates our expectations. Take a quick look at the phrases in the triangles in Figure 2.1. If you have never seen these triangles, you probably read "Paris in the springtime," "Once in a lifetime," and "Bird in the hand." But if you re-examine the words, you will see that what you perceived was not exactly what is written. Do you now see the repeated words? It is easy to miss the repeated word because we don't *expect* to see the word repeated.

Organization of Stimuli

Even though our attention and selection process does reduce the number of stimuli our brain must pro-

cess, the number of stimuli we attend to at any one moment is still substantial. Our brains arrange these stimuli so that they make sense according to organizing principles such as simplicity and pattern.

Simplicity

If the stimuli we attend to are very complex, the brain simplifies the stimuli into some commonly recognized form. Based on a quick look at what a woman is wearing, how she is standing, and the expression on her face, we may perceive her as a business executive, a doctor, or a soccer mom. Similarly, we simplify the verbal messages we receive. For example, after an hour-long performance review in which his boss described four of Tony's strengths and two areas for improvement, Tony might say to Jerry, his coworker, "Well, I'd better shape up or I'm going to get fired!"

We are likely to see what we expect to see.

Pattern

A **pattern** is a set of characteristics used to differentiate some things from others. For example, when you see a crowd of people, instead of perceiving each individual, you may focus on a characteristic of sex and "see" men and women, or you may focus on age and "see" children, teens, adults, and seniors. In our interactions with others, we try to find patterns that help us organize and respond to their behavior. For example, each time Jason and Bill encounter Sara, she hurries over to them and begins an animated conversation. Yet when Jason is alone and runs into Sara, she barely says "Hi." After a while, Jason may detect a pattern to Sara's behavior. She is warm and friendly when Bill is around and not so friendly when Bill is absent. Based on this pattern, Jason may construe Sara's friendly behavior as flirting with Bill.

Interpretation of Stimuli

As the brain selects and organizes the information it receives from the senses, it also interprets the information by assigning meaning to it. Look at the three sets of numbers that follow. What do you make of them?

A. 631 7348

B. 285 37 5632

C. 4632 7364 2596 2174

In each of these sets, your mind looks for clues to give meaning to the numbers. Because you use similar patterns of numbers every day, you probably interpret A as a telephone number. How about B? A likely interpretation is a Social Security number.

Figure 2.1

A Sensory Test of Expectation

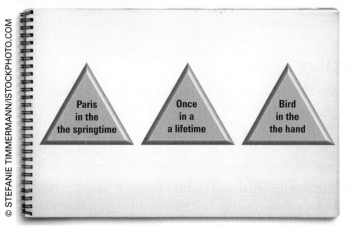

Paris
in the
the springtime

Once
in a
a lifetime

Bird
in the
the hand

© STEFANIE TIMMERMANN/ISTOCKPHOTO.COM

And C? People who use credit cards may interpret this set as a credit card number.

Our interpretation of others' behavior in conversation affects how we interact with them. If Jason believes that Sara is only interested in Bill, he may not participate in conversations that she initiates.

In the remainder of this chapter, we apply this basic information about perception to the study of perceptions of self and others as they influence and are influenced by communication.

© JOAN VICENT CANTÓ ROIG/ISTOCKPHOTO.COM

self-concept
your self-identity

self-esteem
your overall evaluation of your competence and personal worthiness

concept in positive ways. For example, if you perceive that it is easy for you to talk in front of a group of people because you don't feel anxious when doing so, you may conclude that you are a "natural" public speaker.

We place a great deal of emphasis on our first experience with a particular phenomenon, particularly if it is a negative one. For instance, if you get anxious and draw a blank while giving a speech for the first time, you may conclude that you are a poor public speaker. If additional experiences produce similar results, this first perception will be strengthened. Even if the first experience is not immediately repeated, you will probably need more than one contradictory experience to change the original negative perception.

LO² Perceptions of Self: Self-Concept and Self-Esteem

Self-concept and self-esteem are the two perceptions of self that have the greatest impact on how we communicate. Self-concept is your self-identity (Baron, Byrne, & Branscombe, 2006). It is the mental image that you have about your skills, your abilities, your knowledge, your competencies, and your personality. **Self-esteem is your overall evaluation of your competence and personal worthiness** (Mruk, 1999, p. 26). In this section, we describe how you come to understand who you are (self-concept) and how you evaluate yourself (self-esteem). Then we examine what determines how well these self-perceptions match others' perceptions of you. Finally, we discuss the role self-perceptions play when you communicate with others.

Forming and Maintaining a Self-Concept

Our self-concept is essentially our identity—that is, who we think we really are. We develop our self-concept based on our experiences and others' reactions and responses to us.

Personal Experiences

One way we form our self-concept is through our interpretation of our personal experiences regarding our skills, abilities, knowledge, competencies, and personality. Positive experiences shape our self-

Reactions and Responses of Others

Our self-concept is also formed and maintained by how others react and respond to us (Rayner, 2001, p. 43). Other people's comments serve to validate, reinforce, or alter our perception of who and what we are. For example, if during a trip to Cancun your best friend says, "You're really an excellent planner," you may decide that this comment fits your image of who you are. Such comments are especially powerful in affecting our self-concept if we respect the person making the comment. And the power of such comments is increased when the praise is immediate rather than delayed (Hattie, 1992, p. 251).

Our self-concept begins to form early in life, and information we receive from our families shapes our self-concept (Demo, 1987). One of the major responsibilities that family members have is to talk and act in ways that will help develop accurate and positive self-concepts in other family members. For example, the mom who says, "Roberto, your room looks very neat. You are very organized," or the brother who comments, "Kisha, the $20 you lent to Tomika really helped her out. You are very generous," is helping Roberto or Kisha to recognize important parts of their personalities.

Unfortunately, in some families, members do not fulfill these responsibilities. Sometimes family members do real damage to each other's self-concepts. Communicating blame, name-calling, and repeatedly pointing out another's shortcomings are particularly damaging. What are some characteristics of your self-concept and in what specific ways did your family members help shape it?

As we interact with others and with the media, we not only develop an understanding of who we are, but we also form an ideal self-concept, which is what we would like to be. For example, although Jim may know that he is really not naturally athletic, in his ideal self-concept he is a jock. So he plays intramural basketball on his dorm team, hangs out at the gym, and tries to befriend the university scholarship athletes.

LO³ Developing and Maintaining Self-Esteem

You'll recall that our self-esteem is our positive or negative evaluation of our self-concept. Our self-esteem is rooted in our values and develops over time as a result of our experiences. Self-esteem is not just how well or poorly we do things (self-concept) but also the importance or value we place on what we do well or poorly (Mruk, 1999, p. 27). For instance, Chad believes he is good with kids (self-concept). But if he doesn't believe that nurturing children is a valuable attribute for a man to have, then this characteristic is unlikely to help him have positive self-esteem and may even hurt it. High self-esteem requires both the perception of having a characteristic and a belief that the characteristic is valuable. Our self-esteem can affect the types of relationships that we form and who we form them with. For example, research has shown that a person who has high self-esteem is more likely to be committed to a partner who perceives him or her very favorably, whereas a person with low self-esteem is more likely to be committed to a partner who perceives him or her less favorably (Leary, 2002, p. 130). In both cases, the individual finds a partner

who reinforces his or her own self-perceptions, but the person with low self-esteem ends up reinforcing a negative self-image.

The Influence of Gender and Culture on Self-Perceptions

A person's culture has a strong influence on the self-perception process (Samovar, Porter, & McDaniel, 2009). In individualistic cultures, such as the United States, people stress the self and personal achievement. In individualistic cultures, people care about self-concept, self-esteem, and self-image. In fact, all the information thus far in this chapter reflects an individualistic perspective of perception, self-concept, and self-esteem. In an individualistic culture, you tend to think first of what is best for yourself when making a decision, such as taking a new job. You might move far away from family for the job. At work, we want to be paid, judged, and promoted based on our own work rather than how the group is performing. In collectivist cultures, such as China, groups and social norms tend to be more important than individuals. People are expected to be interdependent and to see themselves in terms of the group. Notions of self-concept and self-esteem have little meaning in collectivist cultures. In a collectivist culture, your decision about taking a new job would likely be made collectively by your family, and you would be expected to live near your family. Your salary, performance evaluations, and promotions would naturally be based on how well the entire group, team, or department was functioning. We should note, however, that these generalizations are not absolutes. As more people raised in individualistic cultures and in collectivist cultures live and work together, a blending of values is beginning to emerge.

Similarly, generally speaking, men and women may be socialized to view themselves differently and to value who they are based on whether their characteristics or behaviors correspond to or challenge the characteristics or behav-

UNSURE

CONFIDENT

© ISTOCKPHOTO.COM / © EVELINE KOOIJMAN/ISTOCKPHOTO.COM / © ANDRESR/ISTOCKPHOTO.COM

iors expected of their sex in their culture. There are norms of what it means to be "feminine" and what it means to be "masculine" in any culture. The cultural expectations for your gender inevitably influence your self-perceptions. In the past, boys in the United States were taught to base their self-esteem on their achievements, status, and income, and girls learned that their culture valued their appearance and their relationship skills, so boys and girls formed their self-perceptions based on how well they met these criteria (Wood, 2007).

Today in the United States these definitions of "appropriate" characteristics and behaviors for males and females are becoming less rigid, but they do still exist and are promoted incessantly in popular culture. Consider television sitcoms like *Two and a Half Men, Everybody Loves Raymond,* and *According to Jim,* for example. Such programs continue to portray women as the "natural" caregivers for the family, and when men attempt a caregiver behavior, they make a mess of the situation. Think about your family experiences growing up. How do they compare? Similarly, in terms of appearance, you only need to flip through the pages of any fashion magazine to see the narrowly defined perception of "beauty" for women.

Changing Self-Perceptions

Self-concept and self-esteem are enduring characteristics, but they can be changed. At times, comments that contradict your current self-perception lead you to slowly change it. Certain situations seem to expedite this process, for example, when you experience a profound change in your social environment. When children begin school or go to sleep-away camp, when teens start part-time jobs, when young adults go to college, or when people begin or end jobs or relationships, become parents, or grieve the loss of someone they love, they are more likely to absorb messages that are at odds with their current self-perceptions.

Therapy and self-help techniques can assist us when we want to alter our self-concept and improve our self-esteem. In his analysis of numerous research studies, Christopher Mruk (1999) found that self-esteem is increased through "hard work and practice, practice, practice—there is simply no escaping this basic existential fact" (p. 112).

So why is this important to communication? Because our self-esteem affects with whom we choose to form relationships, how we interact with them, how we participate when we are in small groups, and how comfortable we feel when we are called on to present a speech. Essentially, improving your perception of self will improve how you interact

© MALEWITCH/SHUTTERSTOCK

with others and improving how you interact with others will improve your self-perception.

incongruence
the gap between our inaccurate self-perceptions and reality

Accuracy and Distortion of Self-Perceptions

The accuracy of our self-concept and self-esteem depends on the accuracy of our own perceptions and how we process others' perceptions of us. All of us experience success and failure, and all of us hear praise and criticism. If we are overly attentive to successful experiences and positive responses, our self-concept and self-esteem may become inflated. If you've seen the Disney classic *Beauty and the Beast,* Gaston is a prime example of one with an inflated perception of self. We tend to describe such individuals as "arrogant," "pompous," "haughty," or "snobbish." Who have you known that you might describe in this way? Do you enjoy interacting with them? Conversely, if we perceive and dwell on failures and give little value to our successes, or if we only remember the criticism we receive, our self-concept and our self-esteem may be deflated. Winnie the Pooh's friend Eeyore, the donkey, who is always "having a bad day," is an example of one with a deflated sense of self. We tend to describe such individuals as "depressed," "despondent," "sullen," or "gloomy." Who have you known that you might describe in this way? Do you enjoy interacting with them? In neither case does their self-concept or self-esteem accurately reflect who they are.

Incongruence, the gap between our inaccurate self-perceptions and reality, is a problem because our perceptions of self are more likely than our true abilities to affect our behavior (Weiten, 1998, p. 491). For example, Raul may actually possess all the skills,

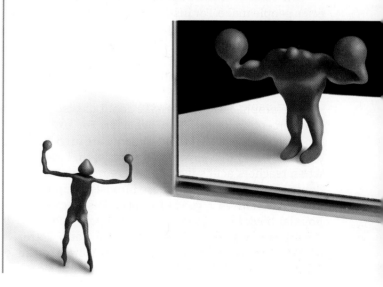

self-fulfilling prophecies
events that happen as a result of being foretold, expected, or talked about

abilities, knowledge, competencies, and personality characteristics for effective leadership, but if he doesn't perceive that he has these characteristics, he won't step forward when leadership is needed. Unfortunately, individuals tend to reinforce their self-perceptions by behaving in ways that conform to their perceived self-perceptions. The inaccuracy of a distorted picture of oneself is magnified through self-fulfilling prophecies, filtering messages, and reliance on media images.

Self-Fulfilling Prophecies

A **self-fulfilling prophecy** is a *false* perception of a situation or characteristic or skill that leads to behaviors that perpetuate that false perception as *true* (Merton, 1968). Self-fulfilling prophesies may be self-created or other-imposed.

Self-created prophecies are predictions you make about yourself. We often talk ourselves into success or failure. For example, researchers have found that when people expect rejection, they are more likely to behave in ways that lead others to reject them (Downey, Freitas, Michaelis, & Khouri, 2004, p. 437). So Aaron, who sees himself as unskilled in establishing new relationships, says to himself, "I doubt I'll know anyone at the party—I'm going to have a miserable time." Because he fears encountering strangers, he feels awkward about introducing himself and, just as he predicted, spends much of his time standing around alone thinking about when he can leave. In contrast, Stefan sees himself as quite social and able to get to know people easily. As a result, he looks forward to the party and, just as he predicted, makes several new acquaintances and enjoys himself.

Self-esteem has an important effect on the prophecies people make. For instance, people with positive self-esteem view success positively and confidently prophesy that they can repeat successes; people with low self-esteem attribute their successes to luck, so they prophesy that they will not repeat them (Hattie, 1992, p. 253).

The prophecies others make about us also affect our perception of self and behavior. For example, when teachers act as if their students are bright, students buy into this expectation and learn. Likewise, when teachers act as if students are not bright, students may "live down" to these imposed prophecies and fail to achieve. A good example takes place in the popular book *Harry Potter and the Order of the Phoenix.* A prophesy was made that suggested Harry Potter would vanquish the Dark Lord (Voldemort). So the Dark Lord sets out to kill Harry Potter. Dumbledore

explains to Harry that the prophecy is only true because the Dark Lord believes it. Still, because the Dark Lord will not rest until he kills Harry, it becomes inevitable that Harry will, in fact, have to kill Voldemort (or vice versa). Have you ever experienced a self-fulfilling prophecy based on what others have said? How did that influence your self-concept and self-esteem?

Filtering Messages

A second way that our self-perceptions can become distorted is through the way we filter what others say to us. We are prone to pay attention to messages that reinforce our current self-image, whereas messages that contradict this image may not "register" or may be downplayed. For example, suppose you prepare an agenda for your study group. Someone comments that you're a good organizer. If you spent your childhood hearing how disorganized you were, you may not really hear this comment, or may downplay it. If, however, you think you are good at organizing, you will pay attention to the compliment and may even reinforce it by responding, "Thanks, I'm a pretty organized person. I learned it from my mom."

Media Images

A third way our perceptions of self can become distorted is through verbal and visual images we see in the media such as on television, in the movies, and in popular magazines. Social learning theory suggests that we strive to copy the characteristics and behaviors of the characters portrayed as perfect examples or "ideal types" (Bandura, 1977). Persistent media messages of violence, promiscuity, use of profanity, bulked-up males, and pencil-thin females have all been linked to distorted perceptions of self among viewers.

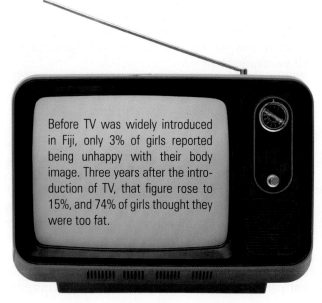

Before TV was widely introduced in Fiji, only 3% of girls reported being unhappy with their body image. Three years after the introduction of TV, that figure rose to 15%, and 74% of girls thought they were too fat.

© GRAFISSIMO/ISTOCKPHOTO.COM

The Effects of Self-Perceptions on Communication

Just as our self-concept and self-esteem affect how accurately we perceive ourselves, so too do they influence our communication by moderating competing internal messages in our self-talk, influencing how we communicate about ourselves with others, thus affecting communication apprehension.

Self-Perceptions Moderate How We Talk to Ourselves

Self-talk (intrapersonal communication) is the internal conversations we have with ourselves. A lot of these conversations are also about ourselves. People who have high self-esteem are more likely to engage in positive self-talk, such as "I know I can do it" or "I did really well on that test." People with low self-esteem are more likely to overemphasize negative self-talk or, ironically, they may overinflate their sense of self-worth to compensate and tell themselves they are good at everything they do.

Self-Perceptions Influence How We Talk about Ourselves with Others

If we feel good about ourselves, we are likely to communicate positively. For instance, people with a strong self-concept and higher self-esteem usually take credit for their successes. Likewise, people with healthy self-perceptions are inclined to defend their views even in the face of opposing arguments. If we feel bad about ourselves, we are likely to communicate negatively by downplaying our accomplishments.

Why do some people put themselves down regardless of what they have done? People who have low self-esteem are likely to be unsure of the value of their contributions and expect others to view them negatively. As a result, people with a poor self-concept or low self-esteem may find it less painful to put themselves down than to hear the criticism of others. Thus, to preempt the likelihood that others will comment on their unworthiness, they do it first.

Self-Perceptions Affect Communication Apprehension

Perhaps one the most unfortunate consequences of a poor self-concept and low self-esteem is a heightened level of communication apprehension. People who harbor fear about speaking with others (whether in one-on-one situations, with certain individuals or groups, or in public speaking situations) tend to engage in negative self-talk that leads to a self-fulfilling prophesy (Richmond & McCroskey, 1995). Even as a young child, Tina was told by friends, family members, and teachers that she was shy. By the time she reached adolescence, she feared going to social events because she "knew nobody would talk to her" and she feared giving speeches because she "would certainly fail." The negative self-talk that leads to communication apprehension can be reversed by replacing negative self-talk with positive self-talk.

self-talk
the internal conversations we have with ourselves

LO⁴ Presenting Self to Others

Your self-concept and self-esteem are the "true" perceptions of what you think of yourself. But when we interact with others, most of us mask some of who we really think we are so that we can meet or violate others expectations. As a result, we create different "selves" to present in different situations and with different people. How differently you present yourself across different social situations and relationships depends on how actively you self-monitor.

Self-Monitoring

When people are in social situations or relationships, they may feel vulnerable. So they analyze and make predications about the situation or relationship and

© JOAN VICENT CANTÓ ROIG/ISTOCKPHOTO.COM

self-monitoring
the internal process of observing and regulating your own behavior based on your analysis of the situation and others' responses to you

role
a pattern of learned behaviors that people use to meet the perceived demands of a particular context

decide how to behave. Self-monitoring is an internal process of being aware of yourself and how you are coming across to others. It involves being sensitive to other people's expressions and reactions (feedback) and using this information in deciding how to act and what roles to play. In other words, it is a process of observing, analyzing, and regulating your own behavior in relation to the response of others (Gangestad & Snyder, 2000). Self-monitoring is an internal thought process, so others probably don't know that you are monitoring and making choices about how to act. Think of the times when you consciously monitored how you were coming across in a situation. If you have ever been in an unfamiliar situation and made a flip remark that was met with stares or glares, you may have said to yourself, "Wow, that was a stupid thing to say! Let me see if I can fix it." Then, based on this self-monitoring, you are able to make a repair.

People differ in when and how carefully they self-monitor. Some people are very cautious and are always vigilant in monitoring situations and relationships. Other people are careful to self-monitor when they perceive themselves to be in a risky or new situation but are less attentive in situations or relationships that they perceive as safer. A few people seem unable to self-monitor. As a result, they tend to say and do the wrong things because they are not paying attention to how they are coming across. You may know someone who seems to always say the wrong thing or act inappropriately. The saying "Think before you speak" is really a call to self-monitor.

We are most likely to self-monitor when we are in a new relationship or an unfamiliar situation. Because we are not sure of how to act in an unfamiliar situation, there is more uncertainty and more analysis about how to present ourselves. When we are communicating in an unfamiliar situation, we may be saying to ourselves things like "Why did I make that silly remark? It sounded lame" or "Well, that seemed to go over well." Even in familiar and comfortable situations, skilled communicators do some self-monitoring by remaining attentive to the feedback they are receiving from others.

Social Construction of Self

While our self-concept and self-esteem are "true" perceptions that we have of ourselves, our self-

monitoring enables us to decide what role we want to play and what persona we want to assume in a certain situation or relationship. As a result, we present differing personas in response to different situations and relationships, and we change ourselves in the process. We socially construct ourselves through the roles we enact. A role is a pattern of learned behaviors that we use to meet the perceived demands of a particular context. For instance, think of your behavior when enacting the role of "sibling" while talking with your sister or brother or the role of "employee" at your job. How is what you say and do different in these contexts than when you are interacting with your classmates or your professor?

Do you have a MySpace or Facebook page? Think of the time and effort you spent creating that "self." Does it accurately reflect all of who you are? Or did you pick and choose what you would present to those who would view your page? The Internet allows you to experiment with a wide variety of roles. Some users experiment with gender and age switching or pretend to have a different job. The ethics of intentionally misrepresenting oneself in cyberspace is problematic because the people with whom you interact have no way to independently access the accuracy of your persona. Nonetheless, many people engage in intentional deception, and child predators are a particular problem. In real life as in cyberspace, we choose what parts of ourselves we allow others to see not only by what we talk about but also by how we behave, and we alter who we are to fit the situation and the relationship.

Let's look at the different personas or selves that Ashley enacts over a few days. As a restaurant server, Ashley is very polite, helpful, agreeable, and attentive to others. She does not talk about herself much or use profanity. She is confident, moves quickly, and cares about being efficient and productive. When Ashley goes out with her friends after work, she is more casual and less concerned about time. She is louder and more boisterous, talks about herself more, occasionally swears, and get into heated debates of issues and ideas. When Ashley visits her grandmother, she behaves in a more childlike way. She never uses profanity, is careful to observe social politeness, is cautious not to mention topics that may offend her grandmother, and listens more than she talks. Online, Ashley may present a party-girl image through a personal profile, photos, and listings of favorite activities, or she may assume totally different identities through avatars in multiplayer games. Ashley will enact other selves when she is at school, when she babysits her five-year-old niece, on a date, and with her rock-climbing partners. Which is Ashley's real self? They all are because our "self" is created in the interactions we have with others. We begin this process at birth and continue it throughout our lives.

LO⁵ Perception of Others

As we encounter others, we are faced with a number of questions: Do we have anything in common? Will others accept and value us? Will we be able to get along? Because this uncertainty makes us uneasy, we try to alleviate it. This process of monitoring the social environment to learn more about self and others is called **uncertainty reduction** (Littlejohn & Foss, 2008). As people interact, they gain information and form impressions of others. For example, when Nicole and Justin meet for the first time at a party, they probably pay much attention to how each other looks, because that's the only source of information they have about each other at first. Then they ask each other questions about their majors, jobs, hobbies, interests, and people they both may know. This small talk helps them gain information so that they can find things they have in common. The more they learn about each other and find commonalities, the less uncertain they are about each other. These perceptions will be reinforced, intensified, or changed as their relationship develops. The factors likely to influence perceptions of others include our observations of their physical characteristics and social behaviors, our interpretation of their messages, our use of stereotyping, and our emotional state.

Observing Others

Can you recall being shown a photo of someone you had not met? What impressions did you form on basis of that photo alone? Recall meeting someone for the first time and forming an impression based on how he or she acted in that situation. Did your impression change once you got to know that person better? Our initial social perceptions or first impressions of others are usually made from our observation of how they look and act. We often judge people to be friendly, intelligent, or "cool" based on how physically attractive we find them (Aronson, 1999, p. 380). And these impressions can influence how we act toward them. For this reason, women in business are advised to wear a suit with pumps or flats as a way of increasing the likelihood that they will be perceived as cred-

ible and move ahead in their field ("How to Dress," 2008).

Likewise, first impressions are also made on the basis of how someone acts. If, on the first day of class, a fellow student strikes up conversations with the strangers sitting near him, makes humorous remarks in class, and gives the best self-introduction in a class activity, you are likely to form the impression that he is confident, extroverted, and friendly. Similarly, if you try to strike up a conversation with someone at a party and the person gives short yes-or-no answers to your questions, you may perceive the person to be unfriendly and dull.

We make similar judgments about people we meet online. We use the profile and other pictures that people post, as well as the nicknames they use for themselves, the personal information they disclose, and the timeliness of their responses to perceive what they are like. Today, potential employers can make judgments about job applicants based on impressions gleaned from the applicants' home pages, profiles, and even the e-mail address they provide. For example, an employer may make different inferences about the character of an applicant whose e-mail address is realhottie@hotmail.com than one whose e-mail address is more generic.

Sometimes we make judgments of other people based on **implicit personality theories** (Asch, 1946), which are assumptions about which physical characteristics and personality traits or behaviors are associated with each other (Michener & DeLamater, 1999, p. 106). Because your own implicit personality theory connects certain traits, you might assume that a person has a whole set of characteristics, traits, and behaviors when you have actually observed only one. When you do this, your perception is based on the **halo effect** (Thorndike, 1920). For instance, Heather sees Martina personally greeting and welcoming every person who arrives at the meeting. According to Heather's implicit personality theory, this behavior is a sign of the characteristic of warmth. She further associates warmth with goodness and goodness with honesty. As a result, she perceives that Martina is good and honest as well as warm.

uncertainty reduction
the process of monitoring the social environment to learn more about self and others

implicit personality theories
assumptions people have developed about which physical characteristics and personality traits or behaviors are associated with another

halo effect
to generalize and perceive that a person has a whole set of characteristics when you have actually observed only one characteristic, trait, or behavior

© YURI ARCURS/SHUTTERSTOCK

stereotypes
attributions that cover up individual differences and ascribe certain characteristics to an entire group of people

prejudice
a rigid attitude that is based on group membership and predisposes an individual to feel, think, or act in a negative way toward another person or group

discrimination
a negative action toward a social group or its members on account of group membership

In reality, Martina may be a con artist who uses her warmth to lure people into a false sense of trust. This example demonstrates a "positive halo" (Heather assigned Martina positive characteristics), but we also use implicit personality theory to inaccurately impute negative characteristics. Given limited amounts of information, we fill in details and come up with a "negative halo." The tendency to do so leads to another factor that influences our perception of others—stereotyping.

Using Stereotypes

One perceptual shortcut that we use in forming our initial perceptions of others is stereotyping. A **stereotype** is "a generalization, usually exaggerated or oversimplified and often offensive, used to describe or distinguish a group" ("Stereotype," 2005). Because it is human nature to name, label, and organize in order to make sense of the stimuli we encounter, we develop or learn generalized perceptions about groups we come in contact with personally or learn about through media portrayals. Subsequently, any number of perceptual cues—skin color, style of dress, a religious medal, gray hair, a loud voice, an expensive car, and so on—can lead us to apply the characteristics associated with a stereotype. A professor may see a student's purple spiked hair and numerous tattoos and assume the student is a rebel who will defy authority, slack off on classroom assignments, and seek attention. In reality, this person may be a polite, quiet, serious honor student who aspires to graduate school. We don't form most of the stereotypes we use from our personal experience (Hall, 2002, p. 201). Instead we learn them from family, friends, coworkers, and media. So we adopt stereotypes before we have any personal proof. And because stereotypes guide what we perceive, they can lead us to attend to information that confirms them and to overlook information that contradicts them.

Unfortunately, stereotyping can lead to prejudice and discrimination. According to B. J. Hall (2002, p. 208), **prejudice** is "a rigid attitude that is based on group membership and predisposes an individual to feel, think, or act in a negative way toward another person or group." Notice the distinction between a stereotype and a prejudice. Whereas a stereotype is a set of beliefs or expectations, a prejudice is a rigid or negative attitude; both relate to group membership. Stereotypes and prejudice are cognitive—that is, things we think.

Discrimination goes a step further in that it involves a negative action toward a social group or its members based on a stereotype and prejudice (Jones, 2002, p. 8). For instance, when Ben discovers that he has been paired with Bobby Jo, a cheerleader, for a class project, he might stereotype her as a ditz who is not too concerned about grades. If he acts on his prejudice, he may discriminate against her by refusing to partner with her. So, without even getting to know Bobby Jo, Ben uses her stereotype to prejudge her and discriminate. Bobby Jo may never get the chance to be known for who she really is, and Ben may have lost an opportunity to get to work with the best student in class. The movie *Legally Blonde* enacts this form of prejudice and discrimination.

© EL GRECO/SHUTTERSTOCK

Emotional State

A final factor that affects how accurately we perceive others is our emotional state at the time of the interaction (Forgas, 1991). For example, if you meet Carol for the first time after you have just received the good news that you got the internship you applied for, your good mood is likely to spill over so that you perceive her more positively than you might under different circumstances. If, however, you just learned that your car needs $1,500 in repairs, your perception of her might be colored by your negative mood and anxiety about paying the bill.

Our emotions also cause us to engage in selective perceptions so that we "see" data that supports our previous knowledge and we ignore inconsistent information. For instance, if Nick is physically attracted to Jessica, he is likely to focus on the positive aspects of Jessica's personality and may overlook or ignore the negative ones that are apparent to others.

Our emotional state also affects our attributions (Forgas, 2000, p. 397). **Attributions** are reasons we give for others' behavior (Heider, 1958). According to attribution theory, what we determine—rightly or wrongly—to be the causes of others' behavior has a direct impact on our perceptions of them. For instance, suppose a coworker with whom you had made a noon lunch date has not arrived by 12:20 p.m. If you like and respect your coworker, you may attribute his lateness to something out of his control: an important phone call at the last minute, the need to finish a job before lunch, or some accident that may have occurred. If you are not particularly fond of your coworker, you are more likely to attribute his lateness to something in his control: forgetfulness, inconsiderateness, or malicious intent. In either case, your attribution will affect your perception of him and probably how you treat him.

Like prejudices, the attributions we make can be so strong that we ignore contrary evidence. If you are not particularly close to your coworker, when he finally arrives and explains that he had an emergency long-distance phone call, you may believe he is lying.

Perceiving Others' Messages

Our observations of others and our emotional state certainly affect how we perceive others. Not only that, they also tend to influence how we perceive the messages others send to us. Two additional factors that influence how we perceive others' messages are context and shared language.

First, we interpret the content and intent of the speaker based on the context. For example, at a family dinner, Jeorge's dad, who dislikes conflict, sought to distract family members from a quarrel between two aunts by looking up at the crystal chandelier hanging above the table and asking, "How do you suppose they clean that chandelier?" Because the aunts were aware that Jeorge's dad hated conflict, they immediately understood "the message" and stopped arguing. Thereafter, regardless of the situation, when anyone in the family wanted to avoid a brewing conflict, they would simply say, "How about that chandelier?" and the potential conflict would usually be diffused. Obviously, people who had not been present at the initial dinner would not have understood the historical context of this message and would likely be confused by it.

The better we know someone, the more likely we are to share an understanding of the context in which our messages are sent and received. When we don't know someone well or when we are speaking with several people or a large audience, there are expanded opportunities for messages to be perceived differently.

Second, even when both participants speak the same language, they might not enjoy a "shared language" in terms of how each one perceives specific words, visual images, and non-verbal cues. To clarify, the sender might use a word with which the receiver is unfamiliar, ambiguously use a word that has multiple meanings, misuse a symbol, or use a personal and idiosyncratic definition of a word. When Justin tells his wife that he's "going out with the guys for an hour or so," she may expect him home in 60 to 90 minutes. When he shows up five hours later, she might be upset. Justin may have figured that "or so" would cover any additional time he was away, but his wife may have viewed it as something less than two hours. Although the message was sent in a language that both "understood," they did not share the meaning because they perceived the message to mean different lengths of time.

Understanding how observations and emotional states, as well as context and shared language, affect our perceptions of others and the messages they send is a first step in improving perceptual accuracy. Now we'll describe four guidelines and a communication skill that you can use to improve the accuracy of your perceptions of others and the messages they send.

attributions
reasons we give for
others' behavior

Improving the Accuracy of Social Perceptions

Because distortions in our perception of others and their messages are common and because they influence how we communicate, improving perceptual accuracy is an important first step in becoming a competent communicator. The following guidelines can aid you in constructing accurate impressions of others and in assessing your perceptions of others' messages.

Question the accuracy of your perceptions. Questioning accuracy begins by saying, "I know what I think I saw, heard, tasted, smelled, or felt, but I could be wrong. What other information should I be aware of?" By accepting the possibility that you have overlooked something, you will become interested in increasing your accuracy.

Seek more information to verify perceptions. If your perception is based on only one or two pieces of information, try to collect additional information so that your perceptions are better grounded. Note that your perception is tentative—that is, subject to change.

The best way to get additional information about people is to talk with them. It's OK to be unsure about

perception check
a message that reflects your understanding of the meaning of another person's non-verbal behavior

how to treat someone from another group. But rather than letting your uncertainty cause you to make mistakes, talk with the person and ask for the information you need to become more comfortable with them.

Realize that your perceptions of a person will change over time. People often base their behavior on perceptions that are old or based on incomplete information. So when you encounter someone you haven't seen for a while, you will want to become reacquainted and let the person's current behavior rather than their past actions or reputation inform your perceptions. A former classmate who was wild in high school may well have changed and become a mature, responsible adult.

Use the skill of perception checking. One way to assess the accuracy of a perception is to verbalize it and see whether others agree with what you see, hear, and interpret. A perception check is a message that reflects your understanding of the meaning of another person's non-verbal behavior. It is a process of describing what you have seen and heard and then asking for feedback from the other person. Perception checking calls for you to (1) watch the behavior of the other person, (2) ask yourself "What does that behavior mean to me?" and (3) describe the behavior and put your interpretation into words to verify your perception.

The following examples illustrate the use of perception checking. In each of the examples, the final sentence is a perception check. Notice that the perception-checking statements do not express approval or disapproval of what is being received—they are purely descriptive statements of the perceptions.

Valerie walks into the room with a completely blank expression. She does not speak to Ann or even acknowledge that Ann is in the room. Valerie sits down on the edge of the bed and stares into space. Ann says, "Valerie, did something happen? You look like you're in a state of shock. Am I right? Is there something I can do?"

While Marsha is telling Jenny about the difficulty of her midterm exam in chemistry class, she notices Jenny smiling. She says to Jenny, "You're smiling. I'm not sure how to interpret it. What's up?" Jenny may respond that she's smiling because the story reminded her of something funny or because she had the same chemistry teacher last year and he purposely gave an extremely difficult midterm to motivate students, but then he graded them on a favorable curve.

Cesar, speaking in short, precise sentences with a sharp tone of voice, gives Bill his day's assignment. Bill says, "From the sound of your voice, Cesar, I get the impression that you're upset with me. Are you?"

So when we use the skill of perception checking, we encode the meaning that we have perceived from someone's behavior and feed it back so that it can be verified or corrected. For instance, when Bill says, "I can't help but get the impression that you're upset with me. Are you?" Cesar may say: (1) "No, whatever gave you that impression?" in which case Bill can further describe the cues that he received; (2) "Yes, I am," in which case Bill can get Cesar to specify what has caused the feelings; or (3) "No, it's not you, it's just that three of my team members didn't show up for this shift." If Cesar is not upset with him, Bill can examine what caused him to misinterpret Cesar's feelings; if Cesar is upset with him, Bill has the opportunity to change the behavior that caused Cesar to be upset.

© JIRI HERA/SHUTTERSTOCK

Checking perceptions enhances their accuracy.

There are even MORE Study Tools for Chapter 2 at www.cengagebrain.com

☑ Speech Builder Express
☑ Printable Flash Cards
☑ Interactive Games
☑ Interactive Video Activities
☑ Chapter Review Cards
☑ Online Quizzes with Feedback
☑ Audio Downloads

Listen Up!

COMM *was designed for students just like you—* busy people who want choices, flexibility, and multiple learning options.

COMM delivers concise, focused information in a fresh and contemporary format. And ... *COMM* gives you a variety of online learning materials designed with you in mind.

At **www.cengagebrain.com**, you'll find electronic resources such as **Printable Flash Cards, Speech Builder Express 3.0™, Interactive Quizzing, Downloads, Games and Simulations,** and **Interactive Video Activities** for each chapter. These resources will help supplement your understanding of core communication concepts in a format that fits your busy lifestyle.

Visit **www.cengagebrain.com** to learn more about the multiple *COMM* resources available to help you succeed!

Communicating *Verbally*

Learning Outcomes

LO[1] Discuss the nature and use of language

LO[2] Identify methods for improving language skills

LO[3] Develop linguistic sensitivity

"*Language affects how people think and what they pay attention to.*"

Sometimes, for a variety of reasons, the way we form our messages makes it difficult for others to understand. Sometimes the problem is what we say; other times it's how we say it. As Thomas Holtgraves (2002), a leading scholar in language use, reminds us, "Language is one of those things that we often take for granted" (p. 8). Yet we could all improve our use of language. In this chapter, we discuss the nature of and purposes for language and improving our verbal language skills.

LO¹ The Nature and Purposes of Language

Language is both a body of symbols (most commonly words) and the systems for their use in messages that are common to the people of the same speech community.

A **speech community**, also called a language community, is a group of people who speak the same language. There are between 3,000 and 4,000 speech communities in the world. Around 60 percent of the world's speech communities have fewer than 10,000 speakers. The five largest speech communities, in order, are: Mandarin Chinese, English, Spanish, Arabic, and Hindi (http://www.ethnologue.com/ethno_docs/distribution.asp?by=size).

Words are symbols used by a speech community to represent objects, ideas, and feelings. Although the word used to represent a particular object or idea varies from language to language, for a word to be a symbol all the members of the speech community must recognize it as standing for the same object, idea, or feeling. Different speech communities use different word symbols for the same phenomenon. For example, the season for planting is called *spring* in English-speaking communities but *printemps* in French-speaking communities.

Speech communities also vary in how they put words together to form messages. The structure a message takes depends on the rules of grammar and syntax that have evolved in a particular speech community. For example, in English a sentence must have at least a subject (a noun or pronoun) and a predicate (a verb). To make a statement in English, the subject is placed before the predicate. In Mandarin Chinese, however, an idea is usually expressed with a verb and a complement (which is rarely a noun and usually another verb or an adjective).

language
a body of symbols (most commonly words) and the systems for their use in messages that are common to the people of the same speech community

speech community
a group of people who speak the same language (also called a language community)

words
symbols used by a speech community to represent objects, ideas, and feelings

What do you think?

It is more important to communicate precise details rather than general ideas.

Strongly Disagree   *Strongly Agree*

| 1 | 2 | 3 | 4 | 5 | 6 | 7 | 8 | 9 | 10 |

© ISTOCKPHOTO.COM

© PRISM68/SHUTTERSTOCK

Fast Facts—Language Games

The mid-20th century German philosopher Ludwig Wittgenstein created what he called "language games" to imagine how the symbols of language (words) acquire their objects or meanings as individuals attempt to convey messages to one another. Wittgenstein's games pictured a builder on a construction project providing commands to his assistant, who supplied materials. When the builder called for a "block," a "pillar," a "slab," or a "beam," the assistant would retrieve the material corresponding with the name in the order that it was requested. Can you imagine a scenario that might illustrate how people might establish a common understanding of the language they are using?

Sapir–Whorf hypothesis
a theory claiming that language influences perception

Language affects how people think and what they pay attention to. This concept is called the Sapir–Whorf hypothesis, named after two theorists, Edward Sapir and Benjamin Lee Whorf (Littlejohn & Foss, 2008). Language allows us to perceive certain aspects of the world by naming them and allows us to ignore other parts of the world by not naming them. For instance, if you work in a job such as fashion or interior design that deals with many different words for color distinctions, you will be able to perceive finer differences in color. Knowing various words for shades of white, such as *ecru, eggshell, cream, ivory, pearl, bone china white,* and *antique white,* actually helps you see differences in shades of white. Similarly, there are concepts that people do not fully perceive until a word is coined to describe them. Think of words added to American English vocabulary in the last few years such as *google, texting, couch potato,* or *mouse potato.* The behaviors to which those words refer certainly existed before the terms were coined. But as a society, we did not collectively perceive these behaviors until language allowed us to name them.

The Relationship Between Language and Meaning

On the surface, the relationship between language and meaning seems perfectly clear: if we select the correct words and structure them using the rules of syntax and grammar agreed upon by our speech community, then people will interpret our meanings correctly. But in fact, the relationship between language and meaning is not nearly so simple for five reasons.

First, the meaning of words is in people, not in the words themselves. If Juan says to Julia that a restaurant is expensive, each of them probably has a different meaning of the word *expensive.* Maybe Juan thinks one meal will cost $40, whereas for Julia *expensive* might mean a $20 meal. All words, especially abstract ones, have multiple meanings depending on

Purposes of Language

Although language communities vary in the words that they use and in their grammar and syntax systems, all languages serve the same purposes.

1. **We use language to designate, label, define, and limit.** So, when we identify music as "punk," we are differentiating it from other music labeled rap, rock, pop, indie, country, or R&B.

2. **We use language to evaluate.** Through language we convey positive or negative attitudes toward our subject. For instance, if you see Hal taking more time than others to make a decision, you could describe Hal positively as "thoughtful" or negatively as "dawdling." Or you might describe a comedy like the movie *Superbad* positively as "hilarious" or negatively as "vulgar." Kenneth Burke (1968), a prominent language theorist, describes this as the power of language to emphasize hierarchy and control. Because language allows us to compare things, we tend to judge them as better or worse, which leads to social hierarchy or a pecking order. Certainly, programs like *What Not to Wear* and *Flip This House* use language to suggest how to judge certain looks as better or worse.

3. **We use language to discuss things outside our immediate experience.** Language lets us talk about ourselves, learn from others' experiences, share a common heritage, talk about past and future events, and communicate about people and things that are not present. Through language, we can discuss where we hope to be in five years, where we plan to go for spring break, or learn about the history that shapes the world we live in. If you ever watch television programs on the Discovery Channel, you are learning from things outside your own experiences.

4. **We use language to talk about language.** We also use language to communicate about how we are communicating. For instance, if your friend said she would see you "this afternoon" but didn't arrive until 5 o'clock and you ask her where she's been, the two of you are likely to discuss your communication and the different interpretations you each bring to the phrase "this afternoon." You might also relate to this if you've ever had a professor tell you an assignment is due "next week" and then asks for it first thing Monday morning with a comment that she "will not accept late papers."

who is using and hearing them. What does *expensive* mean to you?

Second, words have two levels of meaning: denotation and connotation. **Denotation** is the direct, explicit meaning a speech community formally gives a word—it is the meaning found in a dictionary. Different dictionaries may define words in slightly different ways. For instance, the *Encarta World English Dictionary* defines *bawdy* as "ribald in a frank, humorous, often crude way," while the *Cambridge American English Dictionary* defines *bawdy* as "containing humorous remarks about sex." Similar? Yes, but not the same. Not only that, but many words have multiple definitions. For instance, the *Random House Dictionary of the English Language* lists 23 definitions for the word *great*. **Connotation**, the feelings or evaluations we associate with a word, may be even more important to our understanding of meaning than denotation. C. K. Ogden and I. A. Richards (1923) were among the first scholars to consider the misunderstandings resulting from the failure of communicators to realize that their subjective reactions to words are based on their life experiences. For instance, when Tina says "We bought an SUV! I think it's the biggest one Chevy makes," Kim might think "Why in the world would anyone want one of those gas guzzlers that take up so much space to park?" and Lexia might say, "Oh, I envy you. I'd love to own a vehicle that has so much power and sits so high on the road." Word denotation and connotation are important because the only message that counts is the message that is understood, regardless of whether it is the one you intended.

Third, meaning may vary depending on its **syntactic context** (the position of a word in a sentence and the other words around it). For instance, in the same sentence a person might say, "I love to vacation in the mountains, where it's really cool in mornings and you're likely to see some really cool animals." Most listeners would understand that "mornings are really cool" refers to temperature and "see some really cool animals" refers to animals that are uncommon or special.

Fourth, the language of any speech community will change over time. Language changes in many ways, including the creation of new words, the abandonment of old words, changes in word meanings in segments of society, and the influx of words from the mixing of cultures. For instance, the latest edition of *Merriam-Webster's Collegiate Dictionary* contains 10,000 new words and usages. New words are created to express new ideas. For example, younger generations, businesspeople, and scientists, among others, will invent new words or assign different meanings to words to better express the changing realities of their world. For example, *bling* is used to describe flashy jewelry; *marathoning* is the practice of watching an entire season of a TV series in one sitting; a *desktop* is the visual surface we see on our computer screen; and *greenwashing* is the practice of making a misleading claim about the environmental benefits of a product, service, technology, or company practice. In the past 20 years, entire vocabularies have been invented to allow us to communicate about new technologies. So we *google* to get information, use the *wi-fi* on our *laptop*, and listen to a *podcast* while writing a *blog*. Words used by older generations may fade as they no longer describe current realities or are replaced by new words. We once used a *mimeograph*, but now we use a *copy machine*. In addition, some members of the speech community will invent new meanings for old words to differentiate themselves from other subgroups of the language community. For instance, in some parts of the country, young people use the word *bad* to mean "intense," as in "That movie was really bad"; *sick* to mean "cool," as in "That bike is really sick"; or *kickin'* to mean "really great" as in "That concert was really kickin.'"

Fifth, as a society absorbs immigrants who speak different languages and becomes more multicultural, the language of the dominant group gradually absorbs some words from the languages of the immigrants. In English, we use and understand what were once foreign words, such as *petite, siesta, kindergarten,* and *ciao*. Similarly, the slang used by a subgroup may also eventually be appropriated by the larger speech community. For example, the African American

A cool dog?

© WILLEECOLE/SHUTTERSTOCK

denotation
the direct, explicit meaning a speech community formally gives a word

connotation
the feelings or evaluations we associate with a word

syntactic context
the position of a word in a sentence and the other words around it

low-context cultures
cultures in which messages are direct, specific, and detailed

high-context cultures
cultures in which messages are indirect, general, and ambiguous

feminine styles of language
use words of empathy and support, emphasize concrete and personal language, and show politeness and tentativeness in speaking

masculine styles of language
use words of status and problem solving, emphasize abstract and general language, and show assertiveness and control in speaking

slang terms for "girlfriend," *shorty* or *boo*, are now used and understood by a more diverse group of American speakers.

Cultural and Gender Influences on Language Use

Culture and gender both influence how words are used and interpreted. Cultures vary in how much meaning is embedded in the language itself and how much meaning is interpreted from the context in which the communication occurs. In low-context cultures, like the United States and most northern European countries, messages are typically quite direct and language is very specific. Speakers say exactly what they mean, and the verbal messages are very explicit, with lots of details provided. In low-context cultures, what the speaker intends the message to mean is not heavily influenced by the setting or context; rather, it is embedded in the verbal message. In high-context cultures, like Latin American, Asian, and Native American, what a speaker really means for you to understand from the verbal message depends heavily on the setting or context in which it is sent. So verbal messages in high-context cultures may be indirect, using more general and ambiguous language. Receivers in high-context cultures, then, rely on contextual cues to help them understand the speaker's meaning (Samovar, Porter, & McDaniel, 2009).

When people from low-context cultures interact with others from high-context cultures, problems of understanding often occur. Imagine that Isaac from a German company and Zhao from a Chinese company are trying to conduct business.

ISAAC: "Let's get right down to it. We're hoping that you can provide 100,000 parts per month according to our six manufacturing specifications spelled out in the engineering contract I sent you. If quality control finds more than a 2-percent error, we will have to terminate the contract. Can you agree to these terms?"

ZHAO: "We are very pleased to be doing business with you. We produce the highest quality products and will be honored to meet your needs."

ISAAC: "But can you supply that exact quantity? Can you meet all of our engineering specifications? Will you consistently have less than a 2-percent error?"

ZHAO: "We are an excellent, trustworthy company that will send you the highest quality parts."

Isaac is probably frustrated with what he perceives as general, evasive language used by Zhao, and Zhao may be offended by the direct questions, specific language, and perceived threat in Isaac's message. Global migration, business, and travel are increasing the interactions that occur between people accustomed to high- or low-context expectations. As this happens, the likelihood of misunderstanding increases. To be a competent communicator, you will need to be aware of, compensate for, or adapt to the cultural expectations of your conversational partner.

Societal expectations for masculinity and femininity influence language use. According to Wood (2007), **feminine styles of language** typically use words of empathy and support, emphasize concrete and personal language, and show politeness and tentativeness in speaking. **Masculine styles of language** often use words of status and problem solving, emphasize abstract and general language, and show assertiveness and control in speaking.

Feminine language often includes empathic phrases like "I can understand how you feel" or "I've had a similar experience, so I can sense what you are going through." Likewise, feminine language often includes language of support such as "I'm so sorry that you are having difficulty" or "Please let me know if I can help you in any way." Feminine

In what kind of situations would feminine styles of language be best?

What about masculine styles?

© LINDA & COLIN MCKIE/ISTOCKPHOTO.COM / © STACEY NEWMAN/ISTOCKPHOTO.COM language often goes into detail by giving specific examples and personal disclosures. To appear feminine is to speak politely by focusing on others and by not being too forceful with language. Words and phrases like "I may be wrong but," "It's just my opinion," "maybe," "perhaps," and "I don't want to step on anyone's toes here" are associated with feminine styles of speaking.

By contrast, masculine styles of speaking often emphasize status through phrases like "I know that" and "My experience tells me" and communicates problem solving or advice giving through such language as "I would," "You should," and "The way you should handle this is." Masculine styles of communication may favor theoretical or general discussions and avoid giving personal information about oneself. To appear masculine, one's language must be forceful, direct, and in control through such phrases as "definitely," "I have no doubt," "It is clear to me," and "I am sure that."

Women and men can use both masculine and feminine language, although society generally expects women to use feminine language and men to use masculine language. One style is not inherently better than another, but each may be better suited to certain communication situations.

LO² Improving Language Skills

Regardless of whether we are conversing with a friend, working on a task force, or giving a speech, we should strive to use language in our messages that accurately conveys our meanings. We can improve our messages by choosing words that make our meaning clear, choosing language that makes our messages memorable, and choosing language that demonstrates linguistic sensitivity.

Language That Clarifies Meaning

We should strive to choose words that help listeners assign meaning that is similar to what we intended. Compare these two descriptions of a near miss

in a car: "Some nut almost got me a while ago" versus "An hour ago, an older man in a banged-up Honda Civic ran the light at Calhoun and Clifton and almost hit me broadside while I was in the intersection waiting to turn left at the cross street." In the second message, the language is much more specific, so both parties would be more likely to have a more similar perception of the situation than would be possible with the first message.

Often as we try to express our thoughts, the first words that come to mind are general in nature. **Specific words** clear up confusion caused by general words by narrowing what is understood from a general category to a particular group within that category. Specific words are more concrete and precise than general words. What can we do to speak more specifically?

For one, we can select a word that most accurately captures the sense of what we are saying. At first I might say, "Waylon was angry during our work session today." Then I might think, "Was he really showing anger?" So I say, "To be more accurate, he wasn't really angry. Perhaps he was more frustrated or impatient with what he sees as lack of progress by our group." What is the difference between the two statements in terms of words? By carefully choosing words, you can show shades of meaning. Others may respond quite differently to your description of a group member showing anger, frustration, or impatience. The interpretation others get of Waylon's behavior is very dependent on the word or words selected. Specific language is achieved when words are concrete or precise or when details or examples are used.

Concrete words are words that appeal to our senses. Consider the word *speak*. This is an abstract word—that is, we can speak in many different ways. So instead of saying that Jill *speaks in a peculiar way*, we might be more specific

© ROBYN MACKENZIE/ISTOCKPHOTO.COM

Clarify with words that are:

✓ specific

✓ concrete

✓ precise

> **specific words** words that clarify meaning by narrowing what is understood from a general category to a particular item or group within that category

> **concrete words** words that appeal to the senses and help us see, hear, smell, taste, or touch

precise words
words that narrow a larger category

dating information
specifying the time or time period that a fact was true or known to be true

indexing generalizations
the mental and verbal practice of acknowledging the presence of individual differences when voicing generalizations

by saying that Jill *mumbles, whispers, blusters,* or *drones.* Each of these words creates a clearer sense of the sound of her voice.

We speak more specifically when we use **precise words**, narrowing a larger category to a smaller group within that category. For instance, if Nevah says that Ruben is a "blue-collar worker," she has named a general category; you might picture an unlimited number of occupations that fall within this broad category. If instead she is more precise and says he's a "construction worker," the number of possible images you can picture is reduced; now you can only select your image from the specific subcategory of construction worker. So your meaning is likely to be closer to the one she intended. To be even more precise, she may identify Ruben as a "bulldozer operator"; this further limits your choice of images and is likely to align with the one she intended you to have.

Clarity also can be achieved by adding detail or examples. For instance, Linda says, "Rashad is very loyal." The meaning of *loyal* ("faithful to an idea, person, or company," and so on) is abstract, so to avoid ambiguity and confusion, Linda might add, "He defended Gerry when Sara was gossiping about her." By following up her use of the abstract concept of loyalty with a concrete example, Linda makes it easier for her listeners to ground their idea of this personal quality in a concrete or real experience. Likewise, by providing details we clarify our messages. The statement "He lives in a really big house" can be clarified by adding details: "He lives in a 14-room Tudor mansion on a six-acre estate."

We can also increase clarity by dating information. **Dating information** are details that specify the time or period that a fact was true or known to be true. Because nearly everything changes with time, not dating our statements can lead some people to conclude that what we are saying is current when it is not. For instance, Parker says, "I'm going to be transferred to Henderson City." Laura replies, "Good luck—they've had some real trouble with their schools." On the basis of Laura's statement, Parker may worry about the effect his move will have on his children. What he doesn't know is that Laura's information about this problem in Henderson City is over five years old. Henderson City still may have problems, or the situation may have changed. Had Laura replied, "Five years ago, I know they had some

Clarity Is Key!

© DUNCAN GILBERT/ISTOCKPHOTO.COM

X NOT CLEAR: "He lives in a big house"

✓ CLEAR: "He lives in a 14-room Tudor mansion on a six-acre estate"

real trouble with their schools. I'm not sure what the situation is now, but you may want to check," Parker would look at the information differently.

Here are two additional examples:

Undated: Professor Powell is really enthusiastic when she lectures.
Dated: Professor Powell is really enthusiastic when she lectures—at least she was *last semester* in communication theory class.

Undated: You think Mary's depressed? I'm surprised. She seemed her regular, high-spirited self when I talked with her.
Dated: You think Mary's depressed? I'm surprised. She seemed her regular, high-spirited self when I talked with her *last month.*

To date information, before you make a statement (1) consider or find out when the information was true and (2) verbally acknowledge the date or period when the information was true. When you date your statements, you increase the clarity of your messages and enhance your credibility.

Finally, we can increase clarity through indexing generalizations. **Indexing generalizations** is the mental and verbal practice of acknowledging individual differences when voicing generalizations. Although we might assume that someone who buys a Mercedes is rich, that may not be true for all Mercedes buyers. Thus, just because Brent has bought a top-of-the-line, very expensive Mercedes, Brent is not necessarily rich. If we said, "Brent bought a Mercedes; he must be rich," then we should add "Of course not all people who buy Mercedes are rich."

Let's consider another example:

Generalization: Your Toyota should go 50,000 miles before you need a brake job—Jerry's did.
Indexed Statement: Your Toyota may well go 50,000 miles before you need a brake job, Jerry's did, *but of course, all Toyotas aren't the same.*

To index, consider whether what you are about to say applies a generalization to a specific person, place, or thing. If so, qualify it appropriately so that your assertion does not go beyond the evidence that supports it.

To ensure that our listeners decode our messages as we intend them, we can use words that are specific, concrete, and precise. We can also provide details and examples as well as date our information and index our generalizations. Ultimately, our goal is to be understood. Practicing these strategies will help us achieve that goal.

Make Your Messages Memorable

Because your listeners cannot simply re-read what you have said, effective verbal messages use vivid wording and appropriate emphasis to help listeners understand and remember the message. **Vivid wording** is full of life, vigorous, bright, and intense. For example, a novice football announcer might say "Jackson made a great catch," but a more experienced commentator's vivid account would be "Jackson leaped into the air with double-coverage, made a spectacular one-handed catch, and landed somehow with both feet planted firmly in the end zone." The words *spectacular, leaped, one-handed catch,* and *planted firmly* paint an intense verbal picture of the action. Vivid messages begin with vivid thoughts. You are much more likely to *express* yourself vividly when you have physically or psychologically *sensed* the meanings you are trying to convey.

Vividness can be achieved quickly through using similes and metaphors. A **simile** is a direct comparison of dissimilar things and is usually expressed with the words *like* or *as.* Clichés such as

© GEORGE PETERS/ISTOCKPHOTO.COM

"She walks like a duck" and "She sings like a nightingale" are similes. A **metaphor** is a comparison that establishes a figurative identity between objects being compared. Instead of saying that one thing is like another, a metaphor says that one thing *is* another. Thus, a problem car is a "lemon" and an aggressive driver is a "road hog." As you think about and try to develop similes and metaphors, stay away from trite clichés. Although we use similes and metaphors frequently in conversations, they are an especially powerful way to develop vividness when we are giving a speech. Try developing and practicing one or two different original metaphors or similes when you rehearse a speech to see which works best.

Finally, although your goal is to be vivid, be sure to use words that are understood by all your listeners. Novice speakers can mistakenly believe they will be more impressive if they use a large vocabulary, but using big words can be off-putting to the audience and make the speaker seem pompous, affected, or stilted. When you have a choice between a common vivid word or image and one that is more obscure, choose the more common.

Emphasis is the importance you give to certain words or ideas. Emphasis tells listeners what they should seriously pay attention to. Ideas are emphasized through proportion of time, repetition, and transitions. Ideas to which you devote more time are perceived by listeners to be more important, whereas ideas that are quickly mentioned are perceived to be less important. Emphasizing by repeating means saying important words or ideas more than once. You can either repeat the exact words, "A ring-shaped coral island almost or completely surrounding a lagoon is called *an atoll—an atoll,*" or you can restate the idea in different language, "The test will contain about four essay questions; that is, all the questions on the test will be the kind that require you to discuss material in some detail." Emphasizing through transitions means using words that show the relationship between your ideas. For example, some transitions summarize (*therefore, and so, so, finally, all in all, on the whole, in short, thus, as a result*), some clarify (*in fact, for example, that is to say, more specifically*), some forecast (*also, and, likewise, again, in addition, moreover, similarly, further*), and some indicate changes in direction or provide contrasts (*but, however, on the other hand, still, although, while, no doubt*).

vivid wording
wording that is full of life, vigorous, bright, and intense

simile
a direct comparison of dissimilar things

metaphor
a comparison that establishes a figurative identity between objects being compared

emphasis
the weight or importance given to certain words or ideas

jargon
technical terms understood only by select groups

slang
informal vocabulary used by particular groups in society

LO³ Use Linguistic Sensitivity

Linguistic sensitivity means choosing language and symbols that are adapted to the needs, interests, knowledge, and attitudes of the listeners and avoiding language that alienates them. Through appropriate language, we communicate our respect for those who are different from us. To do so, we need to avoid language our listeners might not understand as well as language that might offend them. Linguistic sensitivity can be achieved by using vocabulary our listeners understand, using jargon sparingly, using slang that is appropriate to our listeners and the situation, using inclusive language, and using language that is not offensive.

Adapt your vocabulary to the level of your listener. If you have made a conscious effort to expand your vocabulary, are an avid reader, or have spent time conversing with others who use a large and varied selection of words, then you probably have a large vocabulary. As a speaker, the larger your vocabulary, the more choices you have from which to select the words you want. Having a larger vocabulary, however, can present challenges when communicating with people whose vocabulary is more limited. One strategy for assessing another's vocabulary level is to listen to the types and complexity of words the other person uses and take your signal from your communication partner. When you have determined that your vocabulary exceeds that of your partner, you can use simpler synonyms for your words or use word phrases composed of more familiar terms. Adjusting your vocabulary to others does not mean talking down to them. It is merely polite behavior and effective communication to try to select words that others understand.

Use jargon sparingly. Jargon refers to technical terms whose meanings are understood only by a select group of people based on their shared activity or interests. We may form a special speech community that develops a common language (jargon) based on a hobby or occupation. Medical practitioners speak

A stopwatch, or a chronograph?

a language of their own that people in the medical field understand and those outside the medical field do not. The same is true of lawyers, engineers, educators, and virtually all occupations. For instance, lawyers may speak of briefs and cases, but the general public might associate such terms with underwear (briefs) and packages of beer or soda (cases). If you are an avid computer user, you may know many terms that non–computer users do not. Likewise, there are special terms associated with sports, theatre, wine tasting, and science fiction, to name just a few interest groups. The key to effective use of jargon is to use it only with the people who will understand it or to explain terms the first time you use them. Without explanation, jargon is basically a type of foreign language. Have you ever tried to listen to a professor who uses jargon of his or her field without defining it? If so, how did it affect your learning of the material?

Use slang appropriate to the listeners and to the situation. Slang is informal vocabulary developed and used by particular groups in society. Slang performs an important social function. Slang bonds those in an inner circle who use the same words to emphasize a shared experience. But slang simultaneously excludes others who don't share the terminology. The simultaneous inclusion of some and exclusion of others is what makes slang popular with youth and marginalized people in all cultures. Slang may emerge from teenagers, urban life, college life, gangs, or other contexts. A young adult, for instance, might say "My bad" for "I made a mistake." *Sweet* could be translated as "That's great, fine, or excellent." Using slang appropriately means using it in situations where people understand the slang and avoiding it with people who do not share the slang terminology.

There is a new type of slang developing with digital and Internet technology. Experts in computer-mediated communication (Thurlow, Lengel, & Tomic, 2004) explain that with texting, for example, many of the rules of grammar, style, and spelling are broken. Many people adopt a phonetic type of spelling, which increasingly is understandable to this speech community but may not be understandable to others. Texters know, for example, that *lol* is short for "laugh out loud," *brb* stands for "be right back," and *jk* means "just kidding." Some communication experts who emphasize traditional styles of communication

© TOM HAHN/ISTOCKPHOTO.COM

regard this new language of texters as incorrect, deficient, or inferior. Although this shorthand is convenient in cyberspace, using it in other settings could be problematic.

Use inclusive language. Generic language uses words that apply only to one sex, race, or other group as though they represent everyone. This usage is a problem because it linguistically excludes a portion of the population it ostensibly includes. For example, English grammar traditionally used the masculine pronoun *he* to stand for all humans regardless of gender. According to this rule, we would say, "When a person shops, he should have a clear idea of what he wants to buy." Despite traditional usage, it is hard to picture people of both sexes when we hear the masculine pronoun *he*.

The following techniques can help you be more inclusive. First, use plurals. For instance, instead of saying "Because a doctor has high status, his views may be believed regardless of the topic," you could say "Because doctors have high status, their views may be believed regardless of the topic." Second, use both male and female pronouns: "Because a doctor has high status, his or her views may be believed regardless of the topic." Stewart, Cooper, Stewart, and Friedley (1998, p. 63) cite research showing that when speakers refer to people using "he and she," and to a lesser extent "they," listeners often visualize *both* women and men. Thus, when speakers avoid generic language, it's more likely that listeners will perceive a message that is more gender balanced. Third, avoid using words that are gender specific. For most sex-biased expressions, you can use or create suitable alternatives. For instance, use *police officer* instead of *policeman* and substitute *synthetic* for *man-made*. Instead of saying *mankind*, change the wording—for example, change "all of mankind benefits" to "everyone benefits."

Use nonoffensive language. Finally, you can demonstrate linguistic sensitivity by choosing words that do not offend your listeners. Do you swear when you are with our friends but clean up your act when you are with your grandparents? If so, you are self-monitoring your language so that you don't offend your grandma. Just as you modify your speech when you are with your grandmother, so too you should avoid language that is offensive to those you are talking with.

generic language
using words that may apply only to one sex, race, or other group as though they represent everyone

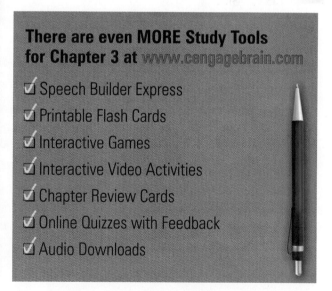

There are even **MORE Study Tools**
for Chapter 3 at www.cengagebrain.com

☑ Speech Builder Express
☑ Printable Flash Cards
☑ Interactive Games
☑ Interactive Video Activities
☑ Chapter Review Cards
☑ Online Quizzes with Feedback
☑ Audio Downloads

© JIM KOLACZKO/ISTOCKPHOTO.COM

4

Learning Outcomes

LO¹ Identify characteristics of non-verbal communication

LO² Identify the different types of non-verbal communication

LO³ Discuss how our self-presentation affects communication

LO⁴ Understand guidelines for improving non-verbal communication

Communicating through *Non-Verbal* Behaviors

© SCOTT HOGGE/ISTOCKPHOTO.COM

"When used effectively, non-verbal communication helps clarify what we are trying to convey verbally."

We've all heard—and said—"actions speak louder than words." In fact, actions are so important to our communication that researchers have estimated that in face-to-face communication as much as 60 percent of the social meaning is a result of nonverbal behavior (Burgoon & Bacue, 2003, p. 179). In other words, the meaning we assign to any communication is based on both the content of the verbal message and our interpretation of the non-verbal behavior that accompanies and surrounds the verbal message.

We begin this chapter by briefly identifying the characteristics of non-verbal communication. Next, we describe the types of non-verbal information we use to communicate with others: use of body (kinesics), use of voice (paralanguage), use of space (proxemics), use of time (chronemics), and self-presentation cues (appearance, including clothing and grooming). Finally, we offer suggestions to help you improve your clarity in sending non-verbal messages and your accuracy in interpreting the non-verbal messages you receive from others.

In the broadest sense, the term *non-verbal communication* describes all human communication messages that transcend spoken or written words (Knapp & Hall, 2006). Specifically, **non-verbal communication behaviors** are those signals that typically accompany our verbal message—our eyes and face, our gestures, our use of voice, and even our appearance. These behaviors are usually interpreted as intentional and have agreed-upon interpretations in a particular culture or speech community (Burgoon & Hoobler, 2002, p. 244).

The widespread use of computer-mediated communication (CMC—e-mail, Facebook, blogs, texting, and so forth) has highlighted non-verbal communication's role in clarifying meaning and conveying emotion. It has become obvious that when CMC is limited to only words, chances for misunderstanding skyrocket (Olaniran, 2002–2003). Recognition of this fact led CMC users to improvise and create **emoticons**: symbolic pictures made with keyboard characters that represent the emotional tone that non-verbal behaviors add to face-to-face verbal messages.

non-verbal communication behaviors
bodily actions and vocal qualities that typically accompany a verbal message

emoticons
symbolic pictures made with keyboard characters that represent the emotional tone that non-verbal behaviors add to face-to-face verbal messages

What do you think?

I don't like it when people stand too close when they're talking to me.

Strongly Disagree   Strongly Agree
1   2   3   4   5   6   7   8   9   10

LO¹ Characteristics of Non-Verbal Communication

When used effectively, non-verbal communication helps clarify what we are trying to convey verbally. Non-verbal communication has four important

kinesics
the interpretation of
body motions used in
communication

characteristics: it is inevitable, it is the primary conveyer of emotions, it is multichanneled, and it is ambiguous.

First, non-verbal communication is *inevitable*. In their germinal book *Pragmatics of Human Communication*, Watzlawick, Bavelas, and Jackson (1967) coined the phrase "We cannot NOT communicate." Though grammatically awkward, this phrase captures the essence of what we mean when we say that non-verbal communication is inevitable. If you are in the presence of someone else, your non-verbal behaviors (whether intentional or not) are sending messages. Moreover, although we can choose what we say in our verbal message, we often don't control our non-verbal behavior and how it is interpreted. When Austin yawns and stares off into the distance during class, his classmates will notice this behavior and assign meaning to it. One classmate may interpret it as a sign of boredom, another might see it as a sign of fatigue, and yet another may view it as a message of disrespect. Meanwhile, Austin may be oblivious to all of the messages that his behavior is sending. Have you ever noticed a classmate checking e-mail or Facebook during class? How did you interpret what you saw? Have you ever done this during a class? If so, what possible messages might your behavior be sending to your instructor and classmates?

Second, non-verbal communication is the *primary conveyor of our emotions*. When we listen to others, we base our interpretation of their feelings and emotions almost totally on their non-verbal behavior. In fact, about 93 percent of the emotional meaning of messages is conveyed non-verbally (Mehrabian, 1972). So, when Janelle says, "I'm fine, but thanks for asking," her sister Renee will understand the real message based on the non-verbal behaviors that accompany it. For example, if Janelle uses a sarcastic tone, Renee may decide that Janelle is angry about something. If Janelle sighs, averts her eyes, tears up, and almost whispers her message, Renee may decide that Janelle is sad and emotionally upset.

Third, non-verbal communication is *multichanneled*. We perceive meaning from a variety of non-verbal behaviors including posture, gestures, body movements, appearance, and vocal mannerisms. When we interpret non-verbal behavior, we usually base our perception on a combination of these behaviors. So, when Anna observes Mimi's failure to sustain eye contact, her bowed head, and her repetitive toe-stubbing in the dirt, she may decide that her daughter is lying about not hitting her brother. The fact that non-verbal communication is multichanneled is one reason people are more likely to believe non-verbal communication when non-verbal behaviors contradict the verbal message (Burgoon, Blair, & Strom, 2008).

Finally, non-verbal communication is *ambiguous*. Very few non-verbal behaviors mean the same thing to everyone. The meaning of one non-verbal behavior can vary, for example, based on culture, sex, gender, and even context or situation. For example, in mainstream American culture, direct eye contact tends to be understood as a sign of respect. That's why parents often tell their children, "Look at me when I'm talking to you." In many Native American, Latin American, Caribbean, and African cultures, however, a direct gaze can be interpreted as disrespectful if the speaker is a superior. In this case, averting one's eyes signals respect. Not only can the meaning of a non-verbal behavior vary in different cultures, but the meaning of the same non-verbal behavior also can differ based on the situation. For example, a furrowed brow might convey Byron's confusion when he did not understand his professor's explanation of the assignment, or Monica's anger when she discovered she did not get the internship she had worked so hard for, or Max's disgust when he was dissecting a frog during biology lab.

LO² Types of Non-Verbal Communication

There are a variety of types of non-verbal messages that we interpret from others and display ourselves. These include the use of the body (kinesics), the voice (vocalics/paralanguage), space (proxemics), and time (chronemics), as well as self-presentation cues.

Use of the Body: Kinesics

Of all the research on non-verbal behavior, you are probably most familiar with kinesics, the technical name for the interpretation of what and how

© JUSTIN HORROCKS/ISTOCKPHOTO.COM

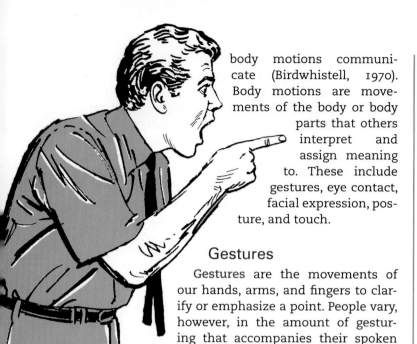

body motions communicate (Birdwhistell, 1970). Body motions are movements of the body or body parts that others interpret and assign meaning to. These include gestures, eye contact, facial expression, posture, and touch.

Gestures

Gestures are the movements of our hands, arms, and fingers to clarify or emphasize a point. People vary, however, in the amount of gesturing that accompanies their spoken messages; for example, some people "talk with their hands" far more than others. Unfortunately, using our hands too much can defeat our purpose and distract listeners from the message we are trying to convey. Some gestures, called **illustrators**, augment the verbal message. When you say "about this high" or "nearly this round," your listeners expect to see a gesture accompanying your verbal description. Other gestures, called **emblems**, can stand alone and substitute completely for words. When you raise your finger and place it vertically across your lips, it signifies "Quiet." An emblem has an automatic agreed-upon meaning in a particular culture, but the meaning assigned to a specific gesture can vary across cultures. For example, the American hand sign for "OK" has an obscene sexual meaning in some European countries and stands for "I'll kill you" in Tunisia. **Adaptors** are gestures that occur unconsciously as a response to a physical need. For example, you may scratch an itch, adjust your glasses, or rub your hands together when they are cold. You do not mean to communicate a message with these gestures, but others do notice and attach meaning to them. Some research suggests differences between how much women and men use adaptors. For example, women tend to play more often with their hair or clothing and tap their fingers more often than men (Pearson, Turner, & West, 1995). Do you know anyone who tends to use a lot of gestures when he or she talks to you? Does it help or hurt message clarity? Why?

Eye Contact

The technical term for **eye contact**, or **gaze**, is oculesics. It has to do with how and how much we look at others when we are communicating. Although the amount of eye contact differs from person to person and from situation to situation, studies show that talkers hold eye contact about 40 percent of the time, and listeners nearly 70 percent of the time (Knapp & Hall, 2006).

Through our eye contact, we both express our emotions and monitor what is occurring in the interaction. How we look at a person can convey a range of emotions such as anger, fear, or affection. The saying "The eyes are the windows to the soul" acknowledges how powerfully we express emotions through eye contact. With eye contact, you can tell whether a person or an audience is paying attention to and interested in what you are saying, as well the person's or the audience's reaction to your comments.

A majority of people in the United States and other Western cultures expect those with whom they are communicating to look them in the eye. Samovar, Porter, and McDaniel (2009) explain, however, that direct eye contact is not a custom throughout the world. For instance, in Japan, prolonged eye contact is considered rude, disrespectful, and threatening.

In the United States, women tend to have more frequent eye contact during conversations than men do (Cegala & Sillars, 1989). Moreover, women tend to hold eye contact longer than men, regardless of the sex of the person they are interacting with (Wood, 2007). It is important to note that these differences, which we have described according to biological sex, are also related to notions of gender and standpoint in society. In other words, people (male or female) will give more eye contact when they are displaying feminine-type behaviors than when they are displaying masculine-type behaviors. Women and men using a feminine style of communication also tend to smile frequently.

gestures
movements of our hands, arms, and fingers that we use to describe or to emphasize

illustrators
gestures that augment a verbal message

emblems
gestures that can substitute for words

adaptors
gestures that respond to a physical need

eye contact (or gaze)
how and how much we look at people with whom we are communicating

© CREATAS/JUPITERIMAGES

facial expression
the arrangement of facial muscles to communicate emotional states or reactions to messages

posture
the position and movement of the body

body orientation
posture in relation to another person

body movement
movement that helps clarify meaning (motivated) or movement that distracts listeners from the point being made (unmotivated)

haptics
the interpretation of touch

Facial Expression

Facial expression is the arrangement of facial muscles to communicate emotional states or reactions to messages. Our facial expressions are especially important in conveying the six basic human emotions of happiness, sadness, surprise, fear, anger, and disgust. Studies show that there are many similarities in non-verbal communication across cultures with regard to facial expressions. For instance, a slight raising of the eyebrow communicates recognition, whereas the wrinkling of one's nose communicates repulsion (Martin & Nakayama, 2000, pp. 183–184). The comedic actor Jim Carrey is notorious for his use of exaggerated facial expressions to reveal emotions in his films (for example, *The Mask, Dumb and Dumber, Liar Liar, The Truman Show,* and *Bruce Almighty*). If you've ever watched the sitcom *Seinfeld*, you may also recall that Kramer (played by Michael Richards) is a master at using facial expressions to make his messages more poignant.

Facial expressions are so important to communicating the emotional part of a message that people often use representative smiley face ☺, sad face ☹, and other emoticons to represent facial expressions when texting, sending e-mail, or posting comments on social networking sites like Facebook (Walther & Parks, 2002).

Posture

Posture is how we position (body orientation) and move our body (body movement). From our posture, others interpret how attentive, respectful, and dominant we are. Body orientation refers to our posture in relation to other people. Facing another person squarely is called *direct body orientation*. When two people's bodies are at angles to each other, this is called *indirect body orientation*. In many situations, direct body orientation signals attentiveness and respect, and indirect body orientation shows inattentiveness and disrespect. In a job interview, you are likely to sit up straight and face the interviewer directly because you want to communicate your interest and respect. Interviewers tend to interpret a slouched posture and indirect body orientation as inattentiveness and disrespect. Yet in other situations, such as talking with friends, a slouched posture and indirect body orientation may be appropriate and may not carry messages about attention or respect. When you are making a speech, an upright stance and squared shoulders will help your audience perceive you as poised and self-confident. When you are giving a speech, be sure to distribute your weight equally on both feet so that you appear confident. Body movement can be motivated (movement that helps clarify meaning) or unmotivated (movement that distracts listeners from the point being made). Pacing, for example, is unmotivated movement.

Haptics

Haptics is the technical term for what and how touch communicates. Touching behavior is a fundamental aspect of non-verbal communication. We use our hands, our arms, and other body parts to pat, hug, slap, kiss, pinch, stroke, hold, embrace, and tickle others. People differ in their use of touching behavior and their reactions to unsolicited touch from others. Some people like to touch others and be touched; other people do not. How we interpret appropriate and inappropriate touch varies not only among individuals but also varies with culture, sex, and gender.

Although American culture uses relatively little contact, we are likely to shake hands to be sociable and polite, pat a person on the back for encouragement, and hug a person to show love. Still, the kinds and amounts of touching behavior within our society vary widely. Touching behavior that seems appropriate to one person may be perceived as overly intimate or threatening by another. Moreover, the perceived appropriateness of touch differs with the context. Touch that is considered appropriate in private may embarrass a person when done in public or in a large group of people. For example, a couple holding hands while strolling in the park or at a shopping mall might seem appropriate, but kissing and fondling each other might not.

Lots of contact and touching is considered normal behavior in some cultures but not encouraged in others (Samovar, Porter, & McDaniel, 2009). Some cultures in South and Central America, as well as many in southern Europe, encourage contact and engage in frequent touching (Neuliep, 2006). In many Arabic countries, for instance, two grown men walking down the street holding hands is a sign of friendship. In the United States, however, it might be interpreted as a sign of an intimate relationship. Many northern European cultures tend to be medium to low in contact, and many Asian cultures are mainly low-contact cultures. The United States,

66 What's an appropriate level of touch in the workplace? 99

© ISTOCKPHOTO.COM / © ISTOCKPHOTO.COM

which is a country of immigrants, is generally perceived to be medium in contact, though there are wide differences between individual Americans due to variations in family heritage.

Some research also suggests that women tend to touch others less than men do, but value touching more than men do. Women view touch as an expressive behavior that demonstrates warmth and affiliation, whereas men view touch as instrumental behavior, something that could lead to sexual activity (Pearson, West, & Turner, 1995, p. 142). Of course, these are generalizations based on gender and standpoints. They do not apply to every woman and man.

Use of the Voice: Vocalics

The interpretation of a verbal message based on the paralinguistic features is called **vocalics**. **Paralanguage** is the voiced but not verbal part of a spoken message. Paralanguage comprises six vocal characteristics: pitch, volume, rate, quality, intonation, and vocalized pauses.

Pitch

Pitch is the highness or lowness of vocal tone. People raise and lower vocal pitch to emphasize ideas and emotions and to indicate questions. People sometimes raise their pitch when they are nervous or afraid. They may lower the pitch to convey peacefulness or sadness (as in a speech given at a funeral) or when they are trying to be forceful. When parents reprimand a child for misbehaving, for example, they typically lower their pitch.

Volume

Volume is the loudness or softness of tone. Whereas some people have booming voices that carry long distances, others are normally soft-spoken. People who speak too loudly run the risk of appearing obnoxious or pushy, whereas people who speak too softly might appear timid and unsure of themselves. Regardless of their normal volume level, however, people also tend to vary their volume depending on the situation, the topic of discussion, and emotional intent. For example, people talk loudly when they wish to be heard in noisy settings. They may speak louder when they are angry and softer when they are being romantic or loving. We should point out here that there are a few cultural and gender variations in the meanings we attach to volume. Samovar, Porter, and McDaniel (2009) suggest, for example, that Arabs tend to speak with a great deal of volume to convey strength and sincerity, whereas soft voices are preferred in Britain, Japan, and Thailand.

Rate

Rate is the speed at which a person speaks. Most people naturally speak between 100 and 200 words per minute. People tend to talk more rapidly when they are happy, frightened, nervous, or excited and more slowly when they are problem solving out loud or are trying to emphasize a point. People who speak too slowly run the risk of boring listeners, and those who speak too quickly may not be intelligible.

Quality (Timbre)

Quality is the sound of a person's voice that distinguishes it from others. Voice quality may be breathy (Marilyn Monroe or Kathleen Turner), strident (Joan Rivers or Marge Simpson), throaty (Nick Nolte or Jack Nicholson), or nasal (Fran Drescher in *The Nanny*). Although each person's voice has a distinct quality, too much breathiness can make people sound frail,

vocalics
the interpretation of the message based on the paralinguistic features

paralanguage
the voiced but not verbal part of a spoken message

pitch
the highness or lowness of vocal tone

volume
the loudness or softness of tone

rate
the speed at which a person speaks

quality
the sound of a person's voice

intonation
the variety, melody, or inflection in one's voice

vocalized pauses
extraneous sounds or words that interrupt fluent speech

proxemics
the interpretation of a person's use of space

personal space
the distance you try to maintain when you interact with other people

too much stridence can make them seem hypertense, too much throatiness can make them seem cold and unsympathetic, and too much nasality can make them sound immature or unintelligent.

Intonation

Intonation is the variety, melody, or inflection in one's voice. Voices with little intonation are described as monotone and tend to bore listeners. If you have ever seen the movie *Ferris Bueller's Day Off*, you may recall the teacher (played by Ben Stein) who is portrayed as boring via a monotone pitch as he questions the class: "Anyone? Anyone? Bueller? Bueller?" Other voices have too much intonation and may be perceived as sing-songy and childlike. Too much intonation is often interpreted as ditzy or even dim-witted. People prefer to listen to voices with a moderate amount of intonation.

In the United States, there are stereotypes about masculine and feminine voices and, thus, how it is appropriate for men and women to sound. Masculine voices are expected to be low-pitched and loud, with moderate to low intonation; feminine voices are expected to be higher-pitched, softer in volume, and more expressive. Although both sexes have the option to portray a range of masculine and feminine paralanguage, most people usually conform to the expectations for their sex (Wood, 2007).

Vocalized Pauses

Vocalized pauses are extraneous sounds or words that interrupt fluent speech. The most common vocalized pauses that creep into our speech include "uh," "um," "er," "well," "OK," and those nearly universal interrupters of American conversations, "you know" and "like." At times we may use vocal pauses to hold our turn when we momentarily search for the right word or idea. Because they are not part of the intended message, occasional vocalized pauses are generally ignored by those who are interpreting the message. However, when we begin to use them to

excess, others are likely to perceive us as nervous or unsure of what we are saying. As the use of vocalized pauses increases, people are less able to understand what we are saying, and they may perceive us as confused and our ideas as not well thought out. For some people, vocalized pauses are so pervasive that listeners are unable to concentrate on the meaning of the message.

We can interpret the paralinguistic part of a message as complementing, supplementing, or contradicting the meaning conveyed by the verbal message. So when Joan says, "Well, isn't that an interesting story," how we interpret her meaning will depend on her paralanguage. If she alters her normal voice so that "Well" is varied both in pitch and tone and the rest of her words are spoken in a staccato monotone, we might interpret the vocalics as contradicting the words and perceive her message as sarcasm. But if her voice pitch rises with each word, we might perceive the vocalics as supplementing the message and understand that she is asking a question.

Use of Space: Proxemics

Have you ever been in the midst of a conversation with someone who you felt was standoffish or pushy? If you had analyzed your feeling, you might have discovered that your impression stemmed from how far the person chose to stand from you. If the person seemed to be farther away than you are accustomed to, you might have interpreted the distance as aloofness. If the distance was less than you would have expected, you might have felt uncomfortable and perceived the person as being overly familiar or pushy. **Proxemics** is the formal term for how space and distance communicate (Hall, 1968). People will interpret how you use the personal space around you, the physical spaces that you control and occupy, and the things you choose to decorate your space.

Personal Space

Personal space is the distance we try to maintain when we interact with other people. Our need for and use of personal space stems from our biological territorial nature, for which space is a protective mechanism. How much space we perceive as

© DUNDANIM/SHUTTERSTOCK

Figure 4.1

Personal Space

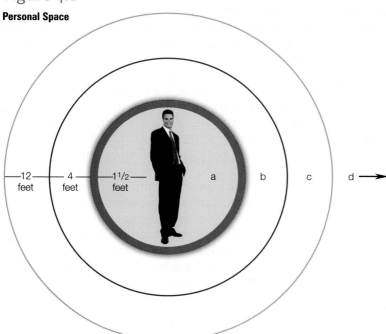

Zone a, **intimate space:** spouses, significant others, family members, and others with whom we have an intimate relationship

Zone b, **personal distance:** friends

Zone c, **social distance:** business associates and acquaintances

Zone d, **public distance:** strangers

appropriate depends on our individual preference, the nature of our relationship to the other person or people, and our culture. Although the absolute amount of space varies from person to person, message to message, and culture to culture, in general the amount of personal space we view as appropriate decreases as the intimacy of our relationship increases. For example, in the dominant U.S. culture, four distinct distances are generally perceived as appropriate and comfortable, depending on the nature of the conversation. *Intimate distance* is defined as up to 18 inches and is appropriate for private conversations between close friends. *Personal distance*, from 18 inches to 4 feet, is the space in which casual conversation occurs. *Social distance*, from 4 to 12 feet, is where impersonal business such as a job interview is conducted. *Public distance* is anything more than 12 feet (Hall, 1966).

Of greatest concern to us is the intimate distance—that which we regard as appropriate for intimate conversation with close friends, parents, and younger children. People usually become uncomfortable when "outsiders" violate this intimate distance. For instance, in a movie theater that is less than one-quarter full, people will tend to leave one or more seats empty between themselves and others whom

they do not know. If a stranger sits right next to us in such a setting, we are likely to feel uncomfortable or threatened and may even move away. Intrusions into our intimate space are acceptable only in certain settings and then only when all involved follow the unwritten rules. For instance, people will tolerate being packed into a crowded elevator or subway and even touching others they do not know, provided that the others follow the "rules." The rules may include standing rigidly, looking at the floor or the indicator above the door, but not making eye contact with others. The rules also include ignoring or pretending that they are not touching.

© KURHAN/SHUTTERSTOCK

physical space
the physical environment over which you exert control

Physical Space

Physical space is the part of the physical environment over which we exert control. Our territorial natures not only lead us to maintain personal distance but also to assert ownership claims to parts of the physical space that we occupy. Sometimes we do not realize the ways we claim space as our own; in other instances, we go to great lengths to visibly "mark" our territory. For example, Ramon arrives early for the first day of class, finds an empty desk, and puts his backpack next to it on the floor and his coat on the seat. He then makes a quick trip to the restroom. If someone comes along while Ramon is gone, moves Ramon's backpack and coat, and sits down at the desk, then that person is violating what Ramon has marked as his territory. If you regularly take the same seat in a class, then that habit becomes a type of marker, signaling to others that a particular seat location is yours. Other students will often leave that seat empty because they have perceived it as yours. Not only can we interpret someone's ownership of space by such markers, but we also can understand a person's status in a group by noting where the person sits and the amount of space over which ownership is claimed. In a well-established group, people with differing opinions will often choose to sit on opposite sides of the table, while allies will sit in adjacent spots. So if you are observant, you can tell where people stand on an issue by noticing where they choose to sit. Many other meanings can be discerned from how people use physical space. Have you ever attended a middle-school dance and noticed how the

artifacts
objects and possessions we use to decorate the physical space we control

chronemics
the interpretation of a person's use of time

monochronic time orientation
a time orientation that emphasizes doing one thing at a time

boys typically sit on one side of the room and the girls on the other? If so, what might that be communicating?

Artifacts

Artifacts are the objects and possessions we use to decorate the physical space we control. When others enter our homes, our offices, or our dorm rooms, they look around and notice what objects we have chosen to place in the space and how we have arranged them. Then they assign meaning to what they see. For example, when Katie visited her boyfriend, Peter, at school, the first thing she noticed was a picture on his bulletin board of him hugging a cute woman she did not recognize. The second thing she noticed was that the framed picture she had given him of her before he left for school was nowhere to be found. From this, she concluded that Peter wasn't honoring his promise not to see anyone at school.

The way we arrange the artifacts in our space also can non-verbally communicate to others. Professors and businesspeople have learned that by choosing and arranging the artifacts in their space, they can influence interactions. We once knew a professor who was very softhearted. So when he had to handle the students who were petitioning to enter closed classes, he turned his desk, which normally faced the window, so that it was directly in front of the door. That way, the students couldn't get into his office, sit down, and break his resolve with their sad stories. Instead, they had to plead their case standing in the very public hall. In this case, his desk served as a barrier and protected him from his softhearted self.

People choose artifacts not just for their function but also for the message that the objects convey about them. When Lee, the baby of his family, got his first job, the first items he purchased for his new apartment were a large flat-screen TV and a stuffed leather couch and chair. He chose these primarily to impress his older and already successful brother. Whether the artifacts you choose are conscious attempts to impress or simply reflect your taste, when others enter your space, they will notice the artifacts and draw conclusions. Have you ever gone to visit someone and been turned off by how messy or dirty the home was? Why? What did the artifacts communicate to you?

As is the case with most forms of non-verbal communication, one's use of space and territory is associated with culture (Samovar, Porter, & McDaniel, 2009). Western cultures like the United States generally demand more space than do collectivist cultures such as India, China, and Japan and will defend space more strongly. Seating and furniture placement may also vary by cultural expectations. For example, Americans in groups tend to talk to those seated opposite them, but Chinese prefer to talk to those seated next to them. Furniture arrangement in the United States and Germany often emphasizes privacy. In France and Japan, furniture is typically arranged for group conversation or participation.

Use of Time: Chronemics

Chronemics is how we interpret use of time and is based largely on cultural context (see, for example, Hall, 1959). People from Western cultures tend to be very time conscious. We carry daily planners and wear digital watches so we can arrive at precisely the "right time." People from many other cultures are far less time conscious. In some Mexican cultures, for example, it's rare to specify an exact time for guests to arrive for dinner. In another example, American executives tend to get right down to business and finish quickly, whereas Japanese executives expect to devote time to social interaction first (Samovar, Porter, & McDaniel, 2009).

Moreover, people can have either a monochronic or a polychronic orientation to time. Those of us with a **monochronic time orientation** tend to concentrate our efforts on one task, and only when it is finished or when the time we have allotted to it is over, do we move on to another task. If we are monochronic, we see time as "real" and think about "spending time," "losing time," and so on. As a result, monochronic people subordinate interpersonal relationships to their schedule (Dahl, 2004, p. 11).

People who have a polychromic time orientation tackle multiple tasks at once.

© NAGY-BAGOLY ARPAD/SHUTTERSTOCK

When Margarite's sister comes into the room and interrupts her study time to share some good news, Margarite, who is monochronic, screams, "Get out! Can't you see I'm studying?" Others of us with a polychronic time orientation tend to tackle multiple tasks at once. For example, while writing a paper, we might periodically check our e-mail and Facebook messages and cook dinner, too. Polychronic people see time as flexible and fluid and view appointment times and schedules as variable and subordinate to interpersonal relationships; they easily alter or adapt their schedule to meet the needs of their relationships (Dahl, 2004, p. 11). For example, George, who is polychronic, shows up for a noon lunch with Raoul at 12:47 p.m. because as he was leaving his office, his coworker stopped him to ask for help on a problem.

How Margarite's sister or Raoul interpreted the time behavior experienced depends on his or her time orientation. If Margarite's sister is also monochronic, she probably apologized, perceiving her own behavior to have been at fault. If Raoul is polychronic, he will not be offended by George's late arrival because he will view George's delay as understandable. We tend to view others' use of time through the lens of the culture from which we come. So if we are monochronic in our orientation

to time, we will view the polychronic time behavior of someone else as being "rude" and vice versa.

As you probably recognize, the dominant U.S. culture has a monochronic time orientation; Swiss and German cultures tend to be even more monochronic. On the other hand, many Latin American and Arab cultures have a polychronic orientation. Immigration has led to an influx of Arab workers into northern Europe and of Latin American workers into the United States. As a result, you are quite likely to encounter people whose use of time is different from your own.

polychronic time orientation
a time orientation that emphasizes doing multiple things at once

endomorph
round and heavy body type

mesomorph
muscular and athletic body type

ectomorph
lean and little muscle development

LO³ Self-Presentation Cues

People learn a lot about us based on how we look. This includes our physical appearance as well as our clothing and grooming.

Physical Appearance

People make judgments about others based on how they look. We can control our physique to some extent through exercise, diet, cosmetic surgery, and so on. But we also inherit much of our physical appearance, including our body type and physical features such as hair and eyes. Our body is one of the first things that others notice about us, and there are culture-based stereotypes associated with each of the three general body shapes. Endomorphs, who are shaped round and heavy, are stereotyped as kind, gentle, and jovial. Mesomorphs, who are muscular and strong, are believed to be energetic, outgoing, and confident. Ectomorphs, whose bodies are lean and have little muscle development, are stereotyped as brainy, anxious, and cautious. Although not everyone fits perfectly into one of these categories, each person tends toward one body type. Even though these stereotypes are far from accurate, there is ample anecdotal evidence to suggest that many of us form our first impressions based on body type stereotypes.

Clothing and Grooming

Our clothing and personal grooming communicate a message about us. Today, more than ever, people use clothing choices, body art, and other personal

© DMITRY MELNIKOV/SHUTTERSTOCK

grooming to communicate who they are and what they stand for. Likewise, when we meet someone, we are likely to form our impression of them from how they are dressed and groomed. Because clothing and grooming can be altered to suit the occasion, we rely heavily on these non-verbal cues to understand who other people are and how to treat them. As a result, you can change how people perceive you by altering your clothing and grooming. For example, a successful sales representative may wear an oversize white T-shirt, baggy shorts, and a backward ball cap when hanging out with his friends; put on khakis and a golf shirt to go to the office; and dress in a formal blue suit to make a major presentation to a potential client group. In each case, he uses what he is wearing to communicate who he is and how others should treat him. Body art (piercings and tattoos) have become quite popular in the United States. Clothing choices vary based on gender, as well. In the United States, feminine clothing is more decorative, and masculine clothing is more functional (Wood, 2007). In professional settings today, masculine clothing (a two-piece suit) is considered most appropriate for both women and men, but women will often wear feminine clothing on a date.

LO4 Guidelines for Improving Non-Verbal Communication

Because non-verbal messages are inevitable, multichanneled, ambiguous, and sometimes unintentional, decoding them accurately can be tricky. Add to this the fact that the meaning for any non-verbal behavior can vary by situation, culture, and gender, and you begin to understand why we so often misread the behavior of others. The following guidelines can help you improve the likelihood that the messages you send will be perceived accurately and that you will accurately interpret the non-verbal messages you receive.

Sending Non-Verbal Messages

Be conscious of the non-verbal behaviors you are displaying. Remember that you are always communicating non-verbally. Some non-verbal cues will always be out of your level of consciousness, but you should work to bring more of your non-verbal behavior into your conscious awareness. Pay attention to what you are doing with your body, voice, space, and self-presentation cues. If you initially have difficulty doing this, ask a friend to point out the non-verbal behaviors you are displaying.

Be purposeful in your use of non-verbal communication. Sometimes, it is important to control what you are communicating non-verbally. For instance, if you want to be persuasive, you should use non-verbal cues that demonstrate confidence and credibility. These may include direct eye contact, a serious facial expression, a relaxed posture, a loud and low-pitched voice with no vocal interferences, and a professional style of clothing and grooming. Although there are no absolute prescriptions for communicating non-verbally, we can make strategic choices to convey the message we desire.

Make sure that your non-verbal cues do not distract from your message. When you are not aware of what non-verbal cues you are displaying or when you are anxious, certain non-verbal behaviors may hinder your communication. Fidgeting, tapping your fingers on a table, pacing, mumbling, and using vocal interferences and adaptors can hinder other people's interpretation

© STEVE DEBENPORT/ISTOCKPHOTO.COM

of your message. Try to use non-verbal behaviors that enhance rather than distract from your message.

Make your non-verbal communication match your verbal communication. When non-verbal messages contradict verbal messages, people are more likely to believe the non-verbal messages, so it is important to have your verbal and non-verbal messages match. In addition, the various kinds of non-verbal communication behavior should match each other. If you are feeling sad, your voice should be softer and less expressive, and you should avoid smiling, which would contradict your voice. People get confused and frustrated by inconsistent messages.

Adapt your non-verbal behavior to the situation. Situations vary in their formality, familiarity among the people, and purpose. Just like you would select different language for different situations, you should adapt your non-verbal messages to the situation. Assess what the situation calls for in terms of body motions, paralanguage, proxemics and territory, artifacts, chronemics, and physical appearance. Of course, you already do some situational adapting with non-verbal communication. You would not dress the same way for a wedding as you do to walk the dog. You do not treat your brother's space and territory the same way you treat your doctor's space and territory. The more you can consciously adapt your non-verbal behavior to what seems appropriate to the situation, the more effective you will be as a communicator.

Interpreting Non-Verbal Messages

Do not automatically assume that a particular behavior means the same to everyone. There is much room for error when people draw quick conclusions about an aspect of non-verbal behavior. Instead, assume multiple possibilities based on culture, gender, and even individual differences. You may have learned over time that your friend grinds her teeth when she is excited. You may never encounter another person who uses this behavior in this way.

Consider non-verbal behaviors as they relate to the context of the message. Because the same non-verbal cue can mean different things in different contexts, take the time to consider how it is intended in a given situation. Realize, too, that you might not understand all the details of the situation. One behavior that often offends teachers is a student answering a cell phone during class. Before assuming the worst, however, it might be best if the teacher tried to discover why the student did so. The student might be in the midst of a serious family situation that demanded instant access.

Pay attention to the multiple non-verbal cues being sent and their relationship to the verbal message. In any one interaction, you are likely to get simultaneous messages from a person's eyes, face, gestures, posture, voice, and use of space and touch. Even in electronic communication, where most non-verbal communication is impossible, facial expression and touch can be communicated through emoticons, paralanguage through capitalization of words, and chronemics through the timing and length of the electronic message. By taking into consideration all non-verbal cues, you will be more effective in interpreting others' messages.

Use perception checking. The skill of perception checking lets you see if your interpretation of another person's message is accurate. By describing the non-verbal behavior you have noticed and tentatively sharing your interpretation of it, you can get confirmation or correction of your interpretation.

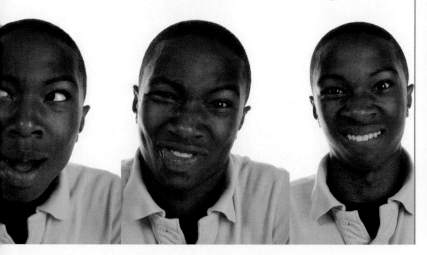

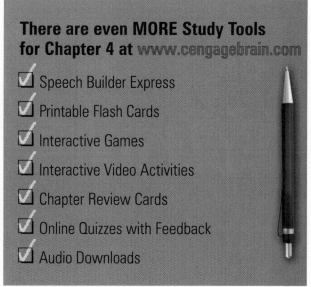

There are even MORE Study Tools for Chapter 4 at www.cengagebrain.com

- ☑ Speech Builder Express
- ☑ Printable Flash Cards
- ☑ Interactive Games
- ☑ Interactive Video Activities
- ☑ Chapter Review Cards
- ☑ Online Quizzes with Feedback
- ☑ Audio Downloads

Listening
and
Responding

Learning Outcomes

1 Define "listening"

2 Identify the five types of listening

3 Identify the five steps of the listening process

> **"** *Listening is important for effective communication because 50 percent or more of the time we spend communicating is spent listening.* **"**

A re you a good listener when you are under pressure? Or do you occasionally find that your mind wanders when others are talking to you? We must not underestimate the importance of listening, because it can provide clarification, connect us to others, build trust and empathy, help us learn and remember material, and improve our ability to evaluate information (Donoghue & Siegel, 2005). We begin this chapter with a discussion of what listening is and the different types of listening. Then, we focus on specific ways you can improve your listening skills during each phase of the listening process.

listening
the process of receiving, constructing meaning from, and responding to spoken and/or non-verbal messages

LO¹ What Is Listening?

People sometimes make the mistake of thinking that listening and hearing are the same thing, but they're not. Hearing is a physiological process, whereas listening is a cognitive process. In other words, listening occurs only when we choose to attach meaning to what we hear. Members of the International Listening Association define listening as "the process of receiving, construct-ing meaning from, and responding to spoken and/or non-verbal messages" (Brownell, 2002, p. 48). One way to understand how listening differs from hearing is to realize that hearing-impaired individuals can still engage in effective listening.

What do you think?

I find it easy to identify with the feelings of the person I am talking to.

Strongly Disagree									Strongly Agree
1	2	3	4	5	6	7	8	9	10

Listening is important for effective communication because 50 percent or more of the time we spend communicating is spent listening (Janusik & Wolvin, 2006). Although most of us have spent a great deal of time learning to read and write, fewer than 2 percent of us have had any formal listening training (International Listening Association). According to research by the International Listening Association, even when we try to listen carefully, most of us remember only about 50 percent of what we hear shortly after hearing it and only about 20 percent two days later. One survey of top-level North American executives revealed that 80 percent believe listening is one of the most important skills needed in the corporate environment (Salopek, 1999). It simply makes sense to improve our listening skills.

LO² Types of Listening

Although we spend most of the time we are communicating listening to what others are saying, the type of listening that is required of us depends

© MARILYN NIEVES/ISTOCKPHOTO.COM

appreciative listening
listening for enjoyment

discriminative listening
listening to understand the meaning of a message

comprehensive listening
listening to learn or remember

empathic listening
listening to understand the speaker's feeling about the message

critical listening
listening to evaluate the truthfulness or honesty of a message

on the situation. So in order to be an effective listener in different situations, you must first consider your purpose for listening. Scholars have identified five types of listening based on five different purposes. These types are appreciative, discriminative, comprehensive, empathic, and critical listening (Wolvin & Coakley, 1996). Each type of listening requires a different degree of psychological processing. By considering your purpose, you can engage in the most appropriate type of listening in a given situation and devote the degree of psychological processing necessary.

Appreciative Listening

In an **appreciative listening** situation, your goal is to listen for enjoyment (Wolvin & Coakley, 1996). With appreciative listening, you do not have to focus as closely or as carefully on specifics as you do in other listening situations. You might use appreciative listening during a casual social conversation while watching a ball game with friends or when listening to your daughter describe the fish she caught on an outing with grandpa. Most people listen to music in this way.

Discriminative Listening

In a discriminative listening situation, your goal is to accurately understand the speaker's meaning. At times this involves listening "between the lines" for meaning conveyed in other ways than the words themselves. Discriminative listening requires us to pay attention not only to the words but also to non-verbal cues such as rate, pitch, inflection, volume, voice quality, inflection, and

gestures. So when a doctor is explaining the results of a test, a patient not only listens carefully to what the doctor is saying but also pays attention to the non-verbal cues that indicate whether these results are troubling or routine. Likewise, we often choose to support political candidates based on whether we believe that we can trust them. If you've ever questioned the truthfulness of a friend's claim, what non-verbal cues helped convince you that they were not telling the whole truth?

Comprehensive Listening

In a **comprehensive listening** situation, your goal is not only to understand the speaker's message but also to learn, remember, and be able to recall what has been said. We listen comprehensively to professors lecturing about key concepts, speakers at training seminars, and broadcast news reports that provide timely information about traffic conditions.

Empathic Listening

When the situation calls for us to try to understand how others are feeling about what they have experienced or are talking about, we use **empathic listening**. Therapists, counselors, psychologists, and psychiatrists engage in empathic listening with their clients, as do those who answer telephone hotlines to support troubled people. When your goal is to be a sounding board or help a friend sort through feelings, you will want to begin with empathic listening.

Critical Listening

In **critical listening** situations, your ultimate goal is to evaluate the worth of a message. Because you need to hear, understand, evaluate, and assign worth to the message, it requires more psychological processing than the other types. Critical listening is the most demanding of the types of listening because it requires that you understand and remember both the verbal and non-verbal message, assess the speaker's credibility, and effectively analyze the truthfulness of the message. Fortunately,

© ISTOCKPHOTO.COM

What kind of listening is best for this situation?

we don't need to do critical listening all the time. But when we are talking with salespeople or listening to political candidates, receiving an apology from someone who has violated our trust, or being solicited for a donation, we need to engage in critical listening.

LO³ Steps of the Listening Process

Listening is a complex process. It is made up of five steps that are each a process. These steps are: (a) attending, (b) understanding, (c) remembering, (d) evaluating, and (e) responding to the message.

Attending

Attending is the process of focusing on what a speaker is saying regardless of the potential distractions of other competing stimuli. Poor listeners have difficulty exercising control over what they attend to, often letting their minds drift to thoughts unrelated to the topic. One reason is that people typically speak at a rate of about 120 to 150 words per minute, but our brains can process between 400 and 800 words per minute (Wolvin & Coakley, 1996). This means that we usually assume we know what a speaker is going to say before he or she finishes saying it, so our mind has lots of time to wander from the message. Moreover, research suggests that the average attention span for adults is 20 minutes or less (Stephens, 1999). Some reports even claim that, thanks to the Internet, our attention span is considerably shorter.

So to be a good listener you must train yourself to focus on or attend to what people are saying regardless of potential distractions. Let's consider five techniques that can help you improve your attending.

Get physically ready to listen. Good listeners create a physical environment that will aid listening, and they adopt a listening posture. They eliminate distractions from the physical environment. If music is playing so loudly that it competes with your roommate who is trying to talk with you, turn it down. If you are checking e-mail or Facebook, stop. Shut down the site so that you won't be tempted to check it while you are supposed to be listening. Similarly, turn off or silence your cell phone. A listening posture is one that moves the listener toward the speaker, allows direct eye contact, and stimulates the senses. For instance, when the professor tells the class that the next bit of information will be on the test, effective listeners are likely to sit upright in their chairs, lean forward slightly, cease any unnecessary physical movement, and look directly at the professor.

Resist mental distractions while you listen. Block out wandering thoughts when they creep into your head while you listen. These thoughts may stem from a visual distraction associated with something you see (such as a classmate who enters the room while the professor is lecturing); an auditory distraction associated with something you hear (such as classmates chatting beside you during class); or a physical distraction associated with body aches, pains, or discomfort (such as wondering what you'll eat for lunch because your stomach is growling). Obviously, the more you can do to eliminate the potential for mental distractions, the less likely you'll be to experience wandering thoughts while you listen.

Resist interrupting others. In conversation, we switch from speaker to listener so frequently that we may find it difficult at times to make these shifts completely. Instead of listening, it is easy to rehearse what we are going to say as soon as we have a chance. It is

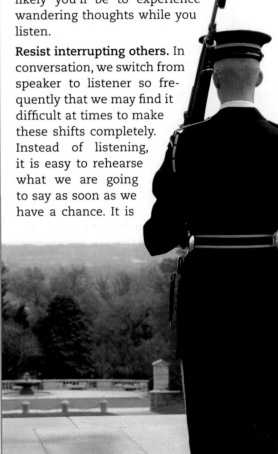

© JAMES STEIDL/SHUTTERSTOCK

attending
the perceptual process of selecting and focusing on specific stimuli from the countless stimuli reaching the senses

understanding
decoding a message accurately to reflect the meaning intended by the speaker

question
a statement designed to get further information or to clarify information already received

paraphrasing
putting into words the ideas or feelings you have perceived from the message

content paraphrase
one that focuses on the denotative meaning of the message

feelings paraphrase
a response that captures the emotions attached to the content of the message

especially important when trying to be a good listener that you let the other person finish before you take your turn to speak. Good listeners resist interrupting others. Especially when you are in a heated conversation or excited about what you just heard, you will consciously need to stop yourself from preparing a response or interrupting the speaker.

Hear a person out before you react. Far too often, we stop listening before the person has finished speaking because we think we know what the person is going to say. Yet often we are wrong. In addition, we often stop listening to people because their mannerisms or words turn us off. Think of the times you may have stopped listening to a professor's lecture and missed important information because of the teacher's accent or gestures. Most of us need to learn the value of patience and silence in allowing others to express themselves and in helping us to listen closely and carefully.

Observe non-verbal cues. Listeners interpret messages more accurately when they observe the non-verbal behaviors accompanying the words. For instance, when your friend says, "Don't worry about me. I'm fine, really," we must interpret cues such as tone of voice, body actions, and facial expression to tell whether she is really fine or whether she is upset but reluctant to tell you about it.

Understanding

Understanding is decoding a message accurately to reflect the meaning intended by the speaker. Sometimes we do not understand because the message is encoded in words that are not in our vocabulary. Other times the meaning that we find in the message may not be the meaning intended by the speaker; and at still other times our misunderstanding may stem from our missing the emotional, non-verbal meaning of a message. We can improve our understanding by asking questions, paraphrasing the message, and empathizing with the speaker.

Ask questions to gain additional information. A question is a statement designed to get further infor-

Steps of the Listening Process

1. Attending
2. Understanding
3. Remembering
4. Evaluating
5. Responding

mation or to clarify information already received. Effective questioning begins by identifying the kind of information you need to increase your understanding. Suppose Maria says to you, "I am totally frustrated. Would you stop at the store on the way home and buy me some more paper?" You may be a bit confused by her request and need more information to understand. Yet if you simply respond "What do you mean?" Maria, who is already frustrated, may become defensive. Instead, you might think about what type of information you need and form a question to meet that need. To increase your understanding, you can ask one of these three types of questions:

- *To get details:* "What kind of paper would you like me to get, and how much will you need?"
- *To clarify word meanings:* "Could you tell me what you mean by *frustrated*?"
- *To clarify feelings:* "What's frustrating you?"

Paraphrase the message to check your understanding. Paraphrasing is putting into words the ideas or feelings you have perceived from the message. For example, during an argument with your sister, after she has stated her concern about your behavior, you might paraphrase what she has said as follows: "You say that you are tired of my talking about work and that you feel that I try to act better than you when I talk about my successes there." Paraphrases may focus on content, on feelings underlying the content, or on both. A **content paraphrase** focuses on the denotative meaning of the message. The first part of the example above ("You say that you are tired of my talking about work") is a content paraphrase. A **feelings paraphrase** is a response that captures the emotions attached to the content of the message. The second part of the example ("you feel that I try to act better than you") is a feelings paraphrase.

By paraphrasing, you give the speaker a chance to verify your understanding. The longer and more complex the message, the more important it is to paraphrase. When the speaker appears to be emotional or when English is not the speaker's native language, paraphrasing is also important.

To paraphrase effectively, (1) listen carefully to the message, (2) notice what images and feelings you have experienced from the message,

(3) determine what the message means to you, and (4) create a message that conveys these images or feelings.

Empathize with the speaker. Empathy is intellectually identifying with or vicariously experiencing the feelings or attitudes of another. To empathize, we generally try to put aside our own feelings or attitudes about another. Three approaches people use when empathizing are empathic responsiveness, perspective taking, and sympathetic responsiveness (Weaver & Kirtley, 1995, p. 131).

- **Empathic responsiveness** occurs when you experience an emotional response parallel to, and as a result of observing, another person's actual or anticipated display of emotion (Omdahl, 1995, p. 4; Stiff, Dillard, Somera, Kim, & Sleight, 1988, p. 199). For instance, when Jackson tells Janis that he is in real trouble financially, and Janis senses the stress and anxiety that Jackson is feeling, we would say that Janis has experienced empathic responsiveness.

- **Perspective taking,** imagining yourself in the place of another, is the most common form of empathizing. Although perspective taking is difficult for many of us (Holtgraves, 2002, p. 122), with conscious effort we can learn to imagine ourselves in the place of another. For example, if Janis personalizes the message by picturing herself in serious financial debt, anticipates the emotions she might experience, and then assumes that Jackson might be feeling the same way, then Janis is empathizing by perspective taking.

- **Sympathetic responsiveness** is feeling concern, compassion, or sorrow for another because of the other's situation or plight. Having sympathy differs from the other two approaches. Rather than attempting to experience the feelings of the other, when you sympathize you translate your intellectual understanding of what the speaker has experienced into your own feelings of concern, compassion, and sorrow for that person. In our previous example, Janis has sympathy for Jackson when she understands that Jackson is embarrassed and worried, but instead of trying to feel those same emotions, she feels concern and compassion for her friend. Because of this difference in perspective, many scholars differentiate sympathy from empathy.

How well you empathize also depends on how observant you are of others' behavior and how clearly you read the non-verbal messages they are sending. To improve your observational skills when another person begins a conversation with you, develop the habit of silently posing two questions to yourself: (1) What emotions do I believe the person is experiencing right now? and (2) On what cues from the person am I basing this conclusion? Consciously asking these questions helps you focus on the non-verbal aspects of messages, which convey most of the information on the person's emotional state.

To further increase the accuracy of reading emotions, you can use the skill of perception checking. This is especially helpful when the other person's culture is different from yours. Atsuko, who was raised in rural Japan (a collectivist culture) and is now studying at a university in Rhode Island, may feel embarrassed when her professor publically compliments her work on a group project. Her friend Meredith might notice Atsuko's reddened cheeks and downcast eyes and comment "Atsuko, you look like I do when I'm embarrassed. Are you uncomfortable that Professor Shank singled you out for praise?"

Remembering

Remembering is being able to retain information and recall it when needed. Too often, people forget almost

---

empathy
intellectually identifying with or vicariously experiencing the feelings or attitudes of another

empathic responsiveness
experiencing an emotional response parallel to, and as a result observing, another person's actual or anticipated display of emotion

perspective taking
imagining yourself in the place of another; the most common form of empathizing

sympathetic responsiveness
feeling concern, compassion, or sorrow for another because of the other's situation or plight

remembering
being able to retain information and recall it when needed

{ Fast Facts—
Professional Mourning }

In ancient cultures, particularly in Egypt and the Near East, it was a common practice to hire professional mourners when someone died, both to lament at the funeral and sometimes to offer a eulogy. A group of mourners can be seen in this relief from a temple of Hatshepsut, near Luxor, Egypt. What empathy roles do you think these kinds of people perform, and what effect do you think they have on others who are mourning, both individually and collectively?

© ISTOCKPHOTO.COM

mnemonic device
any artificial technique used as a memory aid

evaluation
the process of critically analyzing what you have heard to determine its truthfulness

immediately what they have heard. For instance, you can probably think of many times when you were unable to recall the name of a person to whom you had just been introduced.

Think of how much the education system depends on listening and recalling information. Given the common use of lectures, class discussions, and other listening-based learning experiences, it is not surprising that research shows a link between effective listening and school success (Bommelje, Houston, & Smither, 2003). Three techniques that can help you improve your ability to remember information are repeating, constructing mnemonics, and taking notes.

Repeat the information. Repetition—saying something aloud or mentally two, three, or four times immediately after hearing it —helps listeners store information in long-term memory by providing necessary reinforcement (Estes, 1989, p. 7). If information is not reinforced, it will be held in short-term memory for as little as 20 seconds and then be forgotten. When you are introduced to a stranger, increase the chances that you will remember the person's name by immediately using it: "It's nice to meet you, Jack . . . McNeil, right?" If you also mentally say "Jack McNeil, Jack McNeil, Jack McNeil, Jack McNeil" to yourself, you'll further increase your chances of remembering his name. Likewise, when you receive the directions "Go two blocks east, turn left, turn right at the next light, and it's in the next block," immediately repeat to yourself "two blocks east, turn left, turn right at light, next block—that's two blocks east, turn left, turn right at light, next block."

Construct mnemonics. Constructing mnemonics helps listeners put information in forms that are more easily recalled. A **mnemonic device** is any artificial technique used as a memory aid. One of the most common mnemonic techniques is to form

a word with the first letters of a list of items you are trying to remember. For example, a popular mnemonic for the five Great Lakes is HOMES (Huron, Ontario, Michigan, Erie, Superior).

When you want to remember items in a sequence, you can form a sentence with the words themselves or use words starting with the same first letters. For example, most beginning music students learn the mnemonic "*every good boy does fine*" for the notes on the lines of the treble clef (E, G, B, D, F). (And the word *face* is a common mnemonic for the notes on the treble clef spaces, F, A, C, E.)

Take notes. Although note taking would be inappropriate in casual interpersonal encounters, it is a powerful tool for increasing your recall when important information is being shared. Note taking is an important strategy for learners when they attempt to listen to and absorb information from lecture-type speech (Dunkel & Pialorsi, 2005). Note taking does more than provide a written record that you can go back to; it also allows you to take an active role in the listening process (Wolvin & Coakley, 1996, p. 239).

Useful notes may consist of a brief list of main points or key ideas, plus a few of the most significant details. Or they may be a short summary of the entire concept (a type of paraphrase) after the message is completed. For lengthy and detailed information, however, good notes likely will consist of a brief outline of what the speaker has said, including the overall idea, the main points of the message, and key developmental material. Good notes are not necessarily long. In fact, many classroom lectures can be summarized in a simple outline. Figure 5.1 is an example of notes based on the material in this chapter.

Evaluating

The fourth listening process is to evaluate or critically analyze what has been said. **Evaluation** is critically analyzing what you have heard to determine its truthfulness. Critical listening is especially important when you are asked to believe, act on, or support what is being said. For instance, if a person is trying to convince you to vote for a particular candi-

© WOJTEK JARCO/SHUTTERSTOCK

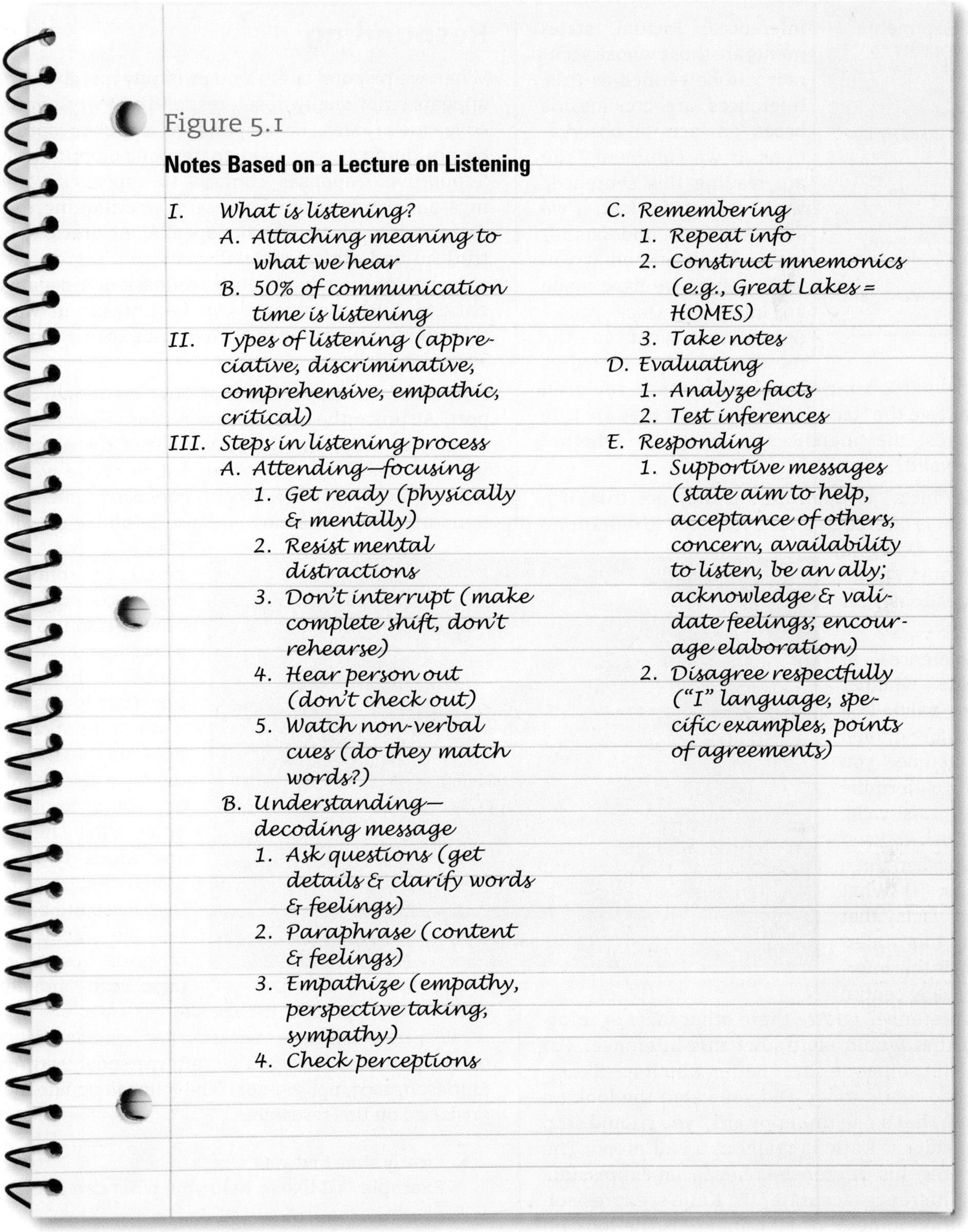

Figure 5.1

Notes Based on a Lecture on Listening

I. What is listening?
    A. Attaching meaning to what we hear
    B. 50% of communication time is listening
II. Types of listening (appreciative, discriminative, comprehensive, empathic, critical)
III. Steps in listening process
    A. Attending—focusing
        1. Get ready (physically & mentally)
        2. Resist mental distractions
        3. Don't interrupt (make complete shift, don't rehearse)
        4. Hear person out (don't check out)
        5. Watch non-verbal cues (do they match words?)
    B. Understanding—decoding message
        1. Ask questions (get details & clarify words & feelings)
        2. Paraphrase (content & feelings)
        3. Empathize (empathy, perspective taking, sympathy)
        4. Check perceptions
    C. Remembering
        1. Repeat info
        2. Construct mnemonics (e.g., Great Lakes = HOMES)
        3. Take notes
    D. Evaluating
        1. Analyze facts
        2. Test inferences
    E. Responding
        1. Supportive messages (state aim to help, acceptance of others, concern, availability to listen, be an ally; acknowledge & validate feelings; encourage elaboration)
        2. Disagree respectfully ("I" language, specific examples, points of agreements)

© OPTIMARC/SHUTTERSTOCK

date, support efforts to legalize gay marriage, or buy an expensive gadget, you will want to listen critically in order to evaluate the information and arguments presented. If you don't critically analyze what you hear, you risk going along with ideas or plans that violate your values, are counterproductive to your interests, or mislead others (including the speaker) who value your judgment.

To evaluate a message, you must learn to separate statements of fact from statements based on

factual statements
statements whose accuracy can be verified or proven

inferences
statements made by the speaker that are based on facts or observations

supportive messages
comforting statements that have a goal to reassure, bolster, encourage, soothe, console, or cheer up

inferences. Factual statements are those whose accuracy can be verified as true. Inferences are conclusions based on facts or observations. If we comment "You are reading this sentence," we have stated a fact. If we say "You are understanding and enjoying what you are reading," we have made an inference. Once you've determined what in the message is being offered as fact and what is being offered as inference, you need to (1) analyze the "facts" to determine if they are true and (2) test the inferences to determine whether they are valid.

Analyze "facts" to determine if they are true. If a statement is offered as a fact, you need to determine if it is true. Doing so often requires asking questions for clarification.

Test inferences to determine whether they are valid. If a statement is offered as an inference, you need to determine whether it is valid. You can ask yourself (or the speaker) three questions: (1) What are the facts that support this inference? (2) Is this information really central

to the inference? (3) Are there other facts or information that would contradict this inference? For example, if someone says "Better watch it—Katie's in one bad mood today. Did you catch the look on her face? That's one unhappy girl," you should stop and consider if Katie is really in a bad mood. The support for this inference is her facial expression. Is this inference accurate? Is Katie's expression one of unhappiness, or is it anger? Is the look on her face enough to conclude that she's in a bad mood? Or are there other cues that those of us who know her would expect to see? Is there anything else about Katie's behavior today that could lead us to believe that she's not in a bad mood? You are listening critically when you separate facts from inferences and then evaluate them as true or valid.

Responding

When we respond to a friend or family member who appears emotionally upset, respond to a work-group colleague's ideas, or respond to a public speech by critiquing it, we need to respond supportively. Supportive responses confirm the speaker's feelings, and when we are disagreeing or critiquing, they demonstrate respect for the speaker. At times, to be truthful and ethical, we will need to disagree with someone or provide negative feedback or a negative critique. Such comments can be phrased in ways that show respect for the other. Let's take a look at several guidelines.

Guidelines for responses that offer emotional support. At times the appropriate response is one that is related to the emotional content of the message we have heard. So the goal of our response will be to reassure, encourage, soothe, console, or cheer up. Supportive response messages are helpful when they create a conversational environment that encourages the other person to talk about and make sense of the situation that is causing distress. Supporting does not mean making false statements or telling someone only what he or she wants to hear. Effective supporting responses are based on the facts but focus on how those facts can provide emotional support for the speaker.

© VALENTIN CASARSA/ISTOCKPHOTO.COM

Research suggests several key characteristics of **supportive messages** in interpersonal settings (Burleson, 2003, pp. 565–568). The following guidelines are based on this research:

- *Clearly state that your aim is to help.*
  Example: "I'd like to help you, what can I do?"

- *Express acceptance or affection; do not condemn or criticize.*
  Example: "I understand that you just can't seem to accept this."

- *Demonstrate care, concern, and interest in the other's situation; do not give a lengthy recount of a similar situation.*
  Example: "What are you planning to do now?" Or "Gosh, tell me more. What happened then?"

- *Indicate that you are available to listen and support the other without intruding.*
  Example: "I know we've not been that close, but sometimes it helps to have someone to listen, and I'd like to do that for you."
- *State that you are an ally.*
  Example: "I'm with you on this." Or "Well, I'm on your side. This isn't right."
- *Acknowledge the other's feelings and situation as well as expressing your sincere sympathy; do not condemn or criticize the other's behavior or feelings.*
  Example: "I'm so sorry to see you feeling so bad. I can see that you're devastated by what has happened."
- *Assure the other that what he or she is feeling is legitimate; do not tell the other how to feel or ignore his or her feelings.*
  Example: "With what has happened to you, you have a right to be angry."
- *Use prompting comments to encourage the other to elaborate on his or her story.*
  Example: "Uh-huh," "yeah," or "I see. How did you feel about that?" Or "What happened before that? Can you elaborate?"

Guidelines for responses that demonstrate respect when disagreeing or critiquing others. When you cannot agree with what a speaker has said, or when you are in a position where it is appropriate for you to critique what someone else has said or done, the following guidelines can help you demonstrate that you respect the person and that your goal is to provide the person with your point of view.

- *Use "I" language so that you clearly own the comments you are making and do not ascribe them to others.*
  Example: "Carla, I really like the way you cited the reference for your opening quotation."
- *Use specific language and specific examples to point out areas of disagreement and areas for improvement.*
  Example: "I apologize, but I can't agree to that deadline or to another meeting about this project until I have had a chance to see the entire presentation. I'd suggest that by Monday at 10:00 a.m. each of us e-mails other team members a copy of the report section we are drafting. Then let's have a short meeting right after class to see if we need to meet again and, if so, to set a time."
- *Find a point to agree with or something positive to say before expressing your disagreement or offering a negative critique.*
  Example: "I really appreciate what you had to say on this topic. But it was hard for me to follow your argument, and I think that if you had

used transitional statements, they could have helped me understand your points better."

In this course, you may be asked to respond to a speech given by one of your classmates. If so, you will want to remember that your goal is to be supportive, honest, and helpful. A good critique will address three topics: the content of the speech, the structure of the speech, and the delivery of the speech.

- When critiquing the content, you can comment on the appropriateness of the speech for that particular audience and the use of facts and inferences. You can also analyze the logic of the arguments and the evidence used to support ideas.
- When critiquing structure, you can focus on the introduction, the use of transitions, the choice of organizational pattern, and the concluding remarks.
- When critiquing delivery, you can comment on how the speaker used voice and gesture, whether the tone was appropriately conversational or formal, and how effectively the speaker used visual aids such as PowerPoint slides.

When you critique a classmate's speech, it is especially important to offer specific suggestions for improvement. Table 5.1 provides examples of ineffective and effective speech critique statements.

Table 5.1

Examples of Effective and Ineffective Speech Critiques

	Ineffective Critique	Effective Critique
CONTENT	"The sources you cited are old and no longer represent current thinking on the topic."	"I noticed you relied heavily on Johnson's 1969 essay about global warming. For me, your argument would be more compelling if you were to cite research that has been published in the last five years."
STRUCTURE	"You were really hard to follow."	"I really appreciate what you had to say on this topic. I would have been able to follow your main points better if I had heard clear transitions between each one. Transitions would have helped me notice the switch from one topic to the next."
DELIVERY	"You talk too fast!"	"I was fascinated by the evidence you offered to support the first main point. It would have been even more compelling for me if you were to slow down while explaining that information. That would give me time to understand the material more fully before we moved on to the next main point."

Table 5.2

A Summary of the Five Aspects of Listening

	Good Listeners	Bad Listeners
ATTENDING	Attend to important information	May not hear what a person is saying
	Ready themselves physically and mentally	Fidget in their chairs, look out the window, and let their minds wander
	Listen objectively regardless of emotional involvement	Visibly react to emotional language
	Listen differently depending on situations	Listen the same way regardless of the type of material
UNDERSTANDING	Assign appropriate meaning to what is said	Hear what is said but are either unable to understand or assign different meaning to the words
	Seek out apparent purpose, main points, and supporting information	Ignore the way information is organized
	Ask mental questions to anticipate information	Fail to anticipate coming information
	Silently paraphrase to solidify understanding	Seldom or never mentally review information
	Seek out subtle meanings based on non-verbal cues	Ignore non-verbal cues
REMEMBERING	Retain information	Interpret message accurately but forget it
	Repeat key information	Assume they will remember
	Mentally create mnemonics for lists of words and ideas	Seldom single out any information as especially important
	Take notes	Rely on memory alone
EVALUATING	Listen critically	Hear and understand but are unable to weigh and consider it
	Separate facts from inferences	Don't differentiate between facts and inferences
	Evaluate inferences	Accept information at face value
RESPONDING SUPPORTIVELY	Provide supportive comforting statements	Pass off joy or hurt; change the subject
	Give alternative interpretations	Pass off hurt; change the subject

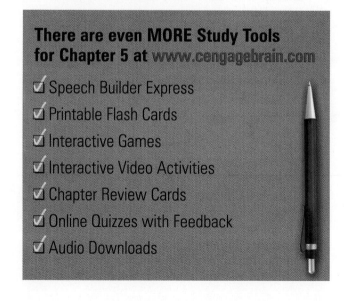

> **❝** Good listeners create a physical environment that will aid listening, and they adopt a listening posture. **❞**

There are even MORE Study Tools for Chapter 5 at www.cengagebrain.com

☑ Speech Builder Express
☑ Printable Flash Cards
☑ Interactive Games
☑ Interactive Video Activities
☑ Chapter Review Cards
☑ Online Quizzes with Feedback
☑ Audio Downloads

Test coming up? Now what?

With COMM you have a multitude of study aids at your fingertips. After reading the chapters, check out these ideas for further help.

Chapter in Review Cards include all learning outcomes, definitions, and visual summaries for each chapter.

Printable Flash Cards give you three additional ways to check your comprehension of key communication concepts.

Other great ways to help you study include **Speech Builder Express 3.0™, Interactive Quizzing, Downloads, Games and Simulations,** and **Interactive Video Activities**.

You can find it all at **www.cengagebrain.com**

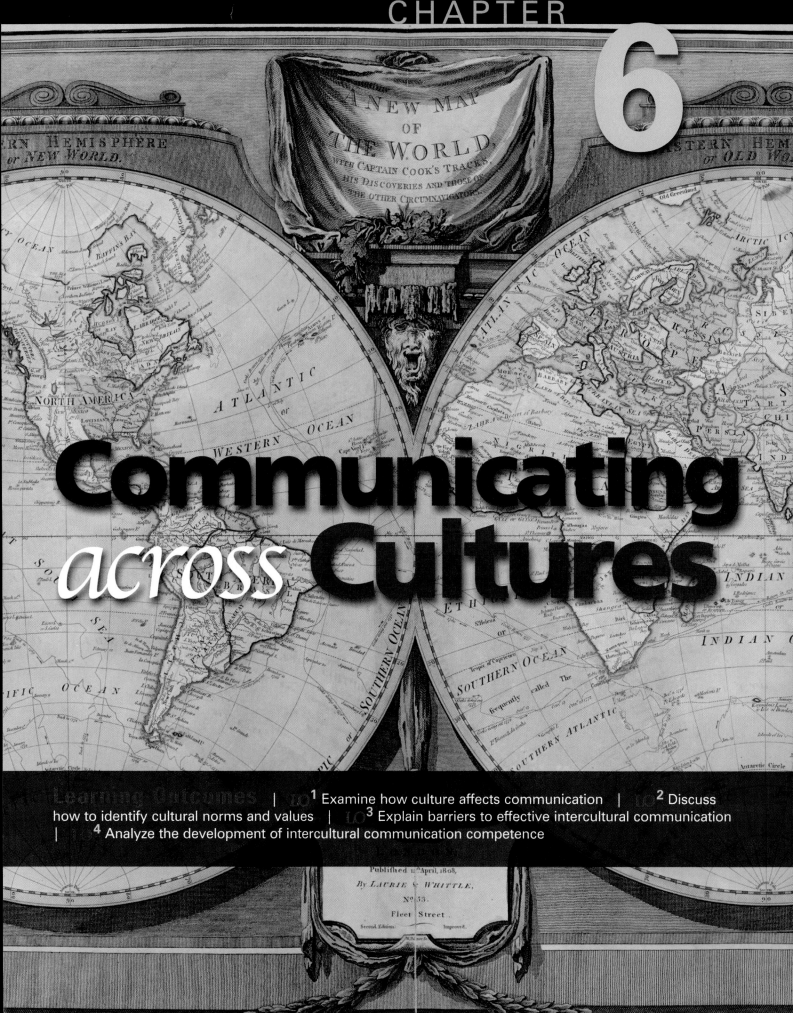

Communicating
across Cultures

© ISTOCKPHOTO.COM

> **"**_Competent intercultural communicators overcome cultural barriers by adopting the correct attitudes toward other cultures, acquiring accurate information about other cultures' values and practices, and developing specific skills needed to be effective across cultures._**"**

Because culture has a profound impact on not only our perceptions but also our communication behavior, in this chapter we examine how culture affects our communication behavior and how it influences our perception of the communication we receive from others. We begin by taking a look at some basic concepts of culture, identifying important values and norms that set cultures apart. Then we discuss the barriers that arise from cultural difference and offer strategies for improving intercultural communication competence.

culture
the values, attitudes, beliefs, orientations, and underlying assumptions prevalent among people in a society

LO¹ Culture and Communication

How often have we heard people observe that the world is getting smaller and the people in it increasingly similar? Today, through the globalization of trade and the Internet, our lives are affected by the decisions and actions of people in other parts of the world, and we can make instant personal contact with people around the globe through the click of a mouse. Some people celebrate this trend as a step toward world unity, but others mourn the loss of local cultures, traditions, and control and feel overwhelmed by the pervasiveness of communication.

Culture is the values, attitudes, beliefs, orientations, and underlying assumptions prevalent among people in a society (Samovar, Porter, & McDaniel, 2009). Yet, we do not have to journey to other countries to meet people of different cultures. As a nation of immigrants, the United States is a multicultural society. Our population includes not only recent immigrants from Asia, Latin America, Eastern Europe, and other countries but also the descendants of earlier immigrants and African slaves brought here against their will as well as native peoples. So understanding how cultural groups vary in their approach to communication can help us as we interact with the people we meet each day.

What do you think?

I feel very comfortable communicating with people of different genders, ages, and ethnicities.

Strongly Disagree   _Strongly Agree_

1   2   3   4   5   6   7   8   9   10

culture shock
the psychological discomfort you may feel when you attempt to adjust to a new cultural situation

intercultural communication
refers to interactions that occur between people whose cultural assumptions are so different that the communication between them is altered

Intercultural Communication

We are so familiar with our own language, gestures, facial expressions, conversational customs, and norms that we may experience anxiety when these familiar aspects of communication are disrupted. This occurs frequently when we interact with people from different cultures. Culture shock is the psychological discomfort you may feel when you attempt to adjust to a new cultural situation (Klyukanov, 2005, p. 33). Because culture shock is caused by an absence of shared meaning, you are likely to feel it most profoundly when you are thrust into another culture through travel, business, or studying abroad. In the film *Lost in Translation*, Bill Murray's character struggles with culture shock when filming a commercial in Japan.

Culture shock can also occur when you have contact with people from another culture within your home country. For example, Brittney, who is from a small town in Minnesota, experienced culture shock when she visited Miami for the first time. She was overwhelmed by the distinct Hispanic flavor of the city, hearing Spanish spoken on the street and seeing signs and billboards written in Spanish, the prevalence of Latin beat music, and the ways people looked and dressed. Brittney was disoriented not only because of the prominence of Spanish but also because

the values, attitudes, beliefs, and behaviors of the people she encountered seemed quite foreign to her. Likewise, if Maria, who lives in Miami, were to visit the small Minnesota town where Brittney grew up, she would also be likely to experience culture shock. Brittney's hometown is like the rural Minnesota towns whose values and customs are humorously highlighted on Garrison Keillor's public radio program *A Prairie Home Companion*.

Intercultural communication refers to interactions between people whose cultural assumptions are so different that the communication between them is altered (Samovar, Porter, & McDaniel, 2009). In other words, when we interact with people whose attitudes, values, beliefs, customs, and behaviors are culturally different from ours, we are communicating across cultural boundaries, which can lead to misunderstandings that would not commonly occur between people who are culturally similar. It is important to recognize that not every exchange between people of different cultures exemplifies intercultural communication. For example, when Brittney is on the beach in Miami and joins a group of Hispanics in a friendly game of beach volleyball, the cultural differences between them are unlikely to affect their game-related exchanges. However, should Brittney decide to join the group for a night of club hopping, she is likely to experience conversations in which cultural differences lead to difficulty in understanding or interpreting what is said.

Dominant Cultures and Co-Cultures

Although the United States is a multicultural society, there are many attitudes,

© CHRISTOPHER FUTCHER/SHUTTERSTOCK

values, beliefs, and customs that a majority of people hold in common. This shared system of meaning constitutes our dominant culture, and like the dominant culture of any country, ours has evolved over time. The dominant culture of the United States once reflected the values of white, Western European, English-speaking, Protestant, heterosexual men. But as we have recognized our diversity, the dominant culture has evolved and incorporated aspects of other cultural groups. The result is a culture that better reflects the diversity of the people in the United States.

Still, there are cultural groups whose values, attitudes, beliefs, and customs differ from the dominant culture. These groups, called co-cultures, exhibit communication that is sufficiently different to distinguish them from the dominant culture. Some of the major contributors to co-cultures in U.S. society today are discussed next.

Race

Traditionally, the term *race* was used to classify people in terms of biological characteristics, such as skin and eye color, hair texture, and body shape. However, scientific justifications for such divisions have proven elusive, and the classification system itself has changed drastically over time (Hotz, 1995). Despite the difficulty of scientifically defining race, people have experienced the social effects of perceived race and have formed communities and cultures based on racialized experiences. So race is an important cultural signifier for many people, and racial identity can influence communication in a number of ways. For example, African Americans "code switch," at times using the linguistic and non-verbal patterns of the dominant culture and at other times using the communication style that is unique to their race (Jackson, 2004). The type of code used may be determined based on their attitude, the topic, or who is listening (Bonvillain, 2003). Likewise, members of co-cultures based on gender, ethnicity, or social class may also change their communication style from time to time to be more similar to or distant from that of the dominant culture.

© YURI ARCURS/SHUTTERSTOCK

Ethnicity

Like race, ethnicity is an inexact distinction. Ethnicity refers to a classification of people based on combinations of shared characteristics such as nationality, geographic origin, language, religion, ancestral customs, and tradition. So people may identify themselves as Italian Americans, Irish Americans, Mexican Americans, and so on. People vary greatly in the importance they attach to their ethnic heritage and the degree to which it affects their attitudes, values, and behavior. If you descend from Italians, this heritage may affect your closeness to family, your religion, the foods you prefer, and many other aspects of your identity. Your roommate may also have Italian ancestors but may not identify herself as Italian and may not follow any family traditions based on this ethnicity.

Language or mother tongue is an obvious influence of ethnicity on communication. Immigrants bring with them the language of their original country, and they may or may not speak English when they arrive. Even after they learn English, many immigrants choose to speak their mother tongue at home, intentionally live close to other people from their home country, and interact with these people in their mother language. As Table 6.1 shows, English is the first language of most people in the United States. But Spanish is quickly becoming a de facto second language. The U.S. Census Bureau data indicates that 15 percent of the U.S. population is Hispanic, and that figure is projected to grow to 30 percent by 2050. Furthermore, 78 percent of those in Hispanic homes report that Spanish is their primary language (U.S. Census Bureau, 2007). So today, most toll-free 800 and 888 numbers offer the option of conversing in English or Spanish, most cable companies have several Spanish-language channels as part of their

dominant culture
the attitudes, values, beliefs, and customs that the majority of people in a society hold in common

co-cultures
groups of people living within a dominant culture but exhibiting communication that is sufficiently different to distinguish them from the dominant culture

ethnicity
a classification of people based on combinations of shared characteristics such as nationality, geographic origin, language, religion, ancestral customs, and tradition

Table 6.1

Languages in the United States with Most Speakers

1. English
2. Spanish
3. Chinese dialects
4. French
5. German
6. Tagalog
7. Vietnamese
8. Italian
9. Korean
10. Russian

Bonjour!
Kamusta?
Bon Giorno!
Guten Tag!

religion

a system of beliefs shared by a group with objects for devotion, rituals for worship, and a code of ethics

social class

an indicator of a person's position in a social hierarchy, as determined by income, education, occupation, and social habits

basic package, and Spanish-language radio stations can be heard across the country.

Sex and Gender

"Frogs and snails and puppy dog tails, that's what little boys are made of." "Sugar and spice and everything nice, that's what little girls are made of." "He's a real man's man." "She's such a girlie girl." These traditional childhood rhymes and sex-specific generalizations capture the traditional thinking about men's and women's co-cultures. Women and men tend to belong to different co-cultures within each larger cultural group. Part of what men and women learn from their co-culture is expectations of how they are to behave and communicate. Because women's co-culture values the nurturing role, women who identify with the feminine co-culture may tend to speak more about their personal relationships, more easily describe their feelings, and be more likely to include others in conversation and actively respond to others. On the other hand, men who identify with masculine co-cultural norms may focus more on tasks or outcomes when they communicate. They may tend to talk more about content and problem solving, emphasize control and status, and be less responsive to others (Wood, 2007). Obviously, people differ in the extent to which they identify with these gendered co-cultures, and those who do not strongly identify with the co-culture may not behave in line with co-cultural expectations. In addition, over time the values and norms of each co-culture can change. For example, in Western societies many of the value differences between men's and women's co-cultures have decreased, but in many Middle Eastern societies such differences still exist.

Religion

A religion is a system of beliefs that is shared by a group and that supplies the group with an entity (or entities) for devotion, rituals for worshipping that entity, and a code of ethics. Although the dominant culture of the United States values religious freedom and diversity, historically it has reflected Judeo-Christian values and practices. All observant practitioners of a religion participate in co-culture. Those who strongly identify with a religious group that is outside the Judeo-Christian tradition have different orientations that shape their relationships and communication behavior. For example, Buddhism advises individuals to embrace rather than resist personal conflict. Adversity, emotional upheaval, and conflict are seen as natural parts of life (Chuang, 2004). Therefore, a Buddhist is apt to communicate openly and calmly during an interpersonal conflict and embrace the positive aspects of conflict in strengthening interpersonal ties. Throughout history, we can point to religious differences as the source of many culture wars. Many of the conflicts in the Middle East today are essentially culture wars based on religious differences.

Sexual Orientation

In most places in the world today, the dominant culture values heterosexuality. Although the dominant cultures of many Western countries have changed their laws reflecting the change in attitudes toward homosexuality, people who are not heterosexual still face discrimination in Western societies and legal and physical threats in many parts of the world. As a result, gay, lesbian, bisexual, and transgender people may participate in and identify with "underground" co-cultural communities. These communities have attitudes, values, customs, rites, and rituals that are supportive of homosexual behavior. So people may frequent gay, lesbian, or bi- bars, join gay churches, sing in local gay men's or women's choruses, and participate in commitment ceremonies where the dominant society has laws against homosexual marriage.

© ANDREW LEVER/SHUTTERSTOCK

Social Class

Social class is a level in the power hierarchy of a society. Membership in each social class is determined by income, education, occupation, and social habits. The dominant culture of the United States is the middle class. Because social class often determines where people live, people of the same social class often establish communities where they reinforce co-cultures with distinct values, rituals, and communication practices. For example, lower-class parents tend to emphasize obedience, acceptance of what others think, and hesitancy in expressing desires to authority figures, whereas middle-class parents more often emphasize self-control, self-direction, and intellectual curiosity.

Such differences in values based on social class may lead those from middle-class backgrounds to speak more directly and assertively than do people from working-class backgrounds (Gilbert & Kahl, 1982).

Age

The period in which we are born and raised can have a strong formative influence on us. People of the same generation form a cultural cohort group whose personal values, beliefs, and behaviors have been influenced by the common life experiences and events they encountered as they aged. People who grew up during the Great Depression tend to be frugal; those alive during World War II value sacrifice of self for cause and country; the baby boomer generation, who came of age during the counterculture 1960s, are likely to question authority; Generation Xers, who were born in the 1960s and 1970s and experienced latchkey childhoods and other consequences of widespread divorce, value self-sufficiency; and those called Generation Next, who came of age after 9/11 and grew up with personal computers, cell phones, and the Internet, tend to value fortune, fame, and tolerance (Pew Research Center, 2007).

Whether in family relationships or in the workplace, when people from different generations interact, their co-cultural orientations can create communication difficulties. Miscommunication, misunderstandings, and conflict are likely to occur when people work with others of different generations. For example, people from earlier generations are unlikely to question authority figures such as parents, teachers, religious leaders, or bosses. They demonstrate respect by using formal terms of address, such as Mr., Ms., Dr., and sir. People who came of age in the 1960s or later, on the other hand, tend to be skeptical of authority and less formal in dealing with authority figures. They are more likely to question their managers and to openly disagree with decisions made by those in authority (Zempke, Raines, & Filipczak, 2000).

Cultural Identity

Recall that your self-concept is the mental image that you have of yourself, and that image is negotiated and reinforced through your communication with others. Membership in the co-cultural groups described above contributes to your cultural identity, but how much your identity is affected by each co-culture depends on the extent to which you identify with it (Ting-Toomey et al., 2000). For example, 20-year-old Kelly is a devout Catholic who attends Mass every morning and is a leader at the Newman Center on campus. She volunteers at the local pregnancy crisis center, where she tutors pregnant teens, and she dates only men who

are Catholic. By contrast, Kelly's roommate, Nicole, is also Catholic but rarely goes to Mass, is not involved at the Newman Center, is pro-choice, and is engaged to a classmate who is Jewish. As you would expect, being a Catholic is central to how Kelly views herself, and it is one of the first things she shares about herself when she meets someone. By contrast, the values of Catholicism don't seem to be central to Nicole's self-image, what she believes, or how she behaves.

LO² Identifying Cultural Norms and Values

Some aspects that identify members of a culture may be easy to spot. We may be able to figure out people's cultural background by the language they speak, their dress, or artifacts such as religious markers they wear as jewelry or place in their home. For example, when people meet Shimon, from his side-curls, his yarmulke, and his black clothes, they can quickly discern that he is a Hassidic Jew. But beyond the style of dress, what does it mean to be a Hassidic Jew? How do Hassidic Jews differ from the dominant culture and from other cultural groups? What are other cultural groups to which they are similar?

The work of Geert Hofstede gives us a way to understand how cultures are similar to and different from one another as well as understand how that variation affects communication. Hofstede (1980) identifies four major dimensions of culture that affect communication: individualism–collectivism, uncertainty avoidance, power distance, and masculinity–femininity. Table 6.2 shows a comparison of different

Table 6.2

Relative Comparison of Dimension Levels between Ten Countries

Individualism	High Uncertainty Avoidance	High Power Distance	Masculinity
USA	Japan	Russia	Japan
Netherlands	Russia	China	Germany
France	West Africa	Indonesia	USA
Germany	France	West Africa	Hong Kong
Russia	Germany	France	China
Japan	China	Hong Kong	Indonesia
Hong Kong	Netherlands	Japan	West Africa
China	Indonesia	USA	France
West Africa	USA	Netherlands	Russia
Indonesia	Hong Kong	Germany	Netherlands
Collectivism	**Low Uncertainty Avoidance**	**Low Power Distance**	**Femininity**

SOURCE: Hofstede, G. H. (1993). Cultural Constraints in Management Theories. *Academy of Management Executive, 7* (1), 81–94.

individualistic culture
emphasizes personal rights and responsibilities, privacy, voicing one's opinion, freedom, innovation, and self-expression

collectivist culture
emphasizes community, collaboration, shared interest, harmony, the public good, and avoiding embarrassment

countries according to these dimensions.

Individualism–Collectivism

In individualistic cultures (for example, the United States, Australia, Great Britain, and Canada as well as northern and eastern European countries), people place primary value on the self and personal achievement. In an individualistic society, people tend to consider the interests of others primarily in relationship to how they affect the interest of the self. If you come from an individualistic culture, you may consider your family and close friends when you act, but mainly because your interests and theirs align. People in individualistic cultures view competition between people as desirable and useful. Because of this, individualistic cultures emphasize personal rights and responsibilities, privacy, voicing one's opinion, freedom, innovation, and self-expression (Andersen, Hecht, Hoobler, & Smallwood, 2003).

In contrast, collectivist cultures (for example, countries in South and Central America, East and Southeast Asia, and Africa) place primary value on the interests of the group and group harmony. In a collectivist society, an individual's decision is shaped by what is best for the group whether it serves the individual's interests or not. Collectivist societies are highly integrated, and maintaining harmony and cooperation are valued over competitiveness and personal achievement. As a result, members of collectivist societies will probably have stronger bonds within the groups to which they belong (family, workplace, and community). Collectivist cultures emphasize community, collaboration, shared interest, harmony, the public good, and maintaining the avoidance of embarrassment (Andersen, Hecht, Hoobler, & Smallwood, 2003).

Notions of individualism and collectivism influence many aspects of communication, including most notably our self-concept formation, conflict management style, and group communication behavior (Samovar, Porter, & McDaniel, 2009). In individualistic cultures, people stress the self and personal achievement, and the individual is treated as the most important element in a social setting. In a collectivist culture, what affects self-concept and self-esteem is not individual achievement; rather, it is whether the group thrives and how people's actions have contributed to their group's success. So if Marie has been raised in an individualist culture and she is the highest-scoring player on her basketball team, she will feel good about herself and identify herself as a "winner" even if her team has a losing season. But if Marie is from a collectivist culture, being the highest-scoring player will have little effect on her self-esteem; the fact that her team had a losing season will likely cause her to feel less personal esteem.

People from each of these cultural perspectives also view conflict differently. In individualistic cultures, the emphasis on the individual leads its members to value and practice assertiveness and confrontational argument, whereas members of collectivist cultures value accord and harmony and thus practice tentativeness and collaboration or avoidance of arguments. In the United States, we teach assertiveness and argumentation as useful skills and expect them in interpersonal and work relationships, politics, consumerism, and other aspects of civic life. By contrast, to maintain harmony and avoid interpersonal clashes, Japanese business has evolved an elaborate process called *nemawashi*, a term that literally means digging around the roots of a tree before transplanting it. In Japan, any subject that might cause conflict at a meeting should be discussed in advance so that the interaction at the meeting will not seem rude or impolite (Samovar & Porter, 2001). In collectiv-

© GREG NICHOLAS/ISTOCKPHOTO.COM / © DIANE DIEDERICH/ISTOCKPHOTO.COM ist societies, a style of communication that respects the relationship is more important than the information exchanged (Jandt, 2001). In collectivist societies, group harmony, sparing others embarrassment, and a modest presentation of oneself are important ways to show respect. A person does not speak directly if it might hurt others in the group.

How people work in groups also depends on the type of culture they come from. Because members of collectivist cultures see group harmony and the welfare of the group to be of primary importance, they strive for consensus on group goals and may, at times, sacrifice optimal outcomes for the sake of group accord. Your cultural assumptions affect how you work to establish group goals, how you interact with other group members, and how willing you are to sacrifice for the sake of the group. Groups with members from both individualistic and collectivist cultures may experience difficulties due to their varying cultural assumptions.

Uncertainty Avoidance

Cultures differ in how their members feel about and deal with unpredictable people, relationships, or events. **Low uncertainty-avoidance cultures** (such as the United States, Sweden, and Denmark) are more tolerant of uncertainty in how people behave, in relationships, and in events, and so put little cultural emphasis on reducing unpredictability. People from cultures with low uncertainty avoidance more easily accept unpredictability and ambiguity in life. They tend to be tolerant of the unusual, prize initiative, take risks, and think that there should be as few rules as possible. People who come from **high uncertainty-avoidance cultures** have a lower tolerance for unpredictable people, relationships, and events. These cultures create systems of formal rules and believe in absolute truth as the way to provide more security and reduce the risk. They also tend to be less tolerant of people or groups with deviant ideas or behavior. Because their culture emphasizes the importance of avoiding uncertainty, they often view life as hazardous and experience anxiety and stress when confronted with unpredictable people,

relationships, or situations. Nations whose cultures are marked by high uncertainty avoidance include Japan, Portugal, Greece, Peru, and Belgium (Samovar, Porter, & McDaniel, 2009).

How our culture has taught us to view uncertainty affects our communication with others. It shapes how we use language, develop relationships, and negotiate with others. People from high uncertainty-avoidance cultures use and value precise language because they believe that careful word choice makes the meaning of a message easier to understand. Imagine a teacher declaring to a class that "the paper must be well researched, with evidence cited, and professional in format and appearance." Students from high uncertainty-avoidance cultures would find the teacher's remarks to be too general and vague. They would most likely experience anxiety and ask a lot of questions about what kind of research is appropriate, how to cite evidence, how much evidence is needed, what writing style to use, and the length of the paper in order to reduce their uncertainty. These students would welcome a specific checklist or rubric that enumerated the exact criteria by which the paper would be graded. By contrast, students from low uncertainty-avoidance cultures would be annoyed by an overly specific list of rules and guidelines, viewing it as a barrier to creativity and initiative. As you can imagine, a teacher with students from both these backgrounds faces a difficult challenge when trying to explain an assignment.

How people approach new relationships and how they communicate in developing them is also affected by their culture's view of uncertainty. As you would expect, people from high uncertainty-avoidance cultures are wary of strangers and may not seek out new relationships or relationships with others they perceive as different (unpredictable). They generally prefer meeting people through friends and family and refrain from being alone with strangers. When developing relationships, people from high uncertainty-avoidance cultures tend to guard their

low uncertainty-avoidance cultures cultures characterized by greater acceptance of, and less need to control, unpredictable people, relationships, or events

high uncertainty-avoidance cultures cultures characterized by a low tolerance for, and a high need to control, unpredictable people, relationships, or events

© IQONCEPT/SHUTTERSTOCK

high power distance
the cultural belief that inequalities in power, status, and rank are "natural" and that these differences should be acknowledged and accentuated

low power distance
the cultural belief that inequalities in power, status, and rank should be underplayed and muted

masculine culture
a culture in which people are expected to adhere to traditional sex roles

privacy, refrain from self-disclosure early in a relationship, and proceed more slowly through relationship development. Members of low uncertainty-avoidance cultures, on the other hand, are likely to initiate relationships with people who differ from them and enjoy the excitement of disclosing personal information in earlier stages of relationship development.

Power Distance

Cultures differ in how accepting they are of wide differences in power held by different groups of people and how people of unequal power expect to be treated. In cultures characterized as having **high power distance**, inequalities in power, status, and rank are viewed as "natural," and these differences are acknowledged by all members of the culture. These cultures believe that everyone in the culture has a rightful place and that members who have higher power, status, and rank should be deferred to by those with less power, status, and rank. High power-distance cultures include most Arab countries of the Middle East as well as India, Malaysia, Guatemala, Venezuela, and Singapore.

In cultures characterized as having **low power distance**, inequalities in power, status, and rank are muted. People know that some individuals have more clout, authority, and influence, but lower-ranking people are not in awe of, are not more respectful toward, and do not fear people with more power. Even though power differences exist, these cultures value democracy and egalitarian behavior. Austria, Finland, Denmark, Norway, the United States, New Zealand, and Israel are examples of countries whose dominant cultures are characterized by low power distance.

Does this greeting indicate high power distance or low power distance?

Our cultural beliefs about power distance affect how we interact with others, including how we communicate with authority figures, our language use, and our non-verbal behavior. If you were a student, unskilled worker, or average citizen in a high power-distance culture, you would not challenge a person in authority because you would expect to be punished for doing so. You would expect the more powerful person to control the interaction and you would listen to what that person said and do what was ordered without question. When talking with more powerful people, you would address them formally by using their title as a sign of respect. Formal terms of address like Mr. or Mrs., proper and polite forms of language, and non-verbal signals of your status differences would be evident in the exchange. If you come from a low power-distance culture, you would be more comfortable challenging those in authority because differences in status are muted. When interacting with a more powerful person, you would feel comfortable directing the course of the conversation and would question or confront them if you needed to. You would not feel compelled to use a formal title when addressing a more powerful person.

Masculinity–Femininity

Cultures differ in how strongly they value traditional sex-role distinctions. Cultures that Hofstede called **masculine cultures** expect people to maintain traditional sex roles and different standards of behavior for men and women. Hofstede called these cultures *masculine* because, for the most part, groups that maintain distinct sex-based roles also value masculine roles more highly than feminine ones. If you come from a masculine culture like the ones that are dominant in Mexico, Italy, and Japan, you are likely to value men when they are assertive and dominant and value women when they are nurturing, caring, and service oriented. When you encounter people who don't meet these expectations, you are likely to be uncomfortable. Overall, however, if you come from a masculine culture, regardless of your sex, you will see masculine behaviors as more worthwhile. Thus, you are likely to value the masculine characteristics of performance, ambition, assertiveness, competitiveness, and material success more

© ISTOCKPHOTO.COM

" Both men and women in feminine cultures learn and are reinforced for demonstrating both traditionally masculine and feminine behaviors . . .

than you value traditionally feminine traits such as service, nurturing, investment in relationships, and helping behaviors (Hofstede, 2000). **Feminine cultures** expect that people, regardless of sex, will assume a variety of roles depending on the circumstances and their own choices; they do not have any sex-role expectations. If you are from a feminine culture, like the national cultures of Sweden, Norway, and Denmark, not only will you feel free to act in ways that are not traditionally assigned to people of your sex, but you will also value traits that have traditionally been associated with feminine roles (Hofstede, 1998).

Whether you come from a masculine or a feminine culture has a significant effect on how much behavioral flexibility you demonstrate. People from masculine cultures have strict definitions of appropriate behavior for people of each sex. As a result, they learn and are reinforced for only those behaviors that are seen to be appropriate for their sex. So men in these cultures are unprepared to engage in nurturing and caring behaviors, such as empathizing and comforting, and women are unprepared to be assertive and argue persuasively. This is one of the reasons why those of us raised in masculine cultures find movies portraying men as bumbling caregivers humorous. Both men and women in feminine cultures learn and are reinforced for demonstrating both traditionally masculine and feminine behaviors. As a result, people from feminine cultures are more flexible in their communication behavior. Both men and women learn to nurture, empathize, assert, and argue, although any single individual may lack skill in one or more behaviors. In fact, some situation comedies created in the United States that have been translated for audiences in feminine cultures have flopped because the humorous anecdotes about men who fail as caregivers don't translate.

LO3 Barriers to Effective Intercultural Communication

Now that you have developed an understanding of culture and the variations that can exist among cultures and co-cultures, you are in a better position to appreciate the specific barriers caused by cultural differences, including anxiety,

> . . . As a result, people from feminine cultures are more flexible in their communication behavior. 99

assumptions of similarity or difference, ethnocentrism, stereotypes and prejudice, incompatible communication codes, and incompatible norms and values.

feminine culture
a culture in which people, regardless of sex, are expected to assume a variety of roles based on the circumstances and their own choices

Anxiety

It is normal to feel some discomfort or apprehension when we recognize that we are different from most everyone else or when we enter a cultural milieu that has unfamiliar customs. Most people experience fear, dislike, and distrust when first interacting with someone from a different culture (Luckmann, 1999). So when Marissa, who is from a barrio in Los Angeles, decided to attend a small liberal arts college in New England, she was nervous and wondered if her decision to attend school in the Northeast had been a good one. The other students had been friendly enough during orientation week, but it had become clear that she didn't really have much in common with them. While the others easily shared stories of spring-break trips with their families and joked about the cars they had wrecked, Marissa found she had little to add—her family always went to see her grandmother in Mexico when her parents took time off from their jobs. She didn't even have a driver's license. When she hesitantly mentioned her *quinceañera* party, everyone turned and stared at her. One guy said, "What in the world is a 'keensy snare yah' party?" and all of the guys laughed. At first, the other women listened politely, but by that time Marissa was so nervous that she stumbled over her words and really didn't do a good job of explaining this coming-of-age tradition that was so important to her community. Most of us are like Marissa when we are anxious—we don't do a good job of sharing our ideas and feelings. So, our anxiety becomes a barrier to our communication.

Assumptions of Similarity or Difference

When people cross into an unfamiliar cultural environment, they often assume that the norms, values, and traditions that applied in their familiar situation match those that apply in the new one. When traveling internationally from the United States, for example, many people expect to eat their familiar hamburgers and fries, provided with rapid and efficient service. Likewise, they may be annoyed with shops and restaurants closing during midday in countries that observe the custom of *siesta*.

ethnocentrism
the belief that one's own culture is superior to others

stereotypes
attributions that cover up individual differences and ascribe certain characteristics to a group of people

prejudice
a rigid attitude based on group membership

It can be just as great a mistake to assume that everything about an unfamiliar culture will be different. With time, Marissa is likely to find that the other students really aren't as different from her friends at home and that school is still school even when there is snow on the ground. As she makes friends, she learns that although Rachel, who is Jewish, didn't have a *quinceañera* party, she did have a bat mitzvah celebration, and Kate, who is Irish Catholic, had a big party to celebrate her confirmation. Because our assumptions guide our communication behavior, incorrectly assuming similarities or differences can lead to miscommunication. The wisest way to overcome this barrier is not to assume anything but to be aware of the feedback you receive, which provides cues to the real similarities and differences that exist between your cultural expectations and those of your interaction partners.

Ethnocentrism

Ethnocentrism is the belief that one's own culture is superior to others. The stereotype of the immigrant in the host country, loudly complaining of how much better everything is back home, is the classic example of ethnocentrism. In varying degrees, ethnocentrism is found in every culture (Haviland, 1993) and can occur in co-cultures as well. An ethnocentric view of the world leads to attitudes of superiority and messages that are directly and subtly condescending in content and tone. As you would expect, these messages are offensive to receivers from other cultures or co-cultures.

Stereotypes and Prejudice

Stereotypes are the attributions that cover up individual differences and ascribe certain characteristics to a group of people. Basing our interactions on stereotypes can lead to misunderstandings and can strain relationships. For example, when Laura anticipates meeting Joey, who she has heard is gay, she may expect him to be effeminate in his manner-

isms and interested in fashion. So she embarrasses him and herself when, early in their conversation, she attempts to find common ground and asks him for advice on what type of cologne to buy her boyfriend—to which he replies, "What is your problem? I may be gay, but I'm not that Clinton Kelly dude from *What Not to Wear!* Just because I'm gay doesn't make me a fashion consultant."

Prejudice is defined as a rigid attitude based on group membership that predisposes us to think, feel, or act in a negative way toward another person or group. Thinking that Amy, a Chinese student in your class, will get the best grade in the course because, supposedly, all Chinese students excel intellectually or assuming that Alberto, who is Mexican, is working in the United States illegally would be examples of prejudice. Colin is prejudiced and believes that all white people try to take advantage of people of color. So when his coworker John, who is white, offers to refer a client to Colin, Colin replies, "Forget it—you're not going to pawn off a deadbeat on me." When we interact based on stereotypes and prejudice, we risk creating messages that are inaccurate and damage our relationships. When we listen with our stereotypes and prejudices in mind, we may misperceive the intent of the person with whom we are talking.

© PRISM68/SHUTTERSTOCK

Incompatible Communication Codes

At times we misunderstand one another because the language or other communication behavior of our culture or co-culture differs from that of another cultural group. For example, Zeke could not understand why those Chinese guys who were continually fighting—screaming at each other and waving their arms—always sat together in the dining hall. Zeke had no idea what they were saying, but from his standpoint they looked pretty angry. Because he didn't understand Mandarin, Zeke was judging the conversation of the Chinese students based on their paralanguage and body movement, which he interpreted as hostile and angry. Zeke did not know that Mandarin is a tonal language. How the words are voiced affects their meaning. The large changes in pitch and volume that he heard were not expression of strong emotion, but only the voicing of different words.

When our conversational partners, people in our group, or audience members speak a different language, it is easy to see that we have incompatible communication codes. But even when people speak the same language, cultural variations can result from their belonging to different co-cultures. For example, people from Great Britain take a *lift* to reach a higher floor, while Americans ride an *elevator*. Even within a national group, co-cultural use of the language can lead to incompatible communication codes. In fact, less powerful co-cultural groups will often purposefully develop in-group codes that are easily understood by co-culture members but are unintelligible to those from the outside. Just try to have a conversation about your computer problem with your friend Sam, who is a "techno geek." As an insider, Sam's vocabulary is likely to be as foreign to you as if he were speaking Icelandic.

One Language, Different Co-Cultures

American English	British English
Parking lot	Car park
Stroller	Perambulator
Gasoline	Petrol
Station wagon	Estate car
Ladybug	Ladybird

© LISA F. YOUNG/SHUTTERSTOCK

People who speak different languages quickly comprehend their inability to communicate verbally and invariably turn to some type of non-verbal signing in an effort to overcome the language barrier.

As we have seen, however, there are also significant differences in the use and meaning of non-verbal behaviors. Not only do incompatible verbal communication codes create barriers to intercultural communication, so do our differences in how we use and interpret non-verbal behavior. For example, in some cultures, belching after eating signifies that the meal did not agree with the diner, whereas in other cultures it is a compliment to the cook. Such cultural differences in non-verbal behavior often account for misunderstandings or embarrassment when people from different cultures attempt to communicate with each other.

Incompatible Norms and Values

All cultures base their communication behaviors on cultural norms and rules and on personal values based on those cultural norms and rules. Sometimes the norms and values of two people of different cultures create barriers that make it difficult for them to understand each other. For example, Jeff and Tabito have been best friends since elementary school. They have shared everything: schoolwork, summer vacations, sports, and camping trips. Now that they are in high school, their interests seem to be changing. One day, Jeff tells Tabito that he has a six-pack of beer and offers to share it with Tabito. Tabito simply says "No" and offers no explanation. Jeff is confused by Tabito's behavior. To Jeff, a fourth-generation American whose family is individualistic in their cultural orientation, drinking a couple of beers is no big deal. He figures, "Even if we get caught, neither of us has ever been in trouble before, so all we'd get is a slap on the wrist." He doesn't consider how his arrest might affect his family and chides Tabito, saying, "Come on, don't wimp out on me now." What Jeff does not understand is that Tabito, coming from a first-generation Japanese American family, has the collectivist values of his parents. Being caught with alcohol would bring great disgrace upon his whole family, and to him, the collectivist goal of maintaining the reputation of his family is much more important than having fun with a friend. Because Tabito and Jeff don't recognize that their cultural backgrounds have led them to have different expectations, they don't discuss it. But both feel the strain that it puts on their conversation and relationship.

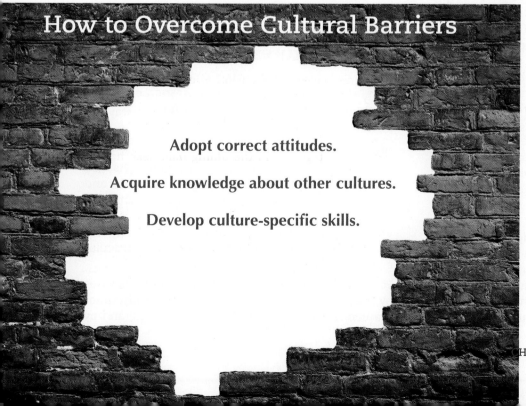

How to Overcome Cultural Barriers

Adopt correct attitudes.

Acquire knowledge about other cultures.

Develop culture-specific skills.

altruism
a display of genuine and unselfish concern for the welfare of others

egocentricity
a selfish interest in one's own needs, to the exclusion of everything else

LO⁴
Intercultural Communication Competence

Competent intercultural communicators overcome cultural barriers by adopting the correct attitudes toward other cultures, acquiring accurate information about other cultures' values and practices, and developing specific skills needed to be effective across cultures.

Adopt Correct Attitudes

The right attitudes for intercultural communication, according to Neuliep (2006), involve one's motivations and flexibility in interacting with others from different cultures. In other words, we must be willing to try and have a desire to succeed when communicating interculturally. We must be willing to try new behaviors rather than expecting the other person to adjust to our style of communicating. Tolerating ambiguity, being open-minded, and acting altruistically enable us to effectively communicate across cultural differences.

Tolerate ambiguity. Communicating with strangers creates uncertainty, and when the stranger also comes from a different culture, we can become anxious about what he or she will expect of us. People beginning intercultural relationships must be prepared to tolerate a high degree of uncertainty about the other person and to tolerate it for a long time. If you enter an intercultural interaction believing that it is OK to be unsure about how to proceed, you are likely to pay closer attention to the feedback you receive from the other person, and you can then work to adjust your behavior and messages so that together the two of you can achieve understanding. Accepting the ambiguity in the interaction can help you work hard to make the conversation successful; you will be much less apt to become frustrated or discouraged by the inevitable false starts and minor misunderstandings.

When Jerome read the Partner Assignment List posted on the bulletin board outside the lab, he discovered that his lab partner had an Indian-sounding name, but he resolved to work hard to make the relationship a success. So when he met Meena in class and found that she was an exchange student from Mumbai, he worked hard to attune his ear to her accent and was pleased to discover that although her accent was at first difficult to understand, her command of English was as good as his. During the semester, Jerome spent a lot of time on understanding Meena's English. He was rewarded, because she really had a much better grasp of chemistry than he did and was willing to tutor him as they worked on assignments.

Be open-minded. An open-minded person is willing to dispassionately receive the ideas and opinions of others. Open-minded people are aware of their own cultural values and recognize that other people's values are different. They resist the impulse to judge the values of other cultures in terms of those of their own culture. In other words, they resist ethnocentrism.

Be altruistic. Altruism is a display of genuine and unselfish concern for the welfare of others. The opposite of altruism is egocentricity, a selfish interest in one's own needs to the exclusion of everything else. Egocentric people are self-centered, whereas altruistic people are other-centered. Altruistic communicators do not neglect their own needs, but they recognize that for a conversation to be successful, both parties must be able to contribute what they want and take what they need from the exchange.

Adopt Correct Attitudes

1. Tolerate ambiguity
2. Be open-minded
3. Be altruistic

Acquire Knowledge about Other Cultures

The more we know about other cultures, the more likely we are to be competent intercultural communicators (Neuliep, 2006). There are several ways to learn about other cultures.

Observe. You can simply watch as members of another culture interact with each other. As you watch, you can notice how their values, rituals, and communication styles are similar to and different from your own and other cultures with which you are familiar. The technique of watching the communication behaviors used by members of a particular culture is called *passive observation*.

Formally study. You can learn about other cultures by reading accounts by their members and ethnographic research studies; by taking courses; and by interviewing members of the culture about their values, rituals, and so on.

Immerse yourself in the culture. You can learn a great deal about another culture by actively participating in it. When you live or work with people whose cultural assumptions are different from yours, you not only acquire obvious cultural information, but you also learn nuances that escape passive observers and are generally not accessible through formal study alone. One reason that study-abroad programs often include home stays is to ensure that students become immersed in the culture of the host country. We hope that you will consider participating in a study-abroad experience. The international or global studies office at your college or university can point you to a variety of study-abroad opportunities and may even guide you to scholarships or grants to help pay your expenses.

Acquire Knowledge about Other Cultures

1. Observe
2. Formally study
3. Immerse yourself in the culture

Develop Culture-Specific Skills

To be effective in intercultural situations, you may need to adapt the basic communication skills that you will learn in this course to the demands of a particular culture. To this end, the three most useful skills that you will study are listening, empathy, and flexibility.

Practice listening. By carefully listening and demonstrating your listening, you can improve your communication with people from other cultures. Because language and non-verbal communication vary across cultures, it is vitally important that you focus closely on the other and listen attentively. There are cultural differences in how people engage in listening and the value that cultures place on listening. In the United States, we listen closely for concrete facts and information and often ask questions while listening. In other cultures, such as Japan, Finland, and Sweden, listeners are more reserved and do not ask as many questions (Samovar, Porter, & McDaniel, 2009). For many cultures in the Far East, listening is much more valued than speaking. Regardless of your cultural background, however, becoming a more skillful listener will help you in your intercultural encounters.

Practice intercultural empathy. Intercultural empathy means imaginatively placing yourself in the other person's cultural world to attempt to experience what he or she is experiencing (Ting-Toomey, 1999). The proverb "Don't judge a person until you have walked a mile in his shoes" captures this idea. By paying close attention to the other person and focusing on the emotions displayed, we can improve our empathic skills.

Develop flexibility. We discussed the concept of flexibility as part of an appropriate attitude toward intercultural encounters, but we can also provide concrete strategies for becoming more flexible in communication. **Flexibility** is the ability to adjust your communication to fit the other person and the situation. With flexibility, you can use a wide variety of communication skills during an interaction and modify your behavior within and across situations. Being flexible means analyzing a situation, making good decisions about how to communicate in that situation, and then modifying your communication when things are not going well.

intercultural empathy
imaginatively placing yourself in the dissimilar other person's cultural world to attempt to experience what he or she is experiencing

flexibility
the ability to adjust your communication to fit the other person and the situation

Develop Culture-Specific Skills

1. Practice listening
2. Practice intercultural empathy
3. Develop flexibility

There are even MORE Study Tools for Chapter 6 at www.cengagebrain.com

☑ Speech Builder Express
☑ Printable Flash Cards
☑ Interactive Games
☑ Interactive Video Activities
☑ Chapter Review Cards
☑ Online Quizzes with Feedback
☑ Audio Downloads

Learning Outcomes

LO^1 Identify the major types of relationships

LO^2 Explain how disclosure and feedback affect relationships

LO^3 Examine levels of communication at various stages in relationships

LO^4 Identify the sources of tension in relationships

Understanding
Interpersonal
Relationships

> **"We engage in impersonal conversations to gain information that may help us connect with other people by discovering that their beliefs, attitudes, and values are similar to our own."**

Interpersonal communication skills help you start, build, and maintain healthy **relationships**—sets of expectations two people have for their behavior based on the pattern of interaction between them (Littlejohn & Foss, 2008). We form relationships to satisfy our innate human need for connection with others. That is, we want to feel a sense of belonging and that someone else is here for us. Relationships run the gamut from impersonal acquaintances to intimate friends. Regardless of the level of intimacy, we seek **good relationships**, ones in which the interactions are satisfying to and healthy for those involved. How we communicate is central to achieving that goal (Littlejohn & Foss, 2008).

In this chapter, we describe three types of interpersonal relationships and provide guidelines for healthy communication in each of them. Next, we talk about the role of self-disclosure and feedback in relationship life cycles. Finally, we talk about the dialectical tensions in relationships and ways to manage them.

relationships
sets of expectations two people have for their behavior based on the pattern of interaction between them

good relationships
ones in which the interactions are satisfying to and healthy for those involved

What do you think?

It is easier to stay in a relationship than to end one.

Strongly Disagree									Strongly Agree
1	2	3	4	5	6	7	8	9	10

LO¹ Types of Relationships

We behave differently depending on whether our relationships are personal or impersonal. Moving on a continuum from impersonal to personal, we can classify our relationships as acquaintances, friendships, and close friends or intimates (Dindia & Timmerman, 2003, p. 687). Specific communication competencies help establish and maintain each type of relationship.

© NENAD AKSIC/ISTOCKPHOTO.COM

acquaintances
people we know by name and talk with when the opportunity arises, but with whom our interactions are largely impersonal

impersonal communication
conversations that can be defined as essentially interchangeable chit-chat

saving face
the process of attempting to maintain a positive self-image in a relational situation

Acquaintances

Acquaintances are people we know by name and talk with when the opportunity arises, but with whom our interactions are limited. Many acquaintance relationships grow out of a particular context. We become acquainted with those who live in our apartment building or dorm or in the house next door, who sit next to us in class, who go to our church, or belong to our club. Thus, Whitney and Paige, who met in calculus class, may talk with each other about class-related issues but make no effort to share personal ideas or see each other outside of class. Most conversations with acquaintances can be defined as **impersonal communication**, which is essentially interchangeable chit-chat (Buber, 1970). In other words, I may talk about the same thing—for instance, the weather—with the grocery clerk, sales associate, bank teller, or server at dinner. If you have an online social networking profile on Facebook, Twitter, or MySpace, many of your online "friends" would probably be most accurately defined as acquaintances if your online conversations are surface-level ones.

Our goals when communicating with acquaintances are usually to reduce uncertainty and maintain face. We engage in impersonal conversations to gain information that may help us connect with other people by discovering that their beliefs, attitudes, and values are similar to our own (Berger, 1987). In doing so, however, either of us may say or do something that produces unintended consequences. That is, we could offend the other person or say something that is taken the wrong way. So our second goal is to monitor verbal and non-verbal feedback and provide opportunities to help the other person save face. **Saving face** is the process of attempting to maintain a positive self-image in a relational situation (Ting-Toomey, 2004).

Acquaintanceship Guidelines

To meet other people and develop acquaintance relationships, it helps to be good at starting and developing conversations. The following guidelines can help you become more competent in conversing with others:

- **Initiate conversations** by introducing yourself, referring to the physical context, referring to your thoughts or feelings, referring to another person, or making a joke. For example, "Hi, I'm Whitney. Do you think it's hot in here, or is it just me?"

- **Develop an other-centered focus** by asking questions, listening carefully, and following up on what has been said. Here is an example:

Whitney:	"Have you ever taken a class from this professor?"
Paige:	"Yeah, I took algebra from her."
Whitney:	"What was she like?"
Paige:	"She was pretty good. Her tests were hard, but they were fair. I learned a lot."
Whitney:	"Did she offer study guides?
Paige:	"Yes, and we reviewed as a class by playing what she called 'algebra jeopardy.' That worked well for me."
Whitney:	"Sounds like I'm going to like this class and this instructor!"

- **Engage in appropriate turn-taking.** Effective conversationalists balance talking with listening and do not interrupt the other. Not only do we need to avoid dominating the conversation, but we also need to uphold our part by talking enough.

  - **Make your comments relevant** to what has previously been said before you change subjects.

- **Be polite.** Consider how your conversational partner will feel about what you say, and work

How's the weather?

© LJUPCO SMOKOVSKI/SHUTTERSTOCK / © GRAHAM KLOTZ/ISTOCKPHOTO.COM to phrase your comments in a way that allows your partner to save face.

Friends

Over time, some acquaintances become our friends. Friends are people with whom we have voluntarily negotiated more personal relationships (Patterson, Bettini, & Nussbaum, 1993, p. 145). As friendships develop, people move toward interactions that are less role bound and more interpersonally satisfying. For example, Whitney and Paige, who are acquaintances in calculus class and have only talked about class-related subjects, may decide to get together after class to work out at the gym. If they find that they enjoy each other's company, they may continue to meet outside of class and eventually become friends.

Some of our friendships are context bound. Thus, people often refer to their tennis friends, office friends, or neighborhood friends. These context friendships may fade if the context changes. For instance, your friendship with a person at the office may fade if you or your friend takes a job with a different company. Did you move a great distance from your hometown to attend college? If so, how many of your high school friends do you still consider friends?

Friendship Guidelines

For friendships to develop and continue, some key behaviors must occur. These behaviors help friendships continue whether you are face to face or separated by distance. Computer-mediated communication and cell phones have proven helpful in maintaining long-distance relationships (Walther & Parks, 2002). The following five competencies can help you develop and maintain your friendships (Samter, 2003):

- **Initiation.** Be proactive in setting up times to spend together. One person must get in touch with the other, and the interaction must be smooth, relaxed, and enjoyable. A friendship is not likely to form between people who rarely interact or who have unsatisfying interactions.

- **Responsiveness.** Each person must listen. Listen to others and respond to what they say. It is difficult to form friendships with people who focus only on themselves or their issues, and it is equally difficult to maintain relationships with people who are uncommunicative.

- **Self-disclosure.** Friends share feelings with each other. Although acquaintances can be maintained by conversations that discuss surface issues or abstract ideas, a friendship is based on the exchange of more personal and specific information, including personal his-

tory, opinions, and feelings. For example, after Paige and Whitney start to spend more time together outside of class, they might have this conversation:

© GRAHAM KLOTZ/ISTOCKPHOTO.COM

friends
people with whom we have negotiated more personal relationships that are voluntary

Paige:	"Can I tell you something and trust you to keep it between us?"
Whitney:	"Of course."
Paige:	"Well, you know I've been seeing David for a while now."
Whitney:	"Yeah, he seems like a nice guy."
Paige:	"Well, the other night we got into a little fight, and he pushed me onto the couch. I actually have a bruise here on my arm from it."

- **Emotional support.** Provide comfort and support when needed. When we are emotionally or psychologically vulnerable, we expect to be helped by those we consider to be friends. When your friends are hurting, they need you to support them by confirming their feelings and helping them make sense of what has happened.

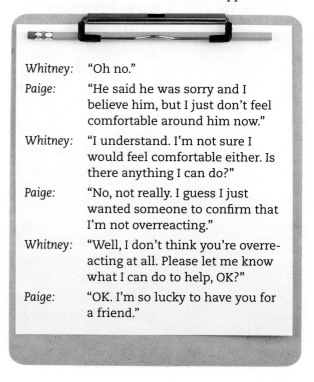

Whitney:	"Oh no."
Paige:	"He said he was sorry and I believe him, but I just don't feel comfortable around him now."
Whitney:	"I understand. I'm not sure I would feel comfortable either. Is there anything I can do?"
Paige:	"No, not really. I guess I just wanted someone to confirm that I'm not overreacting."
Whitney:	"Well, I don't think you're overreacting at all. Please let me know what I can do to help, OK?"
Paige:	"OK. I'm so lucky to have you for a friend."

- **Conflict management.** Manage conflicts so that both parties' needs are met. It is inevitable that friends will disagree about ideas or behaviors. Friendship depends on successfully handling these disagreements through conversation. In fact, by competently managing conflict, people can strengthen their friendship.

Whitney:	"Maybe you should talk to a campus counselor about this."
Paige:	"No, I don't want to make a big deal out of it."
Whitney:	"Paige, you got a bruise. That seems like a big deal to me."
Paige:	"Actually, I bruise really easily. I don't want to see a counselor."
Whitney:	"Well, if anything like this happens again, will you please talk to someone?"
Paige:	"OK, if something happens again, I promise I will."

Close Friends or Intimates

close friends or intimates

people with whom we share a high degree of commitment, trust, interdependence, disclosure, and enjoyment

platonic relationship

an intimate relationship in which the partners are not sexually attracted to each other or do not act on an attraction they feel

romantic relationship

an intimate relationship in which the partners act on their sexual attraction

trust

placing confidence in another in a way that almost always involves some risk

Close friends or intimates are those few people with whom we share close, caring, and trusting relationships characterized by a high degree of commitment, trust, interdependence, disclosure, and enjoyment. We may have countless acquaintances and many friends, but we are likely to have only a few truly intimate relationships. Intimacy is not synonymous with "love" or exclusivity, and both platonic and romantic relationships may become intimate. A platonic relationship is one in which the partners are not sexually attracted to each other or do not act on an attraction they feel. In the television series *Will and Grace*, Will and Grace live together and are intimate friends. But Will is homosexual and Grace is heterosexual, and their relationship is platonic. Conversely, a romantic relationship is one in which the partners act on sexual attraction. Today, many people today use social networking and matchmaking sites to find romantic relationship partners. Sometimes people use ghostwriters to help create the online profile they would like to project.

Regardless of whether the relationship is platonic or romantic, for it to remain intimate, both partners must continue to trust the other. Trust is placing confidence in another in a way that almost always involves some risk. We show trust by having positive expectations of the other person and believing that he or she will behave fairly and honestly. With our close friends, our lives are interdependent or intertwined. We are more likely to share personal, private information about ourselves with close friends. In close relationships, there is some fusion of the self and the other. The partner is perceived as part of yourself. In other words, you come to define who you are, in part, through your close relationships (Aron, Aron, Tudor, & Nelson, 2004). As we disclose personal information, we monitor how well our partner keeps our confidence. Once we perceive our partner to be untrustworthy, we are likely to withdraw and not continue to disclose. As a result, over time the intimacy in the relationship will decrease. When there is a severe breach of trust, we may even abruptly end the relationship.

Research shows that women and men tend to differ on the factors that lead to intimacy in relationships. This may be because society teaches women and men

Men tend to develop close friendships through joint activities, doing favors for each other, and being able to depend on one another.

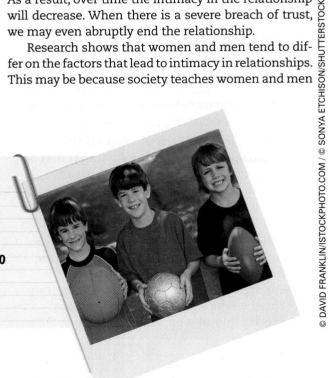

© GRAHAM KLOTZ/ISTOCKPHOTO.COM

© DAVID FRANKLIN/ISTOCKPHOTO.COM / © SONYA ETCHISON/SHUTTERSTOCK

to behave differently, according to the norms of femininity and masculinity. Women tend to develop close relationships with others based on talking, opening up to each other, and sharing personal feelings. By gaining knowledge of the innermost being of their partner, women develop a sense of "we-ness" with others. Men tend to develop close friendships through joint activities, doing favors for each other, and being able to depend on one another. Men are less likely to define a close friend as someone with whom you can share feelings. For men, close friends are the people you can depend on to help you out of a jam and the people you regularly choose for pursuing enjoyable activities together (Wood & Inman, 1993). It is important to note that these differences are more pronounced in same-sex friendships. When men and women develop close friendships or intimate relationships with each other, these distinctions may not apply.

Intimacy Guidelines

Maintaining intimacy depends on developing and maintaining trust in your partner and commitment to your relationship. The following guidelines can help you establish and maintain trust (Boon, 1994, pp. 97–101):

- **Be dependable** so your partner learns that he or she can rely on you at all times and under all circumstances. Of course, nobody is perfect. But striving to be dependable will provide a foundation for understanding when something does come up.

- **Be responsive** in meeting your partner's needs. At times, this will require you to put his or her needs before your own.

- **Be collaborative in managing conflict.** Doing so includes saying you're sorry for something you've done or said, agreeing to disagree, and letting go of the need to be "right."

- **Be faithful** by maintaining your partner's confidential information and by abiding to sexual or other exclusivity agreements between you and your partner. If your partner tells you something in confidence, honor that request.

- **Be transparent** by honestly sharing your real ideas and feelings with your partner.

© DAVID FRANKLIN/ISTOCKPHOTO.COM / © JANI BRYSON/ISTOCKPHOTO.COM

Women tend to develop close relationships with others based on talking, opening up to each other, and sharing personal feelings.

- **Be willing to put your relationship first.** This may mean giving up some activities or relationships to spend time with your partner. This is not to say you should give up all other activities and relationships. Rather, healthy intimate relationships are characterized by a balance between doing things together and doing things apart (Baxter & Montgomery, 1996).

self-disclosure
sharing biographical data, personal ideas, and feelings that are unknown to the other person

feedback
verbal and physical responses to people (and/or their messages) within the relationship

LO² Disclosure and Feedback in Relationship Life Cycles

Relationships are not something we *have* but rather are something we *make* as we communicate with others. Over time, in the give and take of our conversations, we create, recreate, and sometimes even destroy our relationships (Parks, 2006, p. 24). Even though no two relationships develop in exactly the same manner, all relationships tend to move through identifiable stages that include beginning, developing, maintaining, and perhaps deteriorating (Baxter, 1982; Duck, 1987; Knapp & Vangelisti, 2000; Taylor & Altman, 1987). Relationships don't move through these stages in a linear fashion; rather, we seem to cycle back and forth through the stages, so we say that these stages occur within the life cycle of a relationship (Honeycutt, 1993; Duck). How a relationship moves through these stages depends on the interpersonal communication between the partners. In fact, talking is basic to all relationship stages—whether they are beginning, deepening, getting worse, or maintaining at a status quo (Duck). What enables a relationship to move between stages is the disclosure and feedback that occurs between partners. So let's take a look at how disclosure and feedback work together in relationship development.

A healthy interpersonal relationship is marked by an appropriate balance of **self-disclosure** (sharing biographical data, personal ideas, and feelings that are unknown to the other person) and **feedback** (the verbal and physical responses to people and/or their messages) within the relationship. The

Johari window
a tool for examining the relationship between disclosure and feedback in the relationship

Johari window, named after its two originators, Joseph Luft and Harry Ingham, is a tool for examining disclosure and feedback in a relationship (Luft, 1970). The window represents all of the information about you that can be known. You and your partner each may know some (but not all) of this information. The window has four "panes" or quadrants, as shown in Figure 7.1.

The Open Pane

The first quadrant is called the *open* pane of the window because it represents the information about you that both you and your partner know. It includes information that you have disclosed and the observations about you that your partner has shared with you. It might include mundane information that you share with most people, such as your college major, but it also may include information that you disclose to relatively few people. Similarly, it could include simple observations that your partner has made, such as how you doodle when you're bored, or more serious feedback such as how you behave when you're angry.

The Secret Pane

The second quadrant is called the *secret* pane. It contains all those things that you know about your-self but that your partner does not yet know about you. Secret information is made known through the process of self-disclosure. The information moves into the open pane of the window once you share it with your partner. For example, suppose that you had been engaged to be married, but on the day of the wedding your fiancé(e) backed out. You may not want to share this part of your history with casual acquaintances, so it will be in the secret pane of your window in many of your relationships. But when you disclose this fact to a friend, it moves into the open part of your Johari window with this person. As you disclose information, the secret pane of the window becomes smaller and the open pane is enlarged.

The Blind Pane

The third quadrant is called the *blind* pane. This is the place for information that the other person knows about you but about which you are unaware. Most people have blind spots—parts of their behavior or the effects of their behavior of which they are unaware. Information moves from the blind area of the window to the open area through feedback from others. When someone gives you insight about yourself and you accept the feedback, then the information moves into the open pane. Thus, like disclosure, feedback enlarges the open pane of the Johari window, but in this case it is the blind pane that becomes smaller.

The Unknown Pane

The fourth quadrant is called the *unknown* pane. It contains information that neither you nor your partner knows about you. Obviously, you cannot develop a list of this information. So how do we know that it exists? Well, because periodically we discover it. If, for instance, you have never tried hang gliding, then nobody knows how you will react. You might chicken out or follow through, do it well or crash, love every minute of it or be paralyzed with fear. But until you try it, this information is unknown. Once you try it, you gain information about yourself that becomes part of the secret pane, which you can move to the open pane through disclosure. Also, once you have tried it, others who observe your flight will have information about your performance that you may not know unless they give you feedback.

As you disclose and receive feedback, the sizes of the various windowpanes change. These changes reflect the relationships. So the panes of the Johari window you have with different people will vary in size. Figure 7.2 shows examples.

In Figure 7.2A we see an example of a person in a relationship where there is little disclosure or feedback.

Figure 7.1

The Johari Window

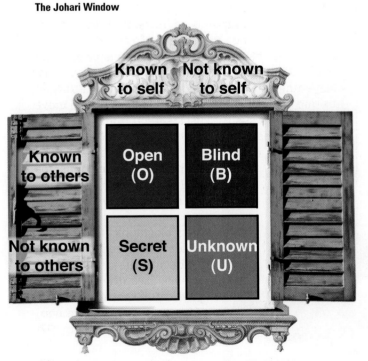

© ISTOCKPHOTO.COM

The open pane is very small because this person has not shared much information with the other and has received little feedback. This pattern is typical of new relationships and ones between casual acquaintances.

Figure 7.2B shows the panes when a person discloses to the partner, but the partner provides little feedback (or the person refuses to accept the partner's feedback). As you can see, the secret pane is smaller than in 7.2A, but the hidden pane is unchanged. Because feedback from others is one of the ways we learn about who we are, relationships in which one partner does not provide feedback can become very unsatisfying to the other individual.

Figure 7.2C shows the panes when a partner is good at providing feedback, but the individual does not disclose. Since most of us disclose only when we trust our partner, this pattern may indicate that the individual does not have confidence in the partner.

Figure 7.2D shows the panes when the individual discloses information and receives feedback. The open pane of the window has enlarged as a result of both processes. Windows that look like this indicate sufficient trust and interest in the relationship that both partners are willing to risk disclosing and giving feedback.

Figure 7.2

Sample Johari Windows

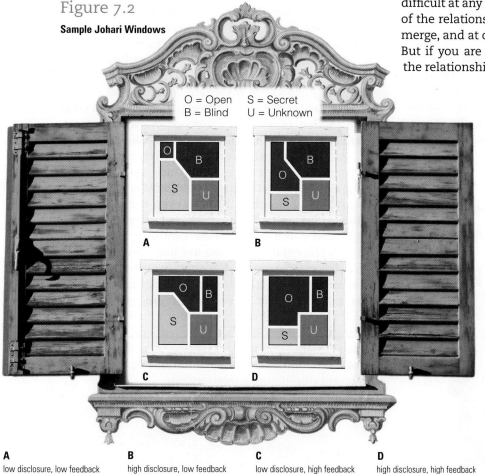

O = Open   S = Secret
B = Blind   U = Unknown

A
B
C
D

A low disclosure, low feedback

B high disclosure, low feedback

C low disclosure, high feedback

D high disclosure, high feedback

Obviously, to get a complete "picture" of a relationship, each partner's Johari window would need to be examined. A balance of appropriate disclosure and feedback for both partners is a sign of a healthy relationship.

LO³ Communication in the Stages of Relationships

Regardless of whether your relationship is with an acquaintance, a friend, or an intimate partner, every relationship develops and changes with time. As noted above, relationships tend to develop along four stages: beginning, developing, maintaining, and deteriorating. Your relationship moves among the stages based on the conversations you have with your partner. Your relationship develops based not only on the information you share with each other but "by the interpretation of such things by the partners" (Duck, 2007, p. 80). In other words, your relationship develops as you and your partner realize the similar ways in which the two of you see the world. Not only that, relationships can alternate almost imperceptibly between stages, so it may be difficult at any point in time to accurately label a stage of the relationship. At times, relationship stages may merge, and at other times, they may be quite distinct. But if you are observant, you can detect which way the relationship is moving over time.

Beginning Relationships

Communication during the beginning stage of a relationship focuses on reducing uncertainty by increasing your knowledge of the other person. Your goal is to understand how he or she sees the world (Berger, 1987). Noted interpersonal communication scholar Steve Duck (1999) conceived the Relationship Filtering Model to explain the process that relationships go through in the beginning stage. When you first meet someone, the model suggests that you assume they are similar to you until what they say or do tells you otherwise. You begin by communicating very generally about noncontroversial topics and ask questions about surface information, such as where she or he grew up and hobbies. Based on what you learn, you make inferences about general attitudes, values, and ways of thinking. If you decide you have enough common interests and attitudes, you will choose to develop the relationship by disclosing more about yourself.

Let's look again at Whitney and Paige, who have decided to become college roommates. At first they are nervous, wondering if they will be compatible as roommates. To reduce this uncertainty, they get to know each other better through disclosure and feedback. They may talk about what they did in high school; what major each is pursuing; what hobbies they like; and their favorite foods, movies, and music. As they learn more about each other, they find that although Whitney is majoring in fine arts and Paige is in pre-med, they both are passionate environmentalists and vegetarians. As they learn more, they begin to relax and find that although they have many differences, they like and respect each other. Over the semester, they each socialize with different friends but continue to have evening meals in the dining hall together. Life in the room they share begins to take on a predictable pattern. When Whitney is working on a class project, materials are strewn all over the room, so Paige accommodates her by studying in the library. When Paige is freaking out over her mid-term exam in chemistry, Whitney gets her a Red Bull from the Quick Mart and then goes to the lounge to watch TV while Paige studies.

Relationships can begin in face-to-face or online environments. Increasingly, the beginning stage may occur online (Ward & Tracy, 2004). Online communication may present a potentially less difficult way to meet others than traditional face-to-face interactions. The initial interaction can occur in the comfort of your own home and at your own pace. You need not be concerned about physical aspects of the self

or the other, and you can more precisely select what you are going to say (Ward & Tracy).

Developing Relationships

As the relationship develops, you disclose more to one another and begin to engage in more physical contact and feel a deepening psychological closeness (Duck, 1999). As healthy relationships develop, partners will identify and capitalize on their similarities and tolerate or negotiate their differences.

As the relationship develops, partners also tend to share greater physical contact. Physical contact may involve sitting closer together, leaning toward each other, more eye contact, and more touch. Such physical behaviors may or may not involve romantic feelings. Even platonic friends increase physical contact with each other as the relationship develops, though females and males may differ in how they show physical contact in same- and opposite-sex friendships. Females may hold hands or hug other female friends, whereas males may high-five each other or punch each other's shoulder. Let's say the relationship between Whitney and Paige is working out well. They spend time together, get to know each other well, and consider themselves to be close friends. By second semester, they hug each other when they return from spring break, share clothes, and do each other's hair, makeup, and nail polish.

Of course, cultural norms also affect how people engage in physical contact in relationships. In some cultures, for instance, male friends who are not romantic partners may hold hands in public or kiss to greet one another. In contrast, for orthodox Jews and observant Muslim women, touching men is abhorred.

As a relationship develops, partners will feel psychologically closer as well (Duck, 1999). Partners who do not feel relaxed and comfortable will remain casual acquaintances and may even decide to avoid having any relationship with one another. If you share no common interests, attitudes, or ways of interpreting the world, you are not likely to choose to develop a deeper relationship. Consider, for example, the people you met during your first weeks on campus. Which ones did not become your friends and why? Most likely, during your initial encounters you gathered information that reduced uncertainty about them, but what you learned was that they did not share enough common interests or attitudes to warrant developing a relationship.

Signs of a Developing Relationship

1. Greater physical contact
2. Closer psychological connection

© ISTOCKPHOTO.COM

Relationships can develop via face-to-face or online interactions. Some people even report that they achieve more closeness in online relationships than in equivalent face-to-face relationships (Walther, 1996). Indeed, rapid and exaggerated intimacy can be part of the fun of online relationships (Rabby & Walther, 2003).

Maintaining Relationships

Maintaining a relationship means that both people participate in ways that keep the relationship at a particular level of closeness. Researchers have catalogued many strategies, such as spending time together, merging friendship networks, sacrifice, and forgiveness that people use to maintain relationships (Rusbult, Olsen, Davis, & Hannon, 2004). You probably unconsciously use many of these techniques to maintain your relationships. Whitney and Paige used these strategies to maintain theirs. Second term, they decided to take a few classes together, join some of the same clubs, and get to know each other's friends. They even visited each other's hometowns and met each other's families and high school friends.

Another relationship maintenance strategy involves a willingness to sacrifice. Sacrifice means putting your own needs or desires on hold. For example, when Whitney was ill, Paige sacrificed a date in order to stay home and take care of her sick roommate. Because all relationships involve give-and-take, being willing at times to do what is best for the other person or for the relationship itself can help maintain the relationship.

Another strategy people sometimes practice is "positive illusion." This means emphasizing others' virtues and downplaying their faults.

Relationships can also be maintained by forgiveness. Because conflict is inevitable in close relationships, we may do or say things that hurt our partner. If not handled properly, such transgressions can harm the relationship and move it to a level of less intimacy. By forgiving minor transgressions, we can keep a relationship at the desired level of closeness. For example, Whitney and Paige each have little habits that annoy the other, but they choose not to let these annoyances get in the way of a good friendship.

Other ways that people maintain their relationships include continuing mutually acceptable levels of affection, self-disclosure, favors, and support.

© SKIP O'DONNELL/ISTOCKPHOTO.COM

Deteriorating and Dissolving Relationships

The less highly developed a relationship is, the more likely it is to dissolve (Parks, 2006). Relationships between acquaintances, casual friends, coworkers, and neighbors will probably end at some point. Over time, a developed relationship may become less satisfying to one or both partners so that a partner will invest less time in the relationship. But this doesn't mean that the relationship will end. Instead, it may revert to a different, less intimate level. The communication in deteriorating relationships is marked by three stages: recognition of dissatisfaction, disengaging, and at times, ending.

The first sign that a relationship is deteriorating is a subtle indication of dissatisfaction. The partners may feel less connected to each other, begin to share fewer activities, and communicate less frequently. They may begin to emphasize each other's faults and downplay virtues. Subjects that once involved deep, private, and frequent communication may become off-limits or sources of conflict. As the relationship begins to be characterized by an increase in touchy subjects and more unresolved conflicts, partners become more defensive and less willing to foster a positive communication climate.

If the relationship continues to be dissatisfying, people begin to drift apart. They become less willing to sacrifice for each other, and they show less forgiveness. Their communication changes from sharing ideas and feelings to making small talk and other "safe" communication and then to having no significant communication at all. It may seem strange that people who once had so much to share can find themselves with nothing to talk about. They depend less on each other and more upon other people for favors and support. Hostility need not be present; rather, this stage is likely to be marked by indifference. Even though Whitney and Paige were very close during their first year at college, they may drift apart over time. Maybe one of them will betray the trust of the other and the tension will lead to their becoming more annoyed with each other's faults. Once this happens, they will probably spend less time together, share fewer activities, talk about less important topics, and generally interact less frequently with each other.

When a relationship can't be maintained at a less developed level, it will end. A relationship has ended when the people no longer interact with each other.

relationship transformation
after an intimate relationship is over, continuing to interact and influence each other through a different type of relationship

dialectic
a tension between conflicting forces

relational dialectics
the competing psychological tensions in a relationship

autonomy
the desire to do things independent of one's partner

connection
the desire to do things and make decisions with one's partner

As Cupach and Metts (1986) show, people give many reasons for terminating relationships, including poor communication, lack of fulfillment, differing lifestyles and interests, rejection, outside interference, absence of rewards, and boredom.

Unfortunately, when people decide to end a relationship, they sometimes look for reasons to blame each other rather than trying to find equitable ways of bringing the relationship to an acceptable conclusion. People sometimes use strategies of manipulation, withdrawal, and avoidance (Baxter, 1982). Though misguided and inappropriate, manipulation involves being indirect and failing to take any responsibility for ending the relationship. Manipulators may purposely sabotage the relationship in hopes that the other person will break it off. Withdrawal and avoidance, also less than competent ways of communicating desires to terminate a relationship, are passive approaches that lead to the slow and often painful death of the relationship.

The most competent way to end a relationship is to be direct, open, and honest. It is important to clearly state your wish to end the relationship while being respectful of the other person and sensitive to the resulting emotions. If two people have had a satisfying and close relationship, they owe it to themselves and to each other to be forthright and fair about communicating during the final stage of the relationship.

Perhaps Whitney and Paige decide, separately, that they want to room with someone else next year. As effective communicators, they would discuss the sensitive topic without blame or manipulation, acknowledge that their relationship is less close than it once was, and move in with new roommates for the second year of college.

Even when the participants agree that their relationship is over, they may continue to interact and influence each other through a different type of relationship. This is called **relationship transformation**. Romantic relationships may transform into friendships, best friends may become casual friends, and even marriages may continue on friendly terms or as a type of business relationship where child-rearing practices and expenses are coordinated (Parks, 2006). After Whitney and Paige graduate, they may try to keep in touch, but as the years pass and they form other attachments, their friendship may wane until they are simply acquaintances who enjoy seeing each other at reunions.

LO⁴ Dialectics in Interpersonal Relationships

Have you ever felt ambivalent about a relationship? On the one hand, you really wanted to become close to someone but at the same time you wanted your "space." Or have you met someone who seemed a bit too nosy but you really wanted to get to know the person? Or have you ever felt that a relationship you were in was in a rut and wished that there could be some excitement like when you first met? If so, you were experiencing what scholars call a relationship dialectic. A **dialectic** is a tension between conflicting forces. **Relational dialectics** are the competing psychological tensions that exist in any relationship. At any one time, one or both people may be aware of these tensions. Let's take a look at the specific dialectics and then discuss how you can use interpersonal communication skills to manage these inevitable tensions in your relationships.

Relational Dialectics

Three dialectics that are common to most relationships are the tugs between autonomy and connection, openness and closedness, and novelty and predictability (Baxter & Montgomery, 1996; Baxter & West, 2003). How these tensions are dealt with can alter the stage and life cycle of a relationship. We'll describe each dialectic and then discuss how you can effectively manage them in your relationships.

Autonomy-Connection

Autonomy is the desire to do things independent of your partner. **Connection** is the desire to link your actions and decisions with your partner. Joel and Shelly have been dating for about a year. At this point in their relationship, Shelly wants to spend most of her free time with Joel and enjoys talking with Joel before acting or making decisions, but Joel has begun to feel hemmed in. For example, he wants to be able to play basketball with the guys without having to clear it first with Shelly. At the same time, however, he doesn't want to hurt Shelly's feelings or ruin the closeness of their relationship. Shelly is at peace and may not recognize any tension between autonomy and connection. On the other hand, Joel is feeling the tension between wanting to be more autonomous without jeopardizing his connection to Shelly. If Joel begins to act autonomously, he may relieve his own tension but at the same time create tension in the relationship.

Openness-Closedness

Openness is the desire to share intimate ideas and feelings with your partner. **Closedness** is the desire to maintain privacy. Let's say that Shelly discloses quite a bit to Joel. She believes it is important to divulge her feelings to Joel, and she expects him to do the same. In other words, the open quadrant of Shelly's Johari window in her relationship with Joel is quite large. Joel, however, is a more private person. He does disclose to Shelly, but not as much as she would like. The secret pane of his Johari window is larger than Shelly would like it to be. The fact that Shelly and Joel differ in their preferred levels of self-disclosure is one source of tension in their relationship. But Shelly does not want complete openness all the time. She realizes that it is appropriate to be closed, or to refrain from self-disclosure with Joel, at times. So she seeks both openness and closedness in this relationship. Likewise, Joel, although wanting more closedness than Shelly does, still wants some openness. So, like Shelly, he wants both forces to occur simultaneously in this relationship.

Novelty-Predictability

Novelty is originality, freshness, and uniqueness in your own or your partner's behavior or in the relationship. **Predictability** is consistency, reliability, and dependability. People experience tension between their desires for novelty and predictability. Because Shelly and Joel have been dating for a year, much of the uncertainty is gone from their relationship. But they do not want to eliminate uncertainty altogether. With no uncertainty at all, a relationship becomes so predictable and so routine that it is boring. Although Shelly and Joel know each other well, can predict much about each other, and have quite a few routines in their relationship, they also want to be surprised and have new experiences with each other. Shelly and Joel may differ in their needs for novelty and predictability. Shelly may yearn for Joel to surprise her with a mystery date, or she

may shock Joel by spontaneously breaking into their favorite song in the middle of the mall. At this point in their relationship, Joel may be comfortable operating by the routines they have established and may be embarrassed and shocked by Shelly's song. Here is another tension between the two that must be managed in their relationship. But they must also cope with the fact that they each need some amount of both novelty and predictability in the relationship.

Although our example of Shelly and Joel is an intimate relationship, it is important to remember that dialectical tensions exist in all relationships—not just romantic ones—and they are always in flux. Sometimes these dialectical tensions are active and in the foreground; at other times they are in the background. Nevertheless, when these tensions are experienced, they change what is happening in the relationship (Wood, 2007).

Managing Dialectical Tensions

You may be wondering how you can cope with dialectical tensions in relationships. How do people satisfy opposite needs at the same time in relationships? Several researchers (Baxter & Montgomery, 1996; Wood, 2007) have studied how people manage dialectical tensions in relationships. Four strategies have been reported: temporal selection, topical segmentation, neutralization, and reframing.

Temporal selection. Temporal selection is the strategy of choosing one desire and ignoring the other for the time being. Perhaps you and a friend realize that you have spent too much time apart lately (autonomy), so you make a conscious decision to pursue connection. That is, you agree that over the next few months to make a point of spending more

openness
the desire to share intimate ideas and feelings with one's partner

closedness
the desire to maintain one's privacy in a relationship

novelty
originality, freshness, and uniqueness in the partners' behaviors or in the relationship

predictability
consistency, reliability, and dependability in a relationship

temporal selection
the strategy of choosing one dialectical tension and ignoring its opposite for a while

© GEMENACOM/SHUTTERSTOCK

**topical
segmentation**
the strategy of choosing certain topics with which to satisfy one dialectical tension and other topics for its opposite

neutralization
the strategy of compromising between the desires of the two partners

reframing
the strategy of changing one's perspective about the level of tension

time together. You schedule lots of activities together so you can be more connected. Over time, however, you may feel that you are spending too much time together and may find yourself cancelling dates. Seesawing like this is one way to temporarily manage a relational dialectic.

Topical segmentation. Topical segmentation is the strategy of choosing certain topics with which to satisfy one desire and other topics for the opposite desire. You and your mom may practice openness by sharing your opinions and feeling about certain topics such as school, work, or politics but maintain your privacy concerning your sex lives. This segmentation satisfies both your needs for balance in the openness-closedness dialectic.

Neutralization. Neutralization is the strategy of compromising between the desires of one person and the desires of the other. Neutralization partially meets the needs of both people but does not fully meet the needs of either. A couple might pursue a moderate level of novelty and spontaneity in their lives, which satisfies both of them. The amount of novelty in the relationship may be less than what one person would ideally want and more than what the other would normally desire, but they have reached a middle point comfortable to both.

Reframing. Reframing is the strategy of changing your perception about the level of tension. Reframing involves putting less emphasis on the dialectical contradiction. It means looking at your desires differently so they no longer seem quite so contradictory. Maybe you are tense because you perceive that you are more open and your partner is more closed. So, you think about how much you disclose to him and how little he discloses to you. You might even discuss this issue with your partner. Perhaps during the conversation, you begin to realize the times that you have held back (closedness) as well as the instances when he was open. After the conversation, you no longer see as strong a contradiction. You see yourselves as more similar than different on this dialectic. You have reframed your perception of the tension.

In most cases when you are developing, maintaining, or trying to repair a deteriorating relationship, it is helpful if you can openly talk with your partner about the tensions that you are feeling and come to an agreement about how you will manage the dialectic going forward. Through self-disclosure and feedback, you and your partner may be able to negotiate a new balance that both of you find satisfying. At times, however, partners will be unable to resolve the tensions. When this happens, it is likely that one or both of you will experience dissatisfaction with the relationship and the relationship may deteriorate or end.

**There are even MORE Study Tools
for Chapter 7 at** www.cengagebrain.com

☑ Speech Builder Express
☑ Printable Flash Cards
☑ Interactive Games
☑ Interactive Video Activities
☑ Chapter Review Cards
☑ Online Quizzes with Feedback
☑ Audio Downloads

© CHRIS SCHMIDT/ISTOCKPHOTO.COM

Speak Up!

COMM was built on a simple principle: to create a new teaching and learning solution that reflects the way today's faculty teach and the way you learn.

Through conversations, focus groups, surveys, and interviews, we collected data that drove the creation of the current version of COMM that you are using today. But it doesn't stop there— in order to make COMM an even better learning experience, we'd like you to SPEAK UP and tell us how COMM worked for you. What did you like about it? What would you change? Are there additional ideas you have that would help us build a better product for next semester's communication students?

At **www.cengagebrain.com** you'll find all of the resources you need to succeed in principles of communication—**Printable Flash Cards, Speech Builder Express 3.0™, Interactive Quizzing, Downloads, Games and Simulations, Interactive Video Activities,** and more!

Speak Up! Go to **www.cengagebrain.com**

Communication Skills in *Interpersonal* Relationships

Learning Outcomes

LO¹ Discuss how to comfort people

LO² Examine the tension between openness and privacy

LO³ Develop ways to negotiate in relationships

LO⁴ Discuss conflict management styles

> ## "*In most long-term relationships, we will encounter incidents when we are expected to respond to the emotional distress of a partner.*"

Every day in your relationships you make decisions about three fundamental issues: (1) how you will respond to the emotional distress of your partner; (2) the information you will share or keep private; and (3) how you will negotiate the differences between your own and your partner's needs, wants, and preferences. The decisions you make and how you choose to behave will affect the degree of intimacy and satisfaction you experience in your relationships. We begin this chapter by discussing emotional support and the communication skills for effective comforting. Next, we discuss how to manage the competing urges between wanting to share information and keeping it to yourself. We conclude the chapter by describing various conflict management styles that can damage your relationships and then present the skills associated with collaboration, a conflict management style that can lead to a win-win situation for both you and your partner.

> **comforting**
> helping people feel better about themselves, their behavior, or their situation by creating a safe conversational space where they can express their feelings and work out a plan for the future

What do you think?

Conflict can help people grow closer together.

Strongly Disagree   *Strongly Agree*
1   2   3   4   5   6   7   8   9   10

LO¹ Comforting Messages

Can you recall a time when you were emotionally distraught? Perhaps someone close to you died unexpectedly, or the person you believed you would spend the rest of your life with dumped you, or someone you trusted betrayed you, or you were unjustly harmed by someone with power over you. If you have experienced any of these or other emotionally devastating events, you probably appreciated the emotional support you received from some of your friends and family members and might have been perplexed, annoyed, or angered by inappropriate statements made by others. In most long-term relationships, we will encounter incidents when we are expected to respond to the emotional distress of a partner. **Comforting** is helping people feel better about themselves, their behavior, or their situation by creating a safe conversational space where they can express their feelings and work out a plan for the future. Effective comforting helps the person who

© VIKTOR PRAVDICA/ISTOCKPHOTO.COM

© HANNAMARIA H/ISTOCKPHOTO.COM / © SUPRI SUHARJOTO/SHUTTERSTOCK

buffering messages
comforting messages that are phrased very politely in ways that address another person's face needs

positive face needs
the desires to be appreciated and approved, liked, and honored

negative face needs
the desires to be free from imposition and intrusion

other-centered messages
comforting messages that encourage relational partners to talk about and elaborate on what happened and how they feel about it

reframing the situation
offerings ideas, observations, information, or alternative explanations that might help a relational partner understand a situation in a different light

is comforted, helping him or her cope with the future and improving his or her relationship with the comforter. Skilled comforting also benefits the comforter, improving his or her self-esteem and relationship with the person being comforted (Burleson, 2003). Comforting rarely happens in a single statement. Instead, it usually occurs over several turns in a conversation or over several conversations that may span weeks, months, or even years.

Skills for Comforting

The following skills can help you succeed when providing emotional comfort.

Clarify Supportive Intentions

When people are experiencing emotional turmoil, they may have trouble trusting the motives of those who want to help. You can clarify your supportive intentions by openly stating that your goal in the conversation is to help your partner. Notice how David does this:

David: (noticing Paul sitting in his cubicle with his head in his lap and his hands over his head): Paul, is everything OK?

Paul: (sitting up with a miserable but defiant look on his face): Like you should care. Yeah, everything is fine.

David: Paul, I do care. You've been working for me for five years. You're one of our best technicians. So if something is going on, I'd like to help, even if all I can do is listen. Now, what's up?

Buffer Face Threats with Politeness

Buffering messages cushion the effect of what is said by using both positive and negative politeness skills. The very act of providing comfort can threaten the positive and negative face needs of your partner. (**Positive face needs** are the desires to be appreciated and approved, liked, and honored. **Negative face needs** are the desires to be free from imposition and intrusion.) On the one hand, your partner might worry that you will respect, like, or value him less because of his situation. On the other hand, the very act of comforting suggests that he cannot independently handle the situation. So comforting messages are phrased very politely in ways that address the other person's face needs. Notice how David says to Paul "You're one of our best technicians," which reaffirms his admiration for Paul's work. David also attends to Paul's need for independence by stating that maybe all he "can do is listen," which implies that Paul will be able to do the rest.

Encourage Understanding through Other-Centered Messages

To reduce emotional distress, people need to make sense out of what has happened (Burleson & Goldsmith, 1998). People feel better if they can re-evaluate specific parts of the situation or change their opinion about what happened. An important way people do this is by repeatedly telling and elaborating on the story (what happened to them). We can help this process by using **other-centered messages**, those that encourage our partner to talk about and elaborate on what happened and how she feels about it. Many of us find this difficult to do because we have been taught it is rude to pry, or we are uncomfortable hearing someone's problems. So, initial reaction may be to change the subject or to talk about similar experiences we have had.

Other-centered messages can be questions that allow the other to elaborate, or they can simply be vocalized encouragement (um, uh-huh, wow, I see). They encourage the person to explore feelings, and they demonstrate understanding and empathy.

Reframe the Situation

When people are in the midst of strong emotions, they are likely to perceive events in a limited way. In these cases, it may be helpful for you to **reframe the situation** by offering ideas, observations, information, or alternative explanations that might help your partner understand the situation in a different light. For example, imagine that Travis returns from class and tells his roommate, Abe, "Well, I'm flunking calculus. It doesn't matter how much I study or how many of the online practice problems I do, I just can't

© SERGHEI VELUSCEAC/ISTOCKPHOTO.COM

get it. I might as well just drop out of school before I flunk out completely. I can ask for a full-time schedule at work and not torture myself with school anymore." To reframe the situation, Abe might remind Travis that he has been putting in many hours at work and ask Travis if he thinks that the heavy work schedule might be cutting into his study time. Or he might tell Travis that he heard calculus instructors curve grades at the end of the term because the material is so difficult. In each case, Abe is offering new observations and providing alternative explanations that can help Travis reframe the situation from an impossible one to a manageable one.

Give Advice

At times, we can comfort people by giving advice—presenting relevant suggestions and proposals that a person can use to resolve a situation. You should not give advice, however, until your supportive intentions have been understood, you have attended to your partner's face needs, and you have sustained other-centered conversation for some time. Only when your partner has had time to make his or her own sense out of what has happened should you move the conversation to addressing next steps. Then you might begin by asking your partner what he or she thinks could help. After listening carefully to the response, you can ask your partner if some feedback and advice would be welcome. Always ask permission and acknowledge that your advice is only one suggestion of many that might work. Present the potential risks or costs associated with your advice, and let your partner know that it's OK if he or she chooses to ignore it.

Gender and Cultural Considerations in Comforting

Many people believe that women expect, need, and provide more emotional support than men. However, a growing body of research suggests that both men and women place a high value on emotional support from their partners in a variety of relationships (siblings, same-sex friendships, opposite-sex friendships, and romantic relationships; Burleson, 2003).

© RENE JANSA/SHUTTERSTOCK

How to Comfort

- Buffer face threats with politeness.
- Encourage understanding through other-centered messages.
- Reframe the situation.
- Give advice.

giving advice
presenting the relevant suggestions and proposals that a person can use to resolve a situation

disclosure
revealing confidential or secret information about others as well as yourself

Studies also find that both men and women report that other-centered messages encouraging them to explore and elaborate on their feelings provide the most comfort. However, men are less likely to use other-centered messages when comforting.

Researchers have also examined cultural differences in comforting. European Americans, more than other American ethnic groups, believe that openly discussing feelings will help a person feel better. Americans are more sensitive to other-centered messages than are Chinese. Both Chinese and Americans view avoidance strategies as less appropriate than approach strategies, but Chinese see avoidance as more appropriate than Americans do. Married Chinese and married Americans both view the emotional support provided by their spouse to be the most important type of social support they receive. African Americans place lower value on their partner's emotional support skills than do European or Asian Americans. This is especially true for African American women. Though these differences exist, it appears that people are more alike than different in the desire for emotional support from close friends and intimate partners.

LO² Managing Privacy and Disclosure in Relationships

In any relationship, both people will at times experience opposite pulls or dialectical tensions. One of these dialectics is the tension between openness and closedness. When we want openness, we use the skills of disclosure to share information and feelings with others. When we are feeling the pull of closedness, we manage our privacy to control what others know about us.

Disclosure is revealing confidential or secret information. Although it includes self-disclosure—which is sharing your own biographical data, personal

© SIL63/SHUTTERSTOCK

privacy management
exercising personal control over confidential information in order to enhance autonomy or minimize vulnerability

ideas, and feelings that were unknown to others—disclosure is a larger concept because it includes confidential information about others as well as yourself (Petronio, 2002). Suppose Jim tells Mark that he wet the bed until he was 12 years old but had never told anyone about it before because he was afraid of being teased. Jim has self-disclosed something confidential to Mark. If Mark later tells someone else that Jim was once a bed wetter, Mark is also disclosing, but he is disclosing Jim's private information, not his own.

Privacy management is the exercise of control over confidential or secret information in order to enhance autonomy or minimize vulnerability (Margulis, 1977, p. 10). The concept of privacy rests on the assumption that people own their personal information and have the right to control it by determining whether that information is to be communicated (Petronio, 2002). Like Jim, you can choose to reveal or conceal personal information from your partner. As your relationship develops, you and your partner will share sensitive information with each other. Then, either one of you could choose to reveal that sensitive information to others outside of the relationship or maintain it within the privacy of your relationship.

If your partner has your permission to share some item of your personal information, then disclosing it to others is unlikely to affect your relationship. However, if you have not given your partner permission to disclose that information and you expect that information to be held privately within your relationship, then its disclosure is likely to damage your trust in your partner and your relationship. So when Jim hears that Mark has "outed" him as a former bed

wetter, he may be embarrassed, hurt, and feel violated because Mark breached his confidentiality, or he may be unaffected if he doesn't care that others know. How Jim reacts to Mark's disclosure of this private information can vary with age. If Jim and Mark are 16 when Jim discloses his bed-wetting, Jim may see this as a very risky disclosure and be much more sensitive than he would if they are 35. The communication or the withholding of personal information is a very complex matter.

People use culture, gender, motivation, context, and risk-benefit analysis as criteria in creating rules for revealing and concealing of information (Petronio, 2002).

Culture

Individualistic cultures value privacy more than collectivist cultures do. Members of individualistic cultures are less likely to disclose personal information to anyone but close intimates.

Gender

Men or women who strongly identify themselves as masculine or feminine are likely to use rules for disclosure and privacy that correspond to sex-role stereotypes (Snell, Belk, & Hawkins, 1986). In cultures where the male stereotype includes "strong and silent" and "competitive," men are likely to keep their feelings to themselves and to avoid disclosing private information that might be used against them.

Motivation

We are more likely to disclose when we have a specific motive. For example, we are more likely to disclose to avoid loneliness or to attract someone we are interested in knowing.

Context

Privacy and disclosure rules, like other communication rules, are influenced by the situation. We may disclose private information to a therapist or counselor in order to cope with a problem. In times of crisis, we may open up to people with whom we do not normally disclose.

Risk-Benefit Analysis

One of the most important criteria we use to decide whether to disclose information or keep it private is the risk-benefit analysis. That is, we weigh the advantages and disadvantages of disclosing information or keeping it private. Common benefits of disclosing include building the relationship, coping with stress, and emotional or psychological catharsis. Benefits of maintaining privacy include control and independence. The risks of disclosing include loss of control, vulnerability, and embarrassment. The risks of maintaining privacy include social isolation and having others misunderstand you.

Although privacy and disclosure decisions affect relationships in many ways, the three most important are related to levels of intimacy, expectations for reciprocity, and information co-ownership—how jointly held private information is shared with others outside the relationship.

What kind of reaction would you expect?

© PHASE4PHOTOGRAPHY/SHUTTERSTOCK

Levels of Intimacy

The effects of privacy and disclosure on intimacy in a relationship are not straightforward. You might think that as relationships develop, people move in a clear-cut way toward deeper disclosure. But research shows that over time, due to the dialectical tensions in relationships, people move back and forth between greater disclosure and moves to re-establish privacy (Altman, 1993).

Sometimes disclosure deepens intimacy. In your relationships, you will probably find yourself and your partner cycling between times when you actively disclose and times when you back off and re-establish privacy boundaries. This can create problems when one partner craves greater intimacy at the same time his or her partner needs to re-establish privacy.

Other times, disclosure can decrease intimacy. People may disclose something to relieve their guilt or stress, as a type of confession. Some disclosures can do irreparable damage to a relationship, such as when one partner in a romantic relationship discloses an infidelity. So, sometimes opting for privacy may preserve the intimacy in a relationship (Hendrick, 1981) and avoid conflict (Roloff & Ifert, 2000). We may choose privacy over disclosure for many legitimate reasons, including protecting the other person's feelings, avoiding unnecessary conflict, sensitivity to the other's face needs, and protecting the relationship. Similarly, people whose religious, social, political, or sexual orientations conflict with the value systems of their partners may choose to keep their orientations private (Petronio, 2002). For example, some gays and lesbians choose not to "come out" to their parents because doing so may lead to estrangement.

Expectations of Reciprocity

Whether your disclosure is matched by similar disclosure from your partner can affect your relationship. Although you may expect reciprocity, recent research (Dindia, 2000b) suggests there can be a long time lag after one person discloses before the other reciprocates. In between, their conversations may center on non-personal topics. One person may not be ready to disclose his or her feelings, even though the conversational partner had revealed private information. After a fourth date, Tom blurts out "Nancy, I love you and I know that I'm going to marry you." Nancy, who thinks she loves Tom but wants to make sure she is not just taken with the idea of being in love, may not voice her feelings for many more months. Nevertheless, the two of them continue to see each other, building common history, and sharing other personal information even though Nancy did not reciprocate at the moment when Tom first declared his love for her.

Information Co-Ownership

A third way that decisions about disclosure and privacy affect relationships has to do with how partners treat the private information that each has shared with the other. When you disclose a secret to your partner, you expect your partner to respect your privacy and not disclose your private information with others. Similarly, you and your partner may share experiences and make decisions that you consider private, and you expect your partner to protect these as well. Whether we hold revealed information in confidence

describing feelings
the skill of naming
the emotions you are
feeling without judging
them

or share it with others may affect the relationship.

As people use technology to develop and maintain their relationships, their decisions about what to disclose and what to keep private as well as the rules that guide those decisions are changing. Both mobile communication technology and the Internet are affecting the disclosure-privacy dialectic by blurring the distinction between what is public and what is private communication (Kleinman, 2007). Cell phones and other wireless technology allow people to carry on private conversations in public spaces. You may IM your friend, and that friend may pass your message around to others you would prefer did not have access to that thought. Social networking sites also blur the edges. Once we post information, it is there for others to take and share with anyone. Whereas paper diaries are considered private thoughts in written form to be guarded from others, online diaries in the form of blogs or tweets are purposely made accessible to friends, acquaintances, and often to hundreds of millions of strangers on the Web.

Guidelines for Appropriate Disclosure

The following communication guidelines can help you make wise decisions regarding disclosure when sharing personal information, sharing feelings, and providing feedback.

Sharing Personal Information

To make good decisions about disclosing personal information, try these strategies:

✓ **Self-disclose the kind of information you want others to disclose to you.** One way to determine what information is appropriate to disclose is to ask yourself whether you would feel comfortable if the other person were to disclose that kind of information to you.

✓ **Self-disclose more intimate information only when the disclosure represents an acceptable risk.** There is always some risk that self-disclosure will distress your partner and damage your relationship, but the better you know your partner, the more likely a difficult self-disclosure will be well received.

✓ **Continue self-disclosure only if it is reciprocated.** Although a self-disclosure may not immediately be reciprocated, when it is apparent that it is not being returned, you should consider limiting the amount of self-disclosure you make. The choice not

to reciprocate indicates that the person does not yet feel comfortable with the level of self-disclosure.

✓ **Gradually move to deeper levels of self-disclosure.** Because receiving self-disclosure can be as threatening as giving it, most people become uncomfortable when the level of disclosure exceeds their expectations. The depth of self-disclosure should gradually increase as the relationship develops. So we should disclose surface information early in a relationship and more personal information in a more developed relationship (Dindia, Fitzpatrick, & Kenny, 1997, p. 408).

✓ **Reserve very personal self-disclosure for ongoing relationships.** Disclosures about intimate matters are appropriate in close, well-established relationships. Making intimate self-disclosures before a bond of trust is established risks alienating the other person. Moreover, people are often embarrassed by and hostile toward others who try to saddle them with intimate information in an effort to establish a personal relationship where none exists.

Sharing Feelings

At the heart of intimate self-disclosure is sharing personal feelings. When we do so, we demonstrate that we trust our partner not to use the information to do us harm. Once we decide to share our feelings, we have to know how to do so appropriately.

The best way to share feelings is by describing them. **Describing feelings** is the skill of naming the emotions you are feeling without judging them. When we describe our feelings, we teach others how to treat us by explaining how what has happened affects us. For example, if you tell Paul that you enjoy it when he visits you, your description of how you feel should encourage him to visit you again. Likewise, when you tell Gloria that it bothers you when she borrows your iPod without asking, she may be more likely to ask the next time. Describing feelings allows you to exercise a measure of control over others' behavior simply by making them aware of the effects their actions have on you.

To practice describing your feelings, try following these four steps:

✓ **Identify the behavior that triggered the feeling.** What has someone said or done to or about you?

✓ **Identify the specific emotion you are experiencing as a result of the behavior.** Sometimes we can't describe our emotions because we don't have the vocabulary to accurately describe what we are feeling. Yes, what we are feeling is similar to anger—but are we annoyed, betrayed, cheated, crushed, disturbed, furious, outraged, or shocked? Each of these words more richly describes a feeling that might less precisely be labeled anger.

✓ **Frame your response as an "I" statement.** For example, "I feel happy/sad/irritated/excited/vibrant." "I" statements help neutralize the impact of an emotional description because they do not blame the other or evaluate the other's behavior. Instead, a first-person message accurately conveys what you are expressing and why. Be careful, however, not to couch a blaming statement as an "I" statement. For example, "I feel like you don't respect me" is a criticism of the other person. It doesn't let the other person know how you feel about what happened. You might have felt hurt, betrayed, or angry. But you haven't disclosed this.

✓ **Verbalize the specific feeling.** Here are two examples of describing feelings effectively. The first one begins with the trigger, and the second one begins with the feeling—either order is acceptable:

Thank you for your compliment [*trigger*]; I [*the person having the feeling*] feel gratified [*the specific feeling*] that you noticed the effort I made.

I [*the person having the feeling*] feel very resentful [*the specific feeling*] when you criticize my cooking after I've worked as many hours as you have [*trigger*].

To begin with, you may find it easier to describe positive feelings: "I felt so much happier after you took me to the movie" or "When you offered to help me with the yard work, I really felt relieved." As you become comfortable describing positive feelings, you can move to describing negative feelings caused by environmental factors: "It's cold and cloudy, and I feel gloomy" or "When there's a thunderstorm, I get jumpy." Finally, you can risk describing the difficult emotions you feel resulting from what people have said or done: "When you use a sarcastic tone while you are saying that what I did pleased you, I really feel confused."

Providing Personal Feedback

Sometimes it is appropriate to go beyond sharing feelings to also disclose our thoughts about another's message or behavior. When personal feedback is shared with sensitivity, it can help the other person develop a more accurate self-concept and can increase the openness in the relationship. Three skills can guide us when giving personal feedback: describing behavior, praising positive behavior, and criticizing negative behavior constructively.

> "When personal feedback is shared with sensitivity, it can help the other person develop a more accurate self-concept and can increase the openness in the relationship."

✓ **Describing behavior.** As is the case when sharing feelings, both effective praising and critiquing are based on being descriptive rather than evaluative as well as being specific rather than vague. Unfortunately, people are quick to share ambiguous conclusions and evaluations. "You're so mean," "She's a tease," "You're a real friend," and countless statements like these are attempts to provide feedback, but they are evaluative and vague. **Describing behavior** is accurately disclosing the specific behaviors of another without commenting on their appropriateness. To describe behavior, we move backward to identify the specific behaviors that led to our perception. What led you to conclude someone was "mean"? Was it something the person said or did? If so, what? Once you have identified the specific behaviors, actions, or messages that led to your conclusion, you can share that information as feedback. For example, "Giorgio, you called me a liar in front of the team, and you know I have no way to prove that I told the truth." "Shana, you came to my graduation even though it was on your twenty-first birthday." "You stayed and comforted me when Tyrone left, and you even volunteered to stay with my son so I could job hunt. You're a real friend."

✓ **Praising positive behavior.** **Praise** is disclosing a specific positive behavior or accomplishment of another person and the effect that behavior has on others. Praise is not the same as flattery. When we flatter someone, we use insincere compliments to ingratiate ourselves to that person. When we praise, our compliments are sincere. Too often we fail to acknowledge the positive and helpful things people say and do. Yet our view of who we are—our identity as well as our behavior—is shaped by how others respond to us. Praise can be used to reinforce positive behavior and to help another develop a positive self-concept.

For praise to be effective, we need to focus on the specific behavior we want to reinforce. If your sister, who tends to be forgetful, remembers your birthday, you might want to praise that behavior. To say "You're so wonderful—you're on top of everything" does not reinforce

describing behavior
accurately recounting the specific behaviors of another without commenting on their appropriateness

praise
describing the specific positive behaviors or accomplishments of another and the effect that behavior has on others

"You're so wonderful—you're on top of everything."

"Thanks for the birthday card. I really appreciate it."

constructive criticism
describing specific behaviors of another that hurt the person or that person's relationships with others

the behavior because it does not identify the behavior. Instead, saying something like "Thanks for the birthday card. I really appreciate it" would be appropriate. The response acknowledges the accomplishment by describing the specific behavior you want to reinforce.

Praise, when appropriate, doesn't cost much, and it is usually appreciated. Not only does praise provide feedback and build esteem, it can also deepen our relationship with that person. To praise behavior effectively, always begin by identifying the specific behavior or accomplishment that you want to reinforce. Then, describe the specific behavior or accomplishment and any positive feelings you or others experienced as a result of the behavior or accomplishment. Finally, phrase your comments so that the level of praise appropriately reflects the significance of the behavior or accomplishment.

Giving constructive criticism. Constructive criticism is disclosing specific behaviors of another that hurt the person or that person's relationships with others. Although the word *criticize* can mean judgment, constructive criticism does not condemn or judge but is based on empathy and a sincere desire to help someone understand the impact of his or her behavior. Use the following guidelines when disclosing your thoughts and providing constructive criticism;

- *Ask the person's permission before giving criticism.* A person who has agreed to hear construc-

tive criticism is likely to be more receptive to it than someone who was not accorded the respect of being asked beforehand.

- *Describe the behavior and its consequences by accurately recounting precisely what was said or done and the reaction of those affected by it.* Your objective description allows the other to maintain face while receiving accurate feedback about the damaging behavior. For example, DeShawn asks "What did you think of the visuals I used when I delivered my report?" If you reply "They weren't very effective," you would be too general and evaluative to be helpful. In contrast, to give descriptive feedback, you might say "Well, the type on the first two was too small, and I had trouble reading them." Notice that this constructive criticism does not attack DeShawn's competence. Instead, it points out a problem and in so doing enables DeShawn to see how to improve.

- *Preface constructive criticism with an affirming statement.* Remember, even constructive criticism threatens the innate human need to be liked and admired. So, prefacing constructive criticism with statements that validate your respect for the other person is important. One way to do this is to offer praise before criticism. You could begin your feedback to DeShawn by saying, "First, the chart showing how much energy we waste helped me see just how much we could improve. The bold colors you chose also really helped me see the problems. But the type size on the first two slides was too small for me to see from the back of the room. It would have helped me read them if they had been larger."

- *When appropriate, suggest how the person can change the behavior.* Because the goal of constructive criticism is to help, it is appropriate to provide suggestions that might lead to positive change. In responding to DeShawn's request for feedback, you might also add, "In my Communication class, I learned that most people in an audience will be able to read 18-point font or larger. You might want to give that a try." By including a positive suggestion, you not only help the person by providing useful information, you also show that your intentions are positive.

Communication Skills for Managing Privacy

Maintaining privacy during interpersonal interactions can be awkward, especially if you want to maintain or further develop your relationship. Because

© VADIM BUKHARIN/ISTOCKPHOTO.COM / © TATIANA POPOVA/ISTOCKPHOTO.COM reciprocal disclosures are part of relationship development, your partner may expect you to respond to his or her disclosure with a similar one of your own. Or you may encounter someone who asks you personal questions that you do not want to answer. In both cases, you will want to respond in a way that maintains your privacy without damaging the relationship. We offer three indirect and one direct communication strategy you can use when you are being pressed to disclose something that you are not comfortable sharing.

Indirect Strategies for Maintaining Privacy

Sometimes you may choose to maintain your privacy by deflecting attention or by simply deceiving the other person. These strategies can be effective in the short term, but don't make them a habit. Over the long term, they may damage the relationship.

✓ **Change the subject.** Partners who are sensitive will recognize a change of subject as signal that you don't want to disclose. For example, when Pat and Eric are leaving economics class, Pat says to Eric, "I got an 83 on the test, how about you?" If Eric doesn't want to share his grade, he might redirect the conversation by saying, "Hey, that's a B. Good going. Did you finish the homework for calculus?"

✓ **Mask feelings.** When you have decided that sharing your feelings is too risky, your may choose to mask your emotions. A good poker player who develops a poker face, a neutral look that is impossible to decipher and stays the same whether the player's cards are good or bad, has learned to mask emotions. Likewise, if Alita laughs along with the others as Manny makes fun of her, this display may mask her feelings of betrayal and embarrassment. On occasion masking your feelings can be an effective strategy. However, if we rely too much on this strategy, we might experience health problems because we are turning our feelings inward and not expressing them. We also run the risk of stunting the growth of our relationships because our partners won't really know or understand us.

✓ **Tell a white lie.** A white lie is a false or misleading statement that might be acceptable if telling the truth would embarrass you or your partner and if the untruth will not cause serious harm to either person or to the relationship. So when Pat asks Eric about his grade on the test, Eric might respond "I'm not sure. I got a few tests back this week."

Direct Strategy for Maintaining Privacy: Establish a Boundary

Changing the subject, masking feelings, and telling white lies are indirect ways to maintain your privacy and generally work in one-time situations. But these strategies will eventually damage your relationships if used repeatedly. When you wish to keep information private over a longer period of time, you will want to use a more direct approach. The skill of **establishing a boundary** allows you to effectively respond to people who expect you to disclose information you prefer to keep private. In essence, it is a polite way to let your partner know that questions requiring you to disclose about a specific topic are out of bounds.

1. Recognize why you are choosing not to share the information.

2. Identify why you made this decision.

3. Form an "I"-centered message that briefly establishes a boundary.

For example, when Pat asks Eric about his test grade, Eric might reply "I know that everyone's different, and I don't mean to be rude, but it's my policy not to ask other people about their grades and not to discuss my own. I know you may think this is weird, but please don't be offended." This lets Pat know that Eric's decision is based on a personal rule rather than an indication of his trust in Pat. Similarly, we sometimes need to establish a boundary regarding private information that another person has entrusted to us. So when Julie asks Ilaria why Emma isn't going on the alternative spring break trip this year, Emma may say "You know, I'd like to share that with you, but Emma told me her reasons in confidence, and I pride myself on honoring commitments I've made to guard others' privacy. I know you can appreciate that."

© ISTOCKPHOTO.COM

establishing a boundary effectively responding to people who expect you to disclose information you prefer to keep private

© JOHANNES NORPOTH/ISTOCKPHOTO.COM

LO³
Negotiating Different Needs, Wants, and Preferences in Relationships

passive behavior not expressing personal preferences or defending our rights because we fear the cost and are insecure in the relationships, have very low self-esteem, or value the other person above ourselves

aggressive behavior belligerently or violently confronting another with your preferences, feelings, needs, or rights with little regard for the situation or for the feelings or rights of others

assertive behavior expressing your personal preferences and defending your personal rights while respecting the preferences and rights of others

Even two people who are in a mutually satisfying, intimate relationship have different needs, wants, and preferences. The dialectical tension between our need for autonomy and our need for connection can affect whether we choose to push to have a preference honored by our partner or whether we are willing to subordinate our wishes to maintain connectedness with our partner. For example, Anna may enjoy watching college football all day every Saturday. But she has begun to date Jack, who hates all sports. So Anna may forego her Saturday habit in order to spend time with Jack. Or Jack may initially indulge Anna by watching with her, getting pleasure from just spending time with her. As they get to know each other better, the person who has made the personal sacrifice may choose to express his or her real preference. How Anna and Jack communicate their preferences and how the other one responds will affect the quality of their relationship. We negotiate our differences in relationships by communicating our personal needs and preferences and by managing the conflict that occurs when our needs, wants, and preferences do not match those of our partner.

Communicating Personal Needs, Wants, and Preferences: Passive, Aggressive, and Assertive Behavior

We can communicate our needs, wants, and preferences in one of three ways. We can be passive, aggressive, or assertive.

Passive Behavior

We exhibit passive behavior when we do not express our personal preferences or defend our rights because we value our connection with the other person more than we value our independence and we fear that we will lose our connection if we stand up for ourselves. We behave passively when we submit to other people's demands even when doing so is inconvenient, against our best interests, or when it violates our rights. For example, Aaron and Katie routinely go to the gym at 10 a.m. Saturday mornings, but Aaron's Friday work schedule has changed and he doesn't get home until 3 a.m. on Saturday morning. Aaron behaves passively if he doesn't say anything to Katie but drags himself out of bed even though he'd much rather sleep.

Aggressive Behavior

We exhibit aggressive behavior when we forcefully make claims for our preferences, feelings, needs, or rights with little or no regard for the situation or for the feelings or rights of our partner. People behave aggressively when they perceive themselves to be powerful, do not value the other person, lack emotional control, or feel defensive. Although aggressive behavior may stem from the need to establish more independence in a relationship, it also weakens feelings of connection and damages relationships. Research shows that people who receive aggressive messages from their partner are likely to feel hurt by them regardless of their relationship (Martin, Anderson, & Horvath, 1996, p. 24). Suppose that, without letting her know of his schedule change, Aaron continues to meet Katie at the gym. If Katie suggests they meet next week at 8 a.m. instead of 10 a.m., Aaron may explode and aggressively reply, "No way! In fact, I don't care if I ever work out on Saturday again!" Katie, who has no context for understanding this aggressive outburst, may be startled, hurt, and confused.

Assertive Behavior

Assertive behavior is expressing our personal preferences and defending our personal rights while respecting the preferences and rights of others. Assertiveness is an effective way to establish our independence while continuing to nurture the relationship because our assertive messages teach our partners how to treat us. When we assert our needs and preferences effectively, we provide our partners with the honest and truthful information they need to understand and meet our needs. When Aaron's schedule changed, he could have behaved assertively and called Katie, explained his situation, and negotiated a more convenient time for working out together.

Figure 8.1

Characteristics of Assertive Behavior

Own your feelings	Assertive individuals acknowledge that the thoughts and feelings expressed are theirs.
Avoid confrontational language	Assertive individuals do not use threats, evaluations, or dogmatic language.
Use specific statements directed to the behaviors at hand	Instead of focusing on extraneous issues, assertive individuals use descriptive statements that focus on the issue that is most relevant.
Maintain eye contact and firm body position	Assertive individuals look people in the eye rather than shifting gaze, looking at the floor, swaying back and forth, hunching over, or using other signs that may be perceived as indecisive or lacking conviction.
Maintain a firm but pleasant tone of voice	Assertive individuals speak firmly but at a normal pitch, volume, and rate.
Avoid hemming and hawing	Assertive individuals avoid vocalized pauses and other signs of indecisiveness.

Assertive messages balance our rights and needs with the rights and needs of others. For a review of the characteristics of assertive behavior, see Figure 8.1.

Here are some useful guidelines for practicing assertive behavior: (1) identify what you are thinking or feeling, (2) analyze the cause of these feelings, (3) identify what your real preferences and rights are; and (4) use describing feelings and describing behavior skills to make "I" statements that explain your position politely.

Cultural Variations in Passive, Aggressive, and Assertive Behavior

Assertiveness is typically valued in individualistic cultures. Whereas North American culture is known for its assertive communication style, Asian and South American cultures, which are collec-

© JASON STITT/SHUTTERSTOCK

tivist, tend to value accord and harmony (Samovar, Porter, & McDaniel, 2007). In collectivist cultures, passive behavior is more prevalent, and personal needs, wants, and preferences are subordinate to the needs of the group. In some cultures, such as Latino or Hispanic societies, men exercise a form of self-expression that goes far beyond the guidelines presented here for assertive behavior. In these societies, the concept of "machismo" guides male behavior. Although what is labeled appropriate behavior varies across cultures, the results of passive and aggressive behaviors seem universal. Passive behavior can cause resentment, and aggressive behavior leads to fear and misunderstanding. When talking with people whose culture, background, or lifestyle differs from your own, you may need to observe their behavior and their responses to your statements before you can be sure about the kinds of behavior that are likely to communicate your intentions effectively.

> **interpersonal conflict**
> when the needs or ideas of one person are at odds with the needs or ideas of another

LO⁴ Managing Conflict in Relationships

When two people have an honest relationship, there will be times when one person's attempt to satisfy his or her own needs will conflict with the other person's desires. When this happens, the partners experience conflict. Interpersonal conflict exists when the needs or ideas of one person are at odds with the needs or ideas of another. In these conflict situations, participants have choices about how they act and how they communicate with each other.

Many people view conflict as a sign of a bad relationship, but in reality conflict occurs in all relationships. Although cultures differ in how they view conflict (for example, Asian cultures see it as

withdrawing
managing conflict by physically or psychologically removing yourself from it

accommodating
managing conflict by satisfying others' needs or accepting others' ideas while neglecting your own

forcing
managing conflict by satisfying your own needs or advancing your own ideas with no concern for the needs or ideas of the other and no concern for the harm done to the relationship

compromising
managing conflict by giving up part of what you want to provide at least some satisfaction for both parties

collaborating
managing conflict by fully addressing the needs and issues of each party and arriving at a solution that is mutually satisfying

dysfunctional), whether conflict hurts or strengthens a relationship depends on how we deal with it. In this section, we discuss five styles people use to manage conflict and how you can skillfully initiate and respond to conflict in your relationships.

Styles of Conflict

Think about the last time you experienced a conflict. How did you react? Did you avoid it? Give in? Force the other person to accept your will? Did you compromise? Or did the two of you use a problem-solving approach? When faced with a conflict, you can withdraw, accommodate, force, compromise, or collaborate (Lulofs & Cahn, 2000, pp. 101–102).

One of the most common ways to deal with conflict is withdrawing. Withdrawing involves physically or psychologically removing yourself from the conflict. You withdraw physically by leaving the site. For instance, imagine Eduardo and Justina getting into an argument about their financial situation. Eduardo may withdraw physically by saying "I don't want to talk about this" and walking out the door. Or he may psychologically withdraw by simply ignoring Justina. When you withdraw repeatedly, you risk damaging your relationship. First, in terms of dialectical tension, withdrawing signals closedness rather than openness and autonomy rather than connection. Further, withdrawing doesn't eliminate the source of the conflict, and it often increases the tension. In many cases, not confronting the problem when it occurs only makes it more difficult to deal with in the long run. Nevertheless, as a temporary strategy, withdrawing may allow tempers to cool and may be appropriate when the issue or the relationship isn't important.

A second style of managing conflict is accommodating, which means satisfying others' needs or accepting others' ideas while neglecting your own. People who adopt the accommodating style use passive behavior. For instance, during a discussion of their upcoming vacation, Mariana and Juan disagree about whether to invite friends to join them. Juan, who would really prefer to be alone with Mariana, uses accommodation when Mariana says,

"I think it would be fun to go with another couple, don't you?" and he replies, "OK, whatever you want."

Accommodating can result in ineffective conflict resolution because important facts, arguments, and positions are not voiced. There are situations, of course, when accommodating is appropriate. When the issue is not important to you but the relationship is, accommodating is the preferred style. Hal and Yvonne are trying to decide where to go for dinner. Hal says, "I really have a craving for some Thai food tonight." Yvonne, who prefers pizza, says, "OK, that will be fine." Yvonne's interest in pizza was not very strong, and because Hal really seemed excited by Thai food, Yvonne accommodated.

A third style of dealing with conflict is forcing. Forcing means satisfying your own needs with no concern for the needs of the other and no concern for the harm done to the relationship. Forcing may use aggressive behavior such as physical threats, verbal attacks, coercion, or manipulation. If you use forcing in a conflict and your partner avoids or accommodates, the conflict seems to subside. If, however, your partner answers your forcing style with a forcing style, the conflict escalates.

Although forcing may result in a person getting her or his own way, it usually hurts a relationship, at least in the short term. There are times, however, when forcing is an effective means to resolve conflict. In emergencies, when quick and decisive action must be taken to ensure safety or minimize harm or when an issue is critical to your own or the other's welfare, or if you are interacting with someone who will take advantage of you if you do not force the issue, this style is appropriate. For example, David knows that, statistically speaking, the likelihood of death or serious injury increases dramatically if one does not wear a helmet when riding a motorcycle. So he insists that his sister wear one when she rides with him, even though she complains bitterly.

A fourth way to manage conflict is compromising, which occurs when partners each give up part of what they want to provide at least some satisfaction for both parties. For example, if Heather and Paul are working together on a class project and need to meet outside of class but both have busy schedules, they may compromise on a time to meet that isn't particularly ideal for either one.

Although compromising is a popular and effective style, there are drawbacks associated with it. One drawback is that the quality of a decision is affected if one of the parties "trades away" a better solution to find a compromise. Compromising is appropriate when the issue is moderately important, when there are time constraints, and when attempts at forcing or collaborating have not been successful.

A fifth style for dealing with conflict is collaboration. When collaborating, you view the disagreement as a problem to be solved, discuss the issues, describe your feelings, and identify the characteristics of an effective solution. With collaboration, both people's needs are met and both sides feel that they have been heard. For example, if Juan and Mariana decide to collaborate on their conflict about asking friends to join them on vacation, Mariana may explain how she thinks that vacationing with friends lower the cost of the trip. Juan may describe his desire to have "alone time" with Mariana. As they explore what each wants from the vacation, they can arrive at a plan that meets both of their needs. So, they may end up vacationing alone but spending several nights camping to lower their expenses. Or they may share a condo with friends but agree to schedule alone time each day.

Guidelines for Collaboration

You may be the person to initiate a conflict, or you may have to respond to a conflict initiated by your partner. In either case, several guidelines can help you guide the conversation. The guidelines below will help you initiate collaborative conflict, and shape a conversation toward collaboration.

There are even MORE Study Tools for Chapter 8 at www.cengagebrain.com

- ☑ Speech Builder Express
- ☑ Printable Flash Cards
- ☑ Interactive Games
- ☑ Interactive Video Activities
- ☑ Chapter Review Cards
- ☑ Online Quizzes with Feedback
- ☑ Audio Downloads

You can initiate a collaborative conflict by:

- *Identifing the problem and own it as your own: "Hi, I'm trying to study and need your help."*

- *Describing the problem in terms of behavior, consequences, and feelings: "When I hear your music, I listen to it instead of studying and then I get frustrated and behind schedule."*

- *Not evaluating the other person's motives. Refrain from blaming or accusing: "That person isn't trying to ruin your study, she's just enjoying her music."*

- *Finding common ground: "I would guess that you have had times when you became distracted from something you needed to do, so I'm hoping that you can help me out by lowering the volume a bit."*

- *Mentally rehearsing so that you can state your request briefly.*

You can shape a conversation toward collaboration by:

- *Disengaging. Mentally "put up your shield" and avoid a defensive response by emotionally disengaging. Remember, your partner has a problem and you want to help.*

- *Responding empathically and with genuine interest and concern. Sometimes you need to allow your partner to vent before the partner will be ready to problem solve: "I can see that you're angry. Tell me about it."*

- *Paraphrasing your understanding of the problem and asking questions to clarify issues: "Is it the volume of my music or the type of music that is making it difficult for you to study?"*

- *Seeking common ground by finding some aspect of the complaint that you can honestly agree with: "I can understand that you would be upset about losing precious study time."*

- *Asking the other person to suggest alternative solutions: "Can you give me a couple of ideas about how we could resolve this so your study is more effective?"*

© STEFANIE TIMMERMANN/ISTOCKPHOTO.COM

Learning Outcomes

LO¹ Discuss how to form and order a series of questions for an interview

LO² Discuss how to conduct information interviews

LO³ Examine how to conduct employment interviews

LO⁴ Discuss interview strategies for job seekers

LO⁵ Identify strategies for dealing with news media

Interviewing

"Although we all are experienced in informal conversation, few people know how to conduct an effective interview, and few of us have practice in effectively presenting ourselves and our ideas in an interview."

Interviewing is a powerful method of collecting or presenting firsthand information that may be unavailable elsewhere. So, it is an important communication skill to master. An **interview** is a highly structured conversation in which one person asks questions and another person answers them. Effective interview participants prepare in advance for the interview conversation, unlike most interpersonal communication. By *highly structured*, we mean that the purpose of the conversation and the questions to be asked are determined ahead of time. Because interviews are highly structured, they can be used to make comparisons. For example, an interviewer may ask two potential employees the same set of questions, compare the answers, and hire the person whose answers fit best with the needs of the organization. Although we all are experienced in informal conversation, few people know how to conduct an effective interview, and few of us have practice in effectively presenting ourselves and our ideas in an interview.

Because the heart of effective interviewing is developing a structured series of good questions, we begin by describing how to do so. Then, we propose some guidelines for conducting both information and employment interviews. Finally, we offer tips about how to present yourself in an employment interview and in a media interview.

interview
a planned, structured conversation in which one person asks questions and another person answers them

interview protocol
an ordered list of questions that have been selected to meet the specific purpose of the interview

What do you think?

I would rather do an interview over the phone than in person.

Strongly Disagree									*Strongly Agree*
1	2	3	4	5	6	7	8	9	10

LO¹ Structuring Interviews

The questions you develop for any interview depend on the specific purpose of the interview. Defining the purpose will give you insight into the major topic areas you will need to cover during the interview conversation. With these topics in mind, you can then structure the interview by forming and ordering a series of questions to use during the meeting.

The Interview Protocol

The **interview protocol** is the list of questions you prepare to elicit the information you want to know from the interviewee. To prepare the interview protocol, begin by

© ISTOCKPHOTO.COM

Figure A.1

Topics for an Interview with a Music Producer

- **Finding artists**
- **Decision process**
- **Criteria**
- **Stories of success and failure**

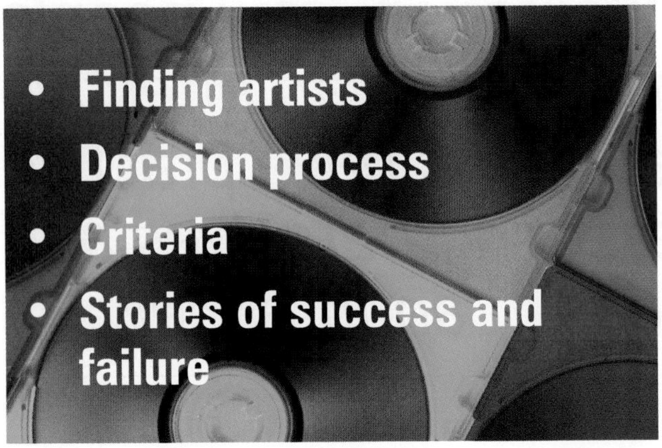

primary questions lead-in questions that introduce one of the major topics of the interview conversation

secondary questions questions designed to prove the answers given to primary questions

open questions broad-based probes that call on the interviewee to provide perspective, ideas, information, feelings, or opinions as he or she answers the question

closed questions narrowly focused questions that require the respondent to give very brief (one- or two-word) answers

listing the topic areas to be covered in the interview. Then prioritize them. Figure A.1 presents a list of topics for an interview with a music producer when the goal is to learn about how producers find and sign new talent.

Effective Questions

Just as the topics in a well-developed speech are structured in an outline with main points, subpoints, and supporting material, an effective interview protocol is structured into primary and secondary questions. The questions should be a mix of open-ended and closed questions as well as neutral and leading questions. Let's briefly examine each type.

Primary and Secondary Questions

Primary questions are lead-in questions about one of the major topics of the interview. They are like the main points of an essay or speech. The interview with the music producer may have four primary questions corresponding to the topics in Figure A.1: (1) How do you find artists to consider for contract? (2) Once an artist has been brought to your attention, what course of action do you follow? (3) What criteria do you use when deciding to offer a contract? (4) Can you tell me the story of how you came to sign one of your most suc-

cessful artists and then one about an unsuccessful artist?

Secondary questions are follow-up questions designed to probe the answers given to primary questions. You can anticipate some of the follow-up questions you may want to ask. For example, if the music producer doesn't mention genre or demographic considerations in his response to your primary question about the criteria used in selecting artists, you might probe with a follow-up question. Some follow-up questions are not as directive and simply encourage the interviewee to continue ("And then?" or "Is there more?"), some probe into what the person has said ("What does 'regionally popular' mean?" or "What were you thinking at the time?"), and some probe the feelings of the person ("How did it feel when her first record went platinum?" or "Did you expect them to become so popular?"). The major purpose of follow-up questions is to encourage the interviewee to expand on an answer she or he has given. Sometimes the interviewee may not understand how much detail you are looking for, and occasionally he or she may be purposely evasive.

Open and Closed Questions

Open questions are broad-based probes that allow the interviewee to provide perspectives, ideas, information, feelings, or opinions as he or she wishes. For example, in a job interview you might be asked, "What one accomplishment has best prepared you for this job?" In a customer service interview, a representative might ask, "What seems to be the problem?" or "Can you tell me the steps you took when you first set up this product?" Open questions encourage the interviewee to talk and allow the interviewer an opportunity to listen and observe. Open questions take time to answer and give respondents more control, which means that interviewers can lose sight of their original purpose if they are not careful (Tengler & Jablin, 1983).

By contrast, closed questions are narrowly focused and control what the interviewee can say. They require very brief (one- or two-word) answers. Closed questions range from those that can be answered yes or no, such as "Have you had a course in marketing?" to those that require only a short answer, such as "How many of the artists you have signed have won Grammys?" By asking closed questions, interviewers can control the interview and obtain specific information quickly. But the answers to closed questions cannot reveal the nuances behind responses, nor are they likely to capture the complexity of the story.

© TATIANA POPOVA/ISTOCKPHOTO.COM

© SN4KE/SHUTTERSTOCK

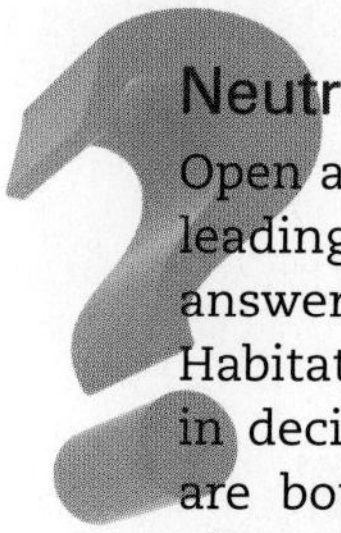

Neutral and Leading Questions

Open and closed questions may be either neutral or leading. Neutral questions do not direct a person's answer. "What can you tell me about your work with Habitat for Humanity?" or "What criteria do you use in deciding whether to offer an artist a contract?" are both neutral questions. The neutral question gives the respondent free rein to answer the question without any knowledge of what the interviewer thinks or believes.

By contrast, leading questions guide respondents toward providing certain types of information and imply that the interviewer prefers one answer over another. "What do you like about working for Habitat for Humanity?" steers respondents to describe only the positive aspects of their volunteer work. "Having a 'commercial sound' is an important criteria, isn't it?" directs the answer by providing the standard for comparison. In most types of interviews, neutral questions are preferable because they are less likely to create defensiveness in the interviewee.

Order and Time Constraints in Interview Protocols

The final step in creating the interview protocol is to develop a sequence for the questions. Here are a few tips about sequencing an interview:

- As in an interpersonal conversation, your initial questions should be short and designed to get the interviewee involved in the conversation. In general, it is better to leave more complex or controversial questions until later, after you have established rapport.

- Be sure to place topics of great importance early in the interview, so that you will have plenty of time for follow-up questions.

- Answering fact questions can be boring for the interviewee, so you might consider spreading these throughout the interview.

- Finally, it is usually easier for people to talk about things in the present than it is for them to remember things from the past or to hypothesize about the future, so begin by asking about current practices or events, then work backward or forward.

Once you have generated a complete question list, you will need to estimate how long it will take to ask and answer all the questions. Typically, allow four minutes for an open question and one minute for a closed question. If your estimate for the length of time needed to answer all the questions exceeds the time allotted for the interview, mark the less-important questions with an asterisk (*) so you can skip them if necessary. You never want an interview to take longer than what you told the interviewee when you scheduled it.

When you have finalized your interview protocol, make a version to use during the interview with enough space between questions for you to take complete notes of the answers.

Figure A.2 shows what an interview protocol for a music producer might look like.

neutral questions questions that do not direct a person's answer

leading questions questions that guide respondents toward providing certain types of information and imply that the interviewer prefers one answer over another

Figure A.2

Protocol for an Interview with a Music Producer

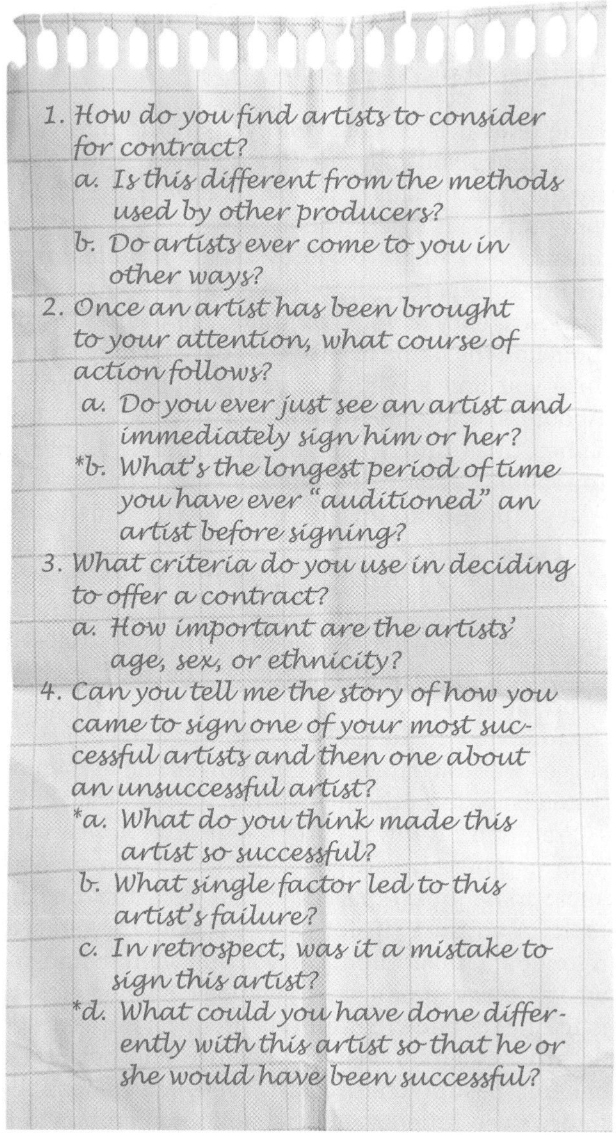

1. How do you find artists to consider for contract?
   a. Is this different from the methods used by other producers?
   b. Do artists ever come to you in other ways?
2. Once an artist has been brought to your attention, what course of action follows?
   a. Do you ever just see an artist and immediately sign him or her?
   *b. What's the longest period of time you have ever "auditioned" an artist before signing?
3. What criteria do you use in deciding to offer a contract?
   a. How important are the artists' age, sex, or ethnicity?
4. Can you tell me the story of how you came to sign one of your most successful artists and then one about an unsuccessful artist?
   *a. What do you think made this artist so successful?
   b. What single factor led to this artist's failure?
   c. In retrospect, was it a mistake to sign this artist?
   *d. What could you have done differently with this artist so that he or she would have been successful?

© SN4KE/SHUTTERSTOCK

© LUMINIS/SHUTTERSTOCK

LO^2 Guidelines for Conducting Information Interviews

Interviewing is a valuable method for obtaining information on nearly any topic. Lawyers and police interview witnesses to establish facts; health care providers interview patients to obtain medical histories before making diagnoses; reporters interview sources for their stories; social workers and sales representatives interview clients; managers interview employees to receive updates on projects; and students interview experts to obtain information for research papers. Assuming you have prepared a good interview protocol, the quality of the information you receive will depend on choosing the right person to interview and effectively conducting the interview conversation.

What kind of research would you need to do to interview this producer?

Doing Research

Sometimes it is obvious who you should interview. Other times you may have to do research to identify the right person or people to interview. Suppose your purpose is to learn about how to get a recording contract. You might begin by asking a professor in the music department for the name of a music production agency in your community or nearby. Or you could find the name of an agency by searching online. Once you find a Web site, you can usually find an "About Us" or "Contact Us" link on it, which will offer names, titles, e-mail addresses, and phone numbers. You should be able to identify someone appropriate to your purpose from this list. Once you have identified the person or people to be interviewed, you should contact them to make an appointment. Today, it is generally best to do so by both e-mail and telephone if possible. When you contact them, be sure to clearly state the purpose of the interview, how the interview information will be used, and how long you expect the interview to take. When setting a date and time, suggest several dates and time ranges and ask which would be best for them.

You don't want to bother your interviewee with information you can get elsewhere. So to prepare appropriate questions, do some research on the topic in advance. If, for instance, you are going to interview a music producer, you will want to find out what a music producer is and does. If your purpose is to understand what criteria producers use to sign an artist or group, you will want to find out first if general "best practices" exist. Then, you can ask the interviewee if he or she has additional criteria, dif-

ferent criteria, or even expand on how the criteria is used in making judgments. Interviewees will be more likely to enjoy talking with you if you're well informed. And being familiar with your subject will enable you to ask better questions.

Conducting an Information Interview

By applying the communication skills we have been discussing in this book, you'll find that you can turn your careful planning into an excellent interview. To guide you in the process, we offer this list of best practices:

Be prompt. Your interviewee deserves your respect, which you can show by being prepared to begin at the time you have agreed to. Remember to allow enough time for potential traffic and parking problems.

Be courteous. Begin by thanking the person for taking the time to talk to you. Remember that although interviewees may enjoy talking about the subject, may be flattered, and may wish to share knowledge, they have nothing to gain from the interview, so you should let them know you are grateful to them for taking the time to talk with you. Most of all, respect what the interviewee says regardless of what you may think of the answers.

If you want to tape-record the interview, ask permission. If the interviewee says no, respect his or her wishes and take careful notes.

Listen carefully. For key information in the interview, paraphrase what the interviewee has said to be sure that you really understand.

Keep the interview moving. You do not want to rush the person, but you do want to get your questions answered during the allotted time.

© DUSTIN STELLER/ISTOCKPHOTO.COM

Make sure that your non-verbal reactions—your facial expressions and your gestures—are keeping with the tone you want to communicate. Maintain good eye contact with the person. Nod to show understanding, and smile occasionally to maintain the friendliness of the interview. How you look and act is likely to determine whether the person will warm up to you and give you an informative interview.

Get permission to quote the interviewee. If you are going to publish the substance of the interview, be sure to get written permission for exact quotes. As a courtesy, offer to let the person see a copy of the article (or at least tell the person exactly when and where it will be published). Under some circumstances, you may want to show the interviewee a draft before it goes into print, if only to allow him or her to double-check the accuracy of direct quotations. If so, provide the draft well before the deadline to give the person the opportunity to read it and to give you time to deal with any suggestions.

Always close the interview by thanking the interviewee for his or her time. This closure leads to positive rapport should you need to follow up later and demonstrates that you realize the person gave up valuable time to visit with you.

LO³ Conducting Employment Interviews

Almost all organizations use interviewing as part of their hiring process. Employment interviews help organizations assess which applicants have the knowledge, experience, and skills to do a job and which applicants will fit into the organization's culture best. Interviews allow organizations to evaluate personal characteristics (such as ambition, energy, and enthusiasm) and interpersonal skills (such as conversing and listening) that cannot be judged from a résumé.

In January 2010, the Bureau of Labor Statistics reported that the unemployment rate in the United States was 9.7 percent, nearly double what it was just two years before, and the highest it's been in 27 years. With more and more people competing for fewer and fewer jobs, this means that we spend more time doing employment interviews both as job seekers and employers than ever before.

Historically, human resource professionals or managers did most of the employment interviewing, but today organizations are relying more and more on coworkers as interviewers. You may have already helped conduct employment interviews, or you may be asked to do so in the near future.

Preparing for the Interview

As with information interviews, your preparation begins by doing research. In the case of employment interviewing, this means becoming familiar with the knowledge, skills, and aptitudes someone must have to be successful in the job. It also means studying the résumés, references, and, if available, the test scores for each person you will interview.

In most employment interviewing situations, you will see several candidates. You will want to make sure that all applicants are asked the same (or very similar) questions and that the questions selected allow applicants to disclose information you will need to know to make an informed hiring decision. To accomplish this, you will want to use a moderate to highly structured interview. This means that you will prepare a general interview protocol to use

© MARCIN BALCERZAK/SHUTTERSTOCK

job seeker
anyone who is looking
for a job or considering
a job change

with all interviewees. Your protocol should have questions designed to probe the interviewees' knowledge, skills, and experiences that are relevant to the job.

It is also important to avoid questions that violate fair employment practice legislation. The Equal Opportunity Commission has detailed guidelines that spell out what questions are unlawful.

Conducting the Interview

As with the information interview, a well-planned employment interview begins with an introduction designed to establish rapport and help the interviewee relax. What follows are some best-practice tips to follow when conducting employment interviews.

Greet the applicant. Warmly greet the applicant by name, shake hands, and introduce yourself. If you will be taking notes or recording the interview, you should explain that as well. If the applicant is extremely nervous, you may want to ask a couple of "warm-up" questions designed to put the applicant at ease. Once the applicant seems comfortable, you can proceed.

Ask the series of prepared questions. Here is where you ask your well-planned questions to determine whether the applicant's knowledge, skills, experiences, personal characteristics, and interpersonal style fit the demands of the job and the organizational culture. It is important to keep the interview moving. You want to give the applicant sufficient

time to answer your questions, but don't waste time by allowing the applicant to over-answer questions.

Consider your verbal and non-verbal cues. As you ask questions, strive to sound spontaneous and to speak in a voice that is easily heard. Be sensitive to the non-verbal messages you are sending. Be careful that you are not leading applicants to answer in certain ways through your non-verbal cues.

Use follow-up questions. You should probe the applicant to expand on answers that are vague or too brief. Remember, your goal is to understand the applicant, which includes his or her strengths, weaknesses, and potential fit with the position and your organization.

Conclude with a clarification of next steps. As the interview comes to an end, tell the applicant what will happen next. Explain how and approximately when the hiring decision will be made as well as how the applicant will be notified. Unless you are the person with hiring authority, remain neutral about the applicant. You don't want to mislead the applicant with false hope or discouragement.

LO⁴ The Steps in Getting a Job

The steps involved in getting a job include preparing a résumé and cover letter, preparing for and participating in the interview, and then following up afterward.

A **job seeker** is anyone who is looking for a job or considering a job change. Some job seekers are unemployed and dedicating 100 percent of their time to finding a job. A job seeker also could be a happily employed person who is recruited to apply for another position. Or a job seeker could be an employed person seeking a more rewarding position. All job seekers must master certain skills to be competitive. As many employment experts will tell you, "As a rule, the best jobs do *not* go to the best-qualified individuals—they go to the best job seekers" (Graber, 2000, p. 29). Successful job seekers begin with a winning résumé and cover letter that helps them get an interview.

Applying for the Job

Because interviewing is time consuming, most organizations do not interview all the people who apply for a job. Rather, they use a variety of screening devices to eliminate people who don't meet their qualifications. Chief among these are evaluating the qualifications presented on the résumé and in the cover letter. The goal of your résumé with cover letter "is to communicate your qualifications in writing and sell yourself to prospective employers" (Kaplan, 2002, p. 6).

© ZSOLT NYULASZI/SHUTTERSTOCK

It All Begins with Research

To write an effective cover letter and résumé that highlight your qualifications for a particular job, you need to know something about the company and the job requirements. The career center advisers at your college or university can assist you with your research. And you can go online to review the company's Web site.

Write an Effective Cover Letter

A cover letter is a short, well-written letter expressing your interest in a particular job. In a cover letter, it is important to focus on the employer's needs—not on your needs. The letter should capture the reader's attention, demonstrate your qualifications, and request an interview. To write your cover letter, follow these simple steps:

Identify the job for which you are applying.

Provide a brief summary of your qualifications. If you have special qualifications that you cannot emphasize adequately in your résumé, you can mention them in your cover letter. Also, be sure to direct the potential employer to the most relevant and impressive parts of your résumé related to the position for which you are applying. Keep in mind, however, that most employers are unlikely to read a cover letter that is longer than two or three paragraphs.

Indicate that you hope to be contacted for an interview and how you can be reached.

Close by saying that you look forward to hearing from them soon.

Figure A.3. provides a sample of a cover letter that follows these steps.

Prepare a Professional Résumé

The résumé is a brief summary of your skills and accomplishments and is your "silent sales representative" (Stewart & Cash, 2000, p. 274). Although there is no universal format for a résumé, there is some agreement on what should be included:

Contact information: Your name, addresses (current and permanent), telephone numbers, and e-mail address. This may sound easy, but consider your contact information from the potential employers' perspective. If you go by a nickname, think twice before using it for your contact information. For example, Thomas sounds more professional and mature than Tommy. Think also about your e-mail address. If your e-mail address is something personal like redwingsfan@yahoo.com or hottee@aol.com, create a separate account with a more professional-sounding name to use on your résumé. Finally, since recruiters typically telephone to set up an interview, think about

© SANDY JONES/ISTOCKPHOTO.COM

your voice-mail message. If you have a novelty phone message such as a recording of Ozzy Osbourne's voice asking the caller to "leave a $%*# message," replace it with a more professional-sounding salutation.

cover letter
a short, well-written letter expressing your interest in a particular job

résumé
a written summary of your skills and accomplishments

Career objective: A one-sentence objective describing your job search goal.

Employment history: A list of your paid work experiences, beginning with the most recent. List the name and address of the organization, your employment dates, your title, key duties, and noteworthy accomplishments. Try not to leave gaps in your work history, because doing so can raise a red flag

Figure A.3

A Sample Cover Letter

2326 Tower Place
Cincinnati, OH 45220
April 8, 2009

Mr. Kyle Jones
Acme Marketing Research Associates
P.O. Box 482
Cincinnati, OH 45201

Dear Mr. Jones:

I am applying for the position of first-year associate at Acme Marketing Research Associates, which I learned about through the Office of Career Counseling at the University of Cincinnati. I am a senior mathematics major at the University of Cincinnati who is interested in a career in marketing research. I am highly motivated, eager to learn, and I enjoy working with all types of people. I am excited by the prospect of working for a firm like Acme Marketing Research Associates, where I can apply my leadership and problem-solving skills in a professional setting.

As a mathematics major, I have developed the analytical proficiency that is necessary for working through complex problems. My courses in statistics have especially prepared me for data analysis, and my more theoretical courses have taught me how to construct an effective argument. My leadership training and experiences have given me the ability to work effectively in groups and have taught me the benefits of both individual and group problem solving. My work on the Strategic Planning Committee has given me an introduction to market analysis by teaching me skills associated with strategic planning. Finally, from my theatrical experience, I have gained the poise to make presentations in front of small and large groups alike. I believe these experiences and others have shaped who I am and have helped me to develop many of the skills necessary to be successful. I am interested in learning more and continuing to grow.

I look forward to having the opportunity for an interview with you. I have enclosed my résumé with my school address and phone number. Thank you for your consideration. I hope to hear from you soon.

Sincerely,
Elisa C. Vardin

to a potential employer. Rather, if you left a paid job while you worked as a stay-at-home parent, say so in a brief line.

Education: List the names and addresses of the schools you have attended (including specialized military schools), the degrees or certificates you have earned (or expect to earn), and the dates of attendance and graduation. Also list academic honors received with degrees or certificates.

Relevant professional affiliations: List the names of the organizations, dates of membership, and offices you held in them.

Military background (if applicable): List branch and dates of service, last rank held, significant commendations, and discharge status.

Special skills: List language fluencies, technical expertise, computer expertise, multimedia competencies, and any other skills related to your job goal.

Community service: List significant involvement in community service organizations, clubs, and other volunteer efforts.

References: List or have available the names, addresses, e-mail addresses, and phone numbers of at least three people who will speak well of your ability, your work product, and your character.

Prepare your résumé so that it is easy to read, highlights your accomplishments, and is short. Good résumés are generally one (and not more than two) pages long. Figure A.4 displays a sample résumé for a recent college graduate.

Electronic Cover Letters and Résumés

Employers like electronic résumés because they can sift through large numbers, looking only for particular qualifications or characteristics. Candidates like electronic résumés because they save time and money. In fact, many large employers now expect to receive your reéumé electronically. As a result, most job search experts now recommend that you have your résumé available in four formats: a print version, a scannable version, a plain text format version, and an e-mail version. These are not separate résumés; rather, they contain the same information but are prepared so that they can be easily received by a prospective employer. Specific information on how to develop each version is available on the Web.

Preparing to Be Interviewed

Once you submit your résumé/cover letter package, you need to prepare for the interview you hope to

Figure A.4

A Sample Résumé

Elisa C. Vardin   2326 Tower Avenue
Cincinnati, Ohio 45220
Phone: (513) 861-2497
E-mail: ElisVardin@UC.edu

PROFESSIONAL OBJECTIVE
To use my intellectual abilities, quantitative capabilities, communication skills, and proven leadership to further the mission of a high-integrity marketing research organization.

EDUCATIONAL BACKGROUND
UNIVERSITY OF CINCINNATI, Cincinnati, OH, B.A. in Mathematics, June 2009. GPA 3.36. Dean's List.
NATIONAL THEATER INSTITUTE at the Eugene O'Neill Theater Center, Waterford, CT. Fall 2008. Acting, Voice, Movement, Directing, and Playwriting.

WORK AND OTHER BUSINESS-RELATED EXPERIENCE
REYNOLDS & DEWITT, Cincinnati, OH. Summer 2008. Intern at brokerage/ investment management firm. Provided administrative support. Created new databases, performance comparisons, and fact sheets in Excel and Word files.
MUMMERS THEATRE GUILD, University of Cincinnati, Spring 2008–Spring 2009. Treasurer. Responsible for all financial/ accounting functions for this undergraduate theater community.
BREAKTHOUGH, CINCINNATI, Cincinnati Country Day School, Cincinnati, OH. Summer 2007. Teacher in program for at-risk junior high students. Taught seventh-grade mathematics, sixth- and seventh-grade speech communication, sign language; academic advisor; club leader. Organized five-hour diversity workshop and three-hour tension-reduction workshop for staff.
STRATEGIC PLANNING COMMITTEE, Summit Country Day School, Cincinnati, OH. Fall 2003–2004. One of two student members. Worked with the board of directors developing the first Strategic Plan for a 1,000-student independent school (pre-K through 12).
AYF INTERNATIONAL LEADERSHIP CONFERENCE, Miniwanca Conference Center, Shelby, MI. Summer 2002–2003. Participant in international student conference sponsored by American Youth Foundation.

PERSONAL
Musical theater: lifetime involvement, including leads and choreography for several shows. A cappella singing group, 2006–2009; director 2007–2008. Swing Club 2007–2009, president and teacher of student dance club. Junior high youth group leader, 2006. Math tutor, 2005. Aerobics instructor, 2008–2009. University of Cincinnati Choral Society, 2005–2009. American Sign Language instructor, Winter 2007, 2008.

TECHNICAL SKILLS AND TRAINING: SAS, SPSS, Excel, Access, Word. Univariate and multivariate statistics (2 courses), regression analysis (2 courses).

REFERENCES: Available on request.

© SANDY JONES/ISTOCKPHOTO.COM

get. In this section, we offer four suggestions to prepare for a job interview: research the organization, prepare a self-summary, practice answering difficult questions, and prepare your questions.

Do your homework. If you haven't yet done extensive research on the position and the organization, do so before you go to the interview. Be sure you know the organization's products and services, areas of operation, ownership, and financial health. Nothing puts off interviewers more than applicants who arrive at an interview knowing little about the organization. You can easily begin your research by looking at the organization's home page online. Be sure to look beyond the "Work for Us" or "Frequently Asked Questions" links. Find more specific information such as pages that target potential investors, report company stock performance, and describe the organization's mission (Slayter, 2006). Likewise, pictures can suggest the type of organizational culture you can expect—formal or informal dress, collaborative or individual work spaces, diversity, and so on. Researching these details will help you decide whether the organization is right for you as well as help you form questions to ask during the interview.

Prepare a self-summary. You should not have to hesitate when an interviewer asks you why you are interested in the job. You should also be prepared to describe your previous accomplishments. Form these statements as personal stories with specific examples that people will remember (Beshara, 2006). Robin Ryan (2000), one of the nation's foremost career authorities, advises job seekers to prepare a 60-second general statement they can share with a potential employer. She advises job seekers to identify which aspects of their training and experience would be most valued by a potential employer. She suggests making a five-point agenda that can (a) summarize your most relevant experience and (b) "build a solid picture emphasizing how you *can* do the job" (p. 10).

Once you have your points identified, practice communicating them fluently in 60 seconds or less.

Prepare a list of questions about the organization and the job. The employment interview should be a two-way street, where you size up the company as they are sizing you up. So you will probably have a number of specific questions to ask the interviewer. For example, "Can you describe a typical workday for the person in this position?" or "What is the biggest challenge in this job?" Make a list of your questions and take it with you to the interview. It can be difficult to come up with good questions on the spur of the moment, so you should prepare several questions in advance. One question we do not advise asking during the interview, however, is "How much money will I make?" Save salary, benefits, and vacation-time negotiations until after you have been offered the job.

Rehearse the interview. Several days before the interview, spend time outlining the job requirements and how your knowledge, skills, and experiences meet those requirements. Practice answering questions commonly asked in interviews, such as those listed in Figure A.5.

Guidelines for Job Interviewees

The actual interview is your opportunity to sell yourself to the organization. Although interviews can be stressful, your preparation should give you the confidence you need to relax and communicate effectively. Believe it or not, the job interview is somewhat stressful for the interviewer as well. Most companies do not interview potential employees every day. Moreover, the majority of interviewers have little or no formal training in the interview process. Your goal is to make the interview a comfortable conversation for both of you.

Figure A.5

FAQs in Interviews

In what ways does your transcript reflect your ability?

Can you give an example of how you work under pressure?

What are your major strengths? Weaknesses?

Can you give an example of when you were a leader and what happened?

Tell me a time when you tried something at work that failed. How did you respond to the failure?

Tell me about a time you had a serious conflict with a coworker. How did you deal with the conflict?

What have you done that shows your creativity?

What kind of position are you looking for?

© THOMAS M PERKINS/SHUTTERSTOCK

Nothing beats preparation.

Use these guidelines to help you have a successful interview.

Dress appropriately. You want to make a good first impression, so it is important to be well groomed and neatly dressed. Although "casual" or "business casual" is common in many workplaces, some organizations still expect employees to be more formally dressed. If you don't know the dress code for the organization, call the human resources department and ask.

Arrive on time. The interview is the organization's first exposure to your work behavior, so you don't want to be late. Find out how long it will take you to travel by making a dry run at least a day before. Plan to arrive 10 or 15 minutes before your appointment.

Bring supplies. Bring extra copies of your résumé, cover letter, and references as well as the list of questions you plan to ask. You will also want to have paper and a pen so that you can make notes.

Use active listening. When we are anxious, we sometimes have trouble listening well. Work on attending, understanding, and remembering what is asked. Remember that the interviewer will be aware of your non-verbal behavior, so be sure to make and keep eye contact as you listen.

Think before answering. If you have prepared for the interview, make sure that as you answer the interviewer's questions you also tell your story. Take a moment to consider how your answers portray your skills and experiences.

Be enthusiastic. If you come across as bored or disinterested, the interviewer is likely to conclude that you would be an unmotivated employee.

Ask questions. As the interview is winding down, be sure to ask the questions you prepared that have not already been answered. You may also want to ask how well the interviewer believes your qualifications match the position and what your strengths are.

Following Up after the Interview

Once the interview is over, you can set yourself apart from the other applicants by following these important steps:

Write a thank-you note. It is appropriate to write a short note thanking the interviewer for the experience and again expressing your interest in the job.

Self-assess your performance. Take time to critique your performance. How well did you do? What can you do better next time?

Contact the interviewer for feedback. If you don't get the job, you might call the interviewer and ask for feedback. Be sure to be polite and indicate that you

TO REVIEW

Before the Job Interview

1. Do your homework.
2. Based on your research, prepare a list of questions about the organization and the job.
3. Rehearse the interview.
4. Dress appropriately.
5. Plan to arrive on time.
6. Bring supplies.

During the Job Interview

1. Use active listening.
2. Think before answering.
3. Be enthusiastic.
4. Ask questions.
5. Avoid discussing salary and benefits.

After the Job Interview

1. Write a thank-you note.
2. Self-assess your performance.
3. Contact the interviewer for feedback.

© RUDYANTO WIJAYA/SHUTTERSTOCK

are only calling to get some help on your interviewing skills. Actively listen to the feedback, using questions and paraphrases to clarify what is being said. Be sure to thank the interviewer for helping you.

LO5 Strategies for Interviews with the Media

Today we live in a media-saturated environment where any individual may be approached by a newsperson and asked to participate in an on-air interview. For example, we have a friend who became the object of media interest when the city council in his town refused to grant him a zoning variance so he could complete building a new home on his property. In the course of three days, his story became front-page news in his town, and reports about his situation made the local radio and TV news shows. You might be asked for an interview at public meetings, at the mall, or within the context of your work or community service. For example, you may be asked to share your knowledge of your organization's programs, events, or activities. Because media interviews are likely to be edited in some way before they are aired and because they reach a wide audience, there are specific strategies you should use to prepare for and participate in them.

Before the Interview

The members of the media work under very tight deadlines, so it is crucial that you respond immediately to media requests for an interview. When people are insensitive to media deadlines, they can end up looking like they have purposefully evaded the interview and have something to hide. When you speak with the media representative, clarify what the focus of the interview will be and how the information will be presented. At times, the entire interview will be presented; however, it is more likely that the information from the interview will be edited or paraphrased and not all of your comments will be reported.

As you prepare for the interview, identify three or four **talking points**—that is, the central ideas you want to present as you answer the questions during a media interview. For example, before our friend was interviewed by the local TV news anchor, he knew that he wanted to emphasize that he was a victim of others' mistakes: (1) he had hired a licensed architect to draw the plans, (2) the city inspectors had repeatedly approved earlier stages of the building process, (3) the city planning commission had voted unanimously to grant him the variance, and (4) he would be out half the cost of the house if he were forced to tear it down and rebuild. Consider how you will tailor your information to the specific audience in terms they can understand. Consider how you will respond to tough or hostile questions.

During the Interview

Media interviews call for a combination of interviewing, non-verbal communication, and public speaking skills (Boyd, 1999). There are many strategies to be followed during a media interview:

Present appropriate non-verbal cues. Inexperienced interviewees can often look or sound tense or stiff. By standing up during a phone interview, your voice will sound more energetic and authoritative. With on-camera interviews, when checking your notes, move your eyes but not your head. Keep a small smile when listening. Look at the interviewer, not into the camera.

Make clear and concise statements. It is important to speak slowly, to articulate clearly, and to avoid technical terms or jargon. Remember that the audience is not familiar with your area of expertise.

Realize that you are always "on the record." Say nothing as an aside or confidentially to a reporter. Do not say anything that you would not want quoted. If you do not know an answer, do not speculate. Instead, indicate that the question is outside your area of expertise. Do not ramble during the interviewer's periods of silence. Do not allow yourself to be rushed into an answer.

Learn how to bridge. Media consultant Joanna Krotz (2006) defines a **bridge** as a transition you create so that you can move from the interviewer's subject to the message you want to communicate. To do this, you first answer the direct question and then use a phrase such as "What's important to remember, however," "Let me put that in perspective," or "It's also important to know."

With careful preparation, specific communication strategies during the interview, and practice, one can skillfully deliver a message in any media interview format.

talking points
the three or four central ideas you will present as you answer the questions that are asked during a media interview

bridge
a transition you create in a media interview so that you can move from the interviewer's subject to the message you want to communicate

There are even MORE Study Tools for Appendix at www.cengagebrain.com

☑ Speech Builder Express
☑ Printable Flash Cards
☑ Interactive Games
☑ Interactive Video Activities
☑ Chapter Review Cards
☑ Online Quizzes with Feedback
☑ Audio Downloads

Communicating in Groups

Learning Outcomes

LO[1]   Analyze the characteristics of an effective work group

LO[2]   Explain various stages of group development

LO[3]   Identify different types of groups

LO[4]   Discuss how to evaluate a group's performance

> ## "Healthy groups are characterized by ethical goals, interdependence, cohesiveness, productive norms, accountability, and synergy."

You probably belong to many formal and informal groups. Each group has different purposes and different expectations of you. But one thing all groups have in common is that their effectiveness depends on members' communication. In fact, year after year, surveys conducted by the National Association of Colleges and Employers report "the ability to work well in groups" is one of the top ten skills sought in college graduates. Although students are often asked to do group projects, very few graduate from college with any formal training in how to participate effectively in groups.

In this chapter and the one that follows, we will help you understand how groups function and how you can communicate most effectively in them. We begin by explaining the characteristics of groups that differentiate them from other collections of people. Next, we describe the stages of development that groups follow over the course of their existence. Then, we identify different types of groups and the communication challenges you might face in each one. We end this chapter by discussing how you can evaluate the effectiveness of groups and group members.

group
a collection of three or more people who interact and attempt to influence each other in order to accomplish a common purpose

group communication
all the verbal and non-verbal messages shared with or among members of the group

What do you think?

Things get done faster when I work with others.

Strongly Disagree | | | | | | | | | Strongly Agree
1   2   3   4   5   6   7   8   9   10

LO¹ Characteristics of Healthy Groups

Take a moment to think about the groups of people you interact with consistently. Examples may range from student clubs to groups of friends you hang out with on weekends to family groups you interact with on special occasions to study groups to online chat rooms or interest groups on social networking sites. What makes each of these a group rather than a mere assembly of people? Scholars generally agree that a **group** is a collection of three or more people who interact and attempt to influence each other in order to accomplish a common purpose. In a social group that purpose may be to have a good time, in a study group to get a good grade, in a work group to help an organization accomplish a task, and in a family to ensure that members survive and thrive. **Group communication**—all the verbal and non-verbal messages shared with or among members of the group—is what makes our participation in

© MICHAEL FLIPPO/ISTOCKPHOTO.COM

healthy group
a group characterized by ethical goals, interdependence, cohesiveness, productive norms, accountability, and synergy

interdependent group
a group in which members rely on each other's skills and knowledge to accomplish the group goals

cohesiveness
the degree of attraction members have to each other and to the group's goal

team-building activities
activities designed to help the group work better together

norms
expectations for the way group members will behave while in the group

ground rules
prescribed behaviors designed to help the group meet its goals and conduct its conversations

these different groups a positive or negative experience. Healthy groups are characterized by ethical goals, interdependence, cohesiveness, productive norms, accountability, and synergy.

Healthy Groups Have Ethical Goals

At times, the goals of a group may not be ethical either because the goal itself is unethical or because fulfilling the goal requires some or all group members to behave in ways that are not in their own best interest. For example, recent news reports have been filled with stories about investment firms built on Ponzi schemes (fraudulent investments) that have financially ruined clients who trusted them. Likewise, some children live in divorced families where the parents' goal seems to be to use the children as foils to harm each other. Criminal gangs are highly effective groups that may make lots of money but do so at the expense of society at large and risk the lives of members to accomplish their illicit goals.

Healthy Groups Are Interdependent

In interdependent groups, members rely on each other's skills and knowledge to accomplish the group goals. One concrete way to understand interdependence is to observe a musical group. Consider, for instance, a symphony orchestra. One reason the music we hear is so beautiful has to do with the fact that the violins, violas, cellos, and basses not only sound different but are each performing a different part made up of differing notes. If any of the musicians did not do their part well, we would hear it. Likewise, in any group, if one person doesn't choose to blend

but instead tries to do all the "work," or if everyone in a group does the same piece of "work" while other pieces are left unattended, that group is not interdependent and is also not as effective as it could be.

Healthy Groups Are Cohesive

Cohesiveness is the force that brings group members closer together (Eisenberg, 2007). In a highly cohesive group, members genuinely like and respect each other and work cooperatively to reach the group's goals (Evans & Dion, 1991). Because cohesiveness is such an important characteristic of healthy groups, many newly formed groups will engage in **team-building activities** designed to build rapport and develop trust among members (Midura & Glover, 2005). Research suggests that five factors help foster cohesiveness in groups (Balgopal, Ephross, & Vassil, 1986; Widmer & Williams, 1991; Wilson, 2005). First, a group develops cohesiveness when members are attracted to its purpose. Daniel, for example, joined the local Lions Club because he was attracted to the group's goal of community service. Second, groups are generally more cohesive when membership in them is voluntary. If Daniel had joined the Lions Club because he felt obligated to do so, cohesiveness would have suffered. Third, members feel free to express their honest opinions even when they disagree with others. Fourth, members support, encourage, and provide positive feedback to each other. Finally, members perceive the group to be achieving its goals and celebrate their accomplishments. When the Lions Club surpassed their previous fundraising record for the annual Journey for Sight 5K Community Run, they celebrated the accomplishment with a picnic in the park, which fostered cohesiveness.

Healthy Groups Develop and Abide by Productive Norms

Norms are expectations about the way group members are to behave while in the group. Healthy groups develop norms that help them achieve their goals (Shimanoff, 1992) and foster cohesiveness (Shaw, 1981). Norms can be developed through formal discussions or informal group processes (Johnson & Johnson, 2003, p. 27). Some groups choose to formulate explicit **ground rules**, prescribed behaviors designed to help the group meet its goals and conduct its conversations. These may include

© DMITRIY SHIRONOSOV/SHUTTERSTOCK

sticking to the agenda, refraining from interrupting others, making brief comments rather than lengthy monologues, expecting everyone to participate, focusing on issues rather than personalities, and sharing decision making. Did your family have formal rules about going out on school nights or curfews? These are also examples of explicit ground rules.

In most groups, however, norms evolve informally. When we join a new group, we act in ways that were considered appropriate in the groups we participated in previously. When members of our new group respond positively to our actions, an informal norm is established. For example, suppose Daniel and two others show up late for a Lions Club meeting. If the latecomers are greeted with disapproving glares, then Daniel and the others will learn that this group has an on-time norm. A group may never actually discuss informal norms, but all veteran group members understand what they are, behave in line with them, and educate new members about them.

Healthy Groups Are Accountable

Accountability means all group members are held responsible for adhering to the group norms and working toward the group's goal. This means a group will sanction a member who violates a group norm. The severity of the sanction depends on the importance of the norm that was violated, the extent of the violation, and the status of the person who violated the norm. Violating a norm that is central to a group's performance or cohesiveness will generally receive a harsher sanction than violating a norm that is less central. Minor violations or violations by a newcomer generally receive more lenient sanctions. As a new Lions Club member, for example, Daniel's sanction was merely a stern look from the others. Group members who have achieved higher status in the group also tend to receive more lenient sanctions or escape sanctioning altogether.

Being accountable can also mean changing counterproductive norms. For example, suppose a few folks tell jokes, tell stories, and generally ignore attempts by others to begin more serious discussion about community service issues at the Lions Club meetings. If the group does not effectively sanction this behavior, then it could become a counterproductive group norm. As a result, work toward the group's goals could be delayed, set aside, or perhaps even forgotten. If counterproductive behavior continues for several meetings and becomes a norm, it will be very difficult (though not impossible) to change.

What can a group member do to try to change a norm? You can help your group change a counterproductive norm by (1) observing the norm and its outcome, (2) describing the results of the norm to the group, and (3) soliciting opinions of other members of the group (Renz & Greg, 2000, p. 52). For instance, Daniel observed that every Lions Club meeting began 15–20 minutes late and that this was making it necessary to schedule additional meetings. When members became frustrated at holding extra meetings, he could bring up his observations and the consequences and ask the group for their reaction.

Healthy Groups Are Synergistic

The old saying "two heads are better than one" captures an important characteristic of healthy groups. **Synergy** is the multiplying force of a group of individuals working together that results in a combined effort greater than any of the parts (Henman, 2003). For instance, the sports record books are filled with "no-name teams" that have won major championships over opponents with more talented players. A healthy group can develop

accountability
group members being held responsible for adhering to the group norms and working toward the group's goal

synergy
a commonality of purpose and a complementariness of each other's efforts that produces a group outcome greater than an individual outcome

© ANDRESR/SHUTTERSTOCK

forming
the initial stage of group development during which people come to feel valued and accepted so that they identify with the group

storming
the stage of group development during which the group clarifies its goals and determines the roles each member will have in the group power structure

a collective intelligence and a dynamic energy that translate into an outcome that exceeds what even a highly talented individual could produce. When a group has ethical goals and is interdependent, cohesive, and held accountable to productive norms, the group is well on its way toward achieving synergy.

LO² Stages of Group Development

Just as interpersonal relationships go through identifiable life cycles, so too do groups move through stages of development. Although numerous models have been proposed to describe the stages of group development,

Synergy is the multiplying force of a group of individuals working together that results in a combined effort greater than any of the parts.

psychologist Bruce Tuckman's (1965) model has been widely accepted because it identifies central issues facing a group at each stage. In this section, we describe each of these stages and the nature of communication during each one.

Forming

Forming is the initial stage of group development and is characterized by orientation, testing, and dependence. Members try to understand precisely what the goal is, what role they will play in reaching the goal, and what the other group members are like. As the goal becomes clearer, members assess how their skills, talents, and abilities might be used in accomplishing it. Members also begin to develop relationships and test what behaviors will be acceptable in the group. Group interactions are likely to be polite and tentative as members become acquainted with each other and find their place in the group. Any real disagreements between people often remain unacknowledged during this stage because members want to be perceived as flexible and likable. During the forming stage, you should express positive attitudes; refrain from abrasive or disagreeable comments; make appropriately benign self-disclosures and wait to see if they are reciprocated; and try to be friendly, open, and interested in others (Anderson, 1988).

Storming

As members figure out the goal and become comfortable with the other group members, they begin to express their honest opinions and vie for power and position. This signals the beginning of the second stage of group development. The storming stage is characterized by conflict and power plays as members seek to have their ideas accepted and strive to find their place within the group's power structure. Constructive disagreements help the group clarify its goal, and the resolution of power plays clarifies the group structure and what is expected of each member. During this storming stage, the politeness exhibited during forming may be replaced by snide comments, sarcastic remarks, or pointedly aggressive exchanges between some members. While storming, members may take sides and form coalitions. Although storming occurs in all groups, some groups manage it better than others. When storming is severe, it can threaten the group's survival. However, if a group does not storm, it may

© SPORTLIBRARY/SHUTTERSTOCK

experience groupthink—a deterioration of mental efficiency, reality testing, and moral judgment that results from in-group pressure to conform (Janis, 1982, p. 9). To avoid groupthink, we should encourage constructive disagreement, avoid name-calling and inflammatory language, and use the active listening skills with an emphasis on paraphrasing and honest questioning (Anderson, 1988).

Norming

Norming is the third stage of group development and is characterized by increased cohesion, collaboration, emerging trust among members, and motivation to achieve the group goal. Having expressed honest opinions, resolved major differences, and sorted out specific roles, members become loyal to each other and to the group goal. During this stage, members come to appreciate their differences, strengthen their relationships, and freely express their ideas and opinions. Members accept the norms established by the group and provide positive and constructive feedback to each other.

Performing

Performing is the fourth stage of group development and is characterized by harmony, productivity, problem solving, and shared leadership. During this stage, the group capitalizes on the skills, knowledge, and abilities of all members to work toward achieving its goal. As well, conversations are focused on sharing task-related information and problem solving. Groups cannot achieve their full potential in this stage unless they have successfully resolved storming conflicts and developed productive norms.

Adjourning

Adjourning is the stage of group development characterized by goal accomplishment, celebration, and disengagement. Adjourning begins when the group recognizes that it has reached its goal. The group will engage in some type of formal or informal celebration during which they recognize their accomplishment and the role that each member played. They may rehash parts of their work and try to capture what they have learned about group process or their own behavior. Finally, group members will begin to disengage from their relationships with each other. The group may formally disband while some members continue to see each other in social settings, or the group may continue to exist with a new goal. The new goal will inevitably cause the members to revisit

the earlier stages of group development, but the cohesion, trust, and norms developed earlier are likely to help the group move quickly and more smoothly through these stages.

With this basic understanding of the stages of group development, we now turn to describing types of groups.

LO³ Types of Groups

Most of us can identify many different groups to which we belong at any point in time; each one is focused on a common purpose, goal, or objective. You have probably noticed that what is expected of you varies from group to group. Scholars who study groups find it useful to categorize groups according to their purpose. This allows scholars to better understand how groups with similar purposes behave and what effects they have on their members. Let's look at the most common group types: families, social friendship groups, support groups, interest groups, service groups, and work groups.

groupthink
a deterioration of mental efficiency, reality testing, and moral judgment that results from in-group pressure

norming
the stage of group development during which the group solidifies its rules for behavior, especially those that relate to how conflict will be managed

performing
the stage of group development when the skills, knowledge, and abilities of all members are combined to overcome obstacles and meet goals successfully

adjourning
the stage of group development in which members assign meaning to what they have done and determine how to end or maintain interpersonal relations they have developed

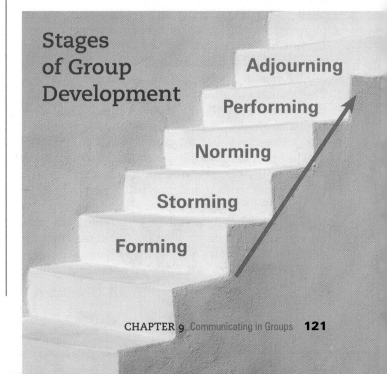

Stages of Group Development

Adjourning

Performing

Norming

Storming

Forming

© MDD/SHUTTERSTOCK

family
a group of intimates who through their communication generates a sense of home and group identity, complete with strong ties of loyalty and emotion, and experiences a history and a future

social friendship group
a group comprised of friends who have a genuine concern about each other's welfare and enjoy spending time together

Families

A family is "a group of intimates who through their communication generates a sense of home and group identity, complete with strong ties of loyalty and emotion, and experiences a history and a future" (Galvin, Byland, & Brommel, 2007). Families can be nuclear (consisting of two parents who live together with their biological or adopted children), single parent (consisting of one adult living with his or her children), extended (consisting of a parent or parents and children living with grandparents, cousins, aunts and uncles, or other relatives), blended (consisting of committed or married adults living with the children of their previous marriages and relationships as well as the children of their union), or mixed (consisting of people of different races).

Not all families work the same way. Contemporary research on families suggests four different ways families function when facing an issue (Koerner & Fitzpatrick, 2002). In protective families, issues are not discussed and are decided solely by the family authority figure. In the movie *The Sound of Music*, prior to Maria's arrival, the Von Trapp family exemplified this family dynamic. In consensual families, all members engage in conversation about an issue, but a family authority figure still makes the final decision. Many television sitcoms from the 1950s and 1960s such as *Father Knows Best*, *Leave It to Beaver*, and *The Brady Bunch* portray families with a benevolent and self-sacrificing father filling this role. In pluralistic families, all members engage in conversation about an issue and everyone participates in the decision making. These families may have formal family meetings to decide important family issues. The popular 1980s television sitcom *Full House*, where three men raised the children together, operated in this way. Finally, in laissez-faire families, members may converse about an issue, but each member makes his or her own decision and is responsible for its consequences. The cartoon family portrayed on *The Simpsons* tends to function this way.

We initially learn how to act in groups based on the ways our family members interacted with each other while we were growing up. Of course, the conversational norms we learned may change as a result of the experiences we have in additional groups throughout our lives. Which family type did you grow up in? Do you think your conversational norms for participating in groups are consistent with what you experienced growing up? Why or why not?

One of the major responsibilities of healthy families is to talk in ways that build one another's self-concept and self-esteem. So it is important that family members (1) praise each other: "Manuel you got a B on that spelling test, good for you!"; (2) offer statements of acceptance and support: "You know that I would rather you go to college, but your mom and I will support your decision to join the Navy"; and (3) verbally express love: "Nevah, you know I love you no matter what."

Social Friendship Groups

A social friendship group is composed of friends who have a genuine concern about each other's welfare and enjoy spending time together. Their interactions are characterized by "interpersonal ties and positive, amiable preexisting relationships among members" (Thompson, 2003, p. 239). Most of us belong to more than one social friendship group during our lives. You may have had a group of friends you were close to in high school, a group of buddies you were close to when you served in the military, or a group of friends you play golf or softball with regularly. Sometimes people who work together evolve into a social friendship group when they begin to get together for social activities outside of work. Social friendship groups may initially form around a shared interest like a book club or Bible study, but as members spend time together and find they enjoy one another's company, they may evolve into a social friendship group. Popular TV programs such as *Friends*,

Family

Social Friendship

Support Group

© DAVID FRANKLIN/ISTOCKPHOTO.COM / © MONKEY BUSINESS IMAGES/SHUTTERSTOCK / © MONKEY BUSINESS IMAGES/SHUTTERSTOCK / © CHRISTOPHER FUTCHER/SHUTTERSTOCK

Interest Group

Service Group

Work Group

© DAVID FRANKLIN/ISTOCKPHOTO.COM / © JOHN NAIRNE/SHUTTERSTOCK /
© TODD S. HOLDER/SHUTTERSTOCK / © ORIONTRAIL/SHUTTERSTOCK

Seinfeld, and *Sex in the City* are recent examples of sitcom friendship groups.

Because social friendship groups fill our needs to be accepted and to belong, communication in these groups should (1) encourage quieter members to participate in conversations: "Hey, Jules, you haven't had a chance to catch us up on how your Dad is doing"; (2) protect members from playful harassment: "Hey Jenna, back off, you've been aiming your put downs at Pam all evening"; (3) provide opportunities for friends to disclose problems and receive support: "Hey, Zach, I heard that your sister was diagnosed with Hodgkin lymphoma. How are you doing?"

Support Groups

Support groups are composed of people who come together to bolster each other by providing encouragement, honest feedback, and a safe environment for expressing deeply personal feelings about a problem common to the members. Support groups include well-known fellowships like Alcoholics Anonymous (AA) and Narcotics Anonymous, survivor or caregiver support groups formed by local chapters of a national organization like the Leukemia and Lymphoma Society or the Alzheimer's Association, grief groups at local synagogues and churches, and neighborhood stay-at-home-dads groups. Until recently, support groups met face-to-face, but today there are thousands of online support groups connecting people who have never met face-to-face.

Support groups must create an environment where members feel safe to disclose highly personal information. So members need to make sure that their messages follow the guidelines in Chapter 8 for comforting, which include clarifying supportive intentions, buffering face threats, using other-centered language, framing, and selectively offering advice.

Interest Groups

An interest group is composed of individuals who come together because they share a concern, hobby, or activity. These groups may be formal with defined goals and tasks (such as a 4-H club or community theater troupe) or may be informal (like a neighborhood book or gardening club). They may be part of a larger organization like La Raza, the Urban League, or the Houston Area Apple Users Group. Some interest groups are externally focused on a common political or social issue and adopt an agenda to achieve change. MADD (Mothers Against Drunk Drivers) is an example. Other interest groups are internally focused on increasing skills or knowledge of their members. Toastmasters, for instance, is focused on helping its members improve their public speaking skills. Some interest groups meet online. Meetup.com is an Internet site that helps people find others who share their interests.

Because interest group members share some passion, all members ought to have an opportunity communicate their expertise by (1) encouraging members to share success stories: "I'm really glad that Brian was able to get Ace Hardware to donate all the bathroom fixtures for our project. Brian, can you tell us what you said and did?" and (2) doing so in ways that all members highlight what they know without demeaning the knowledge or opinions of others: "I really liked hearing Brian's story, and I'd like to hear about how other people approach getting donations."

Service Groups

Service groups are composed of individuals who come together to perform hands-on charitable works or to raise money to help organizations that perform such work. Service groups may be local affiliates of larger secular or religious service organizations like Break Away, Lions Club International, the Red Cross, the

support group
a group comprised of people who come together to bolster each other by providing encouragement, honest feedback, and a safe environment for expressing deeply personal feelings about a problem common to the members

interest group
a group comprised of individuals who come together because they share a common concern, hobby, or activity

service group
a group comprised of individuals who come together to perform hands-on charitable works or to raise money to help organizations that perform such work

work group
a collection of three or more people who must interact and influence each other to solve problems and to accomplish a common purpose

work group goal
a future state of affairs desired by enough members of the group to motivate the group to work toward its achievement

heterogeneous group
group in which various demographics, levels of knowledge, attitudes, and interests are represented

homogeneous group
groups in which members have a great deal of similarity

Salvation Army, B'nai B'rith, and Habitat for Humanity. Other service groups are local and function independently. Small soup kitchens, urban gardening groups, and community beautification groups perform charitable work that may include raising funds and interfacing with government agencies.

Because service groups are both voluntary and task-oriented, they need to be dedicated to the task as well as sensitive to the ego and emotional needs of members. So communication should (1) be clear about individual tasks, roles, and responsibilities: "Jim, as I remember it, today you agreed to work on patching the roof"; (2) encourage and praise member accomplishments: "I was really impressed with how sensitive you were when you turned her down for another bag of groceries"; and (3) be polite: "Mary, it would be great if you would please work with Yvonne on stuffing envelopes for that mailing. Thanks so much!"

Work Groups

A **work group** is a collection of three or more people formed to solve a problem or accomplish a specific task. Examples of work groups include class project groups (established to create a joint presentation, paper, or other learning project) and work teams (established as needed to perform specific activities in the workplace). Effective work groups have clearly defined goals, an appropriate number of members, and diversity in the skills and viewpoints of its members.

An effective **work group goal** is a clearly stated future state of affairs desired by enough members to motivate the group to work toward achieving it (Johnson & Johnson, 2003, p. 73). Effective work group goals are specific. For example, the crew at a local fast food restaurant that began with the goal of "increasing profitability of the restaurant" made the goal more specific in this way: "During the next quarter, the second shift night crew will increase profitability by reducing food costs by 1 percent. They will do so by throwing away less food due to precooking." Effective work group goals are also consistent in that they serve a common purpose. That is, achieving one

goal does not prevent the achievement of another. For the fast food crew, all members must believe that reducing the amount of precooked food on hand will not interfere with maintaining their current level of service. Effective work group goals are challenging. Achieving them will require hard work and team effort. Finally, effective work group goals are acceptable in that all members feel personally committed to achieving them. People tend to support things they help create. So group members who participate in setting the goals are likely to exert a higher effort to achieve them as well.

What is the best size for a work group? In general, research suggests that the best size is the smallest number of people capable of effectively achieving the goal (Sundstrom, DeMeuse, & Futrell, 1990). For many situations, this might mean as few as three to five people. As the size of the group increases, the time spent discussing and deciding also increases. When only Jeff and Sue are in a group, for instance, there is only one relationship to manage. But when a third person, Bryan, joins them, the group now has four relationships to manage (Jeff–Sue; Bryan–Jeff; Bryan–Sue; Bryan–Sue–Jeff). Smaller groups can make decisions more quickly than larger ones. However, if the goals and issues are complex, a group with more members is more likely to have the breadth of information, knowledge, and skills needed to make high-quality decisions. As groups grow in size and complexity, however, the opportunities for each member to participate drop, and because people tend to be more satisfied when they can actively participate, the most desirable size for most work group situations is five to seven members.

More important than the number of people is the right combination of people in the work group. Effective work groups are likely to be composed of people who offer different but relevant knowledge and skills (Valacich, George, Nonamaker, & Vogel, 1994). A **heterogeneous group** is usually better than a homogeneous group. In **homogeneous groups**, members are likely to know the same things, come at the problem from the same perspective, and, consequently, be likely to overlook some important information or take shortcuts in the problem-solving process. In contrast, groups composed of heterogeneous members are more likely to have diverse information, perspectives, and values, and, consequently, discuss issues more thoroughly before reaching a decision. For example, a group composed of seven nurses who are all young white females would be considered a homogeneous group; a group composed of nurses, doctors, nutritionists, and physical therapists who differ in age, race, and sex would be considered a heterogeneous group. The heterogeneous medical group would probably make a more comprehensive decision about a patient's care than the homogeneous group of nurses.

Work groups are usually more task oriented than other groups. So, much of the communication focuses on task-related issues and should (1) seek collaboration to resolve conflicts: "Felicia, I'm having a problem that I need your help with"; (2) update other members on the status of individual efforts: "I thought you all should know that I will be about two days late with that feasibility report, as the woman who was providing me with the cost data is on vacation"; and (3) appropriately credit the contributions of other team members: "Today I am presenting the findings, but I think you should know that Len did the initial research and Mavis did quantitative analysis that led to these conclusions."

LO⁴ Evaluating Group Dynamics

Group dynamics is the way a group interacts to achieve its goal. Effective groups periodically stop and evaluate how their interactions are affecting what they are accomplishing and how members perceive themselves and others. At times, you may be asked to provide a formal evaluation of the group dynamics of a class project group or other work team. One way you might evaluate members is to describe how each member performed his or her specific tasks and how well his or her communication contributed to the cohesiveness, problem solving, and conflict resolution processes in the group. Figure 9.1 is one example you can use for evaluating class project group member participation. Alternatively, in a class project group, members could prepare a "reflective thinking process paper," which details in paragraph form what each member did well and could improve upon as well as a self-analysis of their own contributions and what they could do to improve.

Like the evaluations business managers make of employees, these evaluations serve to document the efforts of group members. They can be submitted to the instructor just as they would be submitted to a supervisor. In business, these documents provide a basis for determining promotion, merit pay, and salary adjustments. In the classroom, they can provide a basis for determining one portion of each member's grade.

© MARK KOLBE/ISTOCKPHOTO.COM

group dynamics
the way a group interacts to achieve its goal

Figure 9.1

Group Dynamics Evaluation Form

Meeting date:
Your name:

Directions
After each required group meeting, provide ethical critiques for both your group members and yourself. Rate each individual on his or her performance in the group. Justify the rating with specific examples taken from the guidelines of ethical group behavior:
• Committed to the group goal
• Fulfills individual assignments
• Manages interpersonal conflicts
• Encourages group participation
• Helps keep the discussion on track

Yourself
Circle overall individual rating
0   1   2   3   4   5   6   7
(poor) (met requirements) (excellent)

Tasks accomplished:

Tasks assigned:

Ethical critique:

Group member
Circle overall individual rating
0   1   2   3   4   5   6   7
(poor) (met requirements) (excellent)

Tasks accomplished:

Tasks assigned:

Ethical critique:

There are even MORE Study Tools for Chapter 9 at www.cengagebrain.com

☑ Speech Builder Express
☑ Printable Flash Cards
☑ Interactive Games
☑ Interactive Video Activities
☑ Chapter Review Cards
☑ Online Quizzes with Feedback
☑ Audio Downloads

Problem Solving
in Groups

Learning Outcomes

LO¹ Identify the steps in the problem-solving process

LO² Discuss shared leadership roles

LO³ Examine ways to make meetings effective

LO⁴ Identify ways that groups can communicate solutions

> **"** *Leaders in business and industry realize that when groups work effectively to solve problems, they provide a deeper analysis of problems, generate a greater breadth of ideas and potential solutions, promote positive group morale, and lead to increased productivity.* **"**

When group meetings are ineffective, it is easy to point the finger at the leader. However, the responsibility for the "waste of time" lies not with one person but with the group and the complex nature of problem solving in groups. Although working in groups can have its disadvantages, it is the preferred approach in business and industry today (O'Hair, O'Rourke, & O'Hair, 2001; Snyder, 2004; Teams, 2004). Leaders in business and industry realize that when groups work effectively to solve problems, they provide a deeper analysis of problems, generate a greater breadth of ideas and potential solutions, promote positive group morale, and lead to increased productivity. You can expect to work in groups to solve problems your organization faces during your professional life. These meetings may be in face-to-face or virtual settings through e-mail, discussion boards, or video conferencing (Tullar & Kaiser, 2000). You will also encounter group problem solving in community groups, interest groups, and even in your family.

What do you think?

When I work in a group, I like to be a follower, not a leader.

Strongly Disagree   *Strongly Agree*

| 1 | 2 | 3 | 4 | 5 | 6 | 7 | 8 | 9 | 10 |

In this chapter, you will learn an effective process for group problem solving, the leadership skills needed to effectively manage group interactions during problem solving, the responsibilities that group members share, and ways that a group can effectively communicate the results of its deliberations to others.

LO¹ The Problem-Solving Process

When a group of people tackles a problem together, it may use an orderly series of steps or a less-structured spiral pattern in which they refine, accept, reject, modify, combine ideas, and circle back to a previous discussion as they go along. To observers, groups that follow an orderly sequence of steps—finishing each before moving to the next one—appear to be more organized and are generally more efficient, completing their deliberations more quickly. Groups that follow a spiral

© PEISEN ZHAO/ISTOCKPHOTO.COM

© ISTOCKPHOTO.COM / © BALONCICI/SHUTTERSTOCK / © ANDREJS PIDJASS/SHUTTERSTOCK / © MARIE-FRANCE BÉLANGER/
© ISTOCKPHOTO.COM / © LVECTOR/SHUTTERSTOCK

problem definition
a formal written statement describing a problem

question of fact
a question asked to determine what is true or to what extent something is true

question of value
a question asked to determine or judge whether something is right, moral, good, or just

sequence of activities may be less efficient, but they can also arrive at effective solutions. For example, when a group is presented with a problem, members will often immediately begin to offer solutions. But after a while, most groups realize they can't decide on a solution until they figure out the criteria for a good solution, or they may realize that each member has a different idea about what the problem is. A group needs to deal with these tasks before it can move to making a decision.

Whether the deliberations are linear or spiral, groups that arrive at high-quality decisions accomplish the six tasks that make up what is known as the Systematic Problem Solving Process (see Figure 10.1). This process, first described by John Dewey in 1933 and since revised by others, is still the best approach to individual or group problem solving (Duch, Groh, & Allen, 2001; Edens, 2000; Levin, 2001). By understanding the steps in problem solving and guiding your group to use them systematically, you can help your group to be both effective and efficient.

Step One: Identify and Define the Problem

The first step is to identify the problem and define it in a way that all group members understand and agree with. Even when a group is commissioned by an outside agency that provides a description of the problem, the group still needs to understand precisely what is at issue and needs to be resolved. Many times what appears to be a problem is only a symptom of a problem, and if the group focuses on solutions that eliminate only a symptom, the underlying problem will remain. For example, let's say that a group's budget crisis is stemming from a recession-related membership drop. How does the group know that the inability to fund the budget is the problem and not just a symptom of the problem? What if their membership drop has some other cause? If that is the case, then cutting the budget may be a temporary fix but will not solve the problem. One way to see if you have uncovered the root cause or real problem is to ask, "If we solve this problem, are we confident that the consequences of the problem will not recur?" If we cut the budget, are we confident that we won't have to cut it further? If not, then we probably need to look further for the root problem. We will need to look more closely at causes for the drop in membership and other ways besides dues for funding the budget. The real problem may be how to fund the budget.

Once your group agrees about the nature of the root problem, you will want to draft a **problem definition**—a formal written statement describing the problem. An effective problem definition is stated as a question of fact, value, or policy; it contains only one central idea; and it uses specific, precise, and concrete language. **Questions of fact** ask the group to determine what is true or to what extent something is true. "What percentage of our projected expenses can be covered with our existing revenue?" is a question of fact. **Questions of value** ask the group to determine or judge whether some-

Deliberations can be:

Spiral

Linear

Figure 10.1

The Systematic Problem Solving Process

Step One: Identify and define the problem

Step Two: Analyze the problem

Step Three: Determine criteria for judging solutions

Step Four: Identify alternative solutions

Step Five: Evaluate solutions and decide

Step Six: Implement the agreed-upon solution

thing is right, moral, good, or just. Questions of value often contain words such as *good, reliable, effective,* or *worthy*—for instance, "What is the most effective way to recruit new members?" **Questions of policy** concern what course of action should be taken or what rules should be adopted to solve a problem— for example, "Should we sponsor an annual fund-raising event with the local Public Relations Society of America (PRSA) chapter in order to help fund our budget?" After some discussion, the student chapter decided that the problem they needed to solve was a policy question that could be best stated as "How can we increase our revenues in order to meet our budget in the current economic conditions?"

Step Two: Analyze the Problem

Analysis of a problem entails finding out as much as possible about the problem. Most groups begin this process with each member sharing information he or she already knows about the problem through previous experiences. Some groups don't move beyond this level of analysis, which maybe OK if the group consists of individuals who are expert in the important areas related to the problem. But when this is not the case, the group needs to search for additional information. Members may be assigned to collect and examine information about the problem that is published in materials available at the library and on the Internet. Other members may interview experts, and still others may conduct surveys to gather information from particular target groups. The information gathered by group members should help the

group to answer key questions about the nature of the problem such as those listed in Figure 10.2.

The PRSA chapter, for example, might interview the dean of Student Affairs to understand how other campus groups have increased their revenues and to learn of any campus policies that govern fund-raising by student groups. Some group members might network with other student groups on campus and PRSA chapters at other schools. Finally, the group could survey former members to understand why they dropped out of the group and what might entice them to rejoin as well as survey eligible students who are not members to find out what would entice them to join.

During the information-gathering and analysis step, it is important to consciously encourage members to share information that is new or contradicts the sentiments or preferences expressed in the group. It is difficult for most of us to give up our pet theories or preferred worldviews. A group that is willing to consider new and unexpected information will more deeply analyze the problem and, therefore, will likely come to a more effective solution.

Step Three: Determine Criteria for Judging Solutions

Criteria are standards or measures used for judging the merits of proposed solutions. They provide a blueprint for how the group will evaluate the virtues of each alternative solution. Research suggests that when groups develop criteria before they think about specific solutions, they are more likely to come to a decision that all members can accept (Young, Wood, Phillips, & Pedersen, 2007). Without clear criteria, group members may argue for their preferred solution without regard to whether it will adequately address the problem and whether it is feasible. Figure 10.3 provides a list of questions that can help a group think about the types of criteria that a solution might need to meet.

Once you've agreed on the list of solution criteria, the group needs to prioritize the list. Although rank ordering the list from most to least important may be unwieldy and counterproductive, it is probably useful to agree on which criteria are major (must meet) and which are minor (would like to see). Based on their research and discussion, the PRSA chapter agreed on three major criteria and one minor criterion. A good plan would comply with the university's policy

question of policy
a question asked to determine what course of action should be taken or what rules should be adopted to solve a problem

criteria
standards or measures used for judging the merits of proposed solutions

Figure 10.2

Questions to Guide Problem Analysis

- What are the symptoms of this problem?
- What are the causes of this problem?
- Can this problem be subdivided into several smaller problems that each may have individual solutions?
- What have others who have faced this problem done?
- How successful have they been with the solutions they attempted?
- How is our situation similar and different from theirs?
- Does this problem consist of several smaller problems? If so, what are their symptoms, causes, previously tried solutions, and so forth?
- What would be the consequences of doing nothing?
- What would be the consequences of trying something and having it fail?

© MARIE-FRANCE BÉLANGER/ISTOCKPHOTO.COM

brainstorming
an uncritical, non-evaluative process of generating possible solutions by being creative, suspending judgment, and combining or adapting ideas

on fund-raising by student groups. It would need to cost less than $500 to implement. It would need to raise at least $4,000. It would not require more than 20 hours of work from each member.

Step Four: Identify Alternative Solutions

Ending up with a good solution depends on having a wide variety of possible solutions to choose from, so one of the most important activities of problem solving is coming up with solution ideas. Many groups fail at generating solution ideas because they criticize the first ideas expressed; this discourages members from taking the risk to put their ideas out for the group to consider. One way to encourage everyone's ideas is to use the technique of brainstorming. Brainstorming is an uncritical, non-evaluative process of generating possible solutions by being creative, suspending judgment, and combining or adapting ideas. When brainstorming, the group agrees to a freewheeling session when members offer ideas without censoring themselves. During this time, other members may build on ideas that have been presented, combine two or more ideas, or even offer off-the-wall thoughts. What members may not do is criticize, poke fun at, or in any other way evaluate the ideas. While the group is brainstorming, one member should be recording the ideas, prefera-

Figure 10.3

Questions to Guide Discussion of Solution Criteria

- What are the quantitative and qualitative measures of success that a solution must be able to demonstrate?
- Are there resource constraints that a good solution must meet (costs, time, manpower)?
- Is solution simplicity a factor?
- What risks are unacceptable?
- Is ease of implementation a consideration?
- Is it important that no constituency be unfairly harmed or advantaged by a solution?

bly in a manner that allows all members to see them (on a whiteboard, smart board, or overhead projector, for instance). When individuals are freed from the fear of criticism, a group may quickly generate 20 or more solution ideas. When members trust each other to abide by the rules, brainstorming is fun and productive.

The PRSA chapter brainstormed and came up with these ideas:

- Place an ad on the communication department's Web site to recruit members.
- Place an ad on the college Web site to recruit members.
- Ask faculty to allow PRSA members to do 2-minute "testimonials" in classes as a way of recruiting members.
- Text-message all the people we know about upcoming PRSA events.
- Run a monthly raffle at the PRSA meetings with the winning ticket to get 4 hours of work from a PRSA member.
- Find PRSA chapter members whose businesses would sponsor student scholarships to the national convention.
- Set up a consulting program to provide public relations help to other student groups for a fee.
- Set up a consulting program to provide public relations help to small businesses for a fee.
- Do a virtual newsletter instead of a printed one.
- Double membership dues.
- Co-sponsor a golf outing with the local PRSA chapter.
- Raffle off a spring break getaway for six to St. Thomas.

Step Five: Evaluate Solutions and Decide

With a list of potential solutions in hand, the group must then sort through them to find the one or ones that will best solve the problem. To do this, the group needs to compare each of the alternatives to the decision criteria they established earlier. If a lot of solutions were generated during brainstorming, the group will probably want to quickly review the list and eliminate those that obviously do not meet the criteria. Then it can concentrate on evaluating the

© MARIE-FRANCE BÉLANGER/ISTOCKPHOTO.COM / © ISTOCKPHOTO.COM

remaining solutions, talking about how well each meets specific criteria and comparing the positive features of each. This discussion may result in only one solution that meets all the criteria, but often there will be more than one viable solution.

Decision making is the process of choosing among alternatives. Sometimes your group may not be responsible for choosing among the remaining alternatives. Instead you will present the results of your work to others who will make the actual decision. At other times your group will make the decision. Five methods are commonly used to reach a group decision. Methods that require greater agreement among members are more time consuming.

The expert opinion method. Once the group has eliminated those alternatives that do not meet the criteria, the group asks the member who has the most expertise to make the final choice. Obviously, this method is quick and useful if one member is much more knowledgeable about the issues or has a greater stake in the implementation of the decision. The PRSA chapter, for instance, might ask its president to make the final choice.

The average group opinion method. In this approach, each group member ranks each of the alternatives that meet all the criteria. Their rankings are then averaged, and the alternative receiving the highest average becomes the choice. This method is useful for routine decisions or when a decision needs to be made quickly. It can also be used as an intermediate straw poll so the group can eliminate low-scoring alternatives before moving to a different process for making the final decision.

The majority rule method. In this method, the group votes on each alternative, and the one that receives a majority of votes (50 percent + 1) is selected. Although this method is considered democratic, it can create problems. If the majority voting for an alternative is slight, then nearly as many members oppose the choice as support it. If these minority members strongly object to the choice, they may sabotage implementation of the solution either actively or passively.

The unanimous decision method. In this method, the group must continue deliberation until every member of the group believes that the same solution is the best. As you would expect, it is very difficult to arrive at a truly unanimous decision, and to do so takes a lot of time. When a group reaches unanimity, however, each member is likely to be committed to selling the decision to others and helping to implement it.

The consensus method. This method is an alternative to the unanimous decision method. In consensus, the group continues deliberation until all members of the group find an acceptable solution, one they can support and are committed to helping implement. Some group members may believe there is a better solution than the one chosen, but all feel that they can live with the chosen solution. Arriving at consensus, though easier than reaching unanimity, is still difficult. Although the majority rule method is widely used, the consensus method is a wise investment if the group needs everyone's support to implement the decision successfully.

Sometimes a group will choose only one solution. But frequently a group will decide on a multi-pronged approach that combines two or three of the acceptable solutions. The PRSA chapter, for instance, reached consensus on a plan to place ads on both the college and department Web sites and to launch a text-message campaign 24 hours before their next meeting. They also decided to approach PRSA chapter members and ask them to sponsor student members to the national convention. Finally, they decided to explore the feasibility of setting up a consulting program.

decision making
the process of choosing among alternatives

Step Six: Implement the Agreed-Upon Solution

Finally, the group may be responsible for implementing the agreed-upon solution or, if the group is presenting the solution to others for implementation, making recommendations for how the solution should be implemented. The group has already considered implementation in terms of selecting a solution but now must fill in the details. What tasks are required by the solution(s)? Who will carry out these tasks? What is a reasonable time frame for implementation generally and for each of the tasks specifically?

LO² Shared Leadership

When we think of leadership, we typically think of a person who is in charge. It was once thought that leaders were "born"—that some people inherited personality and other traits that made them naturally suited to be leaders. Later, the emphasis moved to the notion that leaders were "made" and that if we could identify the specific behaviors of leadership, then any person could learn them and become an effective leader. Then, we recognized that who

informal or emergent leaders
members who gain power because they are liked and respected by the group

shared leadership functions
the sets of roles that group members perform to facilitate the work of the group and help maintain harmonious relationships between members

task roles
sets of behaviors that help a group acquire, process, or apply information that contributes directly to completing a task or goal

maintenance roles
sets of behaviors that help a group develop and maintain cohesion, commitment, and positive working relationships

became a leader and the behaviors that made a leader effective varied depending on the task, the situation, and the followers. The most recent thinking is that leadership is a set of functions that can be performed by one, more than one, or all group members at various times. In other words, leadership is most often a shared activity in which different members perform various functions based on their unique strengths and expertise (Fairhurst, 2001). A group, then, may have a formal leader, but in actuality, throughout the life of the group, a series of informal leaders (also called emergent leaders) will arise to help the group meet the challenges the group faces. People who assume the role of a leader behave and communicate in specific ways that fulfill important leadership functions.

Shared leadership functions are the sets of roles that you or other members perform to facilitate the work of the group and help maintain harmonious relationships between members. A role is a specific pattern of behavior that group members perform based on their skills and their perception about the needs of the group at that time. When leadership roles are effectively performed, the group will function smoothly and members will enjoy each other and working on the task. There are three sets of leadership roles that must be performed by members if a group is to be successful: task roles, maintenance roles, and procedural roles.

Task Roles

Task roles help the group acquire, process, or apply information that contributes directly to completing a task or goal.

- **Information or opinion givers** provide content for the discussion. People who perform this role are well informed on the content of the task and share what they know with the group. Your ability to assume this role depends on your command of high-quality information that the group needs in order to complete its task. "Well, the articles I read seem to agree that" and "Based on how my sorority raised money for the Ronald McDonald House, we could" are statements typical of information and opinion givers.

- **Information or opinion seekers** probe others for their ideas and opinions during group meetings. Typical comments by those performing this role include "Before going further, what information do we have about how raising fees is likely to affect membership?" or "How do other members of the group feel about this idea?"

- **Information or opinion analyzers** help the group scrutinize the content and the reasoning of discussions. They may question what is being said and help members understand the hidden assumptions in their statements. Information or opinion analyzers make statements such as "Enrique, you're generalizing from only one instance. Can you give us some others?"

> The most recent thinking is that leadership is a set of functions that can be performed by one, more than one, or all group members at various times.

Maintenance Roles

Maintenance roles are the sets of behaviors that help the group develop and maintain cohesion, commitment, and positive working relationships. We engage in maintenance leadership any time we manage participation, foster collaboration to resolve conflict, or integrate fun into the group experience. Managing participation means giving everyone an opportunity to share ideas and information with the group and ensuring that no group member or members dominate the discussion. Fostering collaboration to resolve conflict means acting as an unbiased mediator when disagreements between members become heated so that the conflict is resolved as a win-win.

Integrating fun into the group experience means intervening in the group's

© IOFOT/ISTOCKPHOTO.COM

process in order to reduce tension by encouraging the group to relax, laugh, and enjoy each other's company. We know that humor has a positive impact on group communication. Noted psychotherapist and business consultant S. M. Sultanoff (1993) explains that "humor facilitates communication, builds relationships, reduces stress, provides perspective, and promotes attending and energizes" (para 2). Fortune 500 companies such as General Electric, AT&T, Kodak, Lockheed, and IBM all emphasize the value of workplace humor in their training programs.

Members who undertake maintenance leadership roles will be supporters, interpreters, harmonizers, mediators, or interpreters.

- **Supporters** encourage others in the group. When another member contributes to the group, supporters show appreciation through their non-verbal or verbal behavior. Non-verbally, supporters may smile, nod, or vigorously shake their heads. Verbally, they demonstrate support through statements like "Good point, Ming," "I really like that idea, Nikki," or "It's obvious you've really done your homework, Janelle."

- **Interpreters** are familiar with the differences in the social, cultural, and gender orientations of group members and use this knowledge to help group members understand each other. Interpreters are especially important in groups whose members are culturally diverse (Jensen & Chilberg, 1991). For example, an interpreter might say "Paul, Lin Chou is Chinese, so when she says that she will think about your plan she probably means that she does not support your ideas, but she doesn't want to embarrass you in front of the others." Or an interpreter might say "Jim, most of us are from the South and consider it impolite to begin business before we socialize and catch up with one another." When groups do not have a member to serve in the interpreter leadership role and members come from different cultures, effective group process can suffer.

- **Harmonizers** intervene in the group's discussion when conflict is threatening to harm group cohesiveness or the relationship between specific group members. Harmonizers are likely to make statements such as "Tom, Jack, hold it a second. I know you're on opposite sides of this, but let's see where you might have some agreement" or "Cool it, everybody,

we're coming up with some good stuff. Let's not lose our momentum by getting into name-calling."

procedural leadership roles
sets of behaviors that directly support a group process

- **Mediators** are neutral and impartial arbiters who guide the discussion so that members who have conflicting ideas find a mutually acceptable resolution. Mediators do this by maintaining their own neutrality, keeping the discussion focused on issues and not personalities, helping to identify areas of common ground, and working to find a mutually satisfying solution to the disagreement using paraphrasing and perception checking.

- **Tension relievers** recognize when group members are stressed or tired and then intervene to relieve the stress or re-energize the group usually through humor. People who are effective in this leadership role might tell a joke, kid around, or tell a lighthearted story so that the group is refreshed when it returns to the task. In some situations, a single well-placed one-liner will get a laugh, break the tension or monotony, and jolt the group out of its lethargy. Although the tension reliever momentarily distracts the group from its task, this action helps the group remain cohesive.

> Members who undertake maintenance leadership roles will be supporters, interpreters, harmonizers, mediators, or interpreters.

Procedural Roles

Procedural leadership roles are sets of behaviors that directly support the group process. This includes providing logistical support for the group, managing the group's interaction, and keeping records of the group's accomplishments and decisions.

- **Logistics coordinators** arrange for appropriate spaces for group meetings, procure the supplies and equipment that will be needed by the group, and manage other details so that the group's physical needs are met. The logistics coordinator's leadership role is usually carried out behind the scenes, but the successful performance of this role is crucial to a group's ability to be efficient and effective. Making arrangements so that the group has appropriate space, furniture, and equipment and providing for the physical needs of members during the meeting allows the group to efficiently work on its tasks.

© SEMJONOW JURI/SHUTTERSTOCK

agenda
an organized outline of the information and decision items that will be covered during a meeting

- **Expediters** keep track of what the group is trying to accomplish and help move the group through the agenda. When the group has strayed, expediters will make statements like "I'm enjoying this, but I can't quite see what it has to do with resolving the issue" or "Let's see, aren't we still trying to find out whether these are the only criteria that we should be considering?"

- **Gatekeepers** manage the flow of conversation so that all members have an equal opportunity to participate. If one or two members begin to dominate the conversation, the gatekeeper acknowledges this and invites other group members to participate. Gatekeepers also notice non-verbal signals that indicate that a member wishes to speak. The gatekeeper is the one who sees that Juanita is on the edge of her chair, eager to comment, and says, "Let me interrupt you, Doug. We haven't heard from Juanita, and she seems to have something she wants to say."

- **Recorders** take careful notes of what the group has decided and the evidence upon which the decisions are based. Recorders usually distribute edited copies of their notes to group members prior to the next meeting. Sometimes these notes are published as minutes, which become a public record of the group's activities.

LO³ Making Meetings Effective

Disastrous meetings stem from poor meeting arrangement skills by both the meeting facilitator and those who attend the meeting. In a recent survey, business consultant Dike Drummond (2004) discovered that over 50 percent of managers spend at least six hours per week in meetings, and these same managers feel that 50 percent of their meeting time is wasted! To ensure that your meetings are not a waste of your time or that of others, lets look at guidelines for meeting leaders and meeting participants.

Before the meeting . . .

- Leaders need to prepare and distribute an agenda; decide who should attend; manage logistics; speak with each participant.
- Participants need to study the agenda; study the minutes; do homework; list questions; plan to play a leadership role.

Guidelines for Meeting Leaders

Most of us will be responsible for convening a group meeting at some point in our lives. Whether you are leading the meeting for a class project, a task force at work, or substituting for your manager at the monthly department meeting, knowing how to effectively plan for, facilitate, and follow up after meetings are useful skills.

Leadership Roles

- Task roles help the group acquire, process, or apply information that contributes directly to completing a task or goal.
- Maintenance roles are the sets of behaviors that help the group to develop and maintain cohesion, commitment, and positive working relationships.
- Procedural roles are sets of behaviors that directly support the group process.

Before the Meeting

1. **Prepare and distribute an agenda.** An agenda is an organized outline of the information and decision items that will be covered during a meeting. It is a road map that lets the members know the purpose of the meeting and what they are expected to accomplish as a result of attending. Agenda items should move the group toward its goals and should not include things that could be accomplished without the presence (albeit in a face-to-face or virtual environment) of all of the meeting attendees. You can identify the items for your agenda by

- reviewing your notes and the formal minutes of the previous meeting;
- identifying what the group decided would be its work between meetings; and
- identifying what decisions it is expected to make in the next session.

Then you can structure the agenda into information items and decision items, having members report on their assignments and then, based on what has been learned or accomplished, moving to make relevant decisions.

It is critical to distribute the agenda at least 24 hours before the meeting so that members have time to prepare. You can e-mail the agenda, post it to the group's Web page, or hand-deliver it. None of us likes

to come to a meeting and be embarrassed because we have forgotten to complete an assignment, and most of us don't like to be called on to make decisions that we have not had time to think about. Being unprepared is one of the main reasons that time is wasted in meetings. As the meeting leader, you are responsible for providing the information that members need in order to come prepared.

2. **Decide who should attend the meeting.** In most cases, all members of a group will attend meetings. Occasionally, one or more members of the group may not need to attend a particular meeting but may only need to be informed of the outcomes later.

3. **Manage meeting logistics.** You may choose to enact this role or ask another group member to do this. But even if you delegate these tasks, it remains your responsibility to make sure that the meeting arrangements are appropriate. If the group is meeting face-to-face you will want a room that is appropriate to the size and work of the group, and you will want to make sure that all of the equipment that the group needs is on hand and operational. The room should be set up so that it encourages group interaction. This usually means that members can sit around a table or in a circle with plenty of desk/table space for writing. If the entire group or some group members are attending the meeting from remote locations, you will need to make sure that the technology needed to conference them in has been provided. Because groups become less effective in long meetings, a meeting should last no longer than 90 minutes. If a meeting must be planned for a longer period of time, use segments of no longer than 90 minutes with scheduled breaks to avoid fatigue.

4. **Speak with each participant prior to the meeting.** It is important for you as the leader to understand members' positions and personal goals. Time spent discussing issues in advance allows you to anticipate conflicts that might emerge and plan how to manage them so that the group makes effective decisions and maintains cohesiveness.

During the Meeting

1. **Review and modify the agenda.** Begin the meeting by reviewing the agenda and

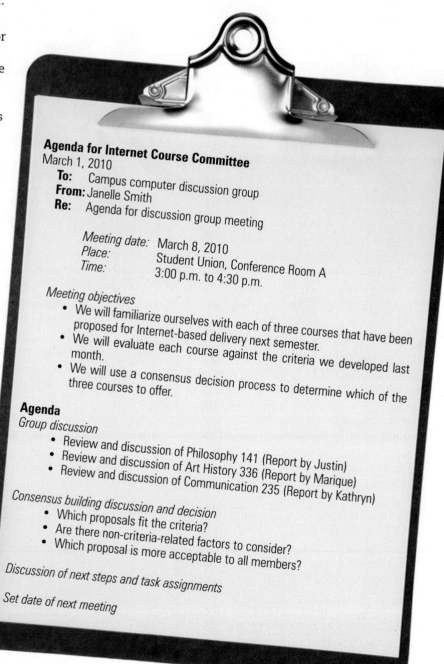

Agenda for Internet Course Committee
March 1, 2010

To: Campus computer discussion group
From: Janelle Smith
Re: Agenda for discussion group meeting

Meeting date: March 8, 2010
Place: Student Union, Conference Room A
Time: 3:00 p.m. to 4:30 p.m.

Meeting objectives
- We will familiarize ourselves with each of three courses that have been proposed for Internet-based delivery next semester.
- We will evaluate each course against the criteria we developed last month.
- We will use a consensus decision process to determine which of the three courses to offer.

Agenda
Group discussion
- Review and discussion of Philosophy 141 (Report by Justin)
- Review and discussion of Art History 336 (Report by Marique)
- Review and discussion of Communication 235 (Report by Kathryn)

Consensus building discussion and decision
- Which proposals fit the criteria?
- Are there non-criteria-related factors to consider?
- Which proposal is more acceptable to all members?

Discussion of next steps and task assignments

Set date of next meeting

© JIM BARBER/SHUTTERSTOCK

modifying it based on members' suggestions. Because things can change between distribution of the agenda and the meeting, reviewing the agenda ensures that the group will be working on items that are still relevant. Reviewing the agenda also gives members a chance to give input into what is to be discussed.

2. **Monitor member interaction.** If other group members are assuming the task-related, maintenance, and procedural functions, you need do nothing. But when there is a need for a particular role and no one is assuming it, you should do so. For example, if you notice that some people are talking more than their fair share and no one is trying to draw out quieter members, you should assume the gatekeeper role and invite reluctant members to comment on the discussion. Similarly, if a discussion becomes too heated, you may need to take on the role of harmonizer so relationships are not unduly strained.

3. **Monitor the time.** It is easy for a group to get bogged down in a discussion. Although another group member may serve as expediter, it is your responsibility as meeting leader to make sure that the group stays on schedule.

4. **Praise in public and reprimand in private.** Meetings provide an excellent opportunity to praise individuals or the entire group for jobs well done. Being recognized among one's peers often boosts self-esteem, group morale, and synergy. Conversely, criticizing individuals or the entire group during a meeting has the opposite effect. The humiliation of public criticism can deflate self-esteem, group morale, and motivation.

5. **Check periodically to see if the group is ready to make a decision.** You should listen carefully for agreement among members and move the group into its formal decision-making process when the discussion is no longer adding insight.

6. **Implement the group's decision rules.** You are responsible for executing the decision-making rule the group has agreed to use. If the group is deciding by consensus, for example, you must make sure all members feel they can support the chosen alternative. If the group is deciding by majority rule, you call for the vote and tally the results.

7. **Summarize decisions and assignments.** You should summarize what has happened and

© KRISTIAN SEKULIC/SHUTTERSTOCK

what is left to accomplish, as well as reiterate task assignments made during the meeting, and review what is left to accomplish or decide.

8. **Set the next meeting.** You should clarify with members when, and if, future meetings are necessary. The overall purposes of the next meeting will dictate what you'll put in the next agenda.

Following Up

1. **Review the meeting outcomes and process.** A good leader learns how to be more effective by reflecting on how well the meeting went. Did the meeting accomplish its goals? Was group cohesion improved or damaged in the process? What will you do differently next time to improve the experience?

2. **Prepare and distribute a meeting summary.** Although in some groups a member serves as the recorder and distributes minutes, many groups rely on their leader. Having a written record of what was agreed to and accomplished, as well as assignments that members agreed to complete prior to the next meeting and the decision items the group agreed to consider next time, gives members an opportunity to review the group's progress and to correct any mistakes in the record. If the group has a recorder, you should review the minutes and compare them to your notes before they are distributed. Summaries are most useful when they are distributed within two or three days of the meeting when everyone's memories are still fresh.

3. **Repair damaged relationships.** If the debate during the meeting was heated, some members may have damaged their relationships or left the meeting angry or hurt. You should help repair relationships by seeking out these participants and talking with them. Through empathetic listening, you can soothe hurt feelings and spark a recommitment to the group.

4. **Conduct informal progress reports.** When participants have been assigned specific task responsibilities, you should periodically check in to see if they have encountered any problems in completing those tasks and how you might help them.

Guidelines for Meeting Participants

Just as there are guidelines for effective conveners/formal leaders to follow before, during, and after meetings, there are also guidelines to help meeting participants.

Before the Meeting

Too often, people think of group meetings as a "happening" that requires attendance but no preparation. Countless times we have observed people arriving at a meeting unprepared even though they are carrying packets of material they received in advance. To be worthwhile, meetings should not be treated as impromptu events but as carefully planned interactions that pool information from well-prepared individuals. Here are some important steps for members to take prior to attending a meeting.

1. **Study the agenda.** Consider the purpose of the meeting and determine what you need to do to be prepared. If you have an assignment, make sure that you will be ready to report on it.

2. **Study the minutes.** If this is one in a series of meetings, read the minutes and your own notes from the previous meeting. What happened at the previous meeting should provide the basis for preparing for the next one.

3. **Do your homework.** Read the material distributed prior to the meeting, and do your own research to become better informed about items on the agenda. If no material is provided, then identify the issues and learn what you need to know to be a productive group member. Bring any materials you find that may help the group accomplish the agenda. If some members will not be able to attend, solicit their ideas about the agenda.

4. **List questions.** Make a list of questions related to agenda items that you would like to have answered during the meeting.

5. **Plan to play a leadership role.** Consider the leadership functions and roles at which you excel. Decide what you will do to play those roles to the best of your ability.

During the Meeting

Go into the meeting planning to be a full participant. If there are five people in the group, all five should be participating.

1. **Listen attentively.** Concentrate on what others are saying so that you can use your material to complement, supplement, or counter what is presented.

2. **Stay focused.** It is easy to get off track during meetings. Keep your comments focused on the specific agenda item under discussion. If others get off the subject, do what you can to get the discussion back on track.

3. **Ask questions.** Honest questions, whose answers you do not already know, help stimulate discussion and build ideas.

During the meeting . . .

- Leaders need to review and modify the agenda; monitor member interaction; monitor the time; praise in public and reprimand in private; check to see if the group is ready to make a decision; implement the group's decision rules; summarize decisions and assignments; set the next meeting.
- Participants need to listen attentively; stay focused; ask questions; take notes; play devil's advocate; monitor contributions.

After the meeting . . .

- Leaders need to review outcomes and process; prepare and distribute summary; repair damaged relationships; conduct informal progress reports.
- Participants need to review and summarize notes; evaluate effectiveness; review decisions; communicate progress; complete tasks; review minutes.

4. **Take notes.** Even if someone else is responsible for providing the official minutes, you'll need notes that help you follow the discussion's line of development. Also, these notes will help you remember what has been said and any responsibilities you have agreed to take on after the meeting.

5. **Play devil's advocate.** When you think an idea has not been fully discussed or tested, be willing to voice disagreement or encourage further discussion.

6. **Monitor your contributions.** Especially when people are well prepared, they have a tendency to dominate the discussion. Make sure that you are neither dominating the discussion nor abdicating your responsibility to share insights and opinions.

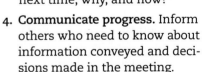

What are some of the difficulties in holding virtual meetings?

© ISTOCKPHOTO.COM

Following these guidelines for participating responsibly in meetings will make them a more pleasant and productive experience. Although most meetings used to be conducted face-to-face, today more meetings are occurring via teleconference, video conference, and online social networks. Engaging responsibly in virtual meetings has some unique challenges, particularly in staying focused and listening attentively.

Following Up

When meetings end, too often people leave and forget about what took place until the next meeting. But what happens in one meeting provides a basis for what happens in the next. You must do your part to prepare to move forward at the next meeting.

1. **Review and summarize your notes.** Try to do this shortly after the meeting while ideas are still fresh in your mind. Make notes of what needs to be discussed next time.

2. **Evaluate your effectiveness.** How effective were you in helping the group move toward achieving its goals? Where were you strong? Where were you weak? What should you do next time to improve and how? For example, if you didn't speak up as much as you would have liked to, perhaps you'll decide to write down questions or topics when they come to you and use them as notes to encourage you to speak up next time.

3. **Review decisions.** Make notes about what your role was in making decisions. Did you do all that you could have done? If not, what will you do differently next time, why, and how?

4. **Communicate progress.** Inform others who need to know about information conveyed and decisions made in the meeting.

5. **Complete your tasks.** Make sure you complete all assignments you received in the meeting.

6. **Review minutes.** Compare the official meeting minutes to your own notes, and report any significant discrepancies to the member who prepared the minutes.

LO⁴ Communicating Group Solutions

Once a group has completed its deliberations, it is usually expected to communicate what it has decided to someone or some other body.

Deliverables are tangible (item, article, entity) or intangible (point, idea, goal) products of your work that must be provided to someone else. Although some deliverables are objects, typically the deliverables from problem-solving groups are communications of the information gathered, analyses, decisions, and recommendations of the group. These kinds of intangible deliverables can be communicated in written formats, oral formats, or visual and audiovisual formats.

Written Formats

Written brief. A written brief is a very short document that describes the problem, background, process, decision, and rationale so that the reader can quickly understand and evaluate the group's product. Most briefs are one or two pages long. When preparing a brief, begin by describing your group's task. What problem were you attempting to solve and why? Then briefly provide the background information the reader will need to evaluate whether the group has adequately studied the problem. Present solution steps and timelines for implementation as bullet points so that the reader can quickly understand what is being proposed. Close with a sentence or very short paragraph that describes how the recommendation will solve the problem as well as any potential side effects.

Comprehensive report. A comprehensive report is a written document that provides a detailed review of the problem-solving process used to arrive at the recommendation. This type of report is usually organized into sections that parallel the problem-solving process.

Because comprehensive reports can be very long, they usually include an executive summary. An **executive summary** is a one-page synopsis of the report. This summary contains enough information to acquaint readers with the highlights of the full document without reading it. Usually, it contains a statement of the problem, some background information, a description of any alternatives, and the major conclusions.

Oral Formats

Oral brief. An oral brief is essentially a summary of a written brief delivered to an audience by a group member. Typically, an oral brief can be delivered in less than 10 minutes.

Oral report. An oral report is similar to a comprehensive report. It provides a more detailed review of a group's problem-solving process. Oral reports can range from 30 to 60 minutes.

Symposium. A symposium is a set of prepared oral reports delivered sequentially by group members before a gathering of people who are interested in the work of the group. A symposium may be organized so that each person's speech focuses on one step of the problem-solving process, or it may be organized so that each speaker covers all of the steps in the problem-solving process as they relate to one of several issues or recommendations that the group worked on or made. In a symposium format, the speakers usually sit together at the front of the room. One member acts as moderator, offering the introductory and concluding remarks and providing transitions between speakers. When introduced by the moderator, each speaker may stand and move to a central spot, usually a lectern. Speakers who are going to use PowerPoint visuals should coordinate their slides so that there can be seamless transitions between speakers. Symposiums often conclude with a question-and-answer session facilitated by the moderator, who directs one or more of the members to answer based on their expertise. Questions can be directed to individuals or to the group as a whole.

Panel discussion. A panel discussion is a structured problem-solving discussion held by a group in front

© KONSTANTIN KAMENETSKIY/SHUTTERSTOCK

deliverables
tangible or intangible products of work that must be provided to someone else

written brief
a very short document that describes a problem, background, process, decision, and rationale so that a reader can quickly understand and evaluate a group's product

comprehensive report
a written document that provides a detailed review of the problem-solving process used to arrive at a recommendation

executive summary
a one-page synopsis of a comprehensive report

oral brief
a summary of a written brief delivered to an audience by a group member

oral report
a detailed review of a group's problem-solving process delivered to an audience by one or more group members

symposium
a set of prepared oral reports delivered sequentially by group members before a gathering of people who are interested in the work of the group

panel discussion
a structured problem-solving discussion held by a group in front of an audience

remote access report (RAR)
a computer-mediated audiovisual presentation of a group's process and outcome that others can receive electronically

streaming video
a pre-recording that is sent in compressed form over the Internet

of an audience. One member serves as moderator, introducing the topic and providing structure by asking a series of planned questions that panelists answer. Their answers and the interaction among them provide the supporting evidence. A well-planned panel discussion seems spontaneous and interactive but requires careful planning and rehearsal to ensure that all relevant information is presented and that all speakers are afforded equal speaking time. After the formal discussion, the audience is often encouraged to question the participants. Perhaps you've seen or heard a panel of experts discuss a topic on a radio or television talk show like *Sports Center* or *The View*.

Virtual Reports

Remote access reports. A remote access report (RAR) is a computer-mediated audiovisual presentation of the group's process and outcome that others can receive through e-mail, Web posting, and so forth. Prepared by one or more members of the group, the RAR is rendered in PowerPoint or other computer software and provides a visual overview

There are even MORE Study Tools for Chapter 10 at www.cengagebrain.com

☑ Speech Builder Express
☑ Printable Flash Cards
☑ Interactive Games
☑ Interactive Video Activities
☑ Chapter Review Cards
☑ Online Quizzes with Feedback
☑ Audio Downloads

of the group's process, decisions, and recommendations. Effective RARs consist of no more than 15 to 20 slides. Slides are titled and content is presented in outline or bullet-point phrases or key words (rather than complete sentences or paragraphs) as well as through visual representations of important information (see Figure 10.4). RARs may be self-running so that the slides automatically forward after a certain number of seconds, but it is better to let the viewer choose the pace and control when the next slide appears. RARs can be silent or narrated. When narrated, a voice-over accompanies each slide, providing additional or explanatory information.

Streaming videos. A streaming video is a prerecording that is sent in compressed form over the Internet. You are probably familiar with streaming video from popular Web sites such as YouTube. Streaming videos are a great way to distribute oral briefs, but they also can be used to distribute recordings of oral reports, symposiums, or panel presentations. Streaming videos are useful when it is inconvenient for some or all the people who need to know the results of the group's work to meet at one time or in one place.

Figure 10.4

Example of a Slide from a Remote Access Report

Future Growth Strategies

- **Expansion into Asian markets**

- **Increase domestic market share**

- **Diversify product line**

SJS, Inc.

More Bang for Your Buck

"I like the lower cost, the size of the book, the lighter reading, and the interactive games and quizzes on the website."

– Jillian Basiger, Student at Lakeland Community College

COMM has it all, and you can too. Between the text and our online offerings, you have everything at your fingertips. Make sure you check out all that COMM has to offer:

- Speech Builder Express
- Printable Flash Cards
- Interactive Games
- Interactive Video Activities
- Chapter Review Cards
- Online Quizzing with Feedback
- Audio Downloads
- And More!

Visit **www.cengagebrain.com** to find the resources you need today!

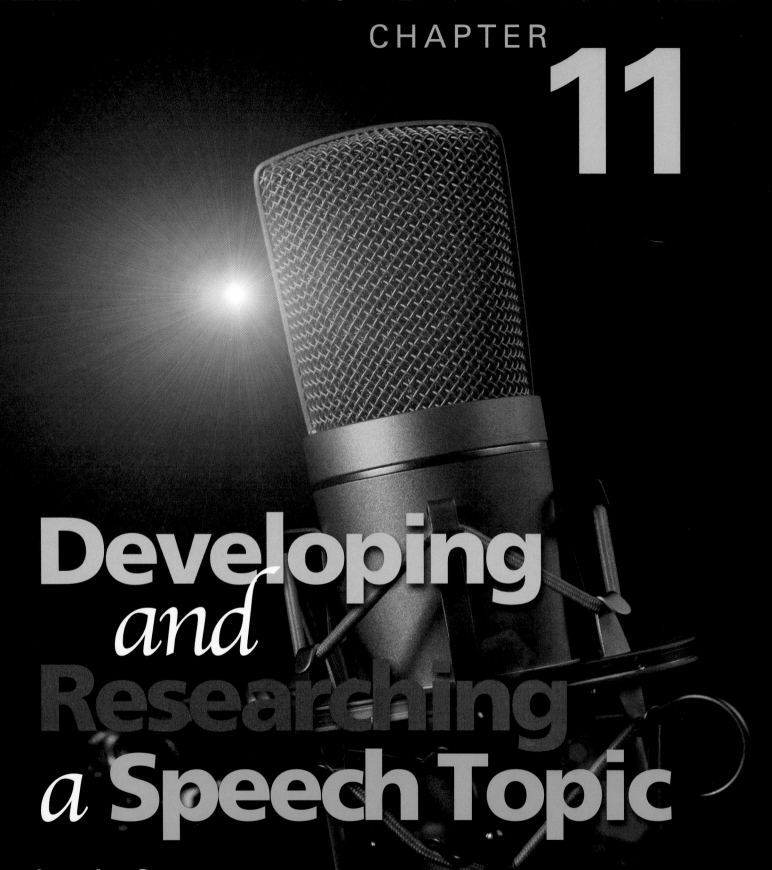

Developing *and* Researching *a* Speech Topic

Learning Outcomes | LO[1] Discuss how to identify topics for your speech | LO[2] Understand how to analyze the audience | LO[3] Understand how to analyze the setting | LO[4] Discuss how to select a topic for your speech | LO[5] Identify the general and specific goals of your speech | LO[6] Develop strategies for locating and evaluating information sources and primary research | LO[7] Evaluate the accuracy, reliability, and validity of information | LO[8] Identify and select relevant information | LO[9] Discuss methods of drawing information from multiple cultural perspectives | LO[10] Explain how to record information | LO[11] Explain how to cite sources in speeches

> **"** *Whether presenting oral reports and proposals, responding to questions, or training other workers, management-level and professional employees spend much of their work lives in activities that include or draw on public speaking skills.* **"**

You may be taking this course as part of a graduation requirement, and the thought of giving a speech can be overwhelming. However, developing public speaking skills is important. Why? Because when you are able to express your ideas to an audience, you are empowered. In a public forum, an effective speaker can stimulate and influence the thinking of others in ways that can improve their lives and the lives of those around them. In the workplace, effective public speaking skills are essential to advancement. Whether presenting oral reports and proposals, responding to questions, or training other workers, management-level and professional employees spend much of their work lives in activities that include or draw on public speaking skills.

Luckily, public speaking skills are not inborn; they are learned. In the chapters that follow, we will explain how you can improve your public speaking through careful preparation. In Chapters 11 through 14, you will learn a simple speech planning process that consists of the five Action Steps listed. Then in the final two chapters, we will present more detailed information on organizing and developing informative and persuasive speeches, which are the two most common types. This chapter is devoted to explaining how to complete the first two action steps.

What do you think?

It makes me nervous to speak in public.

Strongly Disagree   *Strongly Agree*

| 1 | 2 | 3 | 4 | 5 | 6 | 7 | 8 | 9 | 10 |

Speech Action Steps

Action Step 1
Determine a Specific Speech Goal That Fits the Audience and Occasion.

Action Step 2
Gather and Evaluate Information to Develop the Content of Your Speech.

Action Step 3
Organize and Develop Speech Material to Meet the Needs of Your Particular Audience.

Action Step 4
Adapt the Verbal and Visual Material to the Needs of the Specific Audience.

Action Step 5
Practice Presenting the Speech.

© ISTOCKPHOTO.COM

subject
a broad area of knowledge

topic
some specific aspect of a subject

Action Step 1:

Determine a Specific Speech Goal That Fits the Audience and Occasion

Speech planning begins by identifying a goal for your speech. To prepare a specific goal, you will need a list of topics that are appropriate to your specific audience and to the occasion. From these you will be able to select one and write a goal statement for your speech.

LO¹ Identify Topics

Good speech topics are developed from subjects that interest you and that you already know something about. What do you know a lot about? What has interested you enough so that you have gained some expertise? These subjects are a good source for speech topics. What is the difference between subject and topic? A subject is a broad area of knowledge—for example, you may have expertise in the subject of movies, cognitive psychology, computer technology, hip-hop culture, Asian art, or the politics of the Middle East. A topic is narrower and is a subset or specific aspect of a subject. If your subject is movies, you might feel qualified to speak on a variety of topics such as how the Academy Awards nomination process works; the relationships between movie producers, directors, and distributors; or how technology is changing movie production. Similarly, if your subject area is computer technology, you might be able to speak on cloud technology or Web 2.0.

Let's look at how you can identify subject areas that interest you and then, from those subject areas, identify and select specific topics you might use for the speeches you will present.

List Subjects

You can identify potential subjects for your speeches by listing subjects that (1) are important to you—that you find interesting

and exciting—and (2) you know something about. Subjects may be related to careers that interest you, your major area of study, special skills or competencies that you have or admire, your hobbies, or your leisure and volunteer activities as well as your social, economic, or political interests. So if sales and marketing are your majors and your intended career, playing World of Warcraft online and snowboarding are your favorite activities, and you are a literacy volunteer who is concerned about the falling rate of high school graduation, then these are subject areas from which you can identify topics for your speeches.

At this point, it is tempting to think, "The audience is going to be bored if I talk about what interests me." In reality, all subject areas can interest an audience. Have you ever been drawn into a subject because the person you were talking to was so excited by the subject and good at explaining it? If you speak on a topic that you know something about and that really inter-

Holly's list of speeches

Major and career interests
teaching
Web site design
information systems
technology trainer
computer-aided design

Hobbies and activities
social networking
rowing
Big Sisters organization
bird watching
photography

Issues and concerns
endangered birds
child abuse
personal privacy on the Internet
water pollution
parenting & education

© ELENA SCHWEITZER/SHUTTERSTOCK

ests you, you will find it easy to be appear knowl-edgeable and to communicate your enthusiasm to others. At the start of term, Holly, a beginning speech student, created a list of subjects for the speeches she was to give this term in her speech class. She identified subjects under three broad headings: (1) major subject and career interests, (2) hobbies and activities, and (3) issues and concerns.

Brainstorm and Concept Map for Topic Ideas

Since a topic is only one aspect of a subject, you can identify many topics within a subject. Two methods for identifying topics are brainstorming and concept mapping.

Brainstorming is an uncritical, non-evaluative process of generating associated ideas. When you brainstorm, you list as many ideas as you can with-out evaluating them. Holly, for example, decided she wanted to give a speech on the subject of social

networking. By brainstorming, she was able to list topics that included the history of social networking, future trends in social networking, compari-sons between popular social networking sites, the downside of social networking, and the social impacts of online social networks.

A second tool you can use to identify specific topics from a general subject area is concept map-ping. Concept mapping is a visual means of explor-ing connections between a subject and related ideas (Callison, 2001). To generate connections, you might ask yourself questions about your subject, focusing on who, what, where, when, and how. Holly used concept mapping to identify topics related to endan-gered birds. In Figure 11.1, you can see what Holly's concept map looked like.

You can create a list of potential topics by com-pleting Action Step 1.a: Brainstorm and Concept Map for Topics.

> **concept mapping**
> a visual means of exploring connections between a subject and related ideas

Figure 11.1

Concept Map for Endangered Birds

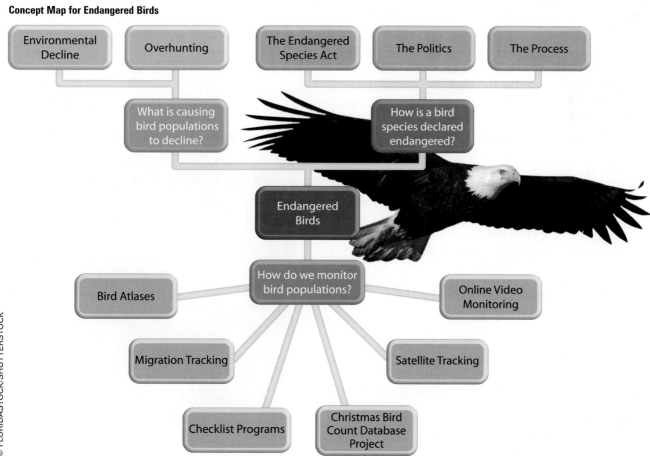

© FLORIDASTOCK/SHUTTERSTOCK

Action Step 1a
Brainstorming and Concept Map for Topics

1. Develop a subject list.
   a. Divide a sheet of paper into three columns. Label column 1 "major or vocational interest," label column 2 "hobby or activity," and label column 3 "concern or issue."
   b. Working on one column at a time, identify subjects of interest to you. Try to identify at least 3 subjects in each column.
   c. Place a check mark next to the subject in each column you would most enjoy speaking about.
   d. Keep these lists for future use in choosing a topic for an assigned speech.
2. For each subject you have checked, brainstorm a list of topics that relate to it.
3. Then, for each subject you have checked, develop a concept map to identify smaller topic areas and related ideas that might be developed into future speeches.

audience analysis
the study of the intended audience for your speech

audience adaptation
the active process of developing a strategy for tailoring your information to the specific speech audience

demographics
data to help you understand basic audience characteristics

LO² Analyze the Audience

Because speeches are presented to a particular audience, before you can finally decide on your topic, you need to understand who will be in your prospective audience. Audience analysis is the study of the intended audience for your speech. Understanding your prospective audience will help you select an appropriate topic from your list. Your audience analysis will also help you in audience adaptation, which is the process of tailoring your speech's information to the needs, interests, and expectations of your audience.

Identify Audience Analysis Information Needs

To begin, you will want to gather information that will help you understand how audience members are alike and different from you and from each other. You will want to gather data to help you understand basic audience characteristics, or demographics. Helpful demographic information includes things such as each audience member's age, education, gender, income, occupation, race, ethnicity, religion, geographic uniqueness, and language. This information will help you make educated inferences about them and adapt your speech accordingly. Figure 11.2 presents a list of questions you can use to obtain necessary demographic information.

Let's look at an example to see how audience analysis data can help you decide on a topic. Suppose that you have decided to give a speech on blogging. If you're not sure your audience understands what blogging is, you may infer what they know by looking at their demographics. Is almost all of the audience young, well educated, and from a middle-class background? If so, you can infer that they will have heard about blogging and know some of the basics. So you will gear your speech to more specialized information. But if your audience is from different demographical groups or if they are a diverse group, then you might need to survey them about what they know about blogging and then use what they tell you to pick an appropriate topic within the general subject of blogging. For example, imagine that one of the topics that interests you is the dangers or "dark side" of blogging. If your audience is made up primarily of 18- to 22-year-old college students, you can assume that they know what blogging is and so this topic would probably be a good one for this audience. If you discover that one or two audience members are older than that, you can avoid marginalizing them by briefly defining blogging in your opening remarks so that they aren't completely lost. But if

HOW WOULD YOU TALK ABOUT BLOGGING TO THIS AUDIENCE?

© ISTOCKPHOTO.COM / © BRITTA KASHOLM-TENGVE/ISTOCKPHOTO.COM

you discover that most of your audience members are older and have never read or written a blog, then this topic may not be appropriate for this audience or you may need to spend more time acquainting the audience with blogging before moving to a discussion of the dangers of blogging.

You will also want to collect subject-related audience data, including how knowledgeable audience members are in your subject area, their initial level of interest in the subject, their attitude toward the subject, and their attitude toward you as a speaker. Once you determine what your audience already knows about your subject, you can eliminate familiar topics that might bore them and choose a topic that will present them with new information and new insights. When you understand the initial level of interest that audience members have regarding your subject, you can choose a topic that builds on that interest or adapt your material so that it captures their interest. Understanding your audience's attitude toward your subject is especially important when you want to influence their beliefs or move them to action. Because there is a limit to how persuasive any one speech can be, knowing your audience members' attitudes toward your subject will enable you to choose a topic that affects your audience's position without alienating them.

Gather Audience Data

There are four main methods you can use to gather the information you need for an audience analysis:

Figure 11.2

Demographic and Subject-Specific Audience Analysis Questions

Age: Average age and age range?
Educational level: Percentage with high school, college, or postgraduate education?
Gender: Percentages of men and women?
Occupation: Single (or dominant) occupation or industry or diverse occupations and industries?
Socioeconomic background: Percentage lower, medium, upper income?
Ethnicity: Dominant culture of group if any? Other co-cultures represented?
Religion: Religions represented? Is one preponderant?
Community: Single neighborhood, city, state, country? Or mixed?
Language: Common spoken language? Other first languages shared by a significant minority?
Knowledge of the subject: What do they know? How varied is their knowledge?
Attitude toward subject: What do they feel or think about the subject?

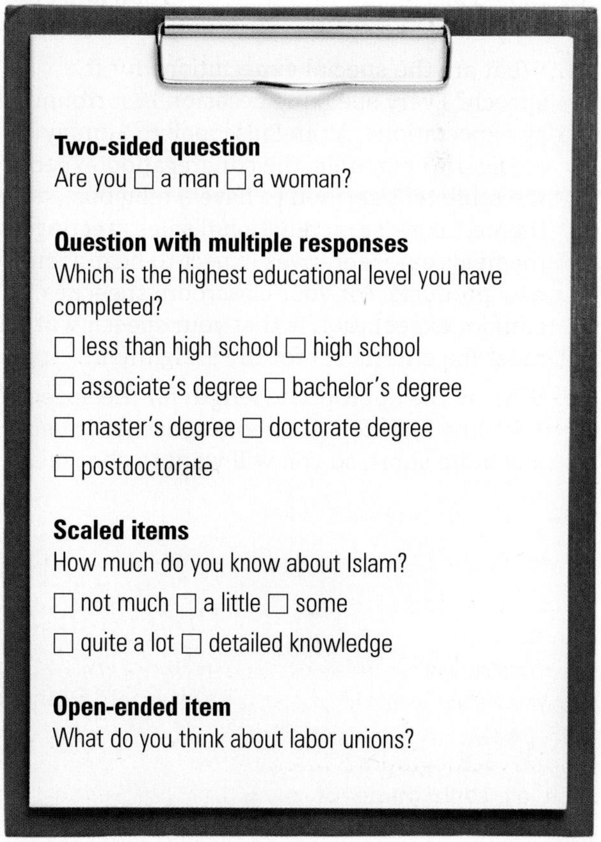

© SERGHEI VELUSCEAC/ISTOCKPHOTO.COM

conducting a survey, observing informally, questioning a representative, and making educated guesses.

Conduct a survey. Although it is not always feasible, the most direct and accurate way to collect audience data is to survey the audience. A survey is a questionnaire designed to gather information from people. Some surveys are done as interviews; others are written forms that are completed by audience members. Survey questions or items can be two-sided items (respondents choose between two answers), multiple response items (respondents choose between several items), scaled items (respondents choose between levels of intensity in a response), or open-ended items (respondents reply in any way they see fit). Figure 11.3 gives examples of each type of question.

Informally observe. If the members of the audience are people whom we know, such as classmates or coworkers, we can learn a lot about them by just watching. For instance, after a couple of classes, we can determine the approximate average age of the class members, the ratio of men to women, and the general cultural makeup. As we listen to classmates talk, we learn about their knowledge of, and interest in, certain issues.

Question a representative. When we are invited to make a speech, we can ask the contact person for

Figure 11.3

Types of Questions

Two-sided question
Are you ☐ a man ☐ a woman?

Question with multiple responses
Which is the highest educational level you have completed?

☐ less than high school ☐ high school

☐ associate's degree ☐ bachelor's degree

☐ master's degree ☐ doctorate degree

☐ postdoctorate

Scaled items
How much do you know about Islam?

☐ not much ☐ a little ☐ some

☐ quite a lot ☐ detailed knowledge

Open-ended item
What do you think about labor unions?

audience information. You should specifically ask for data that are somewhat important for you as you choose a topic or work to adapt your material. For the blogging speech, for example, you would want to know if the audience members have a basic understanding of blogging.

Make educated guesses. If you can't get information in any other way, you can make informed guesses based on indirect data such as the general profile of people in a certain community or the kinds of people likely to attend the event or occasion.

> ## Action Step 1b
> ### Analyzing Your Audience
>
> 1. Decide on the audience characteristics (demographics and subject-specific information that you need in order to choose a topic and adapt to your audience).
> 2. Choose a method for gathering audience information.
> 3. Collect the data.

LO³ Analyze the Setting

The location and occasion make up the speech setting. Answers to several questions about the setting should also guide your topic selection and other parts of your speech planning.

1. **What are the special expectations for the speech?** Every speaking occasion is surrounded by expectations. At an Episcopalian Sunday service, for example, the congregation expects the minister's sermon to have a religious theme. Likewise, at a national sales meeting, the field representatives expect to hear about new products. For your classroom speeches, a major expectation is that your speech will meet the criteria set for the assignment.

2. **What is the appropriate length for the speech?** The time limit for classroom speeches is usually quite short, so you will want to choose a topic that is narrow enough to be accomplished in the brief time allowed. For example, "Two Major Causes of Environmental Degradation" could be presented as a 10-minute speech, but "A History of Human Impact on the Environment" could not. Speakers who speak for more or less time than they have been scheduled can seriously interfere with the program of an event and lose the respect of both their hosts and their audience.

3. **How large will the audience be?** Although audience size may not directly affect the topic you select, it will affect how you adapt your material and how you present the speech. For example, if the audience is small (up to about 50), you can talk without a microphone and move about if you choose to do so. For larger audiences, you might have a microphone that may limit your range of movement.

4. **Where will the speech be given?** Rooms vary in size, shape, lighting, and seating arrangements. Some are a single level, some have stages or platforms, and some have tiered seating. The space affects the speech. For example, in a long narrow room, you may have to speak loudly to be heard in the back row. The brightness of the room and the availability of shades may affect what kinds of visual aids you can use. So you will want to know and consider the layout of the room as you plan your speech. At times, you might request that the room be changed or rearranged so that the space is better suited to your needs.

5. **What equipment is necessary to give the speech?** Would you like to use a microphone, lectern, flip chart, overhead projector and screen, or a hookup for your laptop computer during your speech? If so, you need to check with your host to make sure that the equipment can be made available to you. In some cases, the unavailability of equipment may limit your topic choice. Regardless of what arrangements have been made, however, experienced speakers expect that something may

> ## Action Step 1c
> ### Understanding the Speech Setting
>
> 1. What are the special expectations for the speech?
> 2. What is the appropriate length for the speech?
> 3. How large will the audience be?
> 4. Where will the speech be given?
> 5. What equipment is necessary to give the speech?

© FERENC SZELEPCSENYI/SHUTTERSTOCK

go wrong and are always prepared with alternative plans. For example, although computer slide shows can be very effective, there are often technological glitches that interfere with their use, so many speakers prepare overheads or handouts and bring them along as backup.

LO⁴ Select a Topic

Armed with your topic lists and the information you have collected on your audience and setting, you are ready to select an appropriate topic. Are there some topics on your list that are too simple or too difficult for this audience? Eliminate them. Are some topics likely to bore the audience and you can't think of any way to pique their interest? Eliminate them. How does the audience's demographic profile mesh with each topic? Are some ill suited to this demographic profile? Eliminate them. At the end of this process, you should have several topics that would be appropriate for your audience.

Now consider the setting. Are some of the remaining topics inappropriate for the expectations of the audience or too broad for the time allocated, or do they require equipment that is unavailable in this setting? If so, eliminate them.

From the topics that still remain after considering the audience and the setting, you should choose the one that you would find most enjoyable to share with the audience as your speech topic.

Action Step 1d
Selecting a Topic

Use your responses to Action Steps 1.a, 1.b, and 1.c to complete this step.

1. Write each of the topics that you checked in Action Step 1.a on the lines below:

   _____   _____   _____

   _____   _____   _____

2. Using the information you compiled in Action Step 1.b, the audience analysis, compare each topic to your audience profile. Draw a line through topics that seem less appropriate for your audience.

3. Using the information you compiled in Action Step 1.c, your analysis of the setting, compare the remaining topics to the requirements of the setting. Eliminate topics that seem less suited to the setting.

4. From the topics that remain, choose the one that you would find most enjoyable to present. Circle that topic.

LO⁵ Write a Speech Goal

Once you have chosen your topic, you are ready to identify the general goal of your speech and write a specific goal statement tailored to the audience and setting.

> **general speech goal** the intent of your speech
>
> **specific speech goal** a single statement of the exact response the speaker wants from the audience

Identify Your General Goal

The general goal is the overall intent of the speech. Most speeches generally intend to entertain, inform, or persuade, even though each type can include elements of the other types. Consider the following examples. David Letterman's opening monologue on *Late Night* is intended to entertain, even though it may include material that is persuasive. President Obama's campaign speeches were intended to persuade, even though they may also have been informative. In this book, we focus on the general goals of informing and persuading. These are the kinds of speeches you will most likely present in academic, professional, and community settings.

Phrase a Specific Goal Statement

The specific goal, or specific purpose of your speech, is a single statement that identifies the exact response you want from the audience after they have listened to your speech. A specific goal statement for an informative speech usually specifies whether you want the audience to learn about, understand, or appreciate the topic. "I would like the audience to understand the four major criteria used for evaluating a diamond" is a goal statement for an informative speech. A specific goal statement for a persuasive speech specifies whether you want the audience to accept the belief that you are presenting: "I want my audience to believe that the militarization of space is wrong," or to act a certain way: "I want my audience to donate money to the United Way." Figure 11.4 gives further examples of informative and persuasive speech goals.

To create a well-worded specific goal statement, consider the guidelines that follow:

Write a first draft of your speech goal, using a complete sentence that specifies the response you want from the audience. Julia, who has been

Figure 11.4

Types of Goals

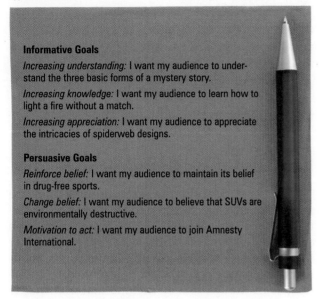

Informative Goals

Increasing understanding: I want my audience to understand the three basic forms of a mystery story.

Increasing knowledge: I want my audience to learn how to light a fire without a match.

Increasing appreciation: I want my audience to appreciate the intricacies of spiderweb designs.

Persuasive Goals

Reinforce belief: I want my audience to maintain its belief in drug-free sports.

Change belief: I want my audience to believe that SUVs are environmentally destructive.

Motivation to act: I want my audience to join Amnesty International.

concerned with and is knowledgeable about the subject of illiteracy, drafts the following statement of her general speech goal: "I want my audience to be informed about the effects of illiteracy." Julia's draft is a complete sentence, and it specifies the response she wants from the audience: to be informed about the effects of illiteracy. Her phrasing tells us that she is planning to give an informative speech.

Revise the draft statement until it focuses clearly on the desired audience reaction. The draft "I want my audience to understand illiteracy" is a good start, but it is extremely broad. Just what is it about illiteracy that Julia wants the audience to understand? She narrows the statement: "I want my audience to understand three effects of illiteracy." This version is more specific than her first draft, but it still does not clearly capture her intention, so she revises it further: "I would like the audience to understand three effects of illiteracy in the workplace." Now the goal is limited by Julia's focus not only on the specific number of effects but also on a specific situation. If Julia wanted to persuade her audience, her specific goal might be "I want my audience to believe that illiteracy in the workplace is a major problem."

Make sure the goal statement contains only one central idea. Suppose Julia had written the following specific goal statement: "I want the audience to understand the nature of illiteracy and innumeracy." This would need to be revised because

it includes two distinct ideas: illiteracy and innumeracy. Although these problems may be related because both make it difficult for people to function in society, the causes of illiteracy and innumeracy are different. It would be difficult to adequately address both within one speech. So Julia would need to realize that this statement includes two topic ideas and should choose between them. If your goal statement includes the word *and*, you may have more than one idea and will need to narrow your focus.

© LINDA & COLIN MCKIE/ISTOCKPHOTO.COM

Action Step 1e
Writing a Specific Goal

Type of speech

1. Write a draft of your general speech goal using a complete sentence that specifies the type of response you want from the audience: to learn about, to understand, or to appreciate the topic.
2. Does it focus on the particular response you want from your audience? Revise it to be more precise.
3. Review the specific goal statement. If it contains more than one idea, select one and redraft your specific goal statement.
4. Test the infinitive phrase. Does the infinitive phrase express the specific audience reaction desired? If not, revise the infinitive phrase.

Write your final wording of the specific goal:

_____

_____

_____

Action Step 2:
Gather and Evaluate Information to Develop the Content of Your Speech

To select and then use the most effective information to support your speech, you must be able to locate and evaluate appropriate sources of information, identify and select the information most relevant to your speech, draw information from multiple cultural perspectives, and then record the information in a way that will help you prepare for and present your speech.

LO⁶ Locate and Evaluate Information Sources

How can you quickly find the best information related to your specific speech goal? It depends. Speakers usually start by assessing their own knowledge, experience, and personal observations. Then they move to secondary resources, which includes information about the topic that has been discovered by other people and is available in public sources. They might do an electronic search for relevant books, articles, general references, and Web sites. Occasionally, when other resources do not have the information needed, they may conduct their own study by doing a survey, interviewing experts, or performing an experiment.

Personal Knowledge, Experience, and Observation

If you have chosen to speak on a topic you know something about, you are likely to have material that you can use as examples and personal experiences in your speech. For instance, musicians have special knowledge about music and instruments, entrepreneurs know about starting up businesses, and marine biologists have an understanding of marine reserves. So Erin, a skilled rock climber, can draw from her own knowledge and experience for her speech "Rappelling Down a Mountain."

For many topics, the knowledge you've gained from experience can be supplemented with careful observation. If, for instance, you were planning to talk about how a small claims court works or how churches help the homeless find shelter and job training, you could learn more by attending small claims sessions or visiting a church's outreach center. By focusing on specific behaviors and taking notes on your observations, you could make a record of specifics to use in your speech.

Sharing your personal knowledge, experience, and observations can also bolster your credibility if you inform your audience about your credentials—your experiences or education that qualifies you to speak with authority on a specific subject. For Erin, establishing her credentials means briefly mentioning her training and expertise as a rock climber before she launches into her observations about unqualified climbers.

Secondary Research

Secondary research is the process of locating information about your topic that has been discovered by other people. Libraries house various sources of secondary research. Most libraries store information about their holdings in electronic databases. Users retrieve the information at computer terminals in the library or over the Internet. If you don't know how to access your school's library resources online, you can call the help desk at your library. If you have difficulty using library search tools, your library probably offers a short seminar or you can ask a research librarian for help. Secondary resources include the following types of materials.

Books

Although books are excellent sources of in-depth material about a topic, most of the information in a book is likely to be at least two years old by the time the book is published. So books are not a good resource if your topic is very new or if you're looking for the latest information on a topic.

Articles

Articles, which may contain more current or highly specialized information on your topic than a book would, are published in periodicals—magazines and journals that appear at regular intervals. The information in periodical articles is often more current than that in books because many periodicals are published weekly, biweekly, or monthly. However, articles don't provide as much in-depth information as you'd find in a book. Articles are often a good source of information for highly specialized topics. Today, most libraries subscribe to electronic databases that

credentials
experience or education that qualifies a person to speak with authority on a specific subject

secondary research
the process of locating information about your topic that has been discovered by other people

periodicals
magazines and journals that appear at fixed intervals

© JOCICALEK/SHUTTERSTOCK

primary research
the process of conducting your own study to acquire information for your speech

index periodical articles. Check with your librarian to learn what electronic indexes your college or university subscribes to.

Newspapers

Newspaper articles are excellent sources of facts about and interpretations of both contemporary and historical issues. Keep in mind, however, that most authors of newspaper articles are journalists who are not experts on the topics they write about. Also keep in mind that journalists sometimes insert their own opinions in an article or present only one side of a controversial issue. So, it is best not to rely solely on newspaper articles for your speech. Most newspapers are available online, which makes them very accessible. Two electronic newspaper indexes that are most useful if they are available to you are (1) *National Newspaper Index*, which indexes five major newspapers: the *New York Times*, the *Wall Street Journal*, the *Christian Science Monitor*, the *Washington Post*, and the *Los Angeles Times*; and (2) *Newsbank*, which provides not only the indexes but also the text of articles from more than 450 U.S. and Canadian newspapers.

Encyclopedias

An encyclopedia can be a good starting point for your research. Encyclopedias give an excellent overview of many subjects and can acquaint you with the basic terminology and ideas associated with a topic. But because encyclopedias provide only overviews, they should never be the sole research base for your speech. Wikipedia, the online collaborative encyclopedia, has become a popular research tool, but it is also a controversial source of information.

Statistical Sources

Statistical sources present numerical information on a wide variety of subjects. When you need facts about demography, continents, heads of state, weather, or similar subjects, access one of the many single-volume sources that report such data. Two of the most popular sources in this category are *The Statistical Abstract of the United States* (available online), which provides numerical information on various aspects of American life, and *The World Almanac and Book of Facts*.

Biographical References

When you need an account of a person's life, you can turn to one of the many biographical references that are available. In addition to full-length biographies and encyclopedia entries, consult such reference books as *Who's Who in America* and *International Who's Who*. Your library may also carry other biographi-

cal references such as *Contemporary Black Biography, Dictionary of Hispanic Biography, Native American Women, Who's Who of American Women, Who's Who Among Asian Americans,* and many more.

Government Documents

If your topic is related to public policy, government documents may provide useful information. Similar documents for other countries, states, and cities may be found by using a search engine.

Internet-Based Resources

In addition to printed resources (many of which you can access online), you may find resources for your speech that are only available on the Internet. For example, you can access electronic databases, bulletin boards, and scholarly and professional electronic discussion groups as well as Web sites and Web pages authored by individuals and groups.

Primary Research

Primary research is the process of conducting your own study to acquire information for your speech. It is much more labor intensive and time consuming than secondary research, and in the professional world it is much more costly. If after making an exhaustive search of secondary sources you cannot locate the information you need you might consider getting it through one of the following primary research methods.

Surveys

You can gather information directly from a group of people through the use of a questionnaire.

Interviews

You can locate an acknowledged expert on your topic and ask for his or her opinions on your topic. The appendix after

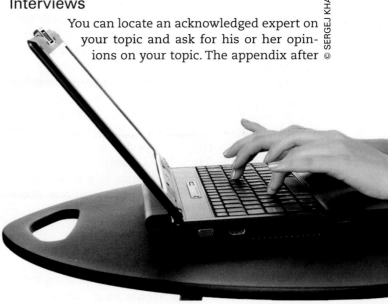

© SERGEJ KHAKIMULLIN/SHUTTERSTOCK

Chapter 8 provides information about conducting interviews.

Experiments

You can design a study to test a hypothesis that you have. Then, based on your analysis, you can report the results in your speech.

LO⁷ Evaluate Sources

Information sources vary in the accuracy, reliability, and validity of the information they present. So before you use the information from a source in your speech, you will want to evaluate it. Four criteria you can use are authority, objectivity, currency, and relevance.

Authority. The first test of a resource is the expertise of its author and/or the reputation of the publishing or sponsoring organization. When the author is named, you can check his or her credentials through biographical references or look on the Internet for a home page listing professional qualifications. Use your library's electronic periodical indexes or check the Library of Congress to see what else the author has published in the field (see *Using Cyber Resources*, 2000).

On the Internet, some information is anonymous or credited to someone whose background is not clear. In these cases, your ability to trust the information depends on evaluating the qualifications of the sponsoring organization. On the Internet, URLs ending in ".gov" (governmental), ".edu" (educational), and ".org" are non-commercial sites with institutional publishers. The URL ".com" indicates that the sponsor is a for-profit organization and may be selling something. If you do not know whether you can trust the source, then do not use the information.

Objectivity. Although all authors have a viewpoint, you will want to be wary of information that is overly slanted. Documents that have been published by business, government, or public interest groups should be carefully scrutinized for obvious biases and good public relations fronts. To evaluate the potential biases in books and articles, read the preface or identify the thesis statement. These often reveal the author's point of view. When evaluating a Web site with which you are unfamiliar, look for its purpose. Most home pages contain a

© ALEXEY STIOP ISTOCKPHOTO.COM

purpose or mission statement (sometimes in a link called *About Us*). Armed with this information, you are in a better position to recognize the biases in the information. Remember, at some level many Web pages can be seen as infomercials, so always be concerned with who created the information and why (Kapoun, 2000).

Currency. In general, newer information is more accurate than older. So when evaluating your sources, be sure to consult the latest information you can find. One of the reasons for using Web-based sources is that they can provide more up-to-date information than printed sources (Munger, Anderson, Benjamin, Busiel, & Pardes-Holt, 2000). But just because a source is found online does not mean that the information is timely. To determine how current the information is, you will need to find out when the book was published, the article was written,

---

Action Step 2a
Locating and Evaluating Information Sources

The goal of this activity is to help you compile a list of potential sources for your speech.

1. Identify gaps in your knowledge that you would like to fill.
2. Identify a person, an event, or a process that you could observe to broaden your personal knowledge base.
3. Brainstorm a list of keywords that are related to your speech goal.
4. Working with your library's catalog, periodical indexes (including InfoTrac College Edition), and general references discussed in this chapter, find and list specific resources that appear to provide information for your speech.
5. Using a search engine, identify organizationally sponsored and personal Web sites that may be sources of information for your speech.
6. Identify a person you could interview for additional information for your speech.
7. Skim the resources you have identified to decide which are likely to be most useful.
8. Evaluate each resource to determine how much faith you can place in the information.

factual statements
statements that can be verified

statistics
numerical facts

examples
specific instances that illustrate or explain a general factual statement

expert opinions
interpretations and judgments made by authorities in a particular subject area

the study was conducted, or the article was placed on the Web or revised. Web page dates are usually listed at the end of the article. If there are no dates listed, you have no way of judging how current the information is.

Relevance. During your research, you will likely come across a great deal of interesting information. Whether that information is appropriate for your speech is another matter. Relevant information is directly related to your topic and supports your main points, making your speech easier to follow and understand. Irrelevant information will only confuse listeners, so you should avoid using it no matter how interesting it is.

LO⁸ Identify and Select Relevant Information

Types of information that you may find in your sources include factual statements, expert opinions, and elaborations.

Factual Statements

Factual statements are those that can be verified. "A recent study confirmed that preschoolers watch an average of 28 hours of television a week" is a statement of of fact that can be verified. One way to verify whether a statement is accurate is to check it against other sources on the same subject. Never use any information that is not carefully documented unless you have corroborating sources. Factual statements may be statistics or examples.

Statistics are numerical facts. "Only five of every ten local citizens voted in the last election" or "The national unemployment rate for May 2009 was 9.4 percent" can provide impressive support for a point, but if statistics are poorly used in a speech, they may be boring and, in some instances, downright deceiving. When you use statistics, follow these guidelines:

- Use only statistics that you can verify to be reliable. Taking statistics from only the most reliable sources and double-checking any startling statistics with another source will guard against the use of faulty statistics.

- Use only timely statistics so your audience will not be misled.

- Use statistics comparatively. You can show growth, decline, gain, or loss by comparing two numbers.

- Use statistics sparingly. A few pertinent numbers are far more effective than a battery of statistics.

- No statistic is completely accurate, and statistics can be manipulated to prove things that a more honest rendering would belie. So before you use a statistic, be sure to evaluate the source and to cross check the method used to collect and interpret the data (Frances, 1994).

Examples are specific instances that illustrate or explain a general factual statement. One or two short examples like the following ones provide concrete detail that makes a general statement more meaningful to the audience: "One way a company increases its power is to buy out another company. Recently, Delta bought out Northwest and thereby became the world's largest airline company" or "Professional billiard players practice many long hours every day. Jennifer Lee practices up to 10 hours a day when she is not in a tournament."

Expert Opinions

Expert opinions are interpretations and judgments made by an authority in a particular subject area. They can help explain what facts mean or put them in perspective. "Watching 28 hours of television

Watching 28 hours of television a week is far too much for young children . . .

© RICK LORD/SHUTTERSTOCK

a week is far too much for young children, but may be OK for adults" and "Having a firewire port on your computer is absolutely necessary" are opinions. Whether they are expert opinions depends on who made the statements. An **expert** is a person who has mastered a specific subject, usually through long-term study, and who is recognized by other people in the field as being a knowledgeable and trustworthy authority.

Elaborations

Both factual information and expert opinions can be elaborated upon through anecdotes and narratives, comparisons and contrasts, or quotable explanations and opinions.

Anecdotes and narratives. Anecdotes are brief, often amusing stories; narratives are accounts, personal experiences, tales, or lengthier stories. Because holding audience interest is important and because audience attention is likely to be captured by a story, anecdotes and narratives are worth looking for or creating. The key to using them is to be sure the point of the story directly addresses the point you are making in your speech. Good stories and narratives may be humorous, sentimental, suspenseful, or dramatic.

Comparisons and contrasts. One of the best ways to give meaning to new ideas or facts is through comparison and contrast. Comparisons illuminate a point by showing similarities, whereas contrasts highlight differences. Although comparisons and contrasts may be literal, like comparing and contrasting the murder rates in different countries or during different eras, they may also be figurative.

- *Figurative comparison:* "In short, living without health insurance is as much of a risk as having uncontrolled diabetes or driving without a safety belt" (Nelson, 2006, p. 24).

- *Figurative contrast:* "If this morning you had bacon and eggs for breakfast, I think it illustrates the difference. The eggs represented 'participation' on the part of the chicken. The bacon represented 'total commitment' on the part of the pig!" (Durst, 1989, p. 325).

Quotations. At times, information you find may be so well stated that you will want to directly quote it in your speech. Because the audience is interested in listening to your ideas and arguments, you should avoid using too many quotations or ones that are too long. But when you find that an author or expert has worded an idea especially well, directly quote it and then verbally acknowledge the person who said or

wrote it. Using quotations or close paraphrases without acknowledging their source is **plagiarism**—the unethical act of representing another person's work as your own.

LO⁹ Draw Information from Multiple Cultural Perspectives

How we perceive facts and what opinions we hold often are influenced by our cultural background. Therefore, it is important to draw information from a variety of cultural perspectives by seeking sources with different cultural orientations and by interviewing experts with diverse cultural backgrounds. For example, when Carrie was preparing for her speech on proficiency testing in grade schools, she purposefully searched for articles written by noted Hispanic, Asian American, African American, and European American authors. In addition, she interviewed two local school superintendents—one from an urban district and one from a suburban district. Because she consciously worked to develop diverse sources of information, Carrie felt confident that her speech would more accurately reflect all sides of the debate on proficiency testing.

LO¹⁰ Record Information

As you find facts, opinions, and elaborations that you want to use in your speech, you need to record the information accurately and keep a careful account of your sources so you can cite them appropriately during your speech.

Prepare Research Cards

How should you keep track of the information you plan to use? Although it may seem easier to record all material from one source on a single sheet of paper (or to photocopy source material), sorting and arranging material is much easier when each item is recorded separately. Recording each piece of information on its own research card allows you to easily

expert
a person who has mastered a specific subject, usually through long-term study

anecdotes
brief, often amusing stories

narratives
accounts, personal experiences, tales, or lengthier stories

comparisons
illuminate a point by showing similarities

contrasts
highlight differences

plagiarism
the unethical act of representing a published author's work as your own

find, arrange, and rearrange individual pieces of information as you prepare your speech.

Make a research card for each factual statement, expert opinion, or elaboration you find. To prepare a research card, begin by writing a keyword or category heading that captures the main idea of this piece of information and identifies the subcategory to which the information belongs. Next, record the specific fact, opinion, or elaboration statement. Any part of the information item that is quoted directly from the source should be enclosed in quotation marks. Finally, record the bibliographic information you will need for your source list.

The exact bibliographic information you record depends on the type of source (such as book, article, or Web site) and the style guide (such as APA or MLA) you are using. Generally, for a book you will record the names of authors, title of the book, the place of publication and the publisher, the date of publication, and the page or pages from which the information is taken. For a periodical or newspaper, you will record the name of the author (if given), the title of the article, the name of the publication, its volume and issue numbers, the date, and the page number from which the information is taken. For online sources, include the URL for the Web site, the heading under which you found the information, the author, the date (if given), and the sponsoring organization or publisher. Be sure to record enough source information so you can relocate the material if you need to. Figure 11.5 provides a sample research card.

The number of sources you will need depends, in part, on the type of speech you are giving and your own expertise. For a narrative/personal experience, you obviously will be the main, if not the only, source. For informative reports and persuasive

Figure 11.5

A Sample Research Card

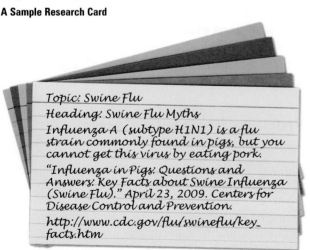

Topic: Swine Flu

Heading: Swine Flu Myths

Influenza A (subtype H1N1) is a flu strain commonly found in pigs, but you cannot get this virus by eating pork.

"Influenza in Pigs: Questions and Answers: Key Facts about Swine Influenza (Swine Flu)." April 23, 2009. Centers for Disease Control and Prevention.

http://www.cdc.gov/flu/swineflu/key_facts.htm

Action Step 2b

Preparing Research Cards: Recording Facts, Opinions, and Elaborations

The goal of this step is to review the source material you identified in Action Step 2.a and to record specific items of information that you might wish to use in your speech.

1. Carefully read all print and electronic sources (including Web site material) you have identified and evaluated as appropriate sources for your speech. Review your notes and any tapes from interviews and observations.

2. As you read an item (fact, opinion, example, illustration, statistic, anecdote, narrative, comparison/contrast, quotation, definition, or description) that you think might be useful in your speech, record it on a research card. If you are using an article from a periodical that you read online, use the periodical research card form.

speeches, however, speakers ordinarily draw from multiple sources. For a five-minute speech on bird flu in which you plan to talk about causes, symptoms, and means of transmission, you might have two or more research cards under each heading. Moreover, the cards should come from a number of different sources. Selecting and using information from several sources helps you develop an original approach to your topic, insures a broader research base, makes it more likely that you will uncover the various opinions related to your topic, and reduces the likelihood that you will plagiarize the ideas of another.

LO¹¹ Cite Sources in Speeches

Although it is important to credit the sources of your information in all of your communication, there are three reasons that it is crucial to cite the sources of your information within your speech. First, speeches, like essays and research papers, are public, so it is plagiarism to present information that you have learned from secondary sources as though it were your own. Second, doing so is also unethical behavior because it prevents the audience from accurately evaluating the source of the information. When a topic is controversial, knowing the source of the information can be critical to the audience's ability to trust it. Third, citing the source of your information adds to your credibility because it demonstrates to the audience that you have studied the topic. You should make a habit of

© SAMUEL KESSLER/ISTOCKPHOTO.COM

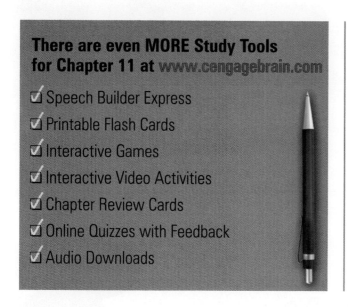

**There are even MORE Study Tools
for Chapter 11 at** www.cengagebrain.com

☑ Speech Builder Express

☑ Printable Flash Cards

☑ Interactive Games

☑ Interactive Video Activities

☑ Chapter Review Cards

☑ Online Quizzes with Feedback

☑ Audio Downloads

using **oral footnotes**, which are references to the original sources, made at the points in the speech where information from those sources is presented. An oral footnote includes enough information for listeners to identify and evaluate the source for themselves.

oral footnote
references to an original source, made at the point in the speech where information from that source is presented

Action Step 2c
Citing Sources

On the back of each research card, write a short phrase that you can use in your speech as an oral footnote.

Figure 11.6

Appropriate Speech Source Citations

Learning Outcomes

LO[1] Describe methods for developing the body of your speech

LO[2] Explain how to create an introduction

LO[3] Explain how to prepare a conclusion

LO[4] Examine guidelines for listing sources

LO[5] Develop a method for reviewing the outline

Organizing Your Speech

© SVEN HOPPE/ISTOCKPHOTO.COM

"Well-constructed speeches have impact."

We often hear speeches that are packed with interesting information and delivered in ways that hold our attention, but when we reflect on what was said, we find it difficult to recall the speaker's main ideas, or even the overall goal of the speech. Although every speech should have an introduction, a body, and a conclusion, not all speeches that have these components are well organized. So, we may listen to a speech and find that even though we have been entertained, the speaker's words have no lasting impact on us.

Well-constructed speeches have impact. When a speech is over, we must remember not only the opening joke or a random story, but we must also remember the main ideas that the speaker presented. In this chapter, we describe the third of the five speech plan action steps. When you have completed this step, you can be confident that your speech not only will maintain your audience's interest but will help your audience understand and remember what you have said.

organizing
the process of selecting and arranging the main ideas and supporting material to be presented in the speech in a manner that makes it easy for the audience to understand

What do you think?

Speeches that are funny are the most memorable.

Strongly Disagree   Strongly Agree
1   2   3   4   5   6   7   8   9   10

Action Step 3:

Organize and Develop Speech Material to Meet the Needs of Your Particular Audience

Organizing, the process of selecting and structuring ideas you will present in your speech, is guided by the audience analysis you conducted during the first step of the speech plan. Your audience will have certain expectations about what you will say and how you will organize it. When the audience's expectations are violated, they may get frustrated and "tune out" or even become hostile.

As you continue your preparation by organizing the information you have gathered, you will (1) develop a thesis statement for the speech tailored to the information needs or persuasive disposition of your audience; (2) select and tailor the speech's main ideas and supporting materials so they are adapted to your particular audience; (3) choose an organizational pattern appropriate to the flow of your ideas; (4) create transitional statements to link main ideas; (5) create an introduction and conclusion to open and close your speech; and (6) prepare a formal sentence outline of the speech so you can be sure that your speech is well structured and your ideas follow an orderly flow.

LO¹ Developing the Body of the Speech

Once you have analyzed the audience, developed a speech goal, and assembled information on your topic, you are ready to craft the body of your

main points
complete sentence representations of the main ideas used in your thesis statement

speech by (a) determining the main points; (b) writing a thesis statement; (c) outlining the body of the speech; (d) selecting and ordering the supporting material (examples, statistics, illustrations, quotations, and so on) that elaborates on or supports each of your main points; and (e) preparing sectional transitions.

 Determine main points

 Write thesis statement

 Outline body of speech

 Select and order supporting material

 Prepare sectional transitions

Determining Main Points

The main points of a speech are the two to five central ideas you want to present, each stated as a complete sentence. You will want to limit the number of main points so that your audience members can keep track of your ideas and so that you can develop each idea with an appropriate amount of supporting material. Usually, the difference between a 5-minute speech and a 25-minute speech with the same speech goal is not the number of main ideas presented but the extent to which each main point is developed.

For some topics and goals, determining the main points is easy. Erin, who plays Division I volleyball for her college, didn't need to do much research for her speech on how to spike a volleyball. And because she would be speaking to a group of athletes, it was easy for her to group the actions into three steps: the proper approach, a powerful swing, and an effective follow-through.

But for other topics and goals, determining main points can be more difficult. For example, Emming wants to speak on choosing a credit card. His specific goal statement is "I want the audience to understand the criteria for choosing a credit card." As he did his research, he uncovered numerous interesting facts related to the topic, but he has had trouble figuring out how to group them. When you find yourself in this situation, you will need to do further work to determine the main ideas you want to present.

How should you proceed? First, list the ideas you have found that relate to your specific goal. Like Emming, you may have a very long list. Second, eliminate ideas that your audience analysis suggests that your audience already understands. Third, see if some of the ideas can be grouped under a broader concept. Fourth, eliminate ideas for which you do not have strong support in the sources you consulted. Fifth, eliminate ideas that might be too complicated for this audience to comprehend in the time you have to explain them. Finally, from the ideas that remain, choose three to five points that are the most important for your audience to understand if you are to accomplish your specific speech goal.

Let's look at how Emming used these steps to identify the main points for his speech on criteria for choosing a credit card. Emming had some thoughts about possible main ideas for the speech, but it wasn't until he completed most of his research, sorted through what he had collected, and thought about it, that he was able to choose his main points.

First, he listed ideas (in this case nine) that were discussed in the research materials he had found about choosing a credit card:

what is a credit card

interest rates

credit ratings

convenience

discounts

annual fee

institutional reputation

reward points

rebates

Second, Emming eliminated the idea "what is a credit card" because he knew that his audience already understood this. This left him with eight ideas—still too many for his speech. Third, Emming noticed that several ideas seemed to be related. "Discounts," "reward points," and "rebates" are all types of incentives that card companies offer to entice people to choose their card. So Emming grouped these three ideas together under the single heading of "incentives." Fourth, Emming noticed that he had uncovered considerable information on interest rates, credit ratings, discounts, annual fees, rebates, and frequent flyer points, but he had very little information on convenience or institutional reputation, so he crossed out those two ideas.

Finally, Emming considered each of the four remaining ideas in light of the five-minute time limit for his speech. He decided to cross out credit ratings because although people's credit ratings influence the types of cards and interest rates for which they might qualify, Emming believed that he could not adequately explain this idea in the short time available. In fact, he believed that explaining credit ratings to this audience might take a lot longer than five minutes and wasn't as basic as some of the other ideas he had listed. When he was finished with his analysis and synthesis, his list looked like this:

This process left Emming with three broad points he could develop in his speech: interest rates, annual fee, and incentives. When you find that you want to talk about a topic that includes numerous forms, types, categories, and so on, follow Emming's steps to reduce the number of your main points to between two and five.

Action Step 3a
Determining Main Points

The goal of this activity is to help you determine three to five main ideas or main points that you will present in your speech.

1. List all the ideas you have found that relate to the specific goal of your speech.
2. If there are more than five:
   a. Draw a line through each idea that you believe the audience already understands, that you have no supporting information for, or that just seems too complicated for the time allowed.
   b. Look for ideas that can be grouped under a larger heading.

From the ideas that remain, choose the two to five that you think will make the best main points for your audience.

Writing a Thesis Statement

A thesis statement is a one- or two-sentence summary of your speech that states your general and specific goals and previews the main points of your speech. Thus, your thesis statement provides a blueprint from which you will organize the body of your speech.

Now let's consider how you arrive at this thesis statement. Recall that Emming determined three main ideas that he wanted to talk about in his speech on choosing a credit card: interest rates, annual fee, and incentives. Based on his general and specific goals and the main points he had determined, Emming was able to write his thesis statement: "Three criteria that you should use to find the most suitable credit card are level of real interest rate, annual fee, and advertised incentives."

thesis statement
a sentence that identifies the topic of your speech and the main ideas you will present

speech outline
a sentence representation of the hierarchical and sequential relationships between the ideas presented in a speech

Action Step 3b
Writing a Thesis Statement

The goal of this activity is to use your specific goal statement and the main points you have identified to develop a well-worded thesis statement for your speech.

1. Write the specific goal you developed in Chapter 11 with Action Step 1.e.
2. List the main points you determined in Action Step 3.a.
3. Now write a complete sentence that includes both your specific goal and your main points.

Outlining the Body of the Speech

Once you have a thesis statement, you can begin to outline your speech. A speech outline is a sentence representation of the hierarchical and sequential relationships between the ideas presented in the speech. Your outline may have three hierarchical levels of information: main points (numbered with Roman numerals), subpoints that support a main point (ordered with capital letters), and sometimes sub-subpoints that support a subpoint (numbered with Arabic numbers). Figure 12.1 shows the general form of the speech outline system.

Writing your main points and subpoints in complete sentences will help you clarify the relationships between main points and subpoints. Once you have worded each main point and determined its relevant subpoints, you will choose a pattern of organization that fits your thesis. The order of your main points will depend on the pattern of organization that you choose.

Wording Main Points

Recall that Emming determined that interest rates, annual fee, and incentives are the three major criteria for finding a suitable credit card and his thesis

© SASHKIN/SHUTTERSTOCK

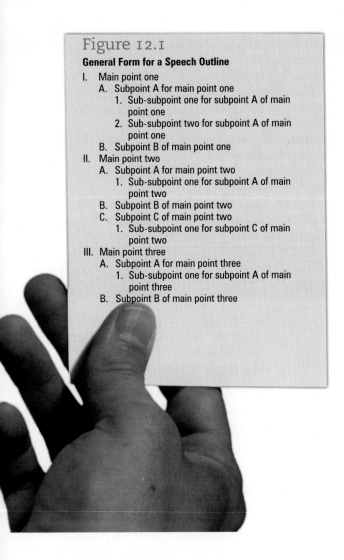

Figure 12.1
General Form for a Speech Outline

I. Main point one
  A. Subpoint A for main point one
    1. Sub-subpoint one for subpoint A of main point one
    2. Sub-subpoint two for subpoint A of main point one
  B. Subpoint B of main point one
II. Main point two
  A. Subpoint A for main point two
    1. Sub-subpoint one for subpoint A of main point two
  B. Subpoint B of main point two
  C. Subpoint C of main point two
    1. Sub-subpoint one for subpoint C of main point two
III. Main point three
  A. Subpoint A for main point three
    1. Sub-subpoint one for subpoint A of main point three
  B. Subpoint B of main point three

Study these statements. Do they seem a bit vague? Sometimes, the first draft of a main point is well expressed and doesn't need additional work. More often, however, our first attempt doesn't quite capture what we want to say. So we need to rework the statements to make them clearer. Testing our main points with two questions can help us as we revise.

Question 1: Is the relationship of each main point statement to the goal statement clearly specified? Based on this question, Emming revised his main points like this:

I. A low interest rate is one criterion that you can use to select a credit card that is suitable for where you are in life.
II. Another criterion that you can use to make sure you find a credit card that is suitable for where you are in life is to look for a card with no annual fee or a very low one.
III. Finding a credit card can also depend on weighing the value of the advertised incentives against the increased annual cost or interest rate, which is the third criterion that you will want to use to be sure that it is suitable for where you are in life.

Question 2: Are the main points parallel in structure? Main points are parallel to each other when their wording follows the same structural pattern, often using the same introductory words. Parallel structure helps the audience recognize main points by recalling a pattern in the wording. Based on this, Emming revised his main points to make them parallel:

I. The first criterion for choosing a credit card is a relatively low interest rate.
II. A second criterion for choosing a credit card is no annual fee or a low annual fee.
III. A third criterion for choosing a credit card is the value of the advertised incentives compared to the increased annual cost or interest rate.

Selecting an Organizational Pattern for Main Points

A speech can be organized in many different ways. Your objective is to use a structure that will help the audience make the most sense of the material. You will want to choose an organizational pattern that makes your main points easy for your audience to understand. Although there are numerous organizational patterns, the four fundamental patterns for beginning speakers are time (or sequential) order, narrative order, topic order, and logical reasons order.

parallel
wording in more than one sentence that follows the same structural pattern, often using the same introductory words

statement was "Three criteria that you should use to find the most suitable credit card are level of real interest rate, annual fee, and advertised incentives." So Emming's first draft of the main points of his speech might look like this:

I. Examining the interest rate is one criterion that you can use to find a credit card that is suitable for where you are in life.
II. Another criterion that you can use to make sure you find a credit card that is suitable for where you are in life is to examine the annual fee.
III. Finding a credit card can also depend on weighing the advertised incentives, which is the third criterion that you will want to use to be sure that it is suitable for where you are in life.

© MIKE FLIPPO/SHUTTERSTOCK

Time order, sometimes called *sequential order* or *chronological order*, arranges main points by a chronological sequence or by steps in a process. When you are explaining how to do something, how to make something, how something works, or how something happened, you will want to use time order. Erin's audience will find it easiest to understand the process of spiking a volleyball if she uses time order for her main points (good approach, powerful swing, good follow-through). Imagine how difficult it would be for her audience if Erin began by talking about a powerful swing, then discussed a good follow-through, and ended by describing a good approach. Could her audience understand her point? Probably. But they would have to work much harder than if she ordered the topics sequentially. Let's look at another example of time order.

Thesis statement: The four steps involved in developing a personal network are to analyze your current networking potential, to position yourself in places for opportunity, to advertise yourself, and to follow up on contacts.

I.   First, analyze your current networking potential.
II. Second, position yourself in places for opportunity.
III. Third, advertise yourself.
IV. Fourth, follow up on contacts.

Although the use of "first," "second," and so on, is not a requirement when using a time order, their inclusion helps audience members keep track of the sequence.

Narrative order dramatizes the thesis with a story or series of stories that includes characters, settings, and a plot. While a narrative may be presented in chronological order, it may also use a series of flash backs or flash forwards to increase the dramatic effect. The main points in a narrative may be the events in a single story that highlights the thesis, or the main points may be individual stories, each of which dramatizes the thesis. Narrative order is a particularly effective way of developing a thesis when you tell stories that are emotionally compelling. Lonna wanted her audience to understand how AIDS affects the lives of survivors, so she chose to develop this thesis by using a narrative order to tell her personal story.

Thesis statement: Today, I want you to understand what it is like to live with AIDS. So I am going to

share the story of my life before contracting AIDS, my life today with AIDS, and my future plans knowing that I have AIDS.

I.   My life before I contracted AIDS was pretty typical for a middle-class white girl.
II. My life today is anything but typical as I balance my schoolwork and social life with weekly visits to the doctor and daily physical and drug therapy.
III. My future life plans have changed dramatically because I have AIDS.

Here's how Lonna could also use a narrative order that shares several stories:

Thesis statement: Today, I want you to understand what it is like to live with AIDS. So I am going to share the stories of Robert, Emma, and me.

I.   Robert's story is about a 27-year-old store manager with AIDS.
II. Emma's story is about a 3-year-old toddler with AIDS.
III. My story is about a 20-year-old college student with AIDS.

Topic order arranges the main points of the speech by categories or divisions of a subject. This is a common way of ordering main points because nearly any subject may be subdivided or categorized in many different ways. The order of the topics may go from general to specific, least important to most important, or some other logical sequence. In the following example, the most important point is presented last and the second most important point is presented first, which is the order that the speaker believes is most suitable for the audience and speech goal.

Thesis statement: To maintain good health, let's discuss three proven methods for ridding our bodies of harmful toxins: staying hydrated, reducing animals foods, and eating natural whole foods.

I.   One proven method for ridding our bodies of harmful toxins is reducing our intake of animal products.

© FELIXCO/SHUTTERSTOCK

time (or sequential) order organizing the main points by a chronological sequence, or by steps in a process

narrative order dramatizes the thesis using a story or series of stories that includes characters, settings, and a plot

topic order organizing the main points of the speech by categories or divisions of a subject

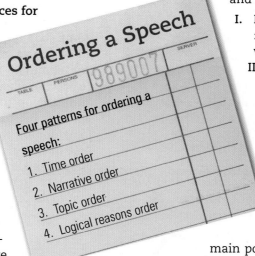

Ordering a Speech

989007

Four patterns for ordering a speech:

1. Time order
2. Narrative order
3. Topic order
4. Logical reasons order

II. A second proven method for ridding our bodies of harmful toxins is eating more natural whole foods.

III. A third proven method for ridding our bodies of harmful toxins is keeping well hydrated.

Logical reasons order is used when the main points are the rationale or proof that supports the thesis.

Action Step 3c
Organizing and Outlining the Main Points of Your Speech

The goal of this activity is to help you phrase and order your main points.

1. Write your thesis statement (Action Step 3.b).
2. Underline the two to five main points determined for your thesis statement.
3. For each underlined item, write one sentence that summarizes what you want your audience to know about that idea.
4. Review the main points as a group.
   a. Is the relationship of each main point statement to the goal statement clearly specified? If not, revise.
   b. Are the main points parallel in structure? If not, revise.
5. Choose an organizational pattern for your main points, and write them in this order. Place an "I" before the main point that you make first, a "II" before your second point, and so on.

Thesis statement: Donating to the United Way is appropriate because your one donation can be divided among many charities, you can stipulate which specific charities you wish to support, and a high percentage of your donation goes to charities.

I. **When you donate to the United Way, your one donation can be divided among many charities.**

II. **When you donate to the United Way, you can stipulate which charities you wish to support.**

III. When you donate to the United Way, you know that a high percentage of your donation will go directly to the charities you've selected.

Although these four organizational patterns are the most basic ones, in Chapters 15 and 16 you will be introduced to several other patterns that are appropriate for informative and persuasive speaking.

Selecting and Outlining Supporting Material

Although the main points provide the basic structure or skeleton of your speech, whether your audience understands, believes, or appreciates what you have to say usually depends on your supporting material—the information you use to develop the main points. You can identify supporting material by sorting your research cards into piles that correspond to each of your main points. The goal is to see what information you have to develop each point. When Emming sorted his research cards, he discovered that for his first point, interest rates, he had the following support:

Once you have listed each of the supporting items, look for relationships between them that will allow you to group ideas under a broader heading and eliminate ideas that don't really belong. Then select the ideas that best support the main idea and develop them into complete sentences. When Emming did this, he came up with two statements for grouping the supporting information about his first main point. These two statements became his subpoints. He also had material that supported each subpoint. Here is Emming's expanded outline for his first main point:

© ISTOCKPHOTO.COM

- Most "zero percent" cards carry an average of 8 percent after a specified 0 percent interest period.
- Some cards carry as much as 21 percent after the first year.
- Some cards offer a grace period.
- Department store interest rates are often higher than bank rates.
- *Variable rate* means that the interest rate can change from month to month.
- Even fixed rates on some cards can be raised to as much as 32 percent if you make a late payment.
- *Fixed rate* means the interest rate will stay the same.
- Many companies offer "zero percent" for up to 12 months.
- Some companies offer "zero percent" for a few months.

I. The first criterion for choosing a credit card is a low interest rate.
   A. Interest rates are the percentages that a company charges you to carry a balance on your card past the due date.
      1. Most credit cards carry an average of 8 percent after a specified 0 percent interest period.
      2. Some cards carry as much as 21 percent after the first year.
      3. Many companies quote low rates (0%–3%) for a specific period.
   B. Interest rates can be variable or fixed.
      1. A variable rate means that the percent charged can vary from month to month.
      2. A fixed rate means that the rate will stay the same.
      3. Even a card with a fixed rate can be raised to as much as 32 percent if you make a late payment.

© OPTIMARC/SHUTTERSTOCK

The outline includes the supporting points of a speech, but it does not include all the development of them. For instance, Emming could use personal experiences, examples, illustrations, anecdotes, statistics, or quotations to elaborate on main points and subpoints. But these are not detailed on the outline. Emming will choose these developmental materials later as he considers how to verbally and visually adapt to his audience.

Preparing Section Transitions and Signposts

Once you have outlined your main points, subpoints, and potential supporting material, you will want to consider how you will move smoothly from one main point to another. **Transitions** are words, phrases, or sentences that show the relationship between or bridge two ideas. Transitions act like tour guides, leading the audience from point to point through the speech. Good transitions are important in writing, but they are even more important in speaking. If listeners get lost or think they have missed something, they cannot check back as they can when reading. Transitions can come in the form of section transitions or signposts.

Section transitions are complete sentences that show the relationship between or bridge major parts of the speech. They may summarize what has just

---

Action Step 3d
Selecting and Outlining Supporting Material

The goal of this activity is to help you develop and outline your supporting material. Complete the following steps for each of your main points.

1. List the main point.
2. Using your research cards, list the key information related to that main point.
3. Analyze that information and cross out items that seem less relevant or don't fit.
4. Look for items that seem related and can be grouped under a broader heading.
5. Try to group information until you have between two and five supporting points for the main point.
6. Write those supporting subpoints in full sentences.
7. Write the supporting sub-subpoints in full sentences.
8. Repeat this process for all main points.
9. Write an outline using Roman numerals for main points, capital letters for supporting points, and Arabic numbers for material related to supporting points.

been said or preview the next main idea. For example, suppose Noel has just finished the introduction of his speech on what it's like to be in a color guard and is now ready to launch into his main points. Before stating his first main point, he might say, "There are many benefits to participating in a color guard, one of which is the physical benefits you get from the workouts." When his listeners hear this transition, they are signaled to mentally prepare to listen to and remember the first main point. When he finishes his first main point, he will use another section transition to signal that he is finished speaking about the first main point and is moving on to the second main point: "Now that we understand some of the physical benefits, we can move on to some of the friendship benefits."

Section transitions are important for two reasons. First, they help the audience follow the organization of ideas in the speech. If every member of the audience were able to pay complete attention to every word, then perhaps section transitions would not be needed. But our attention rises and falls during a speech, so we often find ourselves wondering where we are. Section transitions give us a mental jolt and say, "Pay attention." Second, section transitions are

transitions
words, phrases, or sentences that show the relationship between or bridge ideas

section transition
a complete sentence that shows the relationship between or bridges major parts of the speech

signposts
short word or phrase transitions that connect pieces of supporting material to the main point or subpoint they address

important in helping us retain information. We may remember something that was said once in a speech, but our retention is likely to increase markedly if we hear something more than once.

In a speech, if we forecast main points, then state each main point, and use section transitions between each point, audiences are more likely to follow and remember the organization. To help remember and use section transitions, write them in complete sentences on your speech outline.

Signposts are single words or phrases that connect pieces of supporting material to their main point or subpoint. Signposts are briefer than section transitions, and their only goal is to show relationships among or emphasize important supporting material. Sometimes signposts number ideas: *first, second, third,* and *fourth.* Sometimes they help the audience focus on a key idea: *foremost, most important,* or *above all.* Signposts can also be used to introduce an explanation: *to illustrate, for example, in other words, essentially,* or *to clarify.* Signposts can also signal that a lengthy anecdote, or even the speech itself, is coming to an end: *in short, finally, in conclusion,* or *to summarize.* Just as section transitions serve as the glue that holds your big-picture main points together, signposts connect your subpoints and supporting material within each main point.

LO² Creating the Introduction

Once you have developed the body of the speech, you can decide how to begin your speech. The introduction of your speech establishes your relationship with your audience, so it is worth your time to develop two or three different introductions and then select the one that seems best for this particular audience. Although your introduction may be very short, it should gain the audience's attention and motivate them to listen to all that you have to say. An introduction is generally no more than 10 percent of the length of the entire speech, so for a five-minute speech (approximately 750 words), an introduction of about 30 seconds (approximately 60–85 words) is appropriate.

An effective introduction achieves three goals: it gains attention, it points out how your topic is

Action Step 3e
Preparing Section Transitions

The goal of this exercise is to help you prepare section transitions. Section transitions appear as parenthetical statements before or after each main point. Using complete sentences:
1. Write a transition from your first main point to your second.
2. Write a transition from each remaining main point to the one after it.
3. Add these transitional statements to your outline.

relevant to the listener, and it reveals your thesis statement (specific speech goal and main points). In addition, effective introductions can help you begin to establish your credibility, set the tone for the speech, and create a bond of goodwill between you and the audience.

Gaining Attention

An audience's physical presence does not guarantee that people will actually listen to your speech. Your first goal, then, is to create an opening that will win your listeners' attention by arousing their curiosity and motivating them to continue listening. Although your introductions are limited only by your imagination, let's look at several techniques you can use to get your audience's attention and also to stimulate their interest in what you have to say: startling statements, questions, jokes, personal references, quotations, stories, and suspense.

Startling Statements

A startling statement is a sentence or two that grabs your listeners' attention by shocking them in some way. Because they were shocked, audience members stop what they were doing or thinking about and focus on the speaker. Chris used a startling statement to get his listeners' attention for his speech about how automobile emissions contribute to global warming:

Look around. Each one of you is sitting next to a killer. That's right. You are sitting next to a cold-blooded killer. Before you think about jumping up and running out of this room, let me explain. Everyone who drives an automobile is a killer of the environment. Every time you turn the key to your ignition, you are helping to destroy our precious surroundings.

© REGIEN PAASSEN/SHUTTERSTOCK

Once Chris's startling statement grabbed the attention of his listeners, he went on to state his speech goal and preview his main points.

Rhetorical and Direct Questions

Questions encourage the audience to think about something related to your topic. Questions can be *rhetorical* or *direct*. A rhetorical question seeks a mental rather than a direct response. Notice how a student began her speech on counterfeiting with three short, rhetorical questions:

> **What would you do with this $20 bill if I gave it to you? Take your friend to a movie? Treat yourself to a pizza and drinks? Well, if you did either of these things, you could get in big trouble—this bill is counterfeit! Today I want to explain the extent of counterfeiting in America and what our government is doing to curb it.**

Unlike a rhetorical question, a direct question demands an overt response from the audience, usually by a show of hands. For example, here's how Stephanie introduced her speech on seatbelt safety:

> **By a show of hands, how many of you drove or rode in an automobile to get here today? Of those of you who did, how many of you actually wore your seatbelt?**

Direct questions get audience attention because they require a physical response. However, getting listeners to actually respond can sometimes pose a challenge.

Jokes

A joke is an anecdote or a piece of wordplay designed to be funny and make people laugh. To get audience attention, a joke needs to meet the "three-r test": it must be realistic, relevant, and repeatable (Humes, 1988). In other words, the joke can't be too far-fetched, unrelated to the speech purpose, or potentially offensive to some listeners. For example, one of your authors gave a speech recently about running effective meetings to a group of business professionals. She began with, "As many of you know, I'm a college professor, so I just couldn't resist giving you a quiz." She then handed out a 12-item personal-learning-styles inventory to the audience members. As she distributed it, she explained, "The nice thing about *this* quiz though is that you can't be wrong. You'll all get 100 percent." The audience laughed with relief. Be careful with humorous attention-getters—and consider how you will handle the situation if nobody laughs.

Personal References

A **personal reference** is a brief account of something that happened to you or a hypothetical situation that listeners can imagine themselves in. In addition to getting attention, a personal reference can engage listeners as active participants. A personal reference opening, like this one, may be suitable for a speech of any length:

> **Say, were you panting when you got to the top of those four flights of stairs this morning? I'll bet there were a few of you who vowed you're never going to take a class on the top floor of this building again. But did you ever stop to think that maybe the problem isn't that this class is on the top floor? It just might be that you are not getting enough exercise.**

Quotations

A **quotation** is a comment made by and attributed to someone other than the speaker. A particularly vivid or thought-provoking quotation can make an excellent introduction to a speech of any length, especially if you can use your imagination to relate the quotation to your topic. For instance, notice how Sally Mason, provost at Purdue University, used a quotation to get the attention of her audience, members of the Lafayette, Indiana, YWCA:

> **There is an ancient saying, "May you live in interesting times." It is actually an ancient curse. It might sound great to live in interesting times. But interesting times are times of change and even turmoil. They are times of struggle. They are exciting. But, at the same time, they are difficult. People of my generation have certainly lived through interesting times and they continue today. (Mason, 2007, p. 159)**

rhetorical question
a question seeking a mental rather than a vocal response

direct question
a question that demands an overt response from the audience, usually by a show of hands

joke
an anecdote or a piece of wordplay designed to be funny and make people laugh

personal reference
a brief account of something that happened to you or a hypothetical situation that listeners can imagine themselves in

quotation
a comment made by and attributed to someone other than the speaker

© MARGO HARRISON/SHUTTERSTOCK

© CATHLEEN CLAPPER/ISTOCKPHOTO.COM

story
an account of something that has happened (actual) or could happen (hypothetical)

suspense
wording your attention-getter so that it generates uncertainty and excites the audience

listener relevance link
a statement of how and why your speech relates to or might affect your audience

Stories

A story is an account of something that has happened (actual) or could happen (hypothetical). Most people enjoy a well-told story, so a story can make a good attention getter. One drawback of stories is that they can be lengthy. So use a story only if it is short or if you can abbreviate it to make it appropriate for your speech length. Matt used a story to get audience attention for his speech about spanking as a form of discipline:

> One rainy afternoon, four-year-old Billy was playing "pretend" in the living room. He was Captain Jack Sparrow, staving off the bad guys with his amazing sword-fighting skills. Then it happened. Billy knocked his mother's very expensive china bowl off the table. Billy hung his head and began to cry. He knew what was coming, and sure enough it did. The low thud of his mother's hand on his bottom brought a sting to his behind and a small yelp from his mouth. Billy got a spanking.

Suspense

To create suspense, word your attention-getter so that it generates uncertainty and excites the audience. You have created suspense when your audience wonders, "What is she leading up to?" A suspenseful opening is especially valuable when your audience is not particularly interested in hearing about your topic. Consider the attention-getting value of this introduction:

> It costs the United States more than $116 billion per year. It has cost the loss of more jobs than a recession. It accounts for nearly 100,000 deaths a year. I'm not talking about cocaine abuse—the problem is alcoholism. Today I want to show you how we can avoid this inhumane killer by abstaining from it.

By putting the problem, alcoholism, at the end, the speaker encourages the audience to try to anticipate the answer. And because the audience may well be thinking "narcotics," the revelation that the answer is alcoholism is likely to make them interested in hearing what the speaker has to say.

Establishing Listener Relevance

Even if you successfully get the attention of your listeners, to *keep* their attention you will need to motivate them to listen to your speech. You can do this by creating a clear **listener relevance link**, a statement of how and why your speech relates to or might affect your audience. Sometimes your attention-getting statement will serve this function, but if it doesn't, you will need to provide a personal connection between your topic and your audience. Notice how Tiffany created a listener relevance link for her speech about being a vegetarian by asking her audience to consider the topic in relation to their own lives:

> Although a diet rich in eggs and meat was once the norm in this country, more and more of us are choosing a vegetarian lifestyle to help lower blood pressure, reduce cholesterol, and even help prevent the onset of some diseases. So as I describe my experience, you may want to consider how *you* could alter your diet.

When creating a listener relevance link, answer these questions: Why should my listeners care about what I'm saying? In what way(s) might they benefit from hearing about it? How might my speech address my listeners' needs or desires for such things as health, wealth, well-being, self-esteem, or success?

Stating the Thesis

Because audiences want to know what your speech is going to be about, it's important to state your thesis, which will introduce them to the specific goal and main points of your speech. For his speech about romantic love, after Miguel gained the audience's attention, he introduced his thesis, "In the next five minutes, I'd like to explain to you that romantic love consists of three elements: passion, intimacy, and commitment."

Stating main points in the introduction is necessary unless you have some special reason for not revealing the details of the thesis. For instance, after getting the attention of his audience, Miguel might say, "In the next five minutes, I'd like to explain the three aspects of romantic love," a statement that specifies the number of main points but leaves stating specifics for transition statements immediately preceding main points. Now let's consider three other goals you might have for your introduction.

Establishing Your Credibility

If someone hasn't formally introduced you before you speak, the audience members are going to wonder who you are and why they should pay attention to what you have to say. So another goal of the introduction may be to begin to build your credibility. For instance, it would be natural for an audience to question Miguel's qualifications for speaking on the topic of romantic love. So after his attention-getting statement, he might say, "As a child development and family science major, last semester I took an interdisciplinary seminar on romantic love, and I am now doing an independent research project on commitment in relationships." Remember that your goal is to highlight why you are a credible speaker on this topic, but not to imply that you are *the* or even *a* final authority on the subject.

Setting a Tone

The introductory remarks may also reflect the emotional tone that is appropriate for the topic. A humorous opening will signal a lighthearted tone; a serious opening signals a more thoughtful or somber tone. For instance, a speaker who starts with a rib-tickling story is putting the audience in a lighthearted mood. If that speaker then says, "Now let's turn to the subject of abortion [or nuclear war, or global warming]," the audience will be confused by the introduction that signaled a far different type of subject.

Creating a Bond of Goodwill

In your first few words, you may also establish how your audience will feel about you as a person. If you're enthusiastic, warm, and friendly and give a sense that what you're going to talk about is in the audience's best interest, it will make them feel more comfortable about spending time listening to you.

For longer speeches, you will have more time to accomplish all five goals in the introduction. But for shorter speeches, like those that you are likely to be giving in class, you will first focus on getting attention, establishing listener relevance, and stating the thesis; then you will use very brief comments to try to build your credibility, establish an appropriate tone, and develop goodwill.

Action Step 3f
Writing Speech Introductions

The goal of this activity is to create choices for how you will begin your speech.

1. For the speech body you outlined earlier, write three different introductions—using a startling statement, rhetorical or direct question, joke, personal reference, quotation, story, or suspense—that you believe meet the goals of effective introductions and that you believe would set an appropriate tone for your speech goal and audience.
2. Of the three you drafted, which do you believe is the best? Why?
3. Next, plan how you will introduce your thesis statement.
4. Develop a very short statement that will establish your credibility.
5. Consider how you might establish goodwill during the introduction.
6. Write that introduction in outline form.

LO³ Crafting the Conclusion

Shakespeare said, "All's well that ends well." A strong conclusion will summarize the main ideas and will leave the audience with a vivid impression of what they have learned. Even though the conclusion is a relatively short part of the speech—seldom more than 5 percent (35 to 40 words for a five-minute speech)—it is important that your conclusion be carefully planned. It should achieve two major goals: summarize your speech goal and main points and provide a clincher that leaves a vivid impression of your message in the minds of your audience or compels them to action.

As with your speech introduction, you should prepare two or three conclusions and then choose the one you believe will be the most effective with your audience.

Summary

An effective speech conclusion will include a restatement of your speech goal and summary of the main points. An appropriate summary for an informative speech on how to improve your grades might be, "So I hope you now understand [informative goal] that three techniques to help you improve your grades are to attend classes regularly, to develop a positive attitude toward the course, and to study systematically [main points]." A short ending for a persuasive speech on why you should lift weights might be, "So remember that three major reasons why you should consider lifting weights [persuasive goal] are to improve your appearance, to improve your health, and to accomplish

clincher
a one- or two-sentence
statement that provides
a sense of closure by
driving home the impor-
tance of your speech in
a memorable way

appeal
describes the behavior
you want your listeners
to follow after they have
heard your arguments

both with a minimum of effort [main points]."

Clincher

Although summaries help you achieve the first goal of an effective conclusion, you'll need to develop additional material to achieve the second goal: leaving the audience with a vivid impression or appealing to action. You can achieve this goal with a clincher—a one- or two-sentence statement that provides a sense of closure by driving home the importance of your speech in a memorable way. Very often, effective clinchers also achieve closure by referring back to the introductory comments in some way. You can provide closure and create vivid impressions using any of the attention-getters described earlier in this chapter. For example, in Tiffany's conclusion to her speech about being a vegetarian, she mentioned the personal reference she made in her introduction about a vegetarian Thanksgiving dinner:

> So now you know why I made the choice to become a vegetarian and how this choice affects my life today. As a vegetarian, I've discovered a world of food I never knew existed. Believe me, I am salivating just thinking about the meal I have planned for this Thanksgiving: fennel and blood orange salad; followed by baked polenta layered with tomato, Fontina, and Gorgonzola cheeses; an acorn squash tart, marinated tofu; and with what else but pumpkin pie for dessert!

Sounds good, doesn't it? Clinchers with vivid imagery are effective because they leave listeners with a picture imprinted in their minds.

The appeal to action is a common clincher for a persuasive speech. The appeal describes the behavior that you want your listeners to follow after they have heard your arguments. Notice how David M. Walker, former comptroller general of the United States, concluded his speech on fiscal responsibility with a strong appeal to action:

> The truth is that all sectors of society have a dog in this fiscal fight and transformation effort. If government stays on its current course, we'll

all end up paying a big price, especially our kids and grandkids.

Over its 200-plus years of existence, the United States has faced many great challenges. We've always risen to those challenges, and I'm confident we'll eventually do so this time as well. After all, it's always a mistake to underestimate American resolve when we set our minds to accomplish something.

But we need to act, and act soon. Baby boomers like myself are on course to become the first generation of Americans who leave things in worse shape than when we found them. Fortunately, such a legacy isn't carved in stone. Turning things around won't be easy, and it's not going to happen overnight. But we all need to be part of the solution. By applying our collective energy, expertise, and experience to looming problems; by making some difficult decisions; and by accepting some degree of shared sacrifice, we can ensure a brighter future for this great nation, for our children and grandchildren, and for those who will follow them. (Walker, 2006, p. 762)

All's well that ends well.

© STEVEN WYNN/ISTOCKPHOTO.COM

Action Step 3g
Creating Speech Conclusions

The goal of this activity is to help you create choices for how you will conclude your speech.

1. For the speech body you outlined earlier, write three different conclusions that review important points you want the audience to remember and leave the audience with vivid imagery or an emotional appeal.
2. Which do you believe is the best? Why?
3. Write that conclusion in outline form.

LO⁴ Listing Sources

Regardless of the type or length of speech, you'll want to prepare a list of the sources you are going to use in the speech. Although you may be required to prepare this list for the speeches you give in this course and other courses you take, in real settings this list will enable you to direct audience members to the specific source of the information you have used as well as allow you to quickly find the information at a later date. The two standard methods of organizing source lists are (1) alphabetically by the author's last name or (2) by content category, with items listed alphabetically by author within each category. For speeches with a short list, the first method is efficient. But for long speeches with a lengthy source list, it is helpful to group sources by content categories.

There are many formal bibliographic style formats you can use in citing sources (for example, MLA, APA, Chicago, CBE). The "correct" form differs by professional or academic discipline. Check to see if your instructor has a preference about which style you use for this class.

Regardless of the particular style, however, the specific information you need to record differs somewhat, depending on whether the source is a book, a periodical, a newspaper, or an Internet source or Web site. The elements that are essential to all are author, title of publication, date of publication, and page numbers. Figure 12.2 gives American Psychological Association (APA) citations for the most commonly used sources.

Action Step 3.h helps you compile a list of sources used in your speech. Figure 12.3 gives an example of this activity completed by a student in this course.

LO⁵ Reviewing the Outline

Now that you have created all of the parts of the outline, it is time to put them together in complete outline form and edit them to make sure the outline is well organized and well worded. Use this checklist to complete the final review of the outline before you move into adaptation and rehearsal.

1. *Have I used a standard set of symbols to indicate structure?* Main points are indicated by Roman numerals, major subdivisions by capital letters, minor subheadings by Arabic numerals, and further subdivisions by lowercase letters.

2. *Have I written main points and major subdivisions as complete sentences?* Complete sentences help you to see (1) whether each main point actually develops your speech goal and (2) whether the wording makes your intended point. Unless the key ideas are written out in full, it will be difficult to follow the next guidelines.

3. *Do main points and major subdivisions each contain a single idea?* This guideline ensures that the development of each part of the speech will be relevant to the point. Thus, rather than

   I. **The park is beautiful and easy to get to.**

   divide the sentence so that both parts are separate:

Figure 12.2

Examples of the APA Citation Form for Speech Sources	
Book	Miller, R. B. (2004). *The five paths to persuasion: The art of selling your message.* New York: Warner Business Books.
Edited book	Janzen, R. (2003). Five paradigms of ethnic relations. In L. Samovar & R. Porter (Eds.), *Intercultural communication* (10th ed.) (pp. 36–42) Belmont, CA: Wadsworth.
Academic journal	Barge, J. K. (2004). Reflexivity and managerial practice. *Communication Monographs, 71* (March), 70–96.
Magazine	Krauthammer, C. (2003, September 22). What makes the Bush haters so mad? *Time,* 84.
Newspaper	Cohen, R. (2003, September 17). Wall Street scandal: Whatever the market will bear. *The Cincinnati Enquirer,* p. C6.
Electronic article based on print source	Friedman, T. L. (2003, September 25). Connect the dots. *The New York Times.* Retrieved from http://www.nytimes.com/2003/09/25/opinion/25FRIED.html
Electronic article from Internet-only publication	Osterweil, N., & Smith, M. (2003, September 24). Does stress cause breast cancer? *Web M.D. Health.* Retrieved from http://my.webmd.com/contents/article/74/89170.htm?z3734_00000_1000_ts_01
Electronic article retrieved from database	Grabe, M. (2005). Voluntary use of online lecture notes: Correlates of note use and note use as an alternative to class attendance. *Computers and Education, 44,* 409–421. Retrieved from ScienceDirect.
Movie	Bruckheimer, J. (Producer), & Verbinksi, G. (Director). (2006). *Pirates of the Caribbean: Dead man's chest* [Motion picture]. United States: Walt Disney Pictures.
Television program	Greenberg, D. Z., & Schlattmann, T. (Writers), & Gordon, K. (Director). (2006). Truth be told [Television series episode]. In Manos, J., Jr. (Executive producer), *Dexter.* New York: Showtime Networks.
Music recording	Nirvana. (1991). Smells like teen spirit. On *Nevermind* [CD]. Santa Monica, CA: Geffen.
Personal interview	APA style dictates that personal interviews are not included in a reference list. Rather, cite this type of source orally in your speech, mentioning the name of the person you interviewed and the date of the interview.

I. **The park is beautiful.**

II. **The park is easy to get to.**

The two-point example sorts out distinct ideas so that the speaker can line up supporting material with confidence that the audience will see and understand its relationship to the main points.

4. *Does each major subdivision relate to or support its major point?* This principle, called subordination, insures that you don't wander off point and confuse your audience. For example:

Action Step 3h
Compiling a List of Sources

The goal of this activity is to help you record the list of sources that you used in the speech.

1. Review your research cards, separating those with information you have used in your speech from those you have not.
2. List the sources of information used in the speech by copying the bibliographic information recorded on the research cards.
3. For short lists, organize your list alphabetically by the last name of the first author. Be sure to follow the form shown in Figure 12.2. If you did not record some of the bibliographic information on your research card, you will need to revisit the library, database, or other source to find it.

I. Proper equipment is necessary for successful play.

    A. Good gym shoes are needed for maneuverability.

    B. Padded gloves will help protect your hands.

    C. A lively ball provides sufficient bounce.

    D. And a good attitude doesn't hurt.

Notice that the main point deals with equipment. A, B, and C (shoes, gloves, and ball) all relate to the main point. But D, attitude, is not equipment and should appear under some other main point, if at all.

5. *Are potential subdivision elaborations indicated?* Recall that it is the subdivision elaborations that help to build the speech. Because you don't know how long it might take you to discuss these elaborations, it is a good idea to include more than you are likely to use. During rehearsals, you may discuss each a different way.

Figure 12.3

Sample List of Sources

Dixon, D. (1992). *The practical geologist.* New York: Simon & Schuster.

Klein, C. (1993). *Manual of mineralogy* (2nd ed.) New York: Wiley.

Montgomery, C. W. (1997). *Fundamentals of geology* (3rd ed.) Dubuque, IA: Brown.

© ISTOCKPHOTO.COM

6. *Does the outline include no more than one-third the total number of words anticipated in the speech?* An outline is only a skeleton of the speech—not a complete manuscript with letters and numbers attached. The outline should be short enough to allow you to experiment with different methods of development during practice periods and to adapt to audience reaction during the speech itself. An easy way to judge whether your outline is about the right length is to estimate the number of words that you are likely to be able to speak during the actual speech and compare this to the number of words in the outline (counting only the words in the outline minus speech goal, thesis statement, headings, and list of sources). Because approximate figures are all you need, to compute the approximate maximum words for your outline, start by assuming a speaking rate of 160 words per minute. (Last term, the speaking rate for the majority of speakers in my class was 140 to 180 words per minute.) Thus, using the average of 160 words per minute, a three- to five-minute speech would contain roughly 480 to 800 words, and the outline should be 160 to 300 words. An 8- to 10-minute speech, roughly 1,280 to 1,600 words, should have an outline of approximately 426 to 533 words.

Now that we have considered the various parts of an outline, let us put them together for a final look. The outline in Figure 12.4 illustrates the principles in practice. The commentary to the right of the outline relates each part of the outline to the guidelines we have discussed.

There are even MORE Study Tools
for Chapter 12 at www.cengagebrain.com

☑ Speech Builder Express

☑ Printable Flash Cards

☑ Interactive Games

☑ Interactive Video Activities

☑ Chapter Review Cards

☑ Online Quizzes with Feedback

☑ Audio Downloads

Figure 12.4

Sample Complete Outline

OUTLINE	ANALYSIS

OUTLINE

General goal: I want to inform my audience.
Specific goal: I would like the audience to understand the major criteria for finding a suitable credit card.

Thesis statement: Three criteria that will enable audience members to find the credit card that is most suitable for them are level of real interest rate, annual fee, and advertised incentives.

Introduction

I. How many of you have been hounded by credit card vendors outside the Student Union?
II. They make a credit card sound like the answer to all of your dreams, don't they?
III. Today I want to share with you three criteria you need to consider carefully before deciding on a particular credit card: interest rate, annual fee, and advertised incentives.

Body

I. The first criterion for choosing a credit card is to select a card with a lower interest rate.
   A. Interest rates are the percentages that a company charges you to carry a balance on your card past the due date.
      1. Most credit cards carry an average of 8 percent.
      2. Some cards carry as much as 32 percent.
      3. Many companies offer 0 interest rates for up to 12 months.
      4. Student credit cards typically have higher interest rates.
      5. Some student credit cards carry APRs below 14%.
   B. Interest rates can be variable or fixed.
      1. Variable rates mean that the rate can change from month to month.
      2. Fixed rates mean that the rate will stay the same.
      3. Even cards with fixed rates can be raised to as much as 32% if you make a late payment.

(*Transition:* Now that we have considered interest rates, let's look at the next criterion.)

II. A second criterion for choosing a suitable credit card is to select a card with no annual fee.
   A. The annual fee is the cost the company charges you for extending you credit.
   B. The charges vary widely.
      1. Most cards have no annual fee.
      2. Some companies still charge fees.

(*Transition:* After you have considered interest and fees, you can weigh the incentives that the company promises you.)

III. A third criterion for choosing a credit card is to weigh the incentives.
   A. Incentives are extras that you get for using a particular card.
      1. Some companies promise rebates.
      2. Some companies promise frequent flyer miles.
      3. Some companies promise discounts on "a wide variety of items."
      4. Some companies promise "cash back" on your purchases.
   B. Incentives don't outweigh other criteria.

Conclusion

I. So, if you exercise care in examining interest rates, annual fees, and incentives, you can choose the credit card that's right for you.
II. Then your credit card may truly be the answer to your dreams.

Sources

Bankrate Monitor. Web. <http://www.Bankrate.com>.

Barrett, Lois. "Good Credit 101." *Black Enterprise* Oct. 2006. Web. <http://www.blackenterprise.com/ArchiveOpen.asp?Source=ArchiveTab/2006/10/1006-16.htm>.

"Congratulations, Grads—You're Bankrupt: Marketing Blitz Buries Kids in Plastic Debt." *Business Week*. 2001 May 21: 48. Print.

Hennefriend, Bill. *Office Pro* 64 Oct. 2004: 17–20. Print.

Lankford, Kimberly. "The 31% Credit-card Trap," *Kiplinger's* January 2007: 96–98. Print.

"Protect Your Credit Card." *Kiplinger's* (Dec. 2004): 88. Print.

Ramachandran, Nisha. "Harvesting Rewards." *U.S. News and World Report* 31 July 2005. Web. <http://www.usnews.com/biztech/articles/050808/8rewards.htm>.

ANALYSIS

Write your general and specific goals at the top of the page. Refer to the goal to test whether everything in the outline is relevant.

The thesis statement states the elements that are suggested in the specific goal. In the speech, the thesis serves as a forecast of the main points.

The heading *Introduction* sets the section apart as a separate unit. The introduction attempts to (1) get attention and (2) lead into the body of the speech as well as establish credibility, set a tone, and gain goodwill.

The heading *Body* sets this section apart as a separate unit. In this example, main point I begins a topical pattern of main points. It is stated as a complete sentence.

The two main subdivisions designated by A and B indicate the equal weight of these points. The second-level subdivisions—designated by 1, 2, and 3 for major subpoint A, and 1 and 2 for major subpoint B—give the necessary information for understanding the subpoints.

The number of major and second-level subpoints is at the discretion of the speaker. After the first two levels of subordination, words and phrases may be used in place of complete sentences for elaboration.

This transition reminds listeners of the first main point and forecasts the second.

Main point II, continuing the topical pattern, is a complete sentence that parallels the wording of main point I. Notice that each main point considers only one major idea.

This transition summarizes the first two criteria and forecasts the third.

Main point III, continuing the topical pattern, is a complete sentence paralleling the wording of main points I and II.

Throughout the outline, notice that main points and subpoints are factual statements. The speaker adds examples, experiences, and other developmental material during practice sessions.

The heading *Conclusion* sets this section apart as a separate unit. The content of the conclusion is intended to summarize the main ideas and leave the speech on a high note. The conclusion also provides closure by referring back to the idea mentioned in the introduction that a credit card is the answer to your dreams.

A list of sources should always be a part of the speech outline. The sources should show where the factual material of the speech came from. The list of sources is not a total of all sources available—only those that were used, directly or indirectly. Each of the sources is shown in proper form.

Learning Outcomes

LO¹ Discuss the adaptation of your speech information to your audience

LO² Discuss the adaptation of your visual material to your audience

LO³ Identify different methods for displaying presentational aids

Adapting Verbally
and Visually

© RENÉ MANSI/ISTOCKPHOTO.COM

"Because of the influence of mass media, today's audiences are visually oriented."

Recall from Chapter 11 that audience adaptation is the process of customizing your speech to your specific audience. Audience adaptation depends on audience analysis. You used the results of your audience analysis in Action Step 1.b to identify your topic, decide on a specific purpose, and select main points. Now you are going to learn how to use your audience analysis as you develop that speech. In this chapter, we will look at Action Step 4: Adapt the Verbal and Visual Material to the Needs of the Specific Audience. You will use your knowledge of your audience as you consider what specific verbal material you will present and how you will represent that material visually with presentational aids.

audience adaptation
the process of customizing your speech material to your specific audience

What do you think?

There are few ways to make a speech more engaging for the audience: they're either interested or not.

Strongly Disagree   Strongly Agree
1   2   3   4   5   6   7   8   9   10

Action Step 4:

Adapt the Verbal and Visual Material to the Needs of the Specific Audience

The skill of adapting involves both verbally and visually adapting by preparing presentational aids that facilitate audience understanding.

LO¹ Adapting to Your Audience Verbally

As you select supporting material and make language choices for your speech, you will want to consider how they (1) demonstrate relevance, (2) establish common ground, (3) enhance your credibility and the credibility of the material you are presenting, (4) help the audience comprehend and remember the information, and (5) reflect the cultural diversity in your audience.

Relevance

Your first challenge will be to adapt your speech so the audience sees how it is relevant to them. Listeners pay attention to and are interested in ideas that have a personal impact (when they can answer the question, What does this have to do with me?); they are bored when they don't see how the speech relates to them. You can help the audience perceive your speech as relevant by including supporting material that is timely, proximate, and has a personal impact.

timely
showing how information is useful now or in the near future

proximity
a relationship to personal space

common ground
the background, knowledge, attitudes, experiences, and philosophies that are shared by audience members and the speaker

Establish Timeliness

Listeners are more likely to be interested in information they perceive as **timely**—they want to know how they can use the information *now*. For example, in a speech about the hazards of talking on cell phones while driving, J. J. quickly established the topic's relevance in his introduction:

> Most of us in this room, as many as 90 percent in fact, are a danger to society. Why? Because we talk or text on our cell phones while driving. Although driving while phoning (DWP) seems harmless, a recent study conducted by the Nationwide Mutual Insurance Company reports that DWP is the most common cause of accidents today—even more common than driving under the influence (DUI)! Did you know that when you talk on the phone when you're driving—even if you do so on a hands-free set—you're four times more likely to get into a serious crash than if you're not doing so? That's why several states have actually banned the practice. So this issue is far from harmless and is one each of us should take seriously.

Establish Proximity

Your listeners are more likely to be interested in information that has **proximity**, a relationship to their personal "space." Psychologically, we pay more attention to information that is related to our "territory"—to us, our family, our neighborhood, or our city, state, or country. You have probably heard speakers say something like "Let me bring this closer to home by showing you" and then make their point by using a local example. As you review the supporting material you collect for your speech, look for statistics and examples that have proximity for your audience. For example, J. J. used the latest DWP accident statistics in his state and used a story reported in the local paper of a young mother who was killed while DWPing.

Demonstrate Personal Impact

When you present information that can have a serious physical, economic, or psychological impact on audience members, they are more likely to be interested in what you have to say. For example, notice how your classmates' attention picks up when your instructor says that what is said next "will definitely be on the test." Your instructor understands that this "economic" impact (not paying attention can "cost") is enough to refocus most students' attention on what is being said.

As you prepare your speech, incorporate ideas that create personal impact for your audience. In a speech about toxic waste, you might show a serious physical impact by providing statistics on the effects of toxic waste on the health of people in your state. You may be able to demonstrate serious economic impact by citing the cost to the taxpayers of a recent toxic waste cleanup in your city. Or you might be able to illustrate a serious psychological impact by finding and recounting the stresses faced by one family (that is demographically similar to the audience) with a long-term toxic waste problem in their neighborhood. To drive home the impact of DWP, toward the end of his speech, J. J. introduced John, his high school friend, who had come to class with J. J. and who is now paralyzed and wheelchair bound because his girlfriend crashed into another car while she was texting.

Common Ground

Each person in the audience is unique, with differing knowledge, attitudes, philosophies, experiences, and ways of perceiving the world. They may or may not know others in the audience. So it is easy for them to assume that they have nothing in common with you or with other audience members. Yet when you speak, you will be giving one message to that diverse group. **Common ground** is the background, knowledge, attitudes, experiences, and philosophies that are shared by audience members and the speaker. Effective speakers use their audience analysis to identify areas of similarity; then they use the adaptation techniques of personal pronouns, rhetorical questions, and common experiences to create common ground.

Listeners pay attention to and are interested in ideas that have a personal impact.

© GEORGE FAIRBAIRN/SHUTTERSTOCK

Use Personal Pronouns

The simplest way to establish common ground between yourself and the members of your audience is to use **personal pronouns**: *we, us,* and *our*. For example, in a speech given to an audience whose members are known to be sympathetic to legislation limiting violence in children's programming on TV, notice the different effects of using an unspecific noun and a personal pronoun:

> I know that most *people* are worried about the effects that violence on TV is having on young children.

> I know that most of *us* worry about the effects that violence on TV is having on young children.

By using *us* instead of *people*, the speaker includes the audience members, and this gives them a stake in listening to what is to follow.

Ask Rhetorical Questions

A **rhetorical question** is one whose answer is obvious to audience members and to which they are not really expected to reply. Rhetorical questions create common ground by alluding to information that is shared by audience members and the speaker. They are often used in speech introductions but can also be effective as transitions and in other parts of the speech. For instance, notice how this transition, phrased as a rhetorical question, creates common ground:

> When you have watched a particularly violent TV program, have you ever asked yourself, "Did they really need to be this graphic to make the point"?

Rhetorical questions are meant to have only one answer that highlights similarities between audience members and leads them to be more interested in the content that follows.

Draw from Common Experiences

You can also develop common ground by sharing personal experiences, examples, and illustrations that embody what you and the audience have in common. For instance, in a speech about the effects of television violence, you might allude to a common viewing experience:

> Remember how sometimes at a key moment when you're watching a really frightening scene in a movie, you may quickly shut your eyes? I vividly remember slamming my eyes shut over and over again during the scariest scenes in *The Blair Witch Project*.

To create material that draws on common experiences, you must first analyze how you and your audience members are similar in the exposure you have had to the topic or in other areas that you can then relate to your topic.

Speaker Credibility

Credibility is the confidence that an audience places in the truthfulness of what a speaker says. Some people are widely known as experts in a particular area and have proven to be trustworthy and likeable. When these people give a speech, they don't have to adapt their remarks to establish their credibility. However, most of us—even if we are given a formal introduction to acquaint the audience with our credentials and character—will still need to adapt our remarks to build audience confidence in the truthfulness of what we are saying. Three adaptation techniques can affect how credible we are perceived to be: demonstrating knowledge and expertise, establishing trustworthiness, and displaying personableness.

Demonstrate Knowledge and Expertise

When listeners perceive that you are a knowledgeable expert, they will perceive you as credible. Their

© ISTOCKPHOTO.COM

personal pronouns *we, us,* and *our*; pronouns that refer directly to members of the audience

rhetorical questions questions phrased to stimulate a mental response rather than an actual spoken response on the part of the audience

credibility the level of trust that an audience has or will have in the speaker

How to establish common ground:

Use personal pronouns

Rhetorical Questions

Draw from common experiences

knowledge and expertise
how well you convince your audience that you are qualified to speak on the topic

trustworthiness
both character and apparent motives for speaking

personableness
the extent to which you project an agreeable or pleasing personality

assessment of your knowledge and expertise depends on how well you convince them that you are qualified to speak on this topic. You can demonstrate your knowledge and expertise through direct and indirect means.

You directly establish expertise when you disclose your experiences with your topic, including your formal education, special study, demonstrated skill, and track record. Audience members will also assess your expertise through indirect means, such as how prepared you seem and how much firsthand involvement you demonstrate through personal examples and illustrations. Audiences have an almost instinctive sense of when a speaker is winging it, and most audiences distrust a speaker who does not appear to have command of the material. Speakers who are overly dependent on their notes or who hem and haw, fumbling to find ways to express their ideas, undermine the confidence of the audience. When your ideas are easy to follow and are clearly expressed, audience members perceive you to be more credible.

Similarly, when your ideas are developed through specific statistics, high-quality examples, illustrations, and the personal experiences, audience members are likely to view you as credible. Recall how impressed you are with instructors who always seem to have two or three perfect examples and illustrations and who are able to recall statistics without looking at their notes. Compare them to instructors who seem tied to the textbook and don't appear to know much about the subject beyond their prepared lecture. In which instance do you perceive the instructor to be more knowledgeable?

Establish Trustworthiness

Your **trustworthiness** is the extent to which the audience members believe that what you say is accurate, true, and in their best interests. The more your audience sees you as trustworthy, the more credible you will be. People assess others' trustworthiness by judging their

character and their motives. So you can establish yourself as trustworthy by following ethical standards and by honestly explaining what is motivating you to speak.

As you plan your speech, you need to consider how to demonstrate your character: that you are honest, industrious, dependable, and a morally strong person. For example, when you credit the source of your information as you speak, you confirm that the information is true—that you are not making it up—and you signal your honesty by not taking credit for someone else's ideas. Similarly, if you present the arguments evenly on both sides of an issue, instead of just the side you favor, audience members will see you as fair-minded.

How trustworthy you appear to be will also depend on how the audience views your motives. If people believe that what you are saying is self-serving rather than in their interests, they will be suspicious and view you as less trustworthy. Early in your speech, then, it is important to show how audience members will benefit from what you are saying. For example, in his speech on toxic waste, Brandon might describe how one community's ignorance of the dangers of toxic waste disposal allowed a toxic waste dump to be located in their community, with subsequent serious health issues. He can then share his motive by saying something like "My hope is that this speech will give you the information you need to thoughtfully participate in decisions like these that may face your community."

Display Personableness

We have more confidence in people we like. **Personableness** is the extent to which you project an agreeable or pleasing personality. The more your listeners like you, the more likely they are to believe what you tell them. We quickly decide how much we like a new person based on our first impressions. As a speaker trying to build credibility with an audience, you should look for ways to adapt your personal style to one that will help the audience like you and perceive you as credible.

Besides dressing in a way that is appropriate for the audience and occasion, you can increase the chances that the audience will like you by smiling at individual audience members before beginning your

Who do you think is more personable?

© YURI ARCURS/SHUTTERSTOCK / © SIMON KRZIC/SHUTTERSTOCK

remarks and by looking at individuals as you speak, acknowledging them with a quick nod. You can also demonstrate personableness by using appropriate humor.

Information Comprehension and Retention

Although your audience analysis helped you select a topic that was appropriate for your audience's current knowledge level, you will need to adapt the information you present so that audience members can easily understand it and remember it when you are through. Five guidelines that can aid you are: (1) appealing to diverse learning styles, (2) orienting the audience with basic information, (3) choosing clear language, (4) using vivid language and examples, and (5) comparing unfamiliar ideas with those the audience recognizes.

Appeal to Diverse Learning Styles

A **learning style** is a person's preferred way of receiving information. Because people differ in how they prefer to learn, you should present your ideas in ways that will make it easier for all audience members to understand and remember what you are saying. Kolb's cycle of learning (1984) conceptualizes learning style preferences along four dimensions: feeling, watching, thinking, and doing. Because your audience is likely to have people with a diversity of learning styles, you will want to adapt your ideas so that they can be understood and remembered by people who prefer different styles. Kolb argues that even though individuals might prefer learning in one these four ways, we all learn best when we engage with material in all four ways. So it makes sense to adapt your speech in ways that address all four dimensions. Figure 13.1 illustrates the cycle.

To address the feeling (concrete experience) dimension, you can offer personal stories or examples that appeal to the senses and emotions. J. J. did this when he shared the story about the young mother and when he introduced his wheelchair-bound friend. To address the watching (reflective observation) dimension, you should include visual materials to reinforce important points. You might also integrate rhetorical questions that encourage your listeners to reflect on some of the ideas you present. J. J. did so, for example, when he asked his audience whether they knew that serious automobile accidents are more commonly related to driving while phoning than driving under the influence. To address the thinking (abstract conceptualization) dimension, you should support your ideas with detailed definitions, explanations, facts, and statistics. To address the doing (active experimentation) dimension, you can identify ways that the audience can become personally involved in doing something related to your ideas. J. J. talked about turning off cell phones before starting the car or pulling over to the side of the road to answer or make a call.

learning style
a person's preferred way of receiving information

Orient the Audience with Internal Reviews

Listeners who are confused or have forgotten previous information from your speech lose interest in what is being said. If your speech is more than a couple of minutes long, you can use internal reviews to remind and orient your audience. Suppose your goal is to inform your audience about the three phases of clinical trials that a cancer drug must pass in order to win FDA approval. After explaining the goals of the first phase, the types of patients recruited, the type of information that must be provided to the FDA, and the FDA's review process, you are ready to move on to an explanation of the next phase. But your audience may still be trying to process the information you presented on the first phase. You can use an internal review to summarize the first phase and to preview phase two: "So the goal of the first phase is to see whether a drug that has been found to be safe in animals is safe in humans who have cancer and who have failed other treatments. Phase I trials are not designed to determine whether the drug works or

Figure 13.1

Kolb's Cycle of Learning

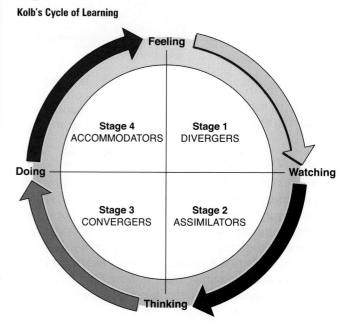

jargon
the unique technical terminology of a trade or profession

slang
informal, non-standard vocabulary and definitions assigned to words by a social group or subculture

sensory language
language that appeals to the senses

not. It is in the next phase, Phase II, that we begin to answer that question."

Choose Specific and Familiar Language

Words can have many meanings, so you want to make sure your listeners understand the meaning you intend. You can do so by using specific language and choosing familiar terms. Specific words clear up the confusion caused by general words by narrowing the focus in some way. For example, saying "a banged-up Honda Civic" is more specific than "a car." Narrowing the meaning encourages your listeners to picture the same thing you are. Similarly, you can narrow a term such as "blue-collar worker" further by saying "construction worker" and even further by saying "bulldozer operator." Choosing specific language is one way to make sure your listeners understand the precise meaning you intend.

Using familiar terms is just as important as using specific words. Avoid **jargon** (the unique technical terminology of a trade or profession) and **slang** (informal, non-standard vocabulary and definitions assigned to words by a social group or subculture) unless (1) you define them clearly the first time you use them and (2) they are central to your speech goal. For instance, in a speech on the major problems faced by functionally illiterate people in the workplace, it will be important to your audience to understand what you mean by "functionally illiterate." Early in the speech, you should offer your definition: "By 'functionally illiterate,' I mean people who have trouble accomplishing simple reading and writing tasks."

The excitement generated by telegrams can be compared to the public response when cell phones became widely available.

Use Vivid Language and Examples

Because listeners cannot reread what you have said, you must speak in ways that help them remember your message. Speaking vividly is one way. Vivid language is full of life—vigorous, bright, and intense. You can do so by using **sensory language** that appeals to the senses of seeing, hearing, tasting, smelling, and feeling. Here is how Marla appealed to the senses when describing the downhill skiing experience:

As you climb the hill, you squint because the bright winter sunshine glistening on the snow is almost blinding [*sight*]. Just before you take off, you gently slip your goggles over your eyes. The bitter cold of them stings your nose [*touch and feel*]. You start the descent, and as you gradually pick up speed, the taste of air and ice and snow in your mouth invigorates you [*taste*]. An odd silence fills the air, and you hear only the swish of your skis against the snow [*sound*] until, at last, you arrive at the bottom of the hill. As you enter the warming house, you feel your fingers thaw in the warm air [*feel*], and the familiar aroma of the wood stove [*smell*] comforts you as you pour yourself a cup of hot chocolate.

Sensory language and examples help audience members understand and remember abstract, complex, and novel material. A vivid example can help us understand a complicated concept. So as you prepare your speech, you will want to adapt by choosing real or hypothetical examples and illustrations to help your audience understand the new information you present.

Compare Unknown Ideas with Familiar Ones

An easy way to adapt your material to your audience is to compare your new ideas with ones the audience already understands. For example, if you want an audience of 18 to 24 year olds to feel the excitement that was generated when telegrams were first introduced, you might compare it to the public response when cell phones became widely available. In the speech on functional illiteracy, if you want your audience of literates to sense what functionally illiterate people experience, you might compare it to the experience of living in a country where one is not fluent in the language.

Adapting to Cultural Differences

Western European speaking traditions inform the approach to public speaking in this book. However,

© ADRIO COMMUNICATIONS LTD/SHUTTERSTOCK /
© STEFAN GLEBOWSKI/SHUTTERSTOCK

public speaking is a social and cultural act. As they prepare and present speeches, speakers from various cultures and subcultures draw on the traditions of their speech communities, and listeners draw on their own cultural expectations when they are part of an audience. When you address an audience composed of people from ethnic and language groups different from your own, you should make three adaptations: being understandable when you are speaking in your second language, showing respect by choosing bias-free language, and creating common ground by choosing culturally appropriate supporting material.

Work to Be Understood When Speaking in Your Second Language

When the first language spoken by audience members is different from yours, they may not be able to understand what you are saying because you may speak with an accent, mispronounce words, choose inappropriate words, and misuse idioms. Speaking in a second language can make you anxious and self-conscious. But most audience members are more tolerant of mistakes made by a second-language speaker than they are of those made by a native speaker. Likewise, they will work hard to understand a second-language speaker.

Nevertheless, when you are speaking in a second language, you have an additional responsibility to make your speech as understandable as possible. You can help your audience by speaking more slowly and articulating as clearly as you can. By slowing your speaking rate, you give yourself additional time to pronounce difficult sounds and choose words whose meanings you know. You also give your audience members additional time to adjust their ears so that they can more easily process what you are saying. You can also use visual aids to reinforce key terms and concepts as you move through you speech. Doing so assures listeners that they've heard you correctly.

One of the best ways to improve when you are giving a speech in a second language is to practice the speech in front of friends and associates who are native speakers. Ask them to take note of words and phrases that you mispronounce or misuse. Then they can work with you to correct the pronunciation or to choose other words that better express your idea. Also, keep in mind that the more you practice speaking the language, the more comfortable you will become with the language and with your ability to relate to the audience members.

Choose Non-Offensive Language

Some words, phrases, and references may be offensive to some cultural groups. When you use these in a speech, you are being disrespectful of the feel-ings of your audience. Respectful language choices are those that will not offend any of your listeners. Disrespectful language includes expressions that some people perceive as sexist, racist, demeaning, insulting, or offensive. Any words, examples, or stories that belittle a person or a group of people based on their race, sex, religion, age, class, education, or occupation are disrespectful.

Profane or vulgar language can also offend some audience members and should be avoided in a public address. Although casual swearing—profanity injected into regular conversation—occurs more today than in the past, research has shown that people who pepper their formal speeches with it are often perceived as abrasive as well as lacking in character and emotional control (DuFrene & Lehman, 2002; O'Connor, 2000). Respectful language is also gender neutral and avoids stereotypes. *Firefighter* rather than *fireman, server* rather than *waitress,* and *flight attendant* rather than *stewardess* are examples of bias-free language choices.

You will also want to avoid offensive examples and stories. Dirty jokes and racist, sexist, or other -ist examples show your disregard for the feelings of some of your audience members and are likely to turn off not only those who you are demeaning but also other members of the audience. You might recall when comedian Chris Rock hosted the 2003 MTV music awards and introduced Eminem as someone who "saves a lot of money on Mother's Day" and P. Diddy as "being sued by more people than the Catholic church." Although some people may have thought that these remarks were funny, others surely did not. And although remarks such as these may be accepted from Chris Rock the comedian, your audience is unlikely to find your use of this type of humor appropriate or effective. As a general rule of thumb: When in doubt, leave it out.

When in doubt, leave it out.

© VIKRAMRAGHUVANSHI/ISTOCKPHOTO.COM

presentational aid
any visual, audio, or audiovisual material used in a speech for the purpose of helping the audience understand some point the speaker is making

Choose Culturally Appropriate Supporting Material

Much of your success in adapting to the audience hinges on establishing common ground and drawing on common experiences. When you are speaking to audiences who are vastly different from you, you should learn as much as you can about their culture so that you can develop the material in a way that is meaningful to them. This may mean conducting additional library research to find statistics and examples that are meaningful to the audience. Or it may require you to elaborate on ideas that would be self-explanatory in your own culture. For example, suppose that Maria, a Mexican American exchange student, was giving a personal narrative speech on her *quinceañera* party when she turned 15 for her speech class at Yeshiva University in Israel. Because students in Israel have no experience with the Mexican coming-of-age tradition of *quinceañera* parties, they would have had trouble understanding the significance of this event if Maria had not used her knowledge of the Bar Mitzvah and Bat Mitzvah coming-of-age ritual celebrations in Jewish culture and related it to them.

LO² Adapting to Audiences Visually

Because of the influence of mass media, today's audiences are visually oriented. As a result, your audience is likely to expect you to use presentational aids to provide a visual component to your speech. A **presentational aid** is any visual, audio, or audiovisual material used in a speech for the purpose of helping the audience understand some point the speaker is making. The most common form of presentational aid is a visual aid—a form of supporting material that allows the audience to see as well as hear information.

There are several benefits to using presentational aids. First, they enable you to adapt to an audience's level of knowledge by clarifying and dramatizing your verbal message. Second, they help audiences retain the information because people are better able to remember what they both see and hear rather than what they only hear (Tversky, 1997). Third, presentational aids help listeners whose learning styles are based on visual cues (Kolb, 1984). Fourth, presentational aids are persuasive. In fact, some research suggests that speakers who use presentational aids are almost two times more likely to convince listeners than those who do not have presentational aids (Hanke, 1998). Finally, using presentational aids helps you feel more confident. Speakers report that when they use presentational aids, they tend to be less anxious and have more confidence (Ayres, 1991).

Types of Presentational Aids

Presentational aids range from those that are ready-made and simple to use to those that require practice to use effectively and must be custom produced for the specific speech. In this section, we describe the types of presentational aids that you can consider using as you prepare your speech.

Actual Objects

Actual objects are inanimate or animate physical samples of the idea you are communicating. Inanimate objects make good visual aids if they are (1) large enough to be seen by all audience members, (2) small enough to carry to the site of the speech, (3) simple enough to understand visually, and

---

Action Step 4a
Adapting to Your Audience Verbally

The goal of this activity is to help you plan how you will verbally adapt your material to the specific audience.

Write your thesis statement: _____

Review the audience analysis that you completed in Action Steps 1.b and 1.c. As you review the speech outline that you completed in Action Steps 3.a–3.h, plan the supporting material you will use to verbally adapt to your audience by answering the following questions:

1. How can I adapt this material so that it is relevant to this audience by showing its timeliness, proximity, and personal impact?
2. How can I establish common ground by using personal pronouns, asking rhetorical questions, and drawing from common experiences?
3. How can I establish my credibility by demonstrating my knowledge and expertise, my trustworthiness, and my personableness?
4. How can I make this material easier for the audience to comprehend by addressing diverse learning styles, orienting them with internal reviews, speaking clearly, using sensory language and examples, and comparing unknowns with what your audience knows?
5. How can I adapt to the cultural differences between my audience and me?

---

(4) safe. A volleyball or a Muslim prayer rug would be appropriate in size for most classroom audiences. A smart phone might be OK if the goal is simply to show what a smart phone looks like, but it might be too small if you want to demonstrate how to use the phone's specialized functions.

Some animate objects also make effective visual aids. On occasion, *you* can be an effective visual aid. For instance, you can use descriptive gestures to show the height of a tennis net, you can use posture and movement to show the motions involved in a golf swing, or you can use your attire to illustrate the native dress of a particular country. Sometimes it can be appropriate to use another person as a visual aid, such as when Jenny used a friend to demonstrate the Heimlich maneuver. Animals can also be effective visual aids. For example, Josh used his American Kennel Club Obedience Champion dog to demonstrate the basics of dog training. But keep in mind that some animals placed in unfamiliar settings can become difficult to control and can distract from your message.

Models

When an object is too large or too small, too complex to understand visually, or potentially unsafe or uncontrollable, a model of the object can be an effective visual aid. A **model** is a three-dimensional scaled-down or scaled-up version of an actual object, and it may also be simplified to aid understanding. In a speech on the physics of bridge construction, a scale model of a suspension bridge would be an effective visual aid. Likewise, in a speech on genetic engineering, a model of the DNA double helix might help the audience understand what happens during these microscopic procedures.

Photographs

If an exact reproduction of material is needed, enlarged still photographs are excellent visual aids. In a speech on smart weapons, enlarged before-and-after photos of target sites would be effective in helping the audience understand the pinpoint accuracy of these weapons.

Simple Drawings and Diagrams

Simple drawings and diagrams are easy to prepare. If you can use a compass and a ruler, you can draw well enough to prepare a simple diagram. Or with a little practice, you can use a basic computer drawing program to prepare one. For instance, if you are making the point that water-skiers must hold their arms straight, their back straight, and their knees bent slightly, a stick figure (see Figure 13.2) will illustrate the point. Stick figures may not be as aesthetically pleasing as professional drawings or photographs, but they

can still be effective. In fact, elaborate, detailed drawings may not be worth the time and effort, and actual photographs may be so detailed that they obscure the point you wish to make. Likewise, a simple **diagram**, a type of drawing that shows how the whole relates to its parts, can be more effective than a photograph because you can choose how much detail to include. Andria's diagram of the human heart, for example, worked well to clarify her message visually (see Figure 13.3).

model
a three-dimensional scaled-down or scaled-up version of an actual object

diagram
a type of drawing that shows how the whole relates to its parts

Figure 13.2

Sample Drawing

Figure 13.3

Sample Diagram

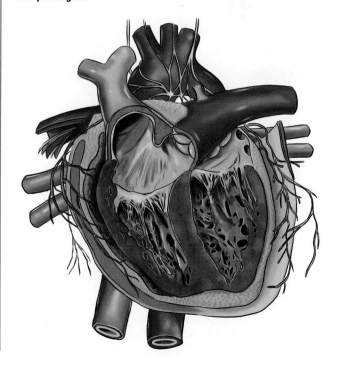

© HKANN/SHUTTERSTOCK

charts
graphic representations that present information in easily interpreted formats

word charts
used to preview, review, or highlight important ideas covered in a speech

flow charts
charts that use symbols and connecting lines to diagram the progressions through a complicated process

graph
a chart that compares information

bar graphs
charts that present information using a series of vertical or horizontal bars

line graphs
charts that indicate changes in one or more variables over time

pie graphs
charts that help audiences visualize the relationships among parts of a single unit

Maps

Like drawings and diagrams, maps are relatively easy to prepare. Simple maps allow you to orient audiences to landmarks (mountains, rivers, and lakes), states, cities, land routes, weather systems, and so on. Commercial maps are available, but simple maps can be customized so that audience members are not confused by visual information that is irrelevant to your purpose. Figure 13.4 shows a map that focuses on poverty levels.

Charts

A **chart** is a graphic representation that distills a lot of information and presents it in an easily interpreted visual format. Word charts, flow charts, and organizational charts are the most

Figure 13.4

Sample Map

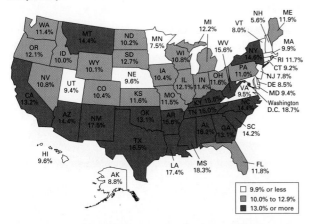

SOURCE: Poverty in the United States: 2005, U.S. Census Bureau, September 2006, Table 19, http://www.census.gov/hhes/www/ poverty/histpov/hstpov19.html.

common. A **word chart** is used to preview, review, or highlight important ideas covered in a speech. In a speech on Islam, a speaker might make a word chart that lists the five pillars of Islam, as shown in Figure 13.5. A **flow chart** uses symbols and connecting lines to diagram the progressions through a complicated process. Organizational charts are a common type of flow chart that shows the chain of command in an

organization. The chart in Figure 13.6 illustrates the organization of a student union board.

Figure 13.5

Sample Word Chart

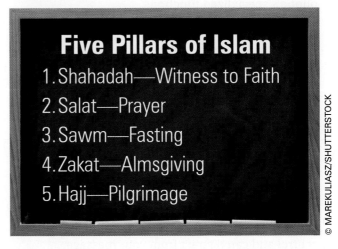

Figure 13.6

Sample Organizational Chart

Graphs

A **graph** is a diagram that presents numerical information. Bar graphs, line graphs, and pie graphs are the most common forms of graphs.

A **bar graph** is a diagram that uses vertical or horizontal bars to show relationships between two or more variables at the same time or at various times on one or more dimensions. For instance, Jacqueline used a bar graph to show the increase of clothing exports by China from 1998 to 2006 (see Figure 13.7).

A **line graph** is a diagram that indicates the changes in one or more variables over time. In a speech on the population of the United States, for example, the line graph in Figure 13.8 helps by showing the population increase, in millions, from 1810 to 2000.

A **pie graph** is a diagram that shows the relationships among parts of a single unit. Ideally, pie graphs should have two to five "slices," or wedges—more than eight make a pie graph difficult to read during a speech. If your graph includes too many wedges, use a different kind of graph or consolidate several less important wedges into a category of "Other," as Tim did in Figure 13.9 to show the percentage of total calories that should come from the various components of food.

Figure 13.7

Sample Bar Graph

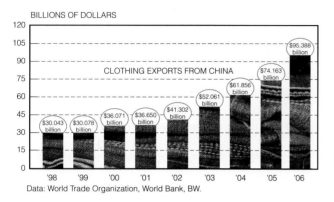

Data: World Trade Organization, World Bank, BW.

Figure 13.8

Sample Line Graph

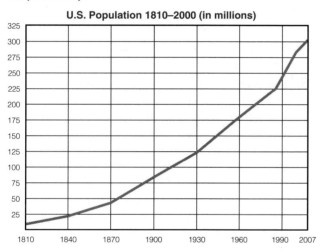

Figure 13.9

Sample Pie Graph

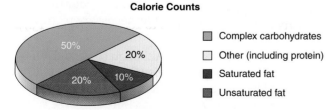

Audio Materials

Audio materials enhance a verbal message through sound. They are especially useful when it is difficult, if not impossible, to describe a sound in words. For example, in David's speech about the three types of trumpet mutes and how they alter the trumpet's sound, he played his trumpet so that listeners could hear what he meant. If you can't or don't want to make your own sounds, you can use recorded excerpts from sources such as famous speeches, radio programs, interviews, and musical recordings or environmental sounds. Before using audio material, make sure you have enough time to present it (it should take no more than about 5 percent of your speaking time) and that you have access to a quality sound system.

Audiovisual Materials

Audiovisual materials enhance a verbal message through sight and sound. You can use short clips from films and videos to demonstrate concepts or processes or to expose audiences to important people. For example, in his speech about the use of robots in automobile production, Chad, who worked as a technician at the local Ford plant, showed a 20-second video clip of a car being painted in a robotic paint booth. As with audio clips, your audiovisual clip should take no more than 5 percent of your speaking time.

Criteria for Choosing Presentational Aids

Now that you understand the various types of presentational aids, you have to decide what content you want to highlight in a presentational aid and the best way to do so. Some simple guidelines can help you make good choices.

- Create aids for important information that the audience needs to understand and remember.

Action Step 4b
Adapting to Your Audience Visually

The goal of this activity is to help you decide which visual aids you will use in your speech.

1. Identify the key ideas in your speech that you could emphasize with a visual presentation to increase audience interest, understanding, or retention.
2. For each idea you have identified, list the type of visual presentation you think would be most appropriate to develop and use.
3. For each idea you plan to present visually, decide on the method or aid you will use to present it.
4. Write a brief paragraph describing why you chose the types of visual aids and methods that you did. Be sure to consider how your choices will affect your preparation time and the audience's perception of your credibility.

- Create aids for ideas that are complex or difficult to explain verbally but would be easy for members to understand visually.

- Create aids that are appropriate for the size of the audience.

- Limit the number of aids so that they do not distract from you as speaker.

- Use media aids only when equipment is readily available and you know how to operate it.

- Consider preparation time and expense when choosing aids.

Designing Effective Presentational Aids

However simple your presentational aids, you still need to produce them carefully. You may need to find or create charts, graphs, diagrams, maps, or drawings. You may need to search for and prepare photographs. You may look for audio or audiovisual snippets and then convert them to a format that you can use at your speech site.

As you approach your design task, you must first determine whether you will design your aids by hand or use computer presentation software. Regardless of which you choose, there are several guidelines that you will want to follow.

1. **Limit the reading required of the audience.** The audience should not spend a long time reading your visual aid; you want them listening to you. So limit the total number of lines on an aid to six or fewer, and write points as short phrases rather than complete sentences.

2. **Customize presentational aids from other sources.** We often get ideas for our aids from other sources, and the tendency is to include everything that was in the original. But if the original source includes information that is irrelevant to your purpose or audience, you should customize your aid to include only the information you want to present. For example, Jia Li was preparing a speech on alcohol abuse by young adults. During her research, she found a graph of the 2005 statistics called "Current, Binge, and Heavy Alcohol Use Among Persons Aged 12 or Older by Age." This graph presented information pertaining to drinkers from ages 12 to 65+, which was much more information than Jia Li needed. So she simplified it for her presentation and used only the information for young adults ages 16 to 29.

3. **Use a photo, print, or type size that can be seen easily by your entire audience.** Check your photo, charts, and lettering for size by moving as far away from the visual aid as the farthest person in your audience will be sitting. If you can see the image, read the lettering, and see the details from that distance, your aid is large enough; if not, create another sample and check it again.

4. **Use a print style that is easy to read.** Avoid fancy print styles; your goal is presentation aids that are easy to read. In addition, some people think that printing in all capital letters creates emphasis, but the combination of uppercase and lowercase letters is easier to read than uppercase only—even when the ideas are written in short phrases.

This print style is easy to read.

THIS PRINT STYLE IS DIFFICULT TO READ.

5. **Make sure information is laid out in a way that is visually pleasing.** Visually pleasing material is artistically arranged while not losing its communicative function. So visuals that will appeal to the audience are neatly prepared, not crowded, have space separating ideas, use color strategically, and use typefaces and indenting to visually display the relationships between the ideas.

6. **Use pictures or other visual symbols to add interest.** A presentational aid should consist of more than just words (Booher, 2003). Even on a word chart, visual symbols can increase retention by appealing to diverse learning styles (Kolb, 1984; Long, 1997). If you are working with computer graphics, consider adding clip art. Most computer graphics packages have a wide variety of clip art that you can import to your document. You can also buy relatively inexpensive software packages that contain thousands of clip art images. A relevant piece of clip art can make the image look both more professional and more dramatic. Be careful, though; clip art can be overdone. Don't let your message be overpowered by unnecessary pictures or animations.

7. **Use color strategically.** Although black and white can work well for your visual aids, you should consider using color. When used strategically, color can emphasize points. Here are some suggestions for incorporating color in your graphics:
   - Choose a single background color to use on all of your presentation aids. Then choose a different color of type for each main point and use it on all visuals related to that main point.

- Use the same color to show similarities and opposite colors (on a color wheel) to depict differences between ideas.
- Use bright colors, such as red, to highlight important information. Be sure to avoid using red and green together, however, since audience members who are color-blind may not be able to distinguish them.
- Make sure that the color of the type can be easily seen on the background.
- Use no more than two or three colors on any presentation aid that is not a photograph.

Pretend you are your audience. Sit as far away as they will be sitting, and evaluate the colors. Assess your color choices for their readability and appeal from the perspective of your audience.

8. **Use presentation software to prepare professional-looking presentational aids.** Presentation software is a type of computer program that enables you to electronically prepare and store your visual aids using a computer. Microsoft's *PowerPoint*, Adobe's *Captivate*, and Apple's *Keynote 3* are popular presentation software programs. The visuals you create on a computer can become overhead transparencies or handouts, or they can be displayed directly on a screen or TV monitor as a computerized slide show. Aids developed with presentation software give a very polished look to your speech and allow you to develop and deliver complex multimedia presentations that are expected in many professional settings.

Computerized slide shows have quickly become the presentational aid of choice today. Unfortunately, too often these shows do not adhere to the most important function of effective presentational aids: to enhance and complement the verbal message, not to replace it. The speaker should not be relegated to the role of projectionist. On the other hand, well-designed and well-presented computerized slide shows greatly enhance audience interest, understanding, and memory as well as the audience's perceptions of the speaker's credibility.

When you are unfamiliar with the software, using it to prepare your presentation aids will be time consuming. But if you start simply, over time you will become more adept at creating professional-quality visuals. Like hand-prepared presentation aids, those you prepare with presentation software need to be created with your specific audience in mind.

Let's see if we can put all of these principles to work. Figure 13.10 contains a lot of important information, but notice how unpleasant it is to the eye. As you can see, this visual aid ignores all princi-

ples. However, with some thoughtful simplification, this speaker could produce the visual aid shown in Figure 13.11, which sharpens the focus by emphasizing the key words (*reduce, reuse, recycle*), highlighting the major details, and adding clip art for a professional touch.

presentation software
a type of computer program that enables you to electronically prepare and store your visual aids using a computer

Figure 13.10

A Cluttered and Cumbersome Visual Aid

> # I WANT YOU TO REMEMBER THE THREE R'S OF RECYCLING
> Reduce the amount of waste people produce like overpacking or using material that won't recycle.
>
> Reuse by relying on cloth towels rather than paper towels, earthenware dishes rather than paper or plastic plates, and glass bottles rather than aluminum cans.
>
> Recycle by collecting recyclable products, sorting them appropriately, and getting them to the appropriate recycling agency.

Figure 13.11

A Simple but Effective Visual Aid

Remember the 3Rs of recycling

Reduce waste

Reuse
✔ cloth towels
✔ dishes
✔ glass bottles

Recycle
✔ collect
✔ sort
✔ deliver

© RENÉ MANSI/ISTOCKPHOTO.COM

flip chart
a large pad of paper
mounted on an easel;
it can be an effective
method for presenting
visual aids

LO³ Methods for Displaying Presentational Aids

Once you have decided on the specific presentational aids for your speech, you will need to choose the method to display them. Methods for displaying aids vary in the type of preparation they require, the amount of specialized training needed to use them effectively, and the professionalism they convey. Some methods, such as writing on a chalkboard, require little preparation. Other methods, such as computerized slide show presentations, can require extensive preparation. Similarly, it's easy to use an object or a flip chart, but you will need training to properly set up and run a computerized slide show presentation. Finally, the quality of your visual presentation will affect your perceived credibility. A well-run computerized slide show is impressive, but technical difficulties can make you look unprepared. Hand-drawn charts and graphs that are hastily or sloppily developed mark you as an amateur, whereas professional-looking visual aids enhance your credibility. Speakers can choose from the following methods for displaying presentational aids.

Posters

The easiest method for displaying simple drawings, charts, maps, photos, and graphs is by mounting them on stiff cardboard or foam core. Then the visual can be placed on an easel or in a chalk tray when it is referred to during the speech. Because posters tend to be fairly small, use them only with smaller audiences.

Whiteboards or Chalkboards

Because a whiteboard or chalkboard is a staple in every college classroom, many novice (and ill-prepared) speakers rely on this method for displaying their visual aids. Unfortunately, the whiteboard or chalkboard is easy to misuse and overuse. Moreover, they are not suitable for depicting complex material. Writing on a whiteboard or chalkboard is appropriate only for very short items of information that can be written in a few seconds. Nevertheless, being able to use a whiteboard or chalkboard effectively should be a part of any speaker's repertoire.

Whiteboards or chalkboards should be written on prior to or during a break in speaking. Otherwise, the visual is likely to be either illegible or partly obscured

Writing on a chalkboard is appropriate only for very short items of information.

by your body as you write. Or you may end up talking to the board instead of to the audience. Should you need to draw or write on the board while you are talking, you should practice doing it. If you are right-handed, stand to the right of what you are drawing. Try to face at least part of the audience while you work. Although it may seem awkward at first, your effort will allow you to maintain contact with your audience and will allow the audience to see what you are doing while you are doing it.

"Chalk talks" are easy to prepare, but they are the most likely to result in damage to speaker credibility. It is the rare individual who can develop well-crafted visual aids on a whiteboard or chalkboard. More often, they signal a lack of preparation.

Flip Charts

A flip chart, a large pad of paper mounted on an easel, can be an effective method for presenting visual aids. Flip charts (and easels) are available in many sizes. For a presentation to four or five people, a small tabletop version works well; for a larger audience, a larger-size pad (30" × 40") is needed.

Flip charts are prepared before the speech, using colorful markers to record the information. At times, a speaker may record some of the information before the speech begins and then add information while speaking.

When you are preparing a flip chart, leave several pages between each visual on the pad. If you discover a mistake or decide to revise, you can tear out that sheet without disturbing the order of other visuals you may have prepared. After you have finished all the visuals, tear out all but one sheet between each of them. This blank sheet serves as both a transition page and a cover sheet. Because you want your audience to focus on your words and not on visual material that is no longer being discussed, you can flip to the empty page until you are ready to talk about the next visual. Also, the empty page between visuals ensures that heavy lines or colors from the next one will not show through.

For flip charts to be effective, information that is handwritten or drawn must be neat and appropriately sized. Flip-chart visuals that are not neatly done detract from speaker credibility. Flip charts can be comfortably used with smaller audiences (less than 100 people) but are not appropriate for larger settings. It is especially important when creating flip charts to make sure that the information is written large enough to be easily seen by all audience members.

Handouts

At times it may be useful for each member of the audience to have a personal copy of the visual aid. For these situations, you can prepare a handout (material printed on sheets of paper). On the plus side, you can prepare handouts quickly, and all the people in the audience can have their own professional-quality copy to refer to and take with them from the speech. On the minus side, distributing handouts is distracting and has the potential for losing audience members' attention when you want them to be looking at you.

Before you decide to use handouts, carefully consider why they would be better than some other method. Handouts are effective for information you want listeners to refer to after the speech, such as a set of steps to follow later, useful telephone numbers and addresses, or mathematical formulas.

If you decide on handouts, distribute them at the end of the speech. If you want to refer to information on the handout during the speech, create another visual aid that you can reveal when discussing it during your speech. Tim used a handout for his flow chart about determining whether someone is overweight. He wanted listeners to take it home with them to refer to later. But for his speech, he also created a flow chart on a poster.

Document Cameras

Another simple way to project drawings, charts, photos, and graphs is using a document camera, such as an Elmo. An Elmo is a document camera that allows you to project images without transferring them to an acetate film. Be sure to transfer drawings, charts, photos, and graphs from their source onto an 8½" × 11"

piece of paper so that you can display them smoothly and professionally.

CD/ DVD Players and LCD Projectors

To show TV, film, and video clips for a classroom speech, a DVD player and a television monitor should be sufficient. For larger audiences, however, you will need to use multiple monitors or, ideally, an LCD multimedia projector. An LCD projector connects to a VCR/DVD player or computer and projects images from them onto a screen, which makes the images easy to see by all members of a large audience. An LCD projector is also ideal for displaying computerized slideshows such as those you create using PowerPoint.

Computer-Mediated Slide Shows

You can present computerized slide shows using an LCD projector or a large monitor connected to an onsite computer that has presentation software compatible with the one you used in making your aids. Because you can't always anticipate problems with onsite projection equipment, come with back-up aids such as transparencies or handouts. When you present your slide show during your speech, ensure that the audience members focus their attention on you when you're not talking about one of your slides. To redirect their attention from your slide show to you, insert blank screens between your slides or press the B key on your computer to display a blank screen.

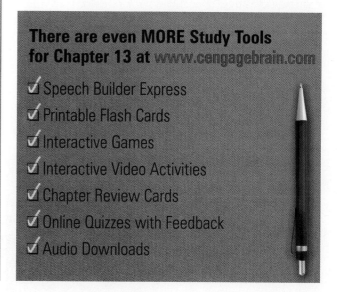

There are even MORE Study Tools for Chapter 13 at www.cengagebrain.com

☑ Speech Builder Express
☑ Printable Flash Cards
☑ Interactive Games
☑ Interactive Video Activities
☑ Chapter Review Cards
☑ Online Quizzes with Feedback
☑ Audio Downloads

Overcoming Speech Apprehension by Practicing Delivery

> **66** *Although some people seem to be naturally fluent and comfortable speaking to a group, most of us are a bit frightened about the prospect and not really comfortable with our abilities to effectively present our ideas.* **99**

The difference between a good speech and a great speech is often how well it is delivered. Although delivery can't compensate for a poorly researched, poorly organized, or poorly developed speech, it can take a well-researched, well-organized, and well-developed speech and make it a powerful vehicle for accomplishing your speech goal. Although some people seem to be naturally fluent and comfortable speaking to a group, most of us are a bit frightened about the prospect and not really comfortable with our abilities to effectively present our ideas.

What do you think?

The best-delivered speeches are the ones that are spontaneous.

Strongly Disagree   *Strongly Agree*

1   2   3   4   5   6   7   8   9   10

Action Step 5:

Practice Presenting the Speech

In this chapter, we're going to explain Action Step 5: Practice Presenting the Speech. We begin by discussing stage fright, or public speaking apprehension, which most of us face. Then, we discuss the characteristics of an effective delivery style and how to use your voice and body effectively when giving a speech. Next, we describe the three most common methods for delivering a speech and introduce a speech practice process designed to make your rehearsal sessions productive. Finally, we offer some criteria you can use to evaluate your speeches, and as an example, we apply the criteria to a sample student speech.

LO¹ Public Speaking Apprehension

Most people feel some fear about speaking in public. So if you're a bit unnerved, you are in good company. In fact, as many as 76 percent of experienced public speakers feel fearful before presenting a speech (Hahner, Sokoloff, & Salisch, 2001). Did you know, for example, that Academy Award–winning actress Meryl Streep, singer Barbra Streisand, and evangelist Billy Graham all experience fear of public speaking?

© OLEG PRIKHODKO/ISTOCKPHOTO.COM

CHAPTER 14 Overcoming Speech Apprehension by Practicing Delivery **191**

public speaking apprehension
a type of communication anxiety (or nervousness); the level of fear you experience when anticipating or actually speaking to an audience

performance orientation
seeing public speaking as a situation in which a speaker must impress an audience with knowledge and delivery, and seeing audience members as hypercritical judges

communication orientation
seeing a speech situation as an opportunity to talk with a number of people about a topic that is important to the speaker and to them

Despite their fear, they are all effective public speakers because they employ the strategies for managing nervousness that you will read about in this chapter. **Public speaking apprehension**, a type of communication anxiety (or nervousness), is the level of fear you experience when anticipating or actually speaking to an audience. Today, you can benefit from the results of a significant amount of research about public speaking apprehension and methods for managing it.

Symptoms and Causes

The symptoms of pubic speaking apprehension vary from individual to individual and range from mild to debilitating. Symptoms can be physical, emotional, or cognitive. Physical symptoms may be stomach upset (or butterflies), flushed skin, sweating, shaking, light-headedness, rapid or heavy heartbeats, and verbal disfluencies such as stuttering and vocalized pauses ("like," "you know," "ah," "um," and so on). Emotional symptoms include feeling anxious, worried, or upset. Cognitive symptoms include negative self-talk, which is also the most common cause of speech apprehension (Richmond & McCroskey, 2000).

In addition to negative self-talk, previous experience and negative reinforcement have also been found to be leading causes of speech apprehension. Previous experience has to do with being socialized to fear public speaking as a result of modeling and negative reinforcement (Richmond & McCroskey, 2000). Modeling has to do with observing how your friends and family members react to speaking in public. If they tend to be quiet and reserved and avoid public speaking, your fears may stem from modeling. Negative reinforcement concerns how others have responded to your public speaking endeavors. If you experienced negative reactions, you might be more apprehensive about speak-

ing in public than if you had been praised for your efforts (Motley, 1997).

Our level of public speaking apprehension is not static. Rather, it varies over the course of giving a speech. Research has identified three phases of speaking anxiety: anticipation, confrontation, and adaptation (Behnke & Carlile, 1971, p. 66). The anticipation phase is the anxiety you experience before giving the speech, both while preparing it and waiting to speak. The confrontation phase is the surge of anxiety you feel as you begin delivering your speech; this usually falls once you get into your speech. The adaptation phase is the period during which your anxiety level gradually decreases; it typically begins about one minute into the presentation and tends to level off after about five minutes.

So researchers have found that the level of apprehension varies over the course of giving a speech and that there are various symptoms and causes of apprehension. But the apprehension we feel does not have to affect how well we present our speeches.

Managing Your Apprehension

Would we be better off if we could be totally free from nervousness? Based on years of study, Gerald Phillips (1977) concluded that "learning proceeds best when the organism is in a state of tension" (p. 37). In fact, it helps to be a little nervous to do your best. Not only that, if you are lackadaisical, you probably won't do a good job (Motley, 1997).

Because at least some tension is constructive, the goal is not to eliminate nervousness but to learn how to manage it. There are five techniques you can use to manage public speaking apprehension: communication orientation, visualization, systematic desensitization, cognitive restructuring, and public speaking skills training.

Communication Orientation

Communication orientation motivation (COM) techniques help you adopt a communication rather than a performance orientation toward speeches (Motley, 1997). When you have a performance orientation, you see public speaking as a situation in which you must *impress* the audience with your knowledge and delivery, and you view audience members as hypercritical judges who will notice and judge even minor mistakes. On the other hand, when you have a communication orientation, you view your speech as an opportunity

© ROBNROLL/SHUTTERSTOCK

to talk with a number of people about a topic that is important to you and to them. You focus on your audience and getting the message across so that they understand your thoughts. You are not concerned about impressing the audience or worried about them judging you.

Visualization

Visualization helps you develop a mental picture of yourself giving a masterful speech. You have probably heard reports of how athletes use visualization to improve sports performance, and you may have used it before athletic competitions yourself. If you visualize yourself going through your entire speech preparation and speech-making process successfully, research has found that you are likely to be more successful when you actually deliver the speech (Ayres & Hopf, 1990, p. 77). By visualizing themselves speaking effectively, people seem to lower their general apprehension and report fewer negative thoughts when they actually speak (Ayres, Hopf, & Ayres, 1994, p. 256). So you will want to use visualization activities as part of your speech preparation.

An interesting study of the use of visualization in sports performances looked at players trying to improve their foul-shooting percentages (Scott, 1997, p. 99). In the study, the players were divided into three groups. One group never practiced, another group practiced, and a third group visualized practicing. As we would expect, those who practiced improved far more than those who didn't. What seems amazing is that those who only visualized practicing improved almost as much as those who practiced. Imagine what can happen when you visualize yourself giving a great speech *and* you practice as well!

Systematic Desensitization

Systematic desensitization can help you reduce apprehension by gradually visualizing and engaging in increasingly more frightening speaking events. The process starts with consciously tensing and then relaxing muscle groups in order to learn how to recognize the difference between the two states. Then, while in a relaxed state, you first imagine yourself and then engage in successively more stressful situations—for example, researching a speech topic in the library, practicing the

© ISTOCKPHOTO.COM/DANIEL BOBROWSKY / © FLIEGENWULF/SHUTTERSTOCK

speech out loud to a roommate, and finally, giving a speech. The ultimate goal of systematic desensitization is to transfer the calm feelings we attain while visualizing to the actual speaking event. Calmness on command—it works.

Cognitive Restructuring

Cognitive restructuring is designed to help you systematically rebuild your thoughts about public speaking by replacing anxiety-arousing negative self-talk with anxiety-reducing positive self-talk. The process consists of four steps:

1. To change your negative thoughts, you must first identify them. Write down all the fears that come to mind when you know you must give a speech.

2. Consider whether or not these fears are rational. (Most are irrational because public speaking is not life threatening.)

visualization
a method to reduce apprehension by developing a mental picture of yourself giving a masterful speech

systematic desensitization
a method to reduce apprehension by gradually visualizing increasingly more frightening speaking events

cognitive restructuring
a method to systematically rebuild thoughts about public speaking by replacing anxiety-arousing negative self-talk with anxiety-reducing positive self-talk

Cognitive Restructuring

Beth decided to try cognitive restructuring to reduce her anxiety about giving speeches in front of her classmates. Here are the positive statements she developed to counter her negative self-talk:

Negative self-talk
1. I'm afraid I'll stumble over my words and look foolish.
2. I'm afraid everyone will be able to tell that I am nervous.
3. I'm afraid my voice will crack.
4. I'm afraid I'll sound boring.

Positive coping statements
1. Even if I stumble, I will have succeeded as long as I get my message across.
2. They probably won't be able to tell I'm nervous, but as long as I focus on getting my message across, that's what matters.
3. Even if my voice cracks, as long as I keep going and focus on getting my message across, I'll succeed at what matters most.
4. I won't sound bored if I focus on how important this message is to me and to my audience. I don't have to do somersaults to keep their attention, because my topic is relevant to them.

public speaking skills training
the systematic teaching of the skills associated with preparing and delivering an effective public speech, with the intention of improving speaking competence and thereby reducing public speaking apprehension

delivery
how a message is communicated orally and visually through the use of voice and body to be conversational and animated

conversational style
an informal style of presenting a speech so that your audience feels you are talking with them, not at them

spontaneity
a naturalness that seems unrehearsed or memorized

animated
lively and dynamic

3. Develop positive coping statements to replace each negative self-talk statement.

4. Incorporate your positive coping statements into your life so they become second nature. You can do this by writing your statements down and reading them aloud to yourself each day as well as before you give a speech. The more you repeat your coping statements, the more natural they will become.

Public Speaking Skills Training

Public speaking skills training is the systematic teaching of the skills associated with preparing and delivering an effective public speech, with the intention of reducing public speaking apprehension. Skills training is based on the assumption that some of our anxiety about speaking in public is due to not knowing how to be successful—we lack the knowledge and behaviors to be effective. Therefore, if we learn the processes and behaviors associated with effective speech making, then we will be less anxious (Kelly, Phillips, & Keaten, 1995, pp. 11–13). Public speaking skills include those associated with the processes of goal analysis, audience and situation analysis, organization, delivery, and self-evaluation.

All five of these methods for reducing public speaking apprehension have successfully helped people manage their anxiety (Dwyer, 2000). For most people, using several of them yields the best results.

LO² Characteristics of an Effective Delivery Style

Think about the best speaker you have ever heard. What made this person stand out in your mind? In all likelihood, how the speaker delivered the speech

had a lot to do with it. **Delivery** is how a message is communicated orally and visually through the use of voice and body.

Use a Conversational Tone

You have probably heard ineffective speakers whose delivery was overly dramatic, too formal, or affected. And you've probably heard ineffective speakers who just read their speeches or sounded mechanical. In contrast, effective delivery has a **conversational style**—your audience feels you are talking *with* them, not *at* them. The hallmark of a conversational style is spontaneity. **Spontaneity** is the ability to sound natural as you speak—as though you are really thinking about the ideas and about getting them across to your audience. Your speech doesn't sound rehearsed, memorized, or read no matter how many times you've practiced it.

How can you make your thoroughly prepared and practiced speech sound spontaneous? One effectively strategy is to learn the *ideas* of the speech instead of trying to memorize its words. You develop spontaneity in public speaking by getting to know the ideas in your speech as well as you know the route you take to school or to work. When you know the ideas this well, you can focus on talking with your audience about your ideas in an organized, professional, and natural way.

Be Animated

Have you ever been bored by a professor reading a well-structured lecture in a monotone voice while looking at the lecture notes rather than the students and making few gestures other than turning the pages? A well-made speech given by an expert can bore an audience unless its delivery is animated—that is, lively and dynamic.

How can you be animated? The secret is to focus on conveying the passion you feel about your topic to your audience through your voice and body. In everyday life, all of us differ in how animated we are when we speak. When we are excited to share something with someone, however, almost all of us become more animated in our delivery. It is this level of liveliness that you want to duplicate when you deliver your speech.

For most of us, appearing conversational and animated requires considerable practice. So, in the next two sections, we'll focus on how you can use your voice and your body to deliver your speech effectively.

© YURI ARCURS/SHUTTERSTOCK

LO³ Effective Use of Your Voice

Your voice is the vehicle that communicates the ideas in your speech to your audience. The sound of your voice affects your success in getting those ideas across. How your voice sounds depends on its pitch, volume, rate, and quality.

Pitch is the highness or lowness of the sounds produced in your larynx by the vibration of your vocal cords. Just as the pitch of a guitar string is changed by making it tighter or looser, the pitch of your voice is changed by tightening and loosening the vocal cords. Natural pitch varies from person to person, but adult men generally have lower voices than women and children.

Volume is how loudly or softly you speak. You control your volume by how forcefully you expel air through your vocal cords. When you push a lot of air through your vocal cords, you speak loudly. When you push less air through, your volume drops.

Rate is how fast you talk. In your speeches, you will want to vary your rate. Present new or difficult ideas more slowly. Speak more quickly when covering material that you expect to be more easily understood.

Quality is the tone or timbre of your voice and what distinguishes it from others—it's how you sound to others. Voices that are nasal, breathy, harsh, or hoarse can be unpleasant to listen to and may distract from the message. The vocal quality that is most easily understood is clear and pleasant to the ear.

By effectively using your pitch, volume, rate, and quality, you can achieve the animated, conversational quality that will help your audience listen to your speech.

As you practice and deliver your speech, take note of *how* you sound. Strive to use your voice so that what you say is both intelligible and vocally expressive.

Speak Intelligibly

To be **intelligible** means to be understandable. All of us have experienced situations in which we couldn't understand what was being said because the speaker was talking too softly or too quickly or had a voice that was compromised in some way. If you are not intelligible, your listeners are bound to struggle with your verbal message. By practicing using appropriate pitch, volume, rate, and vocal quality, you can improve the likelihood that you will be intelligible to your audience.

Most of us speak at a pitch that is appropriate for us and intelligible to listeners. However, some people naturally have voices that are higher or lower in register or become accustomed to talking in tones that are either above or below their natural pitch. Speaking at an appropriate pitch is particularly important if your audience includes people who have hearing loss, as they may find it difficult to hear a pitch that is too high or too low.

In normal conversation, pitch fluctuates frequently, and perhaps even a bit more when giving a speech. For example, in English, a sentence that is meant to be a question is vocalized with rising pitch. If pitch doesn't rise at the end of a question, listeners may interpret the sentence as a statement instead.

The volume of your voice should be loud enough to be heard easily by the audience members in the back of the room but not so loud as to cause discomfort to listeners seated in the front. You can vary your volume to emphasize important information. For example, you may speak louder when as you introduce each of your main points.

The rate at which you speak should be appropriate to the information you are presenting. If you speak too slowly, your listeners' minds may wander from you and your message. If you speak too quickly, especially when sharing complex ideas and arguments, your listeners may not have enough time to process the information completely. Because nervousness may cause you to speak more quickly than normal, monitor your rate and adjust it if you are speaking more quickly than normal.

In addition to vocal characteristics, your articulation and accent can affect intelligibility. **Articulation** is using the tongue, palate, teeth, jaws, and lips to shape vocalized

> If you are not intelligible, your listeners are bound to struggle with your verbal message.

© JAN PAUL SCHRAGE/ISTOCKPHOTO.COM

pitch
the highness or lowness of the sounds produced by the vibration of your vocal cords

volume
the degree of loudness of the tone you make as you expel air through your vocal cords

rate
the speed at which you talk

quality
the tone, timbre, or sound of your voice

intelligible
understandable

articulation
using the tongue, palate, teeth, jaw movement, and lips to shape vocalized sounds that combine to produce a word

pronunciation
the form and accent of various syllables of a word

accent
the articulation, inflection, tone, and speech habits typical of the native speakers of a language

vocal expressiveness
the contrasts in pitch, volume, rate, and quality that affect the meaning an audience gets from the sentences you speak

monotone
a voice in which the pitch, volume, and rate remain constant, with no word, idea, or sentence differing significantly from any other

pauses
moments of silence strategically used to enhance meaning

facial expression
eye and mouth movements

sounds that combine to produce a word. Many of us suffer from minor articulation and pronunciation problems such as adding an extra sound ("athalete" for *athlete*), leaving out a sound ("libary" for *library*), transposing sounds ("revalent" for *relevant*), and distorting sounds ("truf" for *truth*). Accent is the inflection, tone, and speech habits typical of native speakers of a language. When you misarticulate or speak with a heavy accent during a conversation, your listeners can ask you to repeat yourself until they understand you. But in a speech setting, audience members are unlikely to interrupt to ask you to repeat what you have just said. If your accent is strong or very different from that of most of your audience, practice pronouncing key words so that you are easily understood, speak slowly to allow your audience members more time to process your message, and consider reinforcing important points with visual aids.

Use Vocal Expressiveness

Vocal expressiveness is produced by the variety you create in your voice through changing pitch, volume, and rate; stressing certain words; and using pauses. These contrasts clarify the emotional meaning of your message and help animate your delivery. Generally, speeding up your rate, raising your pitch, and increasing your volume reinforce emotions such as joy, enthusiasm, excitement, or anticipation as well as a sense of urgency or fear. Slowing down your rate, lowering your pitch, or decreasing your volume can communicate resolution, peacefulness, remorse, disgust, or sadness.

A total lack of vocal expressiveness produces a **monotone**—a voice in which the pitch, volume, and rate remain constant, with no word, idea, or sentence differing significantly in sound from any other. Although few people speak in a true monotone, many severely limit themselves

by using only two or three pitch levels and relatively unchanging volume and rate. An actual or near monotone not only lulls an audience to sleep but, more important, diminishes the chances of audience understanding. For instance, if the sentence "Congress should pass laws limiting the sale of pornography" is presented in a monotone, listeners will be uncertain whether the speaker is concerned with *who* should take action, what Congress should *do*, or *what* the laws should be.

Pauses, or moments of silence strategically used to enhance meaning, can mark important ideas. If you use one or more sentences in your speech to express an important idea, pause before each sentence to signal that something important is coming or pause afterward to allow the idea to sink in. Pausing one or more times within a sentence can also add impact. Nick included several short pauses within and a long pause after his sentence "Our government has no compassion (*pause*), no empathy (*pause*), and no regard for human feeling" (*longer pause*).

LO⁴ Effective Use of Your Body

Because your audience can see as well as hear you, how you use your body contributes to the impression of conversational and animated delivery. The body language elements that affect delivery are facial expressions, gestures, movement, eye contact, posture, poise, and appearance.

Facial Expressions

Facial expressions are the eye and mouth movements that convey your personableness and can help you animate your speech. When you talk with friends, your facial expressions are naturally animated. Your audiences expect your expressions to be similarly animated when you give a speech. Speakers who do not vary their facial expressions during their speech but instead wear a deadpan expression, a perpetual grin, or a permanent scowl tend to be perceived as boring, insincere, or

© KASIUTEK/SHUTTERSTOCK

stern. Audiences respond positively to natural facial expressions that appear to spontaneously reflect what you're saying and how you feel about it.

Gestures

Gestures—the movements of your hands, arms, and fingers—can help intelligibility. You can use gestures to describe or emphasize what you are saying, refer to presentational aids, or clarify structure. For example, as Aaron began to speak about the advantages of wireless DSL, he said "on one hand" and lifted his right hand face up. When he got to the disadvantages, he lifted his left hand face up as he said "on the other hand."

Some people who are nervous when giving a speech clasp their hands behind their backs, bury them in their pockets, or grip the lectern. Unable to pry their hands free gracefully, they wiggle their elbows weirdly or appear stiff.

As with facial expressions, effective gestures must appear spontaneous and natural even though they are carefully planned and practiced. When you practice and then deliver your speech, leave your hands free so that they will be available to gesture as you normally do.

Movement

Movement is changing the position or location of your entire body. During your speech, it is important to engage only in **motivated movement**, or movement with a specific purpose such as emphasizing an important idea, referencing a presentational aid, or clarifying macrostructure. To emphasize a particular point, you might move closer to the audience. To create a feeling of intimacy before telling a personal story, you might walk out from behind a lectern and sit down on a chair placed at the edge of the stage. Each time you begin a new main point, you might take a few steps to one side of the stage or the other. To use motivated movement effectively, you need to practice when and how you will move.

Avoid such unmotivated movement as bobbing, weaving, shifting from foot to foot, or pacing from one side of the room to the other, as unplanned movements distract the audience from your message. Because many unplanned movements result from nervousness, you can minimize them by paying mindful attention to your body as you speak. At the beginning of your speech, stand up straight on both feet. If you find yourself fidgeting, readjust and position you body with your weight equally distributed on both feet.

Eye Contact

Eye contact is looking directly at the people to whom you are speaking. In speech making, it involves looking at people in all parts of an audience throughout the speech. As long as you are looking at someone (those in front of you, in the left rear of the room, in the right center of the room, and so on) and not at your notes or the ceiling, floor, or window, everyone in the audience will perceive you as having good eye contact with them. Generally, you should look at your audience at least 90 percent of the time, glancing at your notes only when you need a quick reference point. Maintaining eye contact is important for several reasons.

Maintaining eye contact helps audiences concentrate on the speech. If you do not look at audience members while you talk, audience members are unlikely to maintain eye contact with you. This break in mutual eye contact often decreases concentration on your message.

Maintaining eye contact increases the audience's confidence in you, the speaker. Just as you are likely to be skeptical of people who do not look you in the eye as they converse, so too audiences will be skeptical of speakers who do not look at them. In the United States, eye contact is perceived as a sign of sincerity. Speakers who fail to maintain eye contact with audiences are perceived almost always as ill at ease and often as insincere or dishonest (Burgoon, Coker, & Coker, 1986).

Maintaining eye contact helps you gain insight into the audience's reaction to the speech. Because communication is two-way, audience members are communicating with you at the same time you are speaking to them. In public speaking, the audience members typically "speak" through body language. Audience members who are bored might yawn, look out the window, slouch in their chairs, and even sleep. If audience members are confused, they will look puzzled; if they agree with what you

gestures
movements of hands, arms, and fingers that illustrate and emphasize what is being said

movement
changing the position or location of the entire body

motivated movement
movement with a specific purpose, such as emphasizing an important idea, referencing a presentation aid, or clarifying macrostructure

eye contact
looking directly at the people to whom we are speaking

© ANDREY ARMYAGOV/SHUTTERSTOCK

audience contact
when speaking to large
audiences, creating
a sense of looking
listeners in the eye even
though you actually
cannot

posture
the position or bearing
of the body

poise
graceful and controlled
use of the body

appearance
the way we look to
others

say or understand it, they might nod their heads. By monitoring your audience's behavior, you can adjust by becoming more animated, offering additional examples, or moving more quickly through a point.

When speaking to large audiences of 100 or more people, you must create a sense of looking listeners in the eye even though you actually cannot. This process is called **audience contact**. You can create audience contact by mentally dividing your audience into small groups. Then, at random, talk for four to six seconds with each group as you move through your speech.

What would you wear to speak to this audience?

Posture

Posture is the manner in which you hold your body. In speeches, an upright stance and squared shoulders communicate a sense of confidence. As you practice, be aware of your posture and adjust it so that you do not slouch, keeping your weight equally distributed on both feet.

Poise

Poise is a graceful and controlled use of the body that gives the impression that the speaker is self-assured, calm, and dignified. Mannerisms that convey nervousness, such as swaying from side to side, drumming fingers on the lectern, taking off or putting on glasses, jiggling pocket change, smacking the tongue, licking the lips, or scratching the nose, hand, or arm, should be noted during practice sessions and avoided.

Appearance

Some speakers think that what they wear doesn't or shouldn't affect the success of their speech. But your appearance—the way you look to others—is important. Studies show that a neatly groomed and professional appearance sends important messages about a speaker's commitment to the topic and occasion as well as about the speaker's credibility (Bates, 1992; Lawrence & Watson, 1991). Your appearance should complement your message, not detract from it. Three guidelines can help you decide how to dress for your speech.

Consider your audience and the occasion of your speech. Dress a bit more formally than you expect members of your audience to dress. If you dress too formally, your audience is likely to perceive you to be untrustworthy and insincere (Phillips & Smith, 1992), and if you dress too casually, your audience may view you as uncommitted to your topic or disrespectful of them or the occasion (Morris, Gorham, Cohen, & Huffman, 1996).

Consider your topic and purpose. In general, the more serious your topic, the more formally you should dress. For example, if your topic is AIDS and you are trying to convince your audience to be tested for HIV, you will want to look like someone who is an authority by dressing the part. In contrast, if your topic is skateboarding and you are trying to convince your audience that they would enjoy visiting the new skateboard park on campus, you might dress more casually.

Avoid extremes. Your attire shouldn't detract from your speech. Avoid gaudy jewelry, over- or undersized clothing, and sexually suggestive attire. Remember, you want your audience to focus on your message, so your appearance should neutral, not distracting.

All speakers need to practice in order to become effective at using their voice and body in a speech. Even though there are best practices for using your voice and body effectively in a public speaking situation, each of us tends to develop our own unique style. Sometimes a speaker's vocal style or mannerisms become a "signature" and, if the speaker is a celebrity (such as a politician, singer, actor or actress),

© RAIDO VÄLJAMAA/ISTOCKPHOTO.COM / © ISTOCKPHOTO.COM / ISTOCKPHOTO.COM comedians may impersonate him or her for a laugh. Unfortunately, doing so can undermine the person's credibility.

LO⁵ Delivery Methods

Speeches vary in the amount of content preparation and practice you do ahead of time. Each of these factors influences how a speech is delivered. The three most common delivery methods are impromptu, scripted, and extemporaneous.

Impromptu Speeches

At times, you may be called on to speak on the spot. An impromptu speech is one that is delivered with only seconds or minutes of advance notice for preparation and is usually presented without referring to notes of any kind. You may have already been called on in this class to give an impromptu speech, so you know the pressure this delivery method creates.

You can improve your impromptu performances by practicing mock impromptu speeches. For example, if you are taking a class in which the professor calls on students at random to answer questions, you can prepare by anticipating the questions that might be asked on the readings for the day and practice giving your answers. Over time, you will become more adept at organizing your answers and thinking on your feet.

Scripted Speeches

At the other extreme, you might carefully prepare a complete written manuscript of each word you will speak in your presentation. Then you will either memorize or read the text to the audience from a printed document or teleprompter. A scripted speech is one that is prepared by creating a complete written manuscript and delivered by rote memory or reading a written copy.

Obviously, effective scripted speeches take a great deal of time to prepare because both an outline and a word-for-word transcript must be prepared and perhaps memorized. When you memorize a scripted speech, you face the increased anxiety of forgetting your lines. When you read a scripted speech, you must become adept at looking at the script with your peripheral vision so that you don't appear to be reading but instead sound conversational and animated.

Because of the time and skill required to effectively prepare and deliver a scripted speech, scripted speeches are usually reserved for important occasions that have important consequences. Political speeches, keynote addresses at conventions, commencement addresses, and CEO remarks at annual stockholder meetings are examples of occasions when a scripted speech might be worth the effort.

Extemporaneous Speeches

Most speeches, whether in the workplace, in the community, or in class, are delivered extemporaneously. An extemporaneous speech is researched and planned ahead of time, but the exact wording is not scripted and will vary from presentation to presentation. When speaking extemporaneously you may refer to simple notes you have prepared to remind you of the ideas you want to present and the order in which you want to present them.

Extemporaneous speeches are the easiest to give effectively. Unlike impromptu speeches, when speaking extemporaneously you are able to prepare your thoughts ahead of time, have notes to prompt you, and practice what you might actually say. Unlike scripted speeches, extemporaneous speeches do not require as lengthy a preparation process to be effective. In the next section, we describe how to rehearse successfully for an extemporaneous speech.

LO⁶ Rehearsal

Rehearsing is practicing the presentation of your speech aloud. Is it really necessary to practice a speech out loud? A speech that is not practiced out loud is likely to be far less effective than it would have been had you given yourself sufficient time to revise, evaluate, and mull over all aspects of the speech (Menzel & Carrell, 1994, p. 23). Figure 14.1 provides a useful timetable for preparing a classroom speech.

In this section, we describe how to rehearse effectively by preparing speaking notes; handling presentational aids; and recording, analyzing, and refining delivery.

impromptu speech a speech that is delivered with only seconds or minutes of advance notice for preparation and is usually presented without referring to notes

scripted speech a speech that is prepared by creating a complete written manuscript and delivered by rote memory or by reading a written copy

extemporaneous speech a speech that is researched and planned ahead of time, although the exact wording is not scripted and will vary from presentation to presentation

rehearsing practicing the presentation of your speech aloud

Figure 14.1

Sample Timetable for Preparing a Speech

© FENG YU/SHUTTERSTOCK

speaking notes
word or phrase outlines
of your speech

Preparing Speaking Notes

Prior to your first rehearsal session, prepare a draft of your speaking notes. Speaking notes are a word or phrase outline of your speech designed to help trigger your memory. The best notes contain the fewest words possible written in lettering large enough to be seen instantly at a distance.

To develop your notes, begin by reducing your speech outline to an abbreviated outline of key phrases and words. Then, if you have details in the speech that you must cite accurately—such as a specific example, a quotation, or a set of statistics—add these in the appropriate spots. Next, indicate exactly where you plan to share presentational aids. Finally, incorporate delivery cues indicating where you want to make use of your voice and body to enhance intelligibility or expressiveness. For example, indicate where you want to pause, gesture, or make a motivated movement. Capitalize, underline, or highlight words you want to stress. Use slash marks (//) to remind yourself to pause (see Figure 14.2).

For a three- to five-minute speech, you will need no more than three 3 × 5-inch note cards to record your speaking notes. For longer speeches, you might need one card for the introduction, one for each main point, and one for the conclusion. If your speech contains a particularly important and long quotation or a complicated set of statistics, you can record this information in detail on a separate card.

During practice sessions, use the notes as you will when you actually give the speech. If you will use a lectern, set the notes on the speaker's stand or, alternatively, hold them in one hand and refer to them only when needed. How important is it to construct good note cards? Speakers often find that the act of making a note card is so effective in helping cement ideas in the mind that during practice, or later during the speech itself, they rarely use the notes at all.

Handling Presentational Aids

Many speakers think that once they have prepared good presentational aids, they will have no trouble using them in the speech. However, many speeches with good aids have become a shambles because the

Figure 14.2

Sample Note Cards

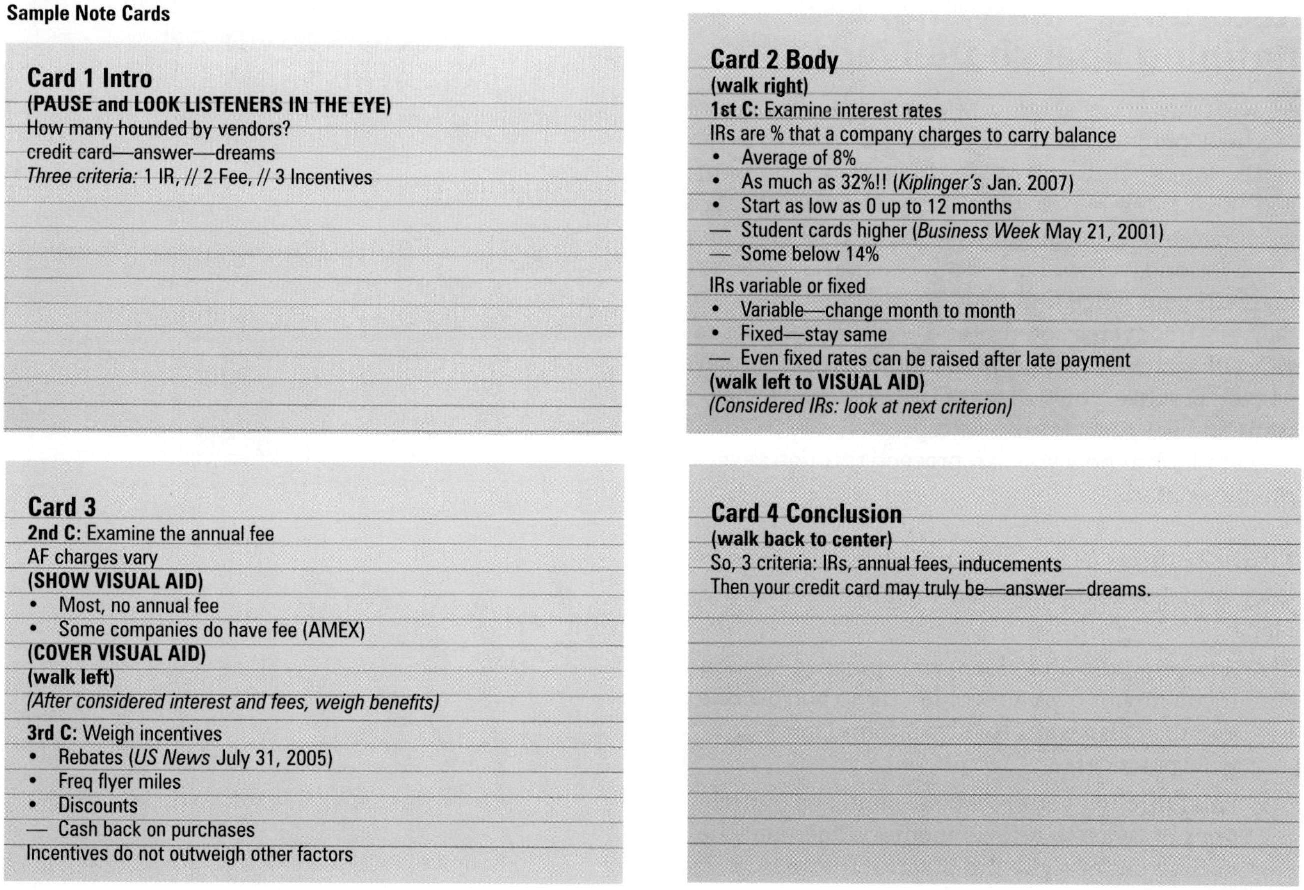

Card 1 Intro
(PAUSE and LOOK LISTENERS IN THE EYE)
How many hounded by vendors?
credit card—answer—dreams
Three criteria: 1 IR, // 2 Fee, // 3 Incentives

Card 2 Body
(walk right)
1st C: Examine interest rates
IRs are % that a company charges to carry balance
• Average of 8%
• As much as 32%!! (*Kiplinger's* Jan. 2007)
• Start as low as 0 up to 12 months
— Student cards higher (*Business Week* May 21, 2001)
— Some below 14%

IRs variable or fixed
• Variable—change month to month
• Fixed—stay same
— Even fixed rates can be raised after late payment
(walk left to VISUAL AID)
(Considered IRs: look at next criterion)

Card 3
2nd C: Examine the annual fee
AF charges vary
(SHOW VISUAL AID)
• Most, no annual fee
• Some companies do have fee (AMEX)
(COVER VISUAL AID)
(walk left)
(After considered interest and fees, weigh benefits)

3rd C: Weigh incentives
• Rebates (*US News* July 31, 2005)
• Freq flyer miles
• Discounts
— Cash back on purchases
Incentives do not outweigh other factors

Card 4 Conclusion
(walk back to center)
So, 3 criteria: IRs, annual fees, inducements
Then your credit card may truly be—answer—dreams.

© STUART BURFORD/ISTOCKPHOTO.COM

aids were not well handled. You can avoid problems by following these guidelines:

Carefully plan when to use presentational aids. Indicate on your outline (and mark on your speaking notes) exactly when you will reveal and conceal each aid. Practice introducing and using your aids until you can use them comfortably and smoothly.

Consider audience needs carefully. As you practice, eliminate any presentational aid that does not contribute directly to the audience's attention to, understanding of, or retention of the key ideas in the speech.

Share a presentational aid only when talking about it. Because presentational aids will draw audience attention, practice sharing them only when you are talking about them and then removing them when they are no longer the focus of attention.

A single visual or audiovisual aid may contain several bits of information. To keep audience attention where you want it, you can prepare the aid so that you only expose the portion you are discussing. This is particularly true when using computerized slideshows. Practice using the "B" key for a black screen when you aren't directly referencing the aid as well as the slideshow animation feature to make

concepts appear only when you are ready to talk about them.

Display visual and audio aids so that everyone in the audience can see and hear them. It's frustrating not to be able to see or hear an aid. Try to practice in the space where you will give your speech so you will know how to adjust the equipment to make visual images easily seen and sounds clearly heard from all points in the room. If you cannot practice in the space ahead of time, be sure to arrive early enough on the day of the presentation to practice quickly with the equipment you will use.

Talk to your audience, not to the presentational aid. Although you will want to acknowledge the presentational aid by looking at it occasionally, it is important to keep your eye contact focused on your audience. As you practice, resist the urge to stare at your presentational aid.

Resist the temptation to pass objects through the audience. People look at, read, handle, and think about whatever they hold in their hands. While they are so occupied, they are not likely to be listening to you. It is better to project the images in front of the audience and save handouts for distribution after the speech.

Recording, Analyzing, and Refining Speech Delivery

As with any other activity, effective speech delivery requires practice, and the more you practice, the better your speech will be. During practice sessions, you have three major goals. First, you will practice wording your ideas so they are clear, inclusive, and vivid. Second, you will practice your speech by working with your voice and body so that your ideas are delivered conversationally and expressively. Third, you will practice using presentational aids. As part of each practice, you will want to analyze how well it went and set goals for the next practice session.

Let's look at how you can proceed through several practice rounds.

First Practice

Your initial rehearsal should include the following steps:

1. Record (audio and video) your practice session. If you do not own a recorder, try to borrow one. You may also want to have a friend sit in on your practice.

2. Read through your complete sentence outline once or twice to refresh memory. Then put the outline out of sight and practice the speech using only the note cards you have prepared.

3. Make the practice as similar to the speech situation as possible, including using the presentational aids you've prepared. Stand up and face your imaginary audience. Pretend that the chairs, lamps, books, and other objects in your practice room are people.

4. Write down the time that you begin.

5. Begin speaking. Regardless of what happens, keep going until you have presented your entire speech. If you goof, make a repair as you would have to do if you were actually delivering the speech to an audience.

6. Write down the time you finish. Compute the length of the speech for this first rehearsal.

Analysis

Listen to and watch the recording, and look at your complete outline. How did it go? Did you leave out any key ideas? Did you talk too long on any one point and not long enough on another? Did you clarify each of your points? Did you adapt to your anticipated audience? (If you had a friend or relative watch and listen to your practice, have him or her help with your analysis.) Were your note cards effective? How well did you do with your presentational aids? Make any necessary changes before your second rehearsal.

Second Practice

Repeat the six steps outlined for the first rehearsal. By practicing a second time right after your analysis, you are more likely to make the kind of adjustments that begin to improve the speech.

Action Step 5a
Rehearsing Your Speech

The goal of this activity is to rehearse your speech, analyze it, and rehearse it again. One complete rehearsal includes a practice, an analysis, and a second practice.

1. Find a place where you can be alone to practice your speech. Follow the six points of the first practice that are shown in the left-hand column of this page.

2. Listen to and watch the recording. Review your outline as you watch and listen and then answer the following questions:

   a. *Are you satisfied with how well*

   The introduction got attention and led into the speech? _____

   Main points were clearly stated? _____

   Well developed? _____

   Material was adapted to the audience? _____

   Section transitions were used? _____

   The conclusion summarized the main points? _____

   The speech was left on a high note? _____

   Presentational aids were used? _____

   Ideas were expressed vividly? _____

   Clearly? _____

   It sounded conversational throughout? _____

   Animated? _____

   Intelligible? _____

   Natural gestures and movement were used? _____

   Eye contact? _____

   Facial expression? _____

   Posture? _____

   Appearance? _____

   b. List the three most important changes you will make in your next practice session:

   One: _____

   Two: _____

   Three: _____

3. Go through the six steps outlined for the first practice again. Did you achieve the goals you set for the second practice? _____

Reevaluate the speech using the checklist, and continue to practice until you are satisfied with all parts of your presentation.

© LOSEVSKY PAVEL/SHUTTERSTOCK

Additional Practices

After you have completed one full rehearsal session, consisting of two practices and the analysis in between them, put the speech away until that night or the next day. Although you should rehearse the speech at least one more time, you will not benefit if you cram all the practices into one long rehearsal time. You may find that a final practice right before you go to bed will be very helpful; while you are sleeping, your subconscious will continue to work on the speech. As a result, you are likely to find significant improvement in your mastery of the speech when you practice again the next day.

How many times you practice depends on many variables, including your experience, your familiarity with the subject, and the length of your speech.

LO⁷ Criteria for Evaluating Speeches

In addition to learning to prepare and present speeches, you are learning to evaluate (critically analyze) the speeches you hear. From an educational standpoint, critical analysis of speeches provides the speaker with an analysis of where the speech went right and where it went wrong, and it also gives you, the critic, insight into the methods that you can incorporate or avoid in your own speeches. In this section, we look at some general criteria for evaluating public speeches.

The critical assumption is that if a speech has good content that is adapted to the audience, is clearly organized, and is delivered well, it is likely to achieve its goal. Thus, you can evaluate any speech by answering questions that relate to the basics of content, structure, and delivery. Figure 14.3 is a speech critique checklist. You can use this checklist to analyze your first speech during your rehearsal period and to critique sample student speeches at the end of this chapter as well as speeches delivered by your classmates.

Figure 14.3

Speech Critique Checklist

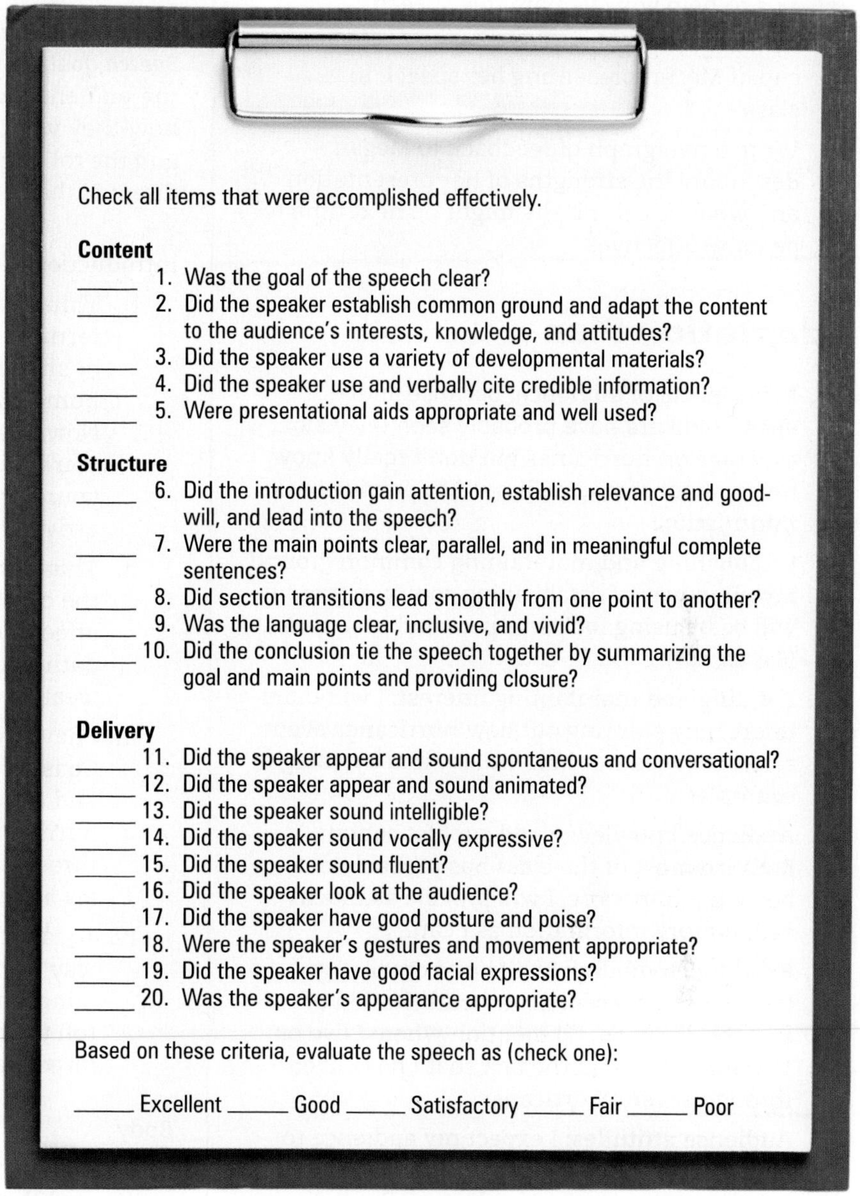

Check all items that were accomplished effectively.

Content
_____ 1. Was the goal of the speech clear?
_____ 2. Did the speaker establish common ground and adapt the content to the audience's interests, knowledge, and attitudes?
_____ 3. Did the speaker use a variety of developmental materials?
_____ 4. Did the speaker use and verbally cite credible information?
_____ 5. Were presentational aids appropriate and well used?

Structure
_____ 6. Did the introduction gain attention, establish relevance and goodwill, and lead into the speech?
_____ 7. Were the main points clear, parallel, and in meaningful complete sentences?
_____ 8. Did section transitions lead smoothly from one point to another?
_____ 9. Was the language clear, inclusive, and vivid?
_____ 10. Did the conclusion tie the speech together by summarizing the goal and main points and providing closure?

Delivery
_____ 11. Did the speaker appear and sound spontaneous and conversational?
_____ 12. Did the speaker appear and sound animated?
_____ 13. Did the speaker sound intelligible?
_____ 14. Did the speaker sound vocally expressive?
_____ 15. Did the speaker sound fluent?
_____ 16. Did the speaker look at the audience?
_____ 17. Did the speaker have good posture and poise?
_____ 18. Were the speaker's gestures and movement appropriate?
_____ 19. Did the speaker have good facial expressions?
_____ 20. Was the speaker's appearance appropriate?

Based on these criteria, evaluate the speech as (check one):

_____ Excellent _____ Good _____ Satisfactory _____ Fair _____ Poor

Sample Informative Speech: Understanding Hurricanes

Adapted from a speech by Megan Soileau from the University of Kentucky*

This section presents a sample informative speech adaptation plan, outline, and transcript by a student in an introductory speaking course.

1. Review the outline and adaptation plan developed by Megan Soileau in preparing her speech on hurricanes.

*Used with permission of Megan Soileau.

© SERGHEI VELUSCEAC/ISTOCKPHOTO.COM

2. Read the transcript of her speech.

3. Use the Speech Critique Checklist from Figure 14.3 to help you evaluate this speech.

4. At www.cengagebrain.com watch a video clip of Megan presenting her speech in class.

5. Write a paragraph of feedback to Megan, describing the strengths of her presentation and what you think she might do next time to be more effective.

Adaptation Plan

1. **Key aspects of audience:** Because audience members have probably seen television coverage on hurricanes but don't really know much about them, I will need to provide basic information.

2. **Establishing and maintaining common ground:** My main way of establishing common ground will be by using inclusive personal pronouns (*we, us, our*).

3. **Building and maintaining interest:** I will build interest by pointing out how hurricanes even affect the weather in Kentucky and by using examples.

4. **Audience knowledge and sophistication:** Because most of the class has probably not been in a hurricane, I will provide as much explanatory information as I can.

5. **Building credibility:** I will build credibility through solid research and oral citation of sources. Early on, I'll mention where I live on the Gulf Coast and the fact that I have lived through several hurricanes.

6. **Audience attitudes:** I expect my audience to be curious about hurricanes, especially since Hurricane Katrina received so much media attention. So I will give them information to help them become more knowledgeable about them.

7. **Adapt to audiences from different cultures and language communities:** Because hurricanes occur on coasts all over the world, I don't need to adapt to different cultures or language communities. However, I will consider how to make the topic relevant to people who do not live on a coast.

8. **Use presentational aids to enhance audience understanding and memory:** I will use several PowerPoint slides to highlight the effects of hurricanes.

Speech Outline: Understanding Hurricanes

General purpose: To inform
Speech goal: In this speech, I am going to familiarize the audience with the overall effects of hurricanes: how they work, ways they affect our whole country, and the toll they have on the people who live in their direct paths.

Introduction

I. Think about a time you've been absolutely terrified (whether it was by a person, event, or situation) and all you wanted to do was go home and be with your family and friends. Now imagine the feeling you might have if you were that afraid, but you had no idea if your home would even be there when you arrived.

II. This is the reality for many people living on the coastlines of the United States. Hurricanes affect the lives of those living in their direct paths, but they can also cause spin-off weather that affects the entire country.

III. I have lived about 45 minutes from the Gulf Coast of Texas my entire life and have seen and experienced the destruction caused by hurricanes firsthand, especially in the past three years. (*Slide 1: Picture of hurricane that hit my hometown last year*)

IV. Today I'd like to speak with you about the way hurricanes work, the ways they affect our entire country, and most importantly, the toll they have on the people who live in their direct paths.

Body

I. To begin, let's discuss how hurricanes form and the varying degrees of intensity of them so we can be better informed when we watch news broadcasts and read newspaper reports about them.

   A. Several basic conditions must be present for a hurricane to form.

      1. According to award-winning Discovery Communications Web site HowStuffWorks.com, hurricanes form "when an area of warm low pressure air rises and cool, high pressure seizes the opportunity to move in underneath it." This causes a center to develop. This center may eventually turn into what is considered a hurricane.

2. The warm and moist air from the ocean rises up into these pressure zones and begins to form storms. As this happens, the storm continues to draw up more warm moist air, and a heat transfer occurs because of the cool air being heated, causing the air to rise again.

3. "The exchange of heat creates a pattern of wind that circulates around a center" (the eye of the storm) "like water going down a drain."

4. The "rising air reinforces the air that is already" being pulled up from the surface of the ocean, "so the circulation and speeds of the wind increase."

B. Classifications of these types of storms help determine their intensity so we can prepare properly for them.

1. Winds that are less than 38 miles per hour are considered tropical depressions.

2. Tropical storms are winds ranging from 39 to 73 miles per hour.

3. And lastly, hurricanes are storms with wind speeds of 74 miles per hour and higher.

4. When storms become classified as hurricanes, they become part of another classification system that is displayed by the Saffir-Simpson Hurricane Scale.

   a. Hurricanes are labeled as Categories 1–5 based on their wind-intensity level or speed. (*Slide 2: Hurricane scale chart*)

   b. Hurricane Ike was labeled differently at different places. (*Slide 3: Map showing the different places Ike was labeled in the different categories*)

Transition: Knowing how and where hurricanes occur helps us determine how our daily lives, even here in Kentucky, may be affected when one hits.

II. A hurricane can affect more than just those living in its direct path, and these effects can actually be seen across the country in terms of the environment and the economy.

A. Hurricanes affect wildlife in negative ways.

1. According to the *Beaumont Enterprise* on October 7, 2008, the storm surge of Hurricane Ike brought up to 14 feet of water in some parts of the Southeast.

2. Dolphins were swept inland with the surge and then, when the waters flowed back out to sea, dolphins were left stranded in the marsh.

3. Some were rescued, but not all. This dolphin was rescued from a ditch. (*Slide 4: Dolphin being rescued*)

B. Hurricanes also affect the economy as prices climb close to all-time highs when hurricanes hit.

1. According to economist Beth Ann Bovino, quoted in the September 29, 2005 issue of *The Washington Post,* gas prices skyrocket when a hurricane like Katrina, Rita, or Ike hit.

   a. Paul Davidson said, in a September 12, 2008 article in *USA Today,* that in anticipation of Hurricane Ike, 12 refineries in Texas were shut down. "This is 17% of the U.S. refining capacity," he said.

   b. That's why even residents here in Lexington saw a dramatic spike in gas prices immediately following Ike's landfall.

2. Energy costs to heat and cool our homes also rise.

   a. When we consumers have to pay more to heat and cool our homes, we also have less to spend eating out at restaurants.

   b. And we have less to spend on non-essentials at the mall.

   c. So, economically we all feel the ripple effect when hurricanes hit.

Transition: So, yes, we all feel the effects of hurricanes, but we should not overlook the dramatic ways in which people who live in the direct path of a hurricane are affected.

III. When a hurricane hits, many of these people become homeless, at least for a while, and suffer emotionally and financially as they evacuate to places all over the country, including Kentucky!

A. People who go through hurricanes suffer extreme emotional effects.

1. Evacuation is stressful because people have to pack up what they can and have no way of knowing if their home will still be standing or inhabitable

when they return. (*Slides 5 and 6: Before and after pictures from Hurricane Ike*)

    2. Even returning home is emotionally taxing because returning home means rebuilding homes, neighborhoods, and even memories.

    3. Though we try to get back to a "normal" life, it can never really be the same as it once was. Instead, it's what Silicon Valley venture capitalist and investor Roger McNamee calls the "new normal" in his book: *The New Normal: Great Opportunities in a Time of Great Risk.*

B. Because they have to rebuild their homes and lives, people also go through financial difficulties.

    1. People battle with insurance companies about whether a home has wind or water damage as they seek financial assistance. (Insurance companies will often claim that it is the one—wind or water—the homeowner is uninsured for.)

    2. Price gouging is another financial challenge hurricane victims face.

      a. When families and businesses begin the process of rebuilding, people come from outside areas to help with labor and materials and will charge exorbitant fees.

      b. An example of this is when my father needed people to help remove two trees from our home in September 2005 after Hurricane Rita.

Conclusion

I. Hurricanes affect victims who live in their direct path and the country as a whole.

II. To understand these effects, we talked about how hurricanes work, how they affect our country and daily lives, and the impacts they have on the lives of people who live through them.

III. Maybe knowing some of these facts will help each of us appreciate our homes and our families just a little bit more. (*Handout: Hurricane tracking charts*)

References

Associated Press. (2008, October 8). Windstorm costs insurers $550M. *Newark Advocate*, p. x.

Bovino, B. A. (2005, September 29). Hurricanes impact national economy. *The Washington Post*, Retrieved from http://washingtonpost.com/wp-dym/content/discussion/2005/09/28/D1200509280I431.html

Davidson, P. (2008, September 12). "Ike blows gasoline prices higher." *USA Today*, p. x.

Marshall, B., Freudenrich, C., & Lamb, R. How hurricanes work. Retrieved from http://www.howstuffworks.com/hurricanes.htm

McNamee, R. (2004). *The new normal: Great opportunities in a time of great risk.* New York: Penguin.

Rappleye, C. (2008, October 7). Hurricane strands marine mammals, damages facility for the stranded. *Beaumont Enterprise*.

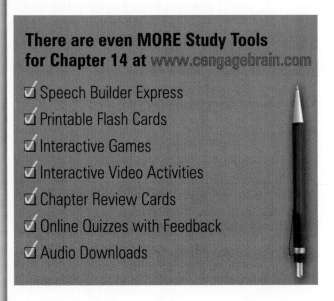

© ROB WILSON/SHUTTERSTOCK

EVACUATION ROUTE

There are even MORE Study Tools for Chapter 14 at www.cengagebrain.com

☑ Speech Builder Express

☑ Printable Flash Cards

☑ Interactive Games

☑ Interactive Video Activities

☑ Chapter Review Cards

☑ Online Quizzes with Feedback

☑ Audio Downloads

Speech and Analysis

Speech

Think about a time you've been absolutely terrified, whether it was by a person, event, or situation and all you wanted to do was go home and be with your family and friends.

Now imagine the feeling you might have if you were that afraid, but you had no idea if your home would even be there when you arrived. This is the reality for many people living on the coastlines of the United States. Hurricanes affect the lives of those living in their direct paths, but they can also affect the entire country.

I have lived about forty-five minutes from the Gulf Coast of Texas my entire life and have seen and experienced the destruction caused by hurricanes first hand, especially in the past three years. (Slide 1: Picture of hurricane that hit my hometown last year.) This is a picture of my hometown when a hurricane hit it last year.

Today I'd like to speak with you about the way hurricanes work, the ways they affect our whole country and, most importantly, the toll they have on the people who live in their direct paths.

To begin, let's discuss how hurricanes form and the varying degrees of intensity of them so we can be better informed when we watch news broadcasts and read newspaper reports about them.

Several basic conditions must be present for a Hurricane to form. According to award-winning Discovery Communications Web site HowStuffWorks.com, hurricanes form "when an area of warm low pressure air rises and cool, high pressure seizes the opportunity to move in underneath it." This causes a center to develop. This center may eventually turn into what is considered a hurricane. The warm and moist air from the ocean rises up into these pressure zones and begins to form storms. As this happens the storm continues to draw up more warm moist air and a heat transfer occurs because of the cool air being heated, causing the air to rise again. "The exchange of heat creates a pattern of wind that circulates around a center" (the eye of the storm) "like water going down a drain." The "rising air reinforces the air that is already" being pulled up from the surface of the ocean, "so the circulation and speeds of the wind increase."

Classifications of these types of storms help determine their intensity so we can prepare properly for them. Winds that are less than 38 miles per hour are considered tropical depressions. Tropical storms have winds that range from 39 to 73 miles per hour. And lastly hurricanes are storms with wind speeds of 74 miles per hour and higher.

Analysis

Megan opens by using an analogy to help get her audience emotionally involved in her speech, then quickly introduces her topic.

Notice how Megan establishes her credibility by sharing that she grew up near the Gulf Coast of Texas and has been a hurricane victim herself. The first slide adds emotional appeal to her point.

Megan concludes her introduction by previewing her main points clearly.

Megan does a nice job of incorporating a listener relevance link into her first main point statement.

Here Megan offers an oral footnote to add credibility. Noting that the Web site is an award-winning one helps her here.

When storms become classified as a hurricane, they become part of another classification system that is displayed by the Saffir-Simpson Hurricane Scale. Hurricanes are labeled as categories 1–5 based on their wind intensity level or speed. (*Slide 2: Hurricane scale chart*) Hurricane Ike was labeled differently at different places. (*Slide 3: Map showing the different places Ike was labeled in the different categories*)

Showing the hurricane scale chart and the map depicting Hurricane Ike at different categories visually reinforces what Megan describes in her verbal message.

Knowing how and where hurricanes occur helps us determine how our daily lives, even here in Kentucky, may be affected when one hits.

A hurricane can affect more than just those living in its direct path, and these effects can actually be seen across the country in terms of the environment and the economy.

Megan does a nice job tieing together the two main points, which makes for a fluent section transition.

Hurricanes affect wildlife in negative ways. According to the *Beaumont Enterprise* on October 7, 2008, Christine Rappleye reported that the storm surge, which is basically a wall of water, that Hurricane Ike brought in across some parts of Southeast Texas was about 14 feet in some places. Dolphins were swept inland with the surge and then, when the waters flowed back out to sea, dolphins were left stranded in the marsh. Some were rescued, but not all. This dolphin was rescued from a ditch. (*Slide 4: Dolphin being rescued*)

Here Megan not only describes the 14-foot wall of water Hurricane Ike transported into Texas but also reinforces it with the picture on her PowerPoint slide.

Hurricanes also affect the economy. Prices of goods climb close to all time highs when hurricanes hit. According to economist Beth Ann Bovino, quoted in the September 29, 2005 issue of *The Washington Post*, gas prices skyrocket when a hurricane like Katrina, Rita, or Ike hit. Paul Davidson said in a September 12, 2008 article in *USA Today* that in anticipation of Hurricane Ike, 12 refineries in Texas were shut down. "This is 17% of the U.S. refining capacity," he said. That's why even residents here in Lexington saw a dramatic spike in gas prices immediately following Ike's landfall.

Indicating that Beth Ann Bovino is an economist makes this oral footnote stand out as very credible.

Here Megan reminds her audience that even in Lexington, Kentucky, hurricanes have an impact, which is felt in higher gas prices and energy costs.

Energy costs to heat and cool our homes also rise. When consumers have to pay more to heat and cool our homes, we also have less to spend eating out at restaurants. And we have less to spend on non-essentials at the mall. So, economically we all feel the ripple effect when hurricanes hit.

Here Megan could have developed her main point with an example or a concrete story.

So, yes, we all feel the effects of hurricanes, but we should not overlook the dramatic ways in which people who live in the direct path of a hurricane are affected.

Again, Megan offers a clear and fluent section transition.

When a hurricane hits, many of these people become homeless, at least for a while, and suffer emotionally and financially as they evacuate to places all over the country, including Kentucky!

People who go through hurricanes suffer extreme emotional effects. Evacuation is stressful because people have to pack up what they can and have no way of knowing if their home will still be standing or inhabitable when they return. (*Slides 5 and 6: Before and after pictures from Hurricane Ike*)

Even returning home is emotionally taxing because returning home means rebuilding homes, neighborhoods, and even memories. Though we try to get back to a "normal" life, it can never really be the same as it once was. Instead, it's what Silicon Valley venture capitalist and investor Roger McNamee calls the "new normal" in his book *The New Normal: Great Opportunities in a Time of Great Risk*.

Because they have to rebuild their homes and lives, people also go through financial difficulties. People battle with insurance companies about whether a home has wind or water damage as they seek financial assistance. (Insurance companies will often claim that it is the one—wind or water—the homeowner is uninsured for.)

Price gouging is another financial challenge hurricane victims face. When families and businesses begin the process of rebuilding, people come from outside areas to help with labor and materials and will charge exorbitant fees. An example of this is when my father needed people to help remove two trees from our home in September 2005 after Hurricane Rita.

To close, I'd like to remind you that hurricanes affect victims who live in their direct path and the country as a whole. To understand some of these effects, we talked about how hurricanes work, how they affect our country and daily lives, and the impacts they have on the lives of people who live through them. Maybe knowing some of these facts will help each of us appreciate our homes and our families just a little bit more. (*Handout: Hurricane tracking charts*)

Again, Megan makes her emotional appeal stronger by showing before and after pictures.

Megan could have developed this point a bit more, perhaps by giving a specific example.

Megan does a nice job concluding her speech by summarizing her main points and tying back to her introduction.

Notice how Megan waits until the end of her speech to distribute her handout. That way, she kept the focus on her message during the speech.

All in all, this is a well-presented, informative speech with sufficient documentation.

15

Informative Speaking

Learning Outcomes

LO**1** Identify the characteristics of effective informative speaking

LO**2** Describe methods for conveying information

LO**3** Discuss common frameworks for structuring informative speeches

> ## "*Effective informative speeches are intellectually stimulating, relevant, creative, memorable, and address diverse learning styles.*"

An informative speech is one whose goal is to explain or describe facts, truths, and principles in a way that stimulates interest, facilitates understanding, and increases the likelihood of remembering. In short, informative speeches are designed to educate audiences. Informative speeches answer questions about a topic, such as who, when, what, where, why, and how. For example, your informative speech might describe who popular singer-songwriter Lady Gaga is, define what Scientology is, compare and contrast the similarities and differences between Twitter and Facebook as social networking sites, narrate the story of Al Franken's campaign for U.S. Senate, or demonstrate how to create and post a video on a Web site like YouTube. Informative speaking is different from other speech forms (such as speaking to persuade, to entertain, or to celebrate) in that your goal is simply mutual understanding about an object, person, place, process, event, idea, concept, or issue.

informative speech
a speech that has a goal to explain or describe facts, truths, and principles in a way that increases understanding

intellectually stimulating
information that is new to audience members

What do you think?

I can learn a lot from listening to a speech.

Strongly Disagree   Strongly Agree
1   2   3   4   5   6   7   8   9   10

In this chapter, we describe five distinguishing characteristics of informative speeches and five methods of informing. Then, we discuss two common types of informative speeches (process and expository speeches) and provide an example of an informative speech.

LO¹ Characteristics of Effective Informative Speaking

Effective informative speeches are intellectually stimulating, relevant, creative, memorable, and address diverse learning styles.

Intellectually Stimulating

Your audience will perceive information to be **intellectually stimulating** when it is new to them and when it is explained in a way that piques their curiosity and excites their interest. By *new* information, we mean information that most of your audience is unfamiliar with or new insights into a topic with which they are already familiar.

If your audience is unfamiliar with your topic, you should consider how you might tap the members' natural curiosity. Imagine that you are an anthropology major

© ISTOCKPHOTO.COM

© ANTONIO JORGE NUNES/SHUTTERSTOCK

listener relevance links
statements that clarify how a particular point may be important to a listener

creative
using information in a way that yields different or original ideas and insights

who is interested in prehistoric humans, which is not an interest shared by most members of your audience. You know that in 1991, a 5,300-year-old man, Ötzi, as he has become known, was found surprisingly well preserved in an ice field in the mountains between Austria and Italy. Even though the discovery was big news at the time, it is unlikely that most of your audience knows much about it. You can draw on their natural curiosity, however, as you present "Unraveling the Mystery of the Iceman," in which you describe scientists' efforts to understand who Ötzi was and what happened to him.

If your audience members are familiar with your topic, you will need to identify information that will be new to them. Begin by asking yourself, What about my topic do listeners probably not know? Then consider depth and breadth as you answer the question. *Depth* has to do with going into more detail than people's general knowledge of the topic. If you've ever watched programs on the *Food Channel,* that's what they do. Most people know basic recipes, but these programs show new ways to cook the same foods. *Breadth* has to do with how your topic relates to associated topics. Trace did this when he informed his audience about type 1 diabetes. He discussed not only the physical and emotional effects of diabetes on the person who has it but also the emotional and relational effects on family and friends. As you can see, when your topic is one that audience members are familiar with, you will need to explore a new angle on it if you are going to stimulate them intellectually.

Relevant

A general rule to remember when preparing your informative speeches is this: Don't assume your listeners will recognize how the information you share is relevant to them. Incorporate **listener relevance links**—statements that clarify how a particular point

may be important to a listener—throughout the speech. As you prepare each main point, ask yourself, How would knowing this information make my listeners happier, healthier, wealthier, and so forth? Or you can compare unfamiliar aspects of your topic to something your listeners are likely to be familiar with. Trace did this when he compared the relational effects of living with diabetes to living with other diseases such as heart disease, eating disorders, and diverticulitis.

Creative

Your audience will perceive your information to be **creative** when it yields different or original ideas and insights. You may never have considered yourself to be creative, but that may be because you have never worked to develop innovative ideas. Contrary to what you may think, creativity is not a gift that some have and some don't; rather, it is the result of hard work. Creativity comes from good research, time, and productive thinking.

Creative informative speeches begin with good research. The more you learn about the topic, the more you will have to think about and develop creatively. Speakers who present information creatively have given themselves lots of supporting material to work with.

For the creative process to work, you have to give yourself time. Rarely do creative ideas come just before a deadline. Instead, they are likely to come when we least expect them—when we're driving our car, preparing for bed, or daydreaming. The creative process depends on having time to mull over ideas. If you complete a draft of your outline several days before you speak, you'll have time to consider how to present your ideas creatively.

For the creative process to work, you have to think productively. Productive thinking occurs when we contemplate something from a variety of perspectives. Then, with numerous ideas to choose from, we can select the ones that are best suited to our particular audience.

© APOLLOFOTO/SHUTTERSTOCK

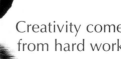

Creativity comes from hard work.

Figure 15.1

Temperature and Precipitation Highs and Lows in Select U.S. Cities

City	Yearly Temperature (in degrees Fahrenheit) High	Yearly Temperature (in degrees Fahrenheit) Low	Precipitation (in inches) July	Precipitation (in inches) Annual
Chicago	95	−21	3.7	35
Cincinnati	98	−7	3.3	39
Denver	104	−3	1.9	15
Los Angeles	104	40	trace	15
Miami	96	50	5.7	56
Minneapolis	95	−27	3.5	28
New Orleans	95	26	6.1	62
New York	98	−2	4.4	42
Phoenix	117	35	0.8	7
Portland, ME	94	−18	3.1	44
St. Louis	97	−9	3.9	37
San Francisco	94	35	trace	19
Seattle	94	23	0.9	38

Let's look at how productive thinking can help to identify different approaches to a topic. Suppose you want to give a speech on climatic variation in the United States, and in your research you ran across the data shown in Figure 15.1. By looking at the data from different perspectives, you can identify several possible ways to develop your speech. For instance, you might notice that the yearly high temperatures vary less than the yearly low temperatures. Most people wouldn't understand why this is so and would be curious. Or you might notice that it hardly ever rains on the West Coast in the summer. In fact, Seattle, a city that most of us consider to be rainy, receives less than an inch of rain in July, which is three inches less than any eastern city and five inches less than Miami. Again, an explanation

of this anomaly would probably interest most audience members. Looking at these data in yet another way reveals that although most of us might think of July as a month that is relatively dry, cities in the Midwest and on the East Coast get more rainfall than we might expect in July.

Productive thought can also help us to create alternative ways to make the same point. Again, using the information in Figure 15.1, we can quickly create two ways to support the point "Yearly high temperatures in U.S. cities vary far less than yearly low temperatures."

> *Alternative A:* Of the 13 cities in this table, 10 cities, or 77 percent, had yearly highs of 95 degrees or more. Four cities, or 30 percent, had yearly lows above freezing; only three cities, or 23 percent, had low temperatures of more than 15 degrees below zero.

> *Alternative B:* Cincinnati, Miami, Minneapolis, New York, and St. Louis—cities at different latitudes—all had yearly high temperatures of 95 to 98 degrees. In contrast, the lowest temperature for Miami was 50 degrees, whereas the lowest temperatures for Cincinnati, Minneapolis, New York, and St. Louis were −7, −27, −2, and −9 degrees, respectively.

Memorable

If your speech is really informative, your audience will hear a lot of new information but will need your help in remembering what's most important. Emphasizing your specific goal and making sure your main points are stated in parallel language are good starting points. Figure 15.2 summarizes ways to use

Figure 15.2

Techniques for Making Informative Speeches Memorable

TECHNIQUE	USE	EXAMPLE
Presentational aids	To provide audience members with a visual or auditory memory of important or difficult material	A diagram of the process of making ethanol
Repetition	To give the audience a second or third chance to retain important information by repeating or paraphrasing it	"The first dimension of romantic love is passion—that is, it can't really be romantic love if there is no sexual attraction."
Transitions	To help the audience understand the relationship between the ideas being presented, including primary and supporting information	"So the three characteristics of romantic love are passion, intimacy, and commitment. Now let's look at each of the five ways you can keep love alive. The first is through small talk."
Humor and other emotional anecdotes	To create an emotional memory link to important ideas	"True love is like a pair of socks, you have to have two, and they've got to match. So you and your partner need to be mutually committed and compatible."
Mnemonics and acronyms	To provide an easy memory prompt for a series or a list	"You can remember the four criteria for evaluating a diamond as the four Cs: carat, clarity, cut, and color." "As you can see, useful goals are SMART: S for specific, M for measurable, A for action oriented, R for reasonable, and T for time bound. That's SMART."

© SERGEY SKLEZNEV/SHUTTERSTOCK / © AQUATIC CREATURE/SHUTTERSTOCK

description

the informative method used to create an accurate, vivid, verbal picture of an object, geographic feature, setting, or image

presentational aids, repetition, transitions, humor, and mnemonics and acronyms to help your audience remember information you believe to be most important.

Address Diverse Learning Styles

Because the members of your audience learn differently, you will be most successful at informing all your audience when you present your information in ways that appeal to all styles of learning (see Figure 13.1). You can appeal to people who prefer to learn through the feeling dimension by providing concrete and vivid images, examples, stories, and testimonials. Address the watching dimension by using visual aids that encourage audience members to reflect. Address the thinking dimension by including and rhetorical questions, definitions, explanations, and statistics. Address the doing dimension by encouraging your listeners to do something during the speech or afterward. Rounding the learning cycle in this way ensures that you address the diverse learning style preferences of your audience and helps to make the speech understandable, meaningful, and memorable for all.

LO² Methods of Informing

We can inform through description, definition, comparison and contrast, narration, and demonstration. Let's look more closely at each of these patterns.

Description

Description is the informative method used to create an accurate, vivid, verbal picture of an object, geographic feature, setting, event, person, or image. This method usually answers an overarching who, what, or where question. If the thing to be described is simple and familiar (like a light bulb or a river), the description may not need to be detailed. But if the thing to be described is complex and unfamiliar (like a sextant or holograph), the description will need to be more exhaustive. Descriptions are, of course,

easier if you have a presentational aid, but verbal descriptions that are clear and vivid can create mental pictures that are also informative. To describe something effectively, you can explain its size, shape, weight, color, composition, age, condition, and spatial organization. Although your description may focus on only a few of these, each characteristic is helpful to consider as you create your description.

You can describe size subjectively, such as large or small, and objectively by noting specific numerical measures. For example, you can describe New York City subjectively as the largest city in the United States or more objectively as home to more than 8 million people with more than 26,000 people per square mile.

You can describe shape by reference to common geometric forms like round, triangular, oblong, spherical, conical, cylindrical, or rectangular, or by reference to common objects such as a book or a milk carton. For example, the Lower Peninsula of Michigan is often described as a left-hand mitten. Shape is made more vivid by using adjectives, such as *smooth*, *jagged*, and so on.

You can describe weight subjectively, such as heavy or light, and objectively by pounds and ounces or kilograms and grams. As with size, you can clarify weight with comparisons. For example, you can describe a Humvee (Hummer) as weighing about 7,600 pounds or about as much as three Honda Civics.

Good informative speeches address the thinking dimension and the doing dimension.

You can describe color by coupling a basic color (such as black, white, red, or yellow) with a common object. For instance, instead of describing something as puce or ocher, you might describe the object as "eggplant purple" or "clay pot orange."

You can describe the composition of something by indicating what it is made of, such as by saying the building was made of brick, concrete, wood, or siding. In some cases, you might be clearer by describing what it looks like rather than what it is. For example, you might say something looks metallic, even if it is made of plastic rather than metal.

You can describe something by its age and by its condition. For example, describing a city as old and well kept gives different mental pictures than does describing a city as old and war torn.

Finally, you can describe by spatial organization going from top to bottom, left to right, outer to inner, and so on. A description of the Sistine Chapel, for example, might go from the floor to the ceiling, and a description of a NASCAR automobile might go from the body to the engine to the interior.

Definition

Definition is a method of informing that explains the meaning of something. There are four ways to define something.

First, you can define a word or idea by classifying it and differentiating it from similar ideas. For example, in a speech on vegetarianism, you might use information from the Vegan Society's Web site (http://www.vegansociety.com) to develop a definition of a vegan: "A vegan is a vegetarian who is seeking a lifestyle free from animal products for the benefit of people, animals, and the environment. Vegans eat a plant-based diet free from all animal products including milk, eggs, and honey. Vegans also don't wear leather, wool, or silk and avoid other animal-based products."

Second, you can define a word by explaining its derivation or history. For instance, the word *vegan* is made from the beginning and end of the word *vegetarian* and was coined in the United Kingdom in 1944, when the Vegan Society was founded. Offering this etymology will help your audience to remember the meaning of *vegan*.

Third, you can define a word by explaining its use or function. For example, in vegan recipes, you can use tofu or tempeh to replace meat and soy milk to replace cow's milk.

The fourth and perhaps the quickest way you can define something is by using a familiar synonym or antonym. A synonym is a word that has the same or a similar meaning; an antonym is a word that has the opposite meaning. So you could define a *vegan*

by comparing it to the word *vegetarian,* which is a synonym, or to the word *carnivore,* which is an antonym.

Comparison and Contrast

Comparison and contrast is a method of informing that focuses on how something is similar to and different from other things. For example, in a speech on vegans, you might tell your audience how vegans are similar and different from other types of vegetarians. You can point out that like vegetarians, vegans don't eat meat. In contrast, semi-vegetarians eat fish or poultry. Like lacto-vegetarians, vegans don't eat eggs, but unlike this group and lacto-ovo-vegetarians, vegans don't use dairy products. So of all vegetarians, vegans have the most restrictive diet. Because comparisons and contrasts can be figurative or literal, you can use metaphors and analogies as well as make direct comparisons.

Narration

Narration is a method of informing that recounts an autobiographical or biographical event, a myth, a story, or some other account. Narrations usually have four parts. First, the narration orients the listener by describing when and where the event took place and by introducing the important people or characters. Second, the narration explains the sequence of events that led to a complication or problem, including details that enhance the development. Third, the narration discusses how the complication or problem affected the key people in the narrative. Finally, the narration recounts how the complication or problem was solved. The characteristics of a good narration include a strong story line; use of descriptive language and detail that enhance the plot, people, setting, and events; effective use of dialogue; pacing that builds suspense; and a strong voice (Baerwald, n.d.).

Narrations can be presented in a first-, second-, or third person voice. When you use first person, you report what you have personally experienced or observed, using the pronouns *I, me,* and *my* as you recount the events. "Let me tell you about the

definition
a method of informing that explains something by identifying its meaning

synonym
a word that has the same or a similar meaning

antonym
a word that is a direct opposition

comparison and contrast
a method of informing that explains something by focusing on how it is similar to and different from other things

narration
a method of informing that explains something by recounting events

© ISTOCKPHOTO.COM

demonstration
a method of informing that explains something by showing how something is done, by displaying the stages of a process, or by depicting how something works

process speech
a speech that demonstrates how something is done or made, or how it works

first time I tried to water-ski" might be the opening for a narrative story told in first person. When you use second person, you place your audience at the scene by using the pronouns *you* and *your*. You might say, for example, "Imagine that you have just gotten off the plane in Hong Kong. You look at the signs but can't read a thing. Which way is the terminal?"

When you use third person, you describe to your audience what has happened, is happening, or will happen to other people by using pronouns like *he, her,* and *they*. For example, "When the students arrived in Venice for their study-abroad experience, the first thing they saw was . . . ."

Demonstration

Demonstration is a method of informing that shows how something is done, displays the stages of a process, or depicts how something works. Demonstrations range from very simple with a few easy-to-follow steps (such as how to iron a shirt) to very complex (such as explaining how a nuclear reactor works). Regardless of whether the topic is simple or complex, effective demonstrations require expertise, developing a hierarchy of steps, and using visual language and aids.

In a demonstration, experience with what you are demonstrating is critical. Expertise gives you the necessary background to supplement bare-bones instructions with personal, lived experience. Why are TV cooking shows so popular? Because the chef doesn't just read the recipe and do what it says. Rather, while performing each step, the chef shares tips that aren't mentioned in any cookbook. It is the chef's experience that allows him or her to say that one egg will work as well as two, or how to tell if the cake is really done.

In a demonstration, you organize the steps from first to last so that your audience will be able to remember the sequence of actions accurately. Suppose that you want to demonstrate the steps in using a touch-screen voting machine. If you present 14 separate points, your audience is unlikely to remember them. However, if you group them under the following four headings, chances are much higher that your audience will be able to remember most of the items: I. Get ready to vote, II. Vote, III. Review your choices, and IV. Cast your ballot.

Although you could explain a process with only words, most demonstrations show the audience the process or parts of the process. That's in part why TV shows like *What Not to Wear* and *Flip This House* are so popular. If what you are explaining is relatively simple, you can demonstrate the entire process from start to finish. However, if the process is lengthy or complex, you may choose to pre-prepare the material for some of the steps. Although you will show all stages in the process, you will not have to take the time for every single step as the audience watches. For example, many of the ingredients used by TV chefs are already cut up and measured into little bowls.

Effective demonstrations require practice. Remember that under the pressure of speaking to an audience, even the simplest task can become difficult. (Did you ever try to thread a needle with 25 people watching you?) As you practice, you will want to consider the size of your audience and the configuration of the room. Be sure that all of the audience will be able to see what you are doing. You may find that your demonstration takes longer than the time limit you have been given. In these cases, you might want to pre-prepare the material for a step or two.

LO³ Common Informative Speech Frameworks

Two of the most common frameworks for structuring or organizing informative speech ideas are process frameworks and expository frameworks.

Process Speech Frameworks

The goal of a process speech is to demonstrate how something is done or made, or how it works. Effective process speeches require you to carefully delineate the steps in the process and the order in which they occur. Then you group the steps and develop concrete explanations for each step and substep. Process speeches rely heavily on the demonstration method of informing.

For example, Allie is a floral designer and has been asked by her former art teacher to speak on the basics of floral arrangement to a high school art class. The teacher has allotted five minutes for her presentation. In preparing for the speech, Allie recognized that in five minutes she could not complete arranging one floral display of any size, let alone help students understand how to create various effects. So she opted to demonstrate only parts of the process and bring arrangements in various stages of completion as additional presentational aids. For example, the first step in floral arranging is to choose the right vase and frog (flower holder). So she brought in vases and frogs of various sizes and shapes to display as she explained how to choose a vase and frog based on the types of flowers used and the desired visual effect. The second step is to prepare the basic triangle of blooms, so she began to demonstrate how to place the flowers she had brought to form a triangle. Rather than hurrying and trying to arrange everything perfectly in the few seconds she had, she brought out several partially finished arrangements that she had stored behind a draped table. These showed carefully completed triangles that used other types of flowers. The third step is placing additional flowers and greenery to complete an arrangement and achieve various artistic effects. Again, Allie demonstrated how to place several blooms, and then, as she described them, she brought out several completed arrangements that illustrated various artistic effects. Even though Allie did not physically perform all of each step, her visual presentation was an excellent demonstration of floral arranging.

Although some process speeches require you to demonstrate, others are not suited to demonstrations. For these, you can use visual aids to help the audience see the steps in the process. In a speech on making iron, it wouldn't be possible to demonstrate the process in a classroom; however, a speaker would be able to greatly enhance the verbal description by showing pictures or drawings of each stage.

In process speeches, the steps are the main points, and the speech is organized in time order, so the earlier steps are discussed before later ones.

Expository Speech Frameworks

The goal of an **expository speech** is to provide carefully researched, in-depth knowledge about a complex topic. For example, "understanding the health care debate," "the origins and classification of nursery rhymes," "the sociobiological theory of child abuse," and "viewing gangsta rap as poetry" are all topics on which you could give an interesting expository speech. Lengthy expository speeches are known as lectures.

All expository speeches require that the speaker uses an extensive research base for preparing the presentation, chooses an organizational pattern that

helps the audience understand the material being discussed, and uses a variety of the informative methods to sustain the audience's attention and comprehension of the material presented.

Even college professors who are experts in their fields draw from a variety of source material when they prepare their lectures. You will want to acquire your information from reputable sources. Then as you are speaking, you will want to cite the sources for the information you present. You do so in the form of **oral footnotes**—oral references to the original source of particular information at the point of presenting it during a speech. In this way, you can establish the trustworthiness of the information you present and also strengthen your own credibility.

Expository speakers also must choose an organizational pattern that is best suited to the material they will present. Different types of expository speeches are suited to different organizational patterns, so it is up to the speaker to arrange the main points of the speech so they flow in a manner that aids audience understanding and memory.

Finally, a hallmark of effective expository speaking is that it uses various methods of informing for developing material. Within one speech, a speaker may use descriptions, definitions, comparisons and contrasts, narration, and short demonstrations to develop the main points.

Expository speeches include speeches that explain a political, economic, social, religious, or ethical issue; those that explain events or forces of history; those that explain a theory, principle, or law; and those that explain a creative work.

© VERONIKA TROFER/SHUTTERSTOCK

> **expository speech**
> an informative presentation that provides carefully researched, in-depth knowledge about a complex topic
>
> **oral footnotes**
> oral references to the original source of particular information at the point of presenting it during a speech

Exposition of Political, Economic, Social, Religious, or Ethical Issues

An expository speech can help the audience understand the background or context of a political, economic, social, religious, or ethical issue. In such a speech, you would explain the forces that gave rise to the issue and are continuing to affect it. You may also present the various positions that are held about the issue and the reasoning behind these positions. Finally, you may discuss various ways that have been presented for resolving the issue.

The general goal of your speech is to inform, not to persuade. So you will want to present all sides of controversial issues without advocating which side is better. You will also want to make sure that the sources you are drawing from are respected experts and are objective in what they report. Finally, you will want to present complex issues in a straightforward manner that helps your audience understand them while not oversimplifying knotty issues. Figure 15.3 provides examples of topic ideas for an expository speech about a political, economic, social, religious, or ethical issue.

For example, while researching a speech on drilling for oil and natural gas in Arctic National Wildlife Refuge, you need to be careful to consult articles and experts on all sides of this controversial issue and fairly represent and incorporate their views in your outline. You will want to discuss all important aspects of this complex issue, including the ecological, economic, political (national, state, and local), and technological aspects. If time is limited, you might discuss just one or two of these aspects, but you should at least inform the audience of the other considerations that affect the issue.

Exposition of Historical Events and Forces

A second important type of expository speech is one that explains historical events or forces. It has been said that those who don't understand history may be forced to repeat it. So an expositional speech about historical events and forces can be fascinating for its own sake, but it can also be relevant for what is happening today. As an expository speaker, you have an obligation during your research to seek out stories and narratives that can enliven your speech. You will also want to consult sources that analyze the events you describe so that you can discuss their impact at the time they occurred and the meaning they have today. Although many of us know the historical fact that the United States developed the atomic bomb during World War II, an expository speech on the Manhattan Project that dramatizes the international race to produce the bomb and tells the stories of the main players would add to our understanding of the inner workings of secret, government-funded research projects and might also place modern arms races and the fear of nuclear proliferation in historical context. Figure 15.4 proposes examples of topic ideas for an expository speech about historical events and forces.

Exposition of a Theory, Principle, or Law

The way we live is affected by natural and human laws and principles and is explained by various theories. Yet there are many theories, principles, and laws that we do not completely understand or we don't understand how they affect us. An expository speech can inform us by explaining these important phenomena. The main challenge for an expository speaker is to find material that explains the theory, law, or principle in language that is understandable to the audience. You will want to search for or create examples and illustrations that demystify complicated concepts and terminology. Effective examples and comparing unfamiliar ideas with those that the audience already knows are techniques that can help you with this kind of speech. In a speech on the psychological principles of operant conditioning, a speaker could help the audience understand the difference between continuous reinforcement and intermittent reinforcement with the following explanation:

Figure 15.3

Topic Ideas for Expository Speeches about Political, Economic, Social, Religious, or Ethical Issues

gay marriage	stem cell research	health care
affirmative action	school vouchers	hate speech
school uniforms	media bias	home schooling
immigration	downloading music	eating disorders

Figure 15.4

Topic Ideas for Expository Speeches about Historical Events and Forces

slavery	the papacy	Irish immigration to the U.S.
women's suffrage	the colonization of Africa	the Vietnam War
the Olympics	building the Great Pyramids	the Ming Dynasty
the Crusades	the Industrial Revolution	the Balfour Declaration

© STUART BURFORD/ISTOCKPHOTO.COM

When a behavior is reinforced continuously, each time the person performs the behavior, a reward is given, but when the behavior is reinforced intermittently, the reward is not always given when the behavior is displayed. Behavior that is learned by continuous reinforcement disappears quickly when the reward no longer is provided, but behavior that is learned by intermittent reinforcement continues for long periods of time, even when not reinforced. Every day you can see the effects of how a behavior was conditioned. For example, take the behavior of putting a coin in a machine. If the machine is a vending machine, you expect to be rewarded every time you "play." And if the machine doesn't dispense the item, you might wonder if the machine is out of order and "play" just one more coin or you might bang on the machine. In any case, you are unlikely to put in more than one more coin. But suppose the machine is a slot machine or a machine that dispenses instant winner lottery tickets. How many coins will you "play" before you stop and conclude that the machine isn't going to give you what you want? Why the difference? Because you were conditioned to a vending machine on a continuous schedule, but a slot machine or automatic lottery ticket dispenser "rewards" you on an intermittent schedule.

Figure 15.5 provides some examples of topic ideas for an expository speech about a theory, principle, or scientific law.

Exposition of Creative Work

Courses in art, theatre, music, literature, and film appreciation give students tools by which to recognize the style, historical period, and quality of a particular piece or group of pieces. Yet most of us know very little about how to understand a creative work, so presentations designed to explain creative works like poems, novels, songs, or even famous speeches can be very instructive for audience members.

When developing a speech that explains a creative work, you will want to find information on the work and the artist who created it. You will also want to find sources that educate you about the period in which this work was created and inform you about the criteria that critics use to evaluate works of this type. For example, if you want to give an expository speech on Fredrick Douglass's Fourth of July Oration given in Rochester, New York, in 1852, you might need to orient your audience by first reminding them of who Douglass was. Then you would want to explain the traditional expectations for Fourth of July speakers in the mid-1800s. After this, you might want to summarize the speech and perhaps share a few memorable quotes. Finally, you would want to discuss how speech critics view the speech and why the speech is considered a great speech.

Figure 15.6 presents examples of topics for expository speeches about creative works.

Sample Informative Speech: Making Ethanol

By Louisa Greene*

This section presents a sample expository speech adaptation plan, outline, and transcript given by a student in an introductory speaking course.

1. Review the outline and adaptation plan developed by Louisa Greene in preparing her speech on ethanol.

*Used with permission of Louisa Greene.

© TERRYM/SHUTTERSTOCK

Figure 15.5

Topic Ideas for Expository Speeches about Theories, Principles, or Laws

natural selection	diminishing returns	psychoanalytic theory
gravity	Boyle's law	Maslow's hierarchy of needs
global warming	number theory	intelligent design
feminist theory	color theory	social learning theory

Figure 15.6

Topic Ideas for Expository Speeches about Creative Works

trip-hop music	the films of Alfred Hitchcock	inaugural addresses
Impressionist painting	the love sonnets of Shakespeare	the *Harry Potter* series
salsa dancing	Kabuki theater	iconography
women in cinema	children's book illustration	fad dances

Figure 15.7
Informative Speech Evaluation Checklist

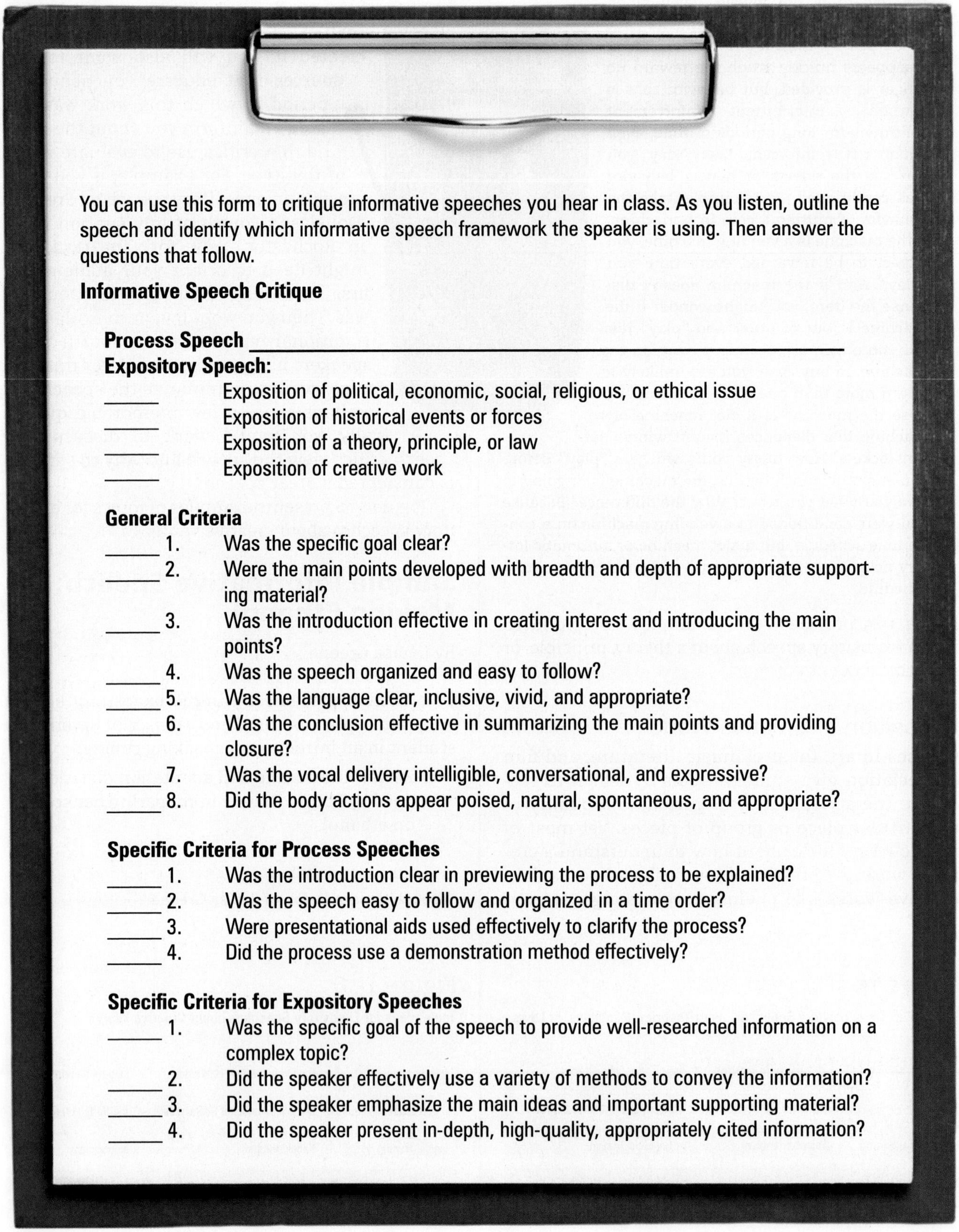

You can use this form to critique informative speeches you hear in class. As you listen, outline the speech and identify which informative speech framework the speaker is using. Then answer the questions that follow.

Informative Speech Critique

Process Speech _____
Expository Speech:

_____ Exposition of political, economic, social, religious, or ethical issue
_____ Exposition of historical events or forces
_____ Exposition of a theory, principle, or law
_____ Exposition of creative work

General Criteria

_____ 1. Was the specific goal clear?
_____ 2. Were the main points developed with breadth and depth of appropriate supporting material?
_____ 3. Was the introduction effective in creating interest and introducing the main points?
_____ 4. Was the speech organized and easy to follow?
_____ 5. Was the language clear, inclusive, vivid, and appropriate?
_____ 6. Was the conclusion effective in summarizing the main points and providing closure?
_____ 7. Was the vocal delivery intelligible, conversational, and expressive?
_____ 8. Did the body actions appear poised, natural, spontaneous, and appropriate?

Specific Criteria for Process Speeches

_____ 1. Was the introduction clear in previewing the process to be explained?
_____ 2. Was the speech easy to follow and organized in a time order?
_____ 3. Were presentational aids used effectively to clarify the process?
_____ 4. Did the process use a demonstration method effectively?

Specific Criteria for Expository Speeches

_____ 1. Was the specific goal of the speech to provide well-researched information on a complex topic?
_____ 2. Did the speaker effectively use a variety of methods to convey the information?
_____ 3. Did the speaker emphasize the main ideas and important supporting material?
_____ 4. Did the speaker present in-depth, high-quality, appropriately cited information?

© SERGHEI VELUSCEAC/ISTOCKPHOTO.COM

2. Read the transcript of her speech.

3. Use the Informative Speech Evaluation Checklist from Figure 15.7 to help you evaluate this speech.

4. At www.cengagebrain.com, watch a video clip of Louisa presenting her speech in class.

5. Write a paragraph of feedback to Louisa, describing the strengths of her presentation and what you think she might do next time to be more effective.

Adaptation Plan

1. **Speaking directly to the audience:** I will begin my speech by asking the audience a question. Throughout the speech I will refer to the audience's previous knowledge and experience.

2. **Building credibility:** Early in the speech I will tell the audience about how I got interested in ethanol when I built a still as a science fair project in high school. I will also tell them that I am now a chemical engineering major and am hoping to make a career in the alternative fuel industry.

3. **Getting and maintaining interest:** Because my audience is initially unlikely to be interested in how to produce ethanol, I will have to work hard to interest them and to keep their interest throughout the speech. I will try to gain their interest in the introduction by relating the production of ethanol, the fuel, to the production of "white lightning," the illegal alcohol, which might be of more interest to the average college student. Throughout the speech, I will use common analogies and metaphors to explain the complex chemical processes. Finally, I will use a well-designed PowerPoint presentation to capture attention.

4. **Facilitating understanding:** Throughout the speech I will use analogies and metaphors and simple language to help the audience understand complex technical and chemical processes. I will use transitions and signposts to differentiate the steps in the process. The PowerPoint slides will provide a visual reinforcement for each step.

5. **Increasing retention:** Early in the speech I will give a brief overview of the four-step process used to make ethanol. Then as I speak about each step, I will use color-coded PowerPoint slides with headers to reinforce the step being discussed. Finally, I will review the steps twice during my conclusion.

Speech Outline

General goal: To inform
Specific goal: I want my audience to understand the process for making ethanol from corn.

Introduction

I. Did you know that cars were originally designed to run on ethanol?
   A. Henry Ford was an ethanol enthusiast.
   B. In World War II about 75% of German and American military vehicles were powered by ethanol.
   C. In 1978 Robert Warren built a still to produce what he called "liquid sunshine," which you may know as ethanol.

II. Both moonshine and ethanol are easily produced using the same method since both are pure or almost pure alcohol.

III. Today, I'm going to explain to you the commercial process that turns corn into alcohol.

Thesis statement: The four steps in the commercial process of making ethanol are first, preparing the corn by making a mash; second, fermenting the mash by adding yeast to make beer; third, distilling the ethanol from the beer; and fourth, processing the remaining whole stillage to produce co-products such as animal feed. (*Slide 1. Shows the four step flow process*)

Body

I. The first step in the commercial process of making ethanol, preparing the mash, has two parts: milling the corn and breaking the starch down into simple sugars. (*Slide 2. Title:* Preparation. *Shows corn flowing from a silo into a hammer mill and then into a holding tank where yeast is added*)
   A. The corn is emptied into a bin and passes into a hammer mill where it is ground into coarse flour.
   B. After milling the corn flour, a starch, must be broken down so that it becomes simple sugars by mixing in water and enzymes to form thick liquid called slurry.
      1. First the water and corn flour are dosed with the enzyme alpha-amylase and heated.
      2. Then the starchy slurry is heated to help the enzyme do its work.
      3. Later gluco-amylase is added to finish the process of turning the starch to simple sugar.

II. The second step of the commercial process for making ethanol is fermenting the slurry or mash by adding yeast. (*Slide 3. Title:* Fermentation. *Shows yeast added to the mash in a fermenter and carbon dioxide being released to form "beer"*)

A. The mash remains in the fermenters for about 50 hours.

B. As the mash ferments, the sugar is turned into alcohol and carbon dioxide.

III. The third step of the commercial process for making ethanol is distilling the fermented mash, now called "beer" by passing it through a series of columns where the alcohol is removed from the mash. (*Slide 4. Title:* Distillation of Ethanol. *Animated slide showing beer flowing into distillation tank, heat being applied to the beer, ethanol vapors being released and captured in a condenser*)

A. Distillation is the process of boiling a liquid and then condensing the resulting vapor in order to separate out one component of the liquid.

B. In most ethanol production, distillation occurs through the use of cooling columns.

C. Once the ethanol has reached the desired purity or proof, it is denatured to be made undrinkable.

IV. The fourth step in commercial production is converting the remaining whole stillage into co-products. (*Slide 5. Title:* Co-product. *Shows a tank with remaining whole solids flowing into a condenser with output flowing into a bin of animal feed*)

Conclusion

I. As you can see, producing ethanol is a simple four-step process: preparing the corn into a slurry or mash, fermenting the slurry into "beer," distilling the "beer" to release the ethanol, and processing the remaining water and corn solids into co-products. (*Slide 6: Same as Slide 1*)

II. With today's skyrocketing gas prices, you can see why this simple process of making liquid sunshine has resulted in an increase of ethanol plants so that cars that can use E-85 fuel.

Works Cited

DENCO. (n.d.). Tour the plant. Retrieved from http://www.dencollc.com/DENCO%20WebSite_files/Tour.htm.

Northwest Iowa Community College Business and Industry Center. (2004, May 7). Module 2: Science and technology. *Ethanol*. Retrieved from http://www.nwicc.com/pages/continuing/business/ethanol/Module2.htm.

Renewable Fuels Association. (n.d.). The industry— Statistics. Retrieved from http://www.ethanolrfa.org/industry/statistics/. Tham, M. T. (1997). *Distillation. An introduction*. Retrieved from http://lorien.ncl.ac.uk/ming/distil/distilo.htm.

Warren, Robert. "Make your own fuel." http://running_on_alcohol.tripod.com/index.html. Last updated 8/18/2006. Accessed 2:30 p.m. CDT 7/3/2007.

© ARTEM EFIMOV/SHUTTERSTOCK

Speech and Analysis

Speech

Did you know that the first Model Ts were designed to run on ethanol and that Henry Ford said that ethanol was the fuel of the future? Or that in World War II about 75 percent of the German and American military vehicles were powered by ethanol since oil for gasoline was difficult to obtain? In 1978, during the first Arab oil embargo, when gas soared from 62 cents a gallon to $1.64, Californian Robert Warren and others built stills to produce what he called, no, not "white lightning" but "liquid sunshine," which we call ethanol.

I became interested in ethanol in high school when I built a miniature ethanol still as a science fair project. I'm now a chemical engineering major and hope to make a career in the alternative fuel industry. So, today, I'm going to explain to you the simple process that takes corn and turns it into liquid sunshine. Specifically I want you to understand the process that is used to make ethanol from corn.

The four steps in the commercial process of making ethanol are first, preparing the corn by making a mash; second, fermenting the mash by adding yeast to make "beer"; third, distilling the ethanol from the "beer"; and fourth, processing the remaining whole stillage to produce co-products like animal feed. (Slide 1)

The first step in the commercial process of making ethanol, preparing the mash, has two parts: milling the corn and breaking the starch down into simple sugars. (Slide 2)

The corn, which has been tested for quality and stored in a silo, is emptied into a bin and passes into a hammer mill where it is ground into coarse flour. This is done to expose more of the corn's starchy material so that these starches can be more easily broken down into sugar.

In your saliva, you have enzymes that begin to break the bread and other starches you eat into sugar. In your stomach, you have other enzymes that finish this job of turning starch to simple sugar so your body can use the energy in the food you eat. In the commercial production of ethanol, a similar transformation takes place.

To break the milled corn flour starch into sugar, the milled flour is mixed with water and alpha-amylase, the same enzyme that you have in your saliva, and is heated. The alpha-amylase acts as Pac-Men and takes bites out of the long sugar chains

Analysis

Louisa begins this speech with a series of rhetorical questions designed to pique the audience's interest in her topic. Because at the time she prepared the speech gasoline prices were once again soaring, these questions coupled with the example of Robert Warren's solution to a similar problem provide a provocative introduction to the general topic of ethanol.

At this point, Louisa personalizes the topic with a self-disclosure that also establishes her credibility. Although the introduction does a good job of gaining attention and interest, it doesn't explain why the audience should care about how ethanol is produced. So this transition to the thesis statement seems abrupt.

This is a clear statement of her thesis. The PowerPoint slide is a simple but effective tool to visually reinforce the verbal description.

Throughout the speech, Louisa does a good job of using signposts to help her audience follow each step of the process. Notice how Louisa has nested two steps: milling and breaking starch into sugar under the more general heading of "preparation." This grouping keeps the main points to a manageable number and will help her audience remember the steps and substeps. Her second slide is simple but effective since it reinforces the two substeps.

One thing Louisa could do better throughout the speech is to offer listener relevance links. Because the audience might not be interested in the topic, she should remind them of its relevance whenever possible.

Louisa helps the audience understand the unfamiliar starch-to-sugar conversion by comparing it to the familiar process of digestion.

The Pac-Man analogy also helps the audience to visualize what is occurring during the starch to sugar conversion.

which are bound together in the starch. What results are broken bits of starch that need further processing to become glucose. So later, gluco-amylase, which is like the enzyme in your stomach, is added, and these new Pac-Men bite the starchy bits into simple glucose sugar molecules. Now this mixture of sugar, water, and residual corn solids, called slurry or mash, is ready to be fermented.

The last sentence in this paragraph is an excellent transition between the two main points.

The second step in the commercial production of ethanol is to ferment the mash by adding yeast in an environment that has no oxygen and allowing the mixture to "rest" while the yeast "works." (Slide 3) This is accomplished by piping the slurry into an oxygen free tank called a fermenter, adding the yeast, and allowing the mixture to sit for about 50 hours. Without oxygen, the yeast feeds on the sugar and gives off ethanol and carbon dioxide as waste products. Eventually, deprived of oxygen, the yeast dies.

Even though she used an effective transition statement, Louisa continues to help the audience stay with her by using the signpost "second step." Her third slide, a visual of the "fermentation equation," nicely simplifies the complex chemistry that underlies fermentation.

This is similar to what happens when we add yeast to bread dough. But in bread the carbon dioxide is trapped in the dough and causes it to rise, while the alcohol is burned off when the bread is baked.

By comparing fermentation in corn mash to bread making, Louisa is able again to make the strange familiar, and she contrasts what happens to the alcohol and the carbon dioxide in ethanol production and bread.

In ethanol production, the carbon dioxide is not trapped in the watery slurry. Since it is as a gas, it bubbles out of mixture and is captured and released into the outside air. The ethanol, however, remains in the mixture that is now called "beer" with the water and the nonfermentable corn solids. At the end of fermentation process, it is the ethanol in the mixture that retains much of the energy of the original sugar. At this point we are now ready to separate or distill the ethanol from the other parts of the beer.

The third step in the commercial production of ethanol is distillation, which is the process of purifying a liquid by heating it and then condensing its vapor. So for example, if you boiled your tap water and condensed the steam that was produced, you would have purified water with no minerals or other impurities. But distilling ethanol is a bit more complicated since both the ethanol and the water in the beer are liquids and can be vaporized into steam by adding heat.

She uses another effective transition statement to signal to her audience that she will be moving to the third step.

Luckily, different liquids boil at different temperatures, and since ethanol boils at 173°F while water boils at 212°F, we can use this boiling point difference to separate the two. So to simplify what is really a more complex process (Slide 4) in the commercial distillation of ethanol, a column or series of columns are used to boil off the ethanol and the water and then to separate these vapors so that the ethanol vapors are captured and condensed back into pure liquid ethanol. The liquid ethanol is then tested to make sure that it meets the specifications for purity and proof. At this point, ethanol is drinkable alcohol

Her fourth slide is much more elaborate than the others. The animation in the slide helps the audience to visualize how distillation works. It would have been more effective, however, had she been able to control the motion so that each stage was animated as she talked about it instead of having quickly moving animation and then a static image.

and would be subject to a $20 per gallon federal excise tax. To avoid this it is "denatured"—made undrinkable by adding gasoline to it. After this, the ethanol is ready to be transported from the plant.

The fourth step in the commercial production process is converting the whole stillage into co-products. (Slide 5) One of the greatest things about producing ethanol is that the water and nonfermentable corn solids which are left after the ethanol is distilled aren't just thrown out as waste. Instead, the remaining water and nonfermentable corn solids can also be processed to make co-products that are primarily used as animal feed.

So as you have seen, the process of making ethanol is really quite simple. (Slide 6) One, prepare the corn by milling and breaking its starch into sugar. Two, ferment the mash using yeast. Three, distill off the ethanol from the beer, and four, process the co-products.

In 1980, when Robert Warren was operating his still, only 175 million gallons of ethanol were being commercially produced in the United States. Twenty-five years later, according to the Renewable Fuels Association, 4.85 billion gallons were produced. That's a whopping 2,674% increase! And it is a trend that is continuing. Automobile manufacturers and service stations are gearing up to satisfy the increased demand for E-85, a fuel that is 85% ethanol. And you may already own a car that is a flexible fuel vehicle. So keep an eye out at your local service station for that green-handled pump. And when you see it, think of the four easy steps, preparation, fermentation, distillation, and processing co-products that were used to produce it.

I'd be happy to answer any questions you may have.

The last sentence serves as an internal conclusion to the fourth step.

A signpost marks the beginning of her brief discussion of the fourth main point. The slide is so simple that it really isn't needed to aid audience understanding, but it is a visual reinforcement of this step, and the audience has been conditioned to expect one slide per point.

Louisa begins the conclusion with a summary of her main points. The sixth slide, a repetition of the first slide, visually closes the loop and reinforces the four steps.

The conclusion then makes a circular reference back to Robert Warren, who was introduced at the beginning of the speech. Then Louisa uses the statistics on ethanol production to drive home the point that ethanol is once again an important fuel source and that in the near future ethanol may be a fuel used by members of the audience.

Notice how cleverly Louisa uses the final statement to once again reinforce the four steps of the ethanol production process. By leaving the sixth slide on the screen until the end of her speech, she is able to point to it as she provides this quick recap.

Louisa could have offered a better ending clincher by tying her final sentence back to her introductory comments about Henry Ford. For example, she might have said, "Almost a century later, it seems that what Henry Ford said will be coming true. Look for a green-handled pump coming soon to a gas station near you."

© SKIP ODONNELL/ISTOCKPHOTO.COM

There are even MORE Study Tools for Chapter 15 at www.cengagebrain.com

☑ Speech Builder Express

☑ Printable Flash Cards

☑ Interactive Games

☑ Interactive Video Activities

☑ Chapter Review Cards

☑ Online Quizzes with Feedback

☑ Audio Downloads

Persuasive Speaking

Learning Outcomes

LO^1 Examine the Elaboration Likelihood Model | LO^2 Consider writing persuasive speech goals as propositions | LO^3 Identify how to develop arguments to support a proposition | LO^4 Discuss how to increase audience involvement | LO^5 Examine how to cue your audience through credibility | LO^6 Discuss how to use incentives to motivate your audience | LO^7 Identify organizational patterns for persuasive speeches

> ## "A persuasive speech is one whose goal is to influence the attitudes, values, beliefs, or behavior of audience members."

Although it is easy to get excited about a powerful speech, real-life attempts to persuade others require speakers to be knowledgeable about forming arguments and adapting them to the needs of the audience. A **persuasive speech** is one whose goal is to influence the attitudes, values, beliefs, or behavior of audience members. It is the most demanding speech challenge because it requires not only the skills you've studied so far but also an understanding of how to convince audience members to alter their attitudes, beliefs, values, or behavior.

persuasive speech
a speech that has a goal to influence the beliefs or behavior of audience members

In this chapter, you will learn how to prepare an effective persuasive speech. We begin by presenting a theoretical model that explains how people process persuasive messages. Then, we use this model to describe how you can meet the challenge of developing an effective persuasive speech. To do this, you will build arguments that are convincing to your audience, use emotion to increase your audience's involvement, develop your credibility by demonstrating goodwill, use incentives to motivate your audience, and choose an effective persuasive organizational pattern.

What do you think?

I am easily persuaded by speeches I hear.

Strongly Disagree   Strongly Agree
1   2   3   4   5   6   7   8   9   10

LO¹ How We Process Persuasive Messages: The Elaboration Likelihood Model (ELM)

Do you remember listening carefully and thoughtfully to an idea someone was trying to convince you about? Do you remember consciously thinking over what had been said and making a deliberate decision? Do you remember other times when you only half-listened and made up your mind quickly based on your gut feeling about the truthfulness of what had been said? What determines how closely we listen to and how carefully we evaluate the hundreds of persuasive messages we hear each day? Richard Petty and John Cacioppo (1996) developed a model that explains how likely people are to spend time elaborating on information (such as the arguments in a speech), using their critical thinking skills, rather than processing the information in a simpler, less critical manner. Called the Elaboration Likelihood Model (ELM), this theory can be used by speakers to develop persuasive speeches that will be influential with audience members, regardless of how they process information.

The model suggests that people process information in one of two ways. One way is intense and time consuming. People using what is called the "central route"

© STEFAN KLEIN/ISTOCKPHOTO.COM

Figure 16.1

The Elaboration Likelihood Model

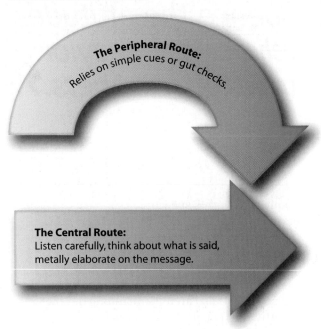

The Peripheral Route:
Relies on simple cues or gut checks.

The Central Route:
Listen carefully, think about what is said,
metally elaborate on the message.

proposition
a declarative sentence
that clearly indicates the
speaker's position on
the topic

proposition of fact
a speech goal designed
to convince the audi-
ence that something is
or is not true

listen carefully, think about what is said, and may even mentally elaborate on the message. The second way, called the "peripheral route," is a shortcut that relies on simple cues such as a quick evaluation of the speaker's credibility, or a gut check on what the listener feels about the message.

According to the ELM, what determines if we use the central or peripheral route is how important we perceive the issue to be for us. When we feel involved with an issue, we are willing to expend the energy necessary for processing on the central route. When the issue is less important to us, we take the peripheral route. So, how closely audience members will follow the speaker's argument depends on how involved they feel with the topic. For example, a person with a chronic illness that is expensive to treat is more likely to pay attention to and evaluate proposals to change health care benefits. Listeners who are healthy will probably quickly agree with suggestions from someone they perceive to be credible or go along with a proposal that seems compassionate.

The ELM also suggests that when listeners form attitudes as a result of central processing (critical thinking), they are less likely to change their minds than when their attitudes are based on peripheral cues. You can probably remember times when you were swayed at the moment by a powerful speaker but on later reflection regretted your decision and changed your mind. Likewise, you probably have some strongly held beliefs that are based on information you have heard and spent time thinking about.

When you prepare a persuasive speech, you will draw on this theory by developing your topic in a way that will increase the likelihood that your audience members feel personally involved with the topic. You will want to develop sound reasons so that audience members who use the central, critical thinking approach to your speech will find your arguments convincing. For members who are less involved, you will want to appeal to their emotions and include information that enables them to see you as credible.

LO² Writing Persuasive Speech Goals as Propositions

A persuasive speech's specific goal is stated as a **proposition.** A proposition is a declarative sentence that clearly indicates the speaker's position on the topic. For example, "I want to convince my audience that pirating copyrighted media (illegally downloading music and movies) is wrong." The goal of a persuasive speech is to get the audience to agree with what the speaker is advocating. The goal may focus on what the audience's attitude or belief should be, what they should value, or how they should act. The three major types of persuasive goals are stated as propositions of fact, value, or policy.

Types of Persuasive Goals

A **proposition of fact** is a statement designed to convince your audience that something did or did not exist or occur in the past, is or is not true in the present, or will or will not occur in the future. A proposi-

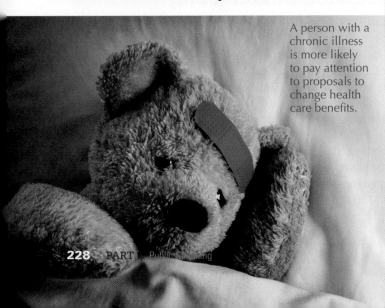

A person with a chronic illness is more likely to pay attention to proposals to change health care benefits.

© CARLOS CAETANO/SHUTTERSTOCK

tion of fact takes a position on something not known for certain but that can be argued for as true or plausible. Although propositions of fact may or may not be true—both positions are arguable—they are stated as true. For example, you could argue a proposition of fact that "Smoking marijuana leads to the use of more dangerous drugs" or "Smoking marijuana is less dangerous than drinking alcohol." Other examples are "There is [or is not] a God"; "Thanks to the messaging opportunities of the Internet, the postal service will eventually cease to exist"; and "Global warming is destroying the earth" are propositions of fact.

A proposition of value is a statement designed to convince your audience that something is good, bad, desirable, undesirable, fair, unfair, moral, immoral, sound, unsound, beneficial, harmful, important, or unimportant (Hill & Leeman, 1997). You can attempt to persuade your audience that something has more value than something else, or you can attempt to persuade them that something meets valued standards. "A low-fat diet is actually better than a fat-free diet" is an example of the former, and "Multilingual education is beneficial to children" is an example of the latter.

A proposition of policy is a statement designed to convince your audience that they should take a specific course of action. Propositions of policy will implore listeners using phrases such as *do it/don't*

do it, should/shouldn't, and *must/must not.* "All college students should be required to take an oral communication skills course in order to graduate" and "We must vote for the tax levy to build a downtown entertainment center" are propositions of policy. Figure 16.2 provides several examples of how propositions of fact, value, and policy can be developed from the same topic idea.

proposition of value
a speech goal designed to convince the audience that something is good, fair, moral, sound, etc., or its opposite

proposition of policy
a speech goal designed to convince the audience that a specific course of action should be taken

target audience
the group of people a speaker most wants to persuade

Tailoring Your Proposition to Your Audience

As you consider your topic and the proposition you will argue, you'll want to understand the opinions your audience members currently have about your topic.

Audience members' opinions about your speech topic can range from highly favorable to highly opposed and can be visualized as lying on a continuum like the one in Figure 16.3. Even though an audience will include individuals with opinions at nearly every point along the continuum, generally their opinions will tend to cluster in one area of the continuum. For instance, most of the audience members represented in Figure 16.3 were "mildly opposed," even though a few people were more hostile and a few had favorable opinions. This cluster point would be your target audience—the group of people you most want to persuade.

The initial attitude of your target audience toward your topic can be classified as "in favor" (already supportive), "neutral" (uninformed, impartial, or apathetic), or "opposed" (against a particular belief or holding an opposite point of view). You develop your proposition based on where your target audience stands initially. Generally, when your target audience is opposed, seek incremental change. When your target audience is neutral, seek agreement. And when your

Figure 16.2

Examples of Persuasive Speech Propositions

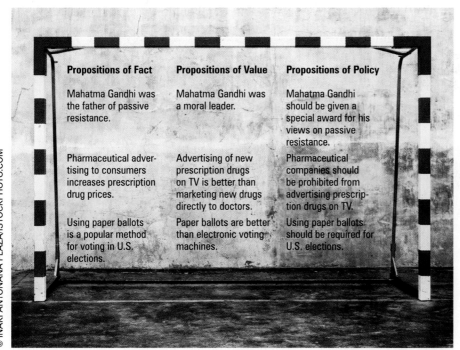

© IÑAKI ANTOÑANA PLAZA/ISTOCKPHOTO.COM

Propositions of Fact	Propositions of Value	Propositions of Policy
Mahatma Gandhi was the father of passive resistance.	Mahatma Gandhi was a moral leader.	Mahatma Gandhi should be given a special award for his views on passive resistance.
Pharmaceutical advertising to consumers increases prescription drug prices.	Advertising of new prescription drugs on TV is better than marketing new drugs directly to doctors.	Pharmaceutical companies should be prohibited from advertising prescription drugs on TV.
Using paper ballots is a popular method for voting in U.S. elections.	Paper ballots are better than electronic voting machines.	Using paper ballots should be required for U.S. elections.

Figure 16.3

Sample Opinion Continuum

NO	Highly opposed	Opposed	Mildly opposed	Neither in favor nor opposed	Mildly in favor	In favor	Highly in favor	YES
	2	2	11	1	2	2	0	

uninformed
not knowing enough about a topic to have formed an opinion

impartial
knowing the basics about a topic but still having no opinion about it

apathetic
having no opinion because one is uninterested, unconcerned, or indifferent to a topic

target audience is in favor, seek action. So for the target audience represented on the continuum in Figure 16.3, you would develop a proposition seeking incremental change in attitude, belief, or value. Let's look a bit closer at each of these types of audiences and how you should focus your speech.

Opposed

If your target audience is very much opposed to your goal, it is unrealistic to believe that you will be able to change their attitude from opposed to in favor in only one short speech. Instead, when dealing with a hostile (strongly opposed) target audience, seek incremental change—that is, attempting them to move only a small degree in your direction. For example, if you determine that your audience is likely to be opposed to the proposition "I want to convince my audience that gay marriage should be legalized," you might rephrase your proposition to "I want to convince my audience that committed gay couples should be able to have the same legal protection that is afforded to committed heterosexual couples through state-recognized civil unions." Then brainstorm potential objections, questions, and criticisms that might arise, and shape your speech around them.

Neutral

If your target audience is neutral, you can be straightforward with the reasons in support of your proposition. But you should consider whether they are uninformed, impartial, or apathetic about your topic. If they are **uninformed**—that is, they do not know enough about a topic to have formed an opinion—you will need to provide the basic arguments and information. For example, if your target audience is uninformed about gay marriage, you might need to begin by highlighting the legal benefits of marriage. Make sure that each of your reasons is well supported with good information. If your target audience is **impartial**—that is, they know the basics about your topic but have no opinion—you will want to provide more elaborate or secondary arguments and more robust evidence. Perhaps your audience knows the legal benefits of marriage but needs to understand how gay partners who do not have these benefits are disadvantaged. When target audience members have no opinion because they are **apathetic**, you will need to find ways to personalize the topic for them so that they see how it relates to them or their needs. In other words, you need to provide answers to a question such as, I'm not gay, so why should I care? You can do this by including listener relevance links for each main point in your speech.

In Favor

If your target audience is only mildly in favor of your proposal, your task is to reinforce and strengthen their beliefs. Audience members who favor your topic will benefit from an elaboration of the reasons for holding these beliefs. They may become further committed to the belief by hearing additional or new reasons and more recent evidence that supports it.

If your audience strongly agrees with your position, then you can consider a proposition that builds on that belief and moves the audience to act on it. So, for example, if the topic is gay marriage and your audience poll shows that most audience members strongly favor the idea, then your goal may be "I want my audience members to walk in Saturday's march in support of gay marriage" or "I want my audience members to e-mail their state representatives and urge them to support

© JON SCHULTE/ISTOCKPHOTO.COM

legislation allowing our state to extend the right to marry to gay couples."

LO³ Developing Arguments (Logos) That Support Your Proposition

Persuasive speeches develop an **argument**, which is the collective reasons and evidence used to support the proposition. Aristotle, the ancient Greek philosopher who is credited with first articulating how people attempt to persuade, used the term logos to denote the logical reasoning used to develop an argument. So the main points of your persuasive speeches are reasons that argue for your proposition. You will choose your reasons and the evidence that supports them from the information you have acquired during your research.

Finding Reasons to Use as Main Points

Reasons are main point statements that summarize several related pieces of evidence and show *why* the listener should believe or do something. For example, suppose your speech proposition is "I want the audience to believe home ownership is good for a society." Based on your research, you develop six potential reasons:

I.   Home ownership builds strong communities.
II. Home ownership reduces crime.
III. Home ownership increases individual wealth.

IV. Home ownership increases individual self-esteem.
V.   Home ownership improves the value of a neighborhood.
VI. Home ownership is growing in the suburbs.

Once you have identified reasons, you can weigh and evaluate each and choose the three or four that have the highest quality. You can judge the quality of each reason by asking the following questions:

- **Is the reason directly related to proving the proposition?** Sometimes we find information that can be summarized into a reason, but that reason doesn't directly argue the proposition. For instance, you may have uncovered a lot of research that supports the notion that "home ownership is growing in the suburbs." Unfortunately, it isn't clear how the growth of home ownership in the suburbs benefits society as a whole. When choosing reasons, eliminate those that are only tangentially related to your proposition.

- **Do I have strong evidence to support a reason?** Some reasons sound impressive but cannot be supported with solid evidence. For example, the second reason, "Home ownership reduces crime," sounds like a good one, but if the only proof you have is an opinion expressed by one person whose expertise is questionable, or if, in your research, you discover that although crime is lower in areas with high home ownership there is little evidence to suggest a cause-and-effect relationship, you should eliminate this reason from consideration.

- **Will this reason be persuasive for this audience?** Suppose that you have a lot of factual evidence to support the reason "Home ownership encourages self-esteem." This reason might be very persuasive to an audience of social workers, psychologists, and teachers, but it would probably be less important to an audience of financial planners, bankers, and economists. Once you have identified reasons that are related to the proposition and have strong evidence to support them, choose to use as main points of your speech the three or four that you believe will be most persuasive for your particular audience.

argument
the process of proving conclusions you have drawn from reasons and evidence

logos
the logical reasoning a speaker uses to develop an argument

reasons
main point statements that summarize several related pieces of evidence and show why you should believe or do something

© FEVERPITCH/SHUTTERSTOCK

Selecting Evidence to Support Reasons

Although a reason may seem self-explanatory, audience members will need information that backs it up before they will believe it. As you researched, you may have discovered more evidence to support a reason than you will have time to use. So you will have to select the pieces of evidence you will present.

Verifiable factual statements are a strong type of evidence to support reasons. Suppose, for example, that you were attempting to convince people that Alzheimer's research should be better funded, and you want to use the reason "Alzheimer's disease is an increasing health problem in the United States." A factual statement that supports this reason would be "According to a 2003 article in the *Archives of Neurology,* the number of Americans with Alzheimer's has more than doubled since 1980 and is expected to continue to grow, affecting between 11.3 and 16 million Americans by the year 2050."

Statements from people who are experts on a subject can also be used as evidence to support a reason. For example, the statement "According to the Surgeon General, 'By 2050, Alzheimer's disease may afflict 14 million people a year'" is an expert opinion.

Let's look at an example of how fact and expert opinion evidence can be used in combination to support a proposition.

Proposition: I want the audience to believe that playing violent video games leads children to become aggressive and violent in real life.

Reason: Playing violent video games increases aggressive emotions in children.

Support: Studies measuring the emotional responses of adolescents to playing violent video games when compared with emotional responses of children playing non-violent games have shown that violent games increase aggressive emotions. [*fact*] Adolescents themselves often seem to recognize this. In their study published in a 1998 issue of *Psychological Reports,* Griffiths and Hunt observed that when asked to name the "bad things" about computer games, many students reported that they make people more moody and aggressive. [*opinion*] And the same study also found that students who were more "addicted" to

video games were significantly more likely to be in a bad mood before, during, and after play than were non-addicted students (Walsh, 2001). [*fact*]

Regardless of whether the evidence is based on expert opinions or facts, you will want to use the best evidence you have found to support your point. You can use the answers to the following questions to help you select evidence that is likely to persuade your audience:

- **Does the evidence come from a well-respected source?** This question involves both the people who offered the opinions or compiled the facts and the book, journal, or Internet source in which they were reported. Just as some people's opinions are more reliable than others, some printed and Internet sources are more reliable than others. Be especially careful of undocumented information. Eliminate evidence that comes from a questionable, unreliable, or biased source.

- **Is the evidence recent and, if not, is it still valid?** Things change, so information that was accurate for a particular time may not be valid today. As you look at your evidence, consider when the evidence was gathered. Something that was true five years ago may not be true today. A trend that was forecast a year ago may have been revised since then. A statistic that was reported last week may be based on data that were collected three years ago. So whether it is a fact or an opinion, you want to choose evidence that is valid today.

  - For example, the evidence "The total cost of caring for individuals with Alzheimer's is at least $100 billion according to the Alzheimer's Association and the National Institute on Aging" was cited in a 2003 NIH publication. But it is based on information from a study using 1991 data that were updated to 1994 data before being published. As a result, we can expect that today, annual costs would be higher. If you choose to use this evidence, you should disclose the age of the data used in the study and indicate that today, the costs would be higher.

- **Does the evidence really support the reason?** Just as reasons need to be relevant to the proposition, evidence needs to be relevant to the reason. Some of the evidence you have found may be only indirectly related to the reason and should be eliminated in favor of evidence that provides more central support.

- **Will this evidence be persuasive for this audience?** Finally, just as when you select your reasons, you will want to choose evidence that your particular audience is likely to find persuasive. So, if you have your choice of two quotations from experts, you will want to use the one from the person your audience is likely to find more credible.

Types and Tests of Arguments

An argument is the logical relationship between the proposition and the reasons or between the reasons and the evidence. If your audience is not convinced that your supporting evidence provides a convincing argument for your reason, they will not agree with it. And if your audience doesn't buy the argument from your reasons, they will not support your proposition.

You can develop several kinds of arguments:

1. *Arguing from example.* You **argue from example** when the reasons you offer are examples of the proposition or when the evidence you offer are examples of the reasons. For instance, if you say "Anyone who studies can get As" and offer as evidence "Tom, Jane, and Josh studied and they all got As," you would be making an argument from example. An argument from example asserts that what is true in some instances is true in all instances. When arguing from example, you can make sure that your argument is valid by answering the following questions:
   - Were enough instances (or examples) cited so listeners understand that they are not isolated or handpicked examples?
   - Were the instances typical and representative?
   - Are the negative instances really atypical?

   If the answer to any of these questions is no, then consider making your argument in a different way.

2. *Arguing from analogy.* You **argue from analogy** when you support your reason with a single comparable example that is so significantly similar to the subject that it offers strong proof. For example, if you support your proposition "Children who play violent video games for two or more hours per day act more aggressively" by saying "Children who watch violent television

programs for two or more hours per day act more aggressively than children who don't," you would be arguing from analogy. An argument from analogy asserts that what is true or will work in one set of circumstances is true or will work in a comparable set of circumstances. When arguing from analogy, make sure your argument is valid by answering these questions:
   - Are the subjects really comparable (for example, are video games really similar to TV programs in all important ways)? If they are not, then your argument is not valid.
   - Are any of the ways that the subjects are dissimilar important to the conclusion? If so, the reasoning is not sound.

3. *Arguing from causation.* You **argue from causation** when you cite evidence that one or more events always or almost always bring about, lead to, create, or prevent a predictable event or set of effects. If you support your proposition "Fewer Americans will be buying new homes in the next year" by saying "Unemployment is higher than it has been in decades" and "Banks are applying tougher standards for loan approvals," you would be arguing from causation. Your argument can be boiled down to "The lack of sufficient funds causes a reduction in the number of homes being bought." The general form of a causal argument is if A, which is known to bring about B, has happened, then we can expect B to occur. To make sure your causal arguments are sound, you should answer the following questions:
   - Are the events alone enough to cause the stated effect?
   - Do other events accompanying the events cited actually cause the effect?
   - Is the relationship between causal events and effect consistent?

   If the answer to one of these questions is "No," the reasoning is not sound.

4. *Arguing from sign.* You **argue from sign** when you offer events as outward signals of the truth of your proposition or reason. For example, you

arguing from example
to support a claim by providing one or more individual examples

arguing from analogy
to support a claim with a single comparable example that is significantly similar to the subject of the claim

arguing from causation
to support a claim by citing events that have occurred to bring about the claim

arguing from sign
to support a claim by citing information that signals the claim

hasty generalization
a fallacy that presents a generalization that is either not supported with evidence or is supported with only one weak example

false cause
a fallacy that occurs when the alleged cause fails to be related to or produce the effect

ad hominem
a fallacy that occurs when one attacks the person making the argument rather than the argument itself

either-or
a fallacy that occurs when a speaker supports a claim by suggesting there are only two alternatives when, in fact, others exist

might support your point that the recession is worsening by noting that the local soup kitchens have experienced an increase in the number of people they are serving. Your argument would be "Longer lines at soup kitchens are a sign of the worsening recession." To test this kind of argument, you should ask the following questions:

- Does the sign cited always or usually signal the conclusion drawn?
- Are a sufficient number of signs present?
- Are contradictory signs also in evidence?

If your answer to the first two of these questions is no, or yes to the third question, then your reasoning is not sound.

Avoiding Fallacies in Your Reasons and Argument

As you are developing your reasons and the argument that you will make, you should make sure that you avoid fallacies or errors in your reasoning. There are five common fallacies:

1. *Hasty generalization.* A hasty generalization presents a generalization that is either not supported with evidence or is supported with only one weak example. Because the supporting material that is cited should be representative of all the supporting material that could be cited, enough supporting material must be presented to satisfy the audience that the instances are not isolated or handpicked. Because you can find an example or statistic to support almost anything, avoiding hasty generalizations requires you to be confident that the instances you cite as support are typical and representative of your claim. For example, someone who argued "All Akitas are vicious dogs" based on the sole piece of evidence that "My neighbor's Akita bit my best friend's sister" would be guilty of a hasty generalization. It is hasty to generalize about the temperament of a whole breed of dogs based on a single action of one dog.

2. *False cause.* A false cause fallacy occurs when the alleged cause fails to be related to or produce the effect. The Latin term for this fallacy is *post hoc, ergo propter hoc,* meaning "after this, therefore because of this." Just because one thing happened after another does not mean that the first necessarily caused the second. Don't be like people who blame monetary setbacks or illness on black cats or broken mirrors, and be careful that you don't present a coincidental event as causal unless you can prove the causal relationship. To claim that school violence is caused by listening to Marilyn Manson's shock rock music is an example of a false cause fallacy. When one event follows another, there may be no connection at all, or the first event might be just one of many causes that contribute to the second.

3. *Ad hominem.* An ad hominem fallacy supports a claim by attacking or praising the character of someone or something. *Ad hominem* literally means "to the man." For example, if Jamal's support for his claim that his audience members should buy an iPhone is that Steve Jobs, co-founder and CEO of Apple Inc., is a genius, he would be making an ad hominem argument. Jobs's intelligence isn't really a reason to buy a particular cell phone. Television commercials that feature celebrities using the product are often guilty of committing ad hominem fallacies.

4. *Either-or.* An either-or fallacy supports a claim by suggesting there are only two alternatives when, in fact, others exist. This kind of fallacy oversimplifies a complex issue. For example, when Robert argued "We'll either have to raise taxes or close the library," he committed an either-or fallacy. He reduced a complex issue to one oversimplified solution when there were many other possible solutions for keeping the library open.

© HÉLÈNE VALLÉE/ISTOCKPHOTO.COM

5. *Straw person.* A **straw person** fallacy occurs when a speaker weakens the opposing position by misrepresenting it in some way and then attacking that misrepresented (straw person) position. For example, in her speech advocating a seven-day waiting period to purchase handguns, Colleen favored regulation, not prohibition, of gun ownership. Bob argued in opposition claiming "It is our constitutional right to bear arms." However, Colleen did not advocate abolishing the right to bear arms. Bob distorted Colleen's position, making it easier for him to refute.

© SONY HO/SHUTTERSTOCK

LO⁴ Increasing Audience Involvement through Emotional Appeal (Pathos)

As you will recall, the ELM suggests that people are more likely to listen to and think about information when they feel personally involved in the topic. We are more likely to be involved in a topic when we have an emotional stake in it. If you can give your audience members an emotional stake in what you are saying, they are more likely to listen to and think about your arguments. Aristotle labeled these appeals to emotion pathos. You can increase your audience members' involvement by evoking negative or positive emotions in your speeches (Nabi, 2002, p. 292).

Negative emotions are disquieting, so when people experience them, they look for ways to eliminate the discomfort. You might tap any number of negative emotions in your speech. The five most common are fear, guilt, shame, anger, and sadness. Notice in the following statement how fear personalizes the statistics on heart disease and piques your interest in listening to what the speaker has to say:

© ISTOCKPHOTO.COM

> One out of every three Americans age 18 and older has high blood pressure. It is the primary cause of stroke, heart disease, heart failure, kidney disease, and blindness. It triples a person's chance of developing heart disease, and boosts the chance of stroke seven times and the chance of congestive heart failure six times. Look at the person on your right; look at the person on your left. If they don't get it, chances are you will. Today, I'd like to convince you that you are at risk of developing high blood pressure.

Positive emotional involvement can also lead audience members to more carefully consider your proposition and arguments. When you evoke positive emotions, audience members will look for ways to sustain or further enhance the feeling. Five of the most common positive emotions you can evoke are happiness/joy, pride, relief, hope, and compassion. For example, notice how the speaker used the emotion of pride to pique interest in a speech designed to get the audience to sign up for an alternative spring break experience with Habitat for Humanity:

> Imagine that you are an Olympian who has won your event and stand on the podium with a medal around your neck as they play your national anthem. Imagine opening your mail and finding out that you have gotten into the top ranked graduate program in the country. Now imagine that you are standing on the front porch of a brand new home that you have helped to build and are being hugged by the mother of four children who, thanks to your selfless work, will no longer have to share a one-bedroom fifth-floor walk-up. Imagine the pride? How long has it been since you felt so good? Well, folks, that's just what you'll experience and much more when you sign up to work with the Habitat for Humanity house being constructed in your community.

Some of the techniques you might use to appeal to emotions in your speeches include vivid stories

straw person
a fallacy that occurs when a speaker weakens the opposing position by misrepresenting it in some way and then attacks that weaker (straw person) position

pathos
appeals to emotion

ethos
appeals to credibility

goodwill
the audience percep-
tion that the speaker un-
derstands, empathizes
with, and is responsive
to them

and testimonials, startling statistics, emotion-packed listener relevance links, striking presentational aids, provocative language, and animated vocal delivery and body language.

LO⁵ Cueing Your Audience through Credibility (Ethos): Demonstrating Goodwill

You cannot expect that everyone in your audience will choose the central processing route when listening to your speech. Some will still pay minimal attention to your arguments and instead will use simple cues and process your message using the peripheral route. The most important cue for those who process information along the peripheral route is the credibility of the speaker. Aristotle used the term **ethos** to characterize such appeals to credibility. One crucial characteristic for motivating uninvolved audience members to believe what you are saying is your goodwill. Goodwill is the audience members' perception that the speaker (1) understands, (2) empathizes with, and (3) is responsive to them. In other words, goodwill is the audience members' belief that your intentions toward them are for their good. Audience members who perceive the speaker as exhibiting goodwill toward them are more willing to believe what the speaker is saying.

You can demonstrate that you understand your audience by personalizing your information. Information you gleaned from your audience analysis can help you. For example, Meg, a union rep trying to convince the membership to accept a new contract change to health care benefits, might build goodwill by personalizing one aspect of the proposal:

> I know that about 40 percent of you have little use for eye care, which is part of the new package. But for the 60 percent of you who wear glasses or have dependents who wear glasses, this plan will not only pay for your annual eye exam, but it will also pay 30 percent of the cost of new glasses or 25 percent of the new cost of contact lenses. This will mean about $250 in your pocket each year, and with less overtime predicted for this year, that's a real benefit.

Speakers also demonstrate goodwill by empathizing with their audience. Empathizing requires you to go beyond understanding and identify emotionally with audience members' views. This doesn't mean, however, that you accept their views as your own. It means only that you acknowledge their views as valid. Even when your speech is designed to change audience members' views, the sensitivity you show to their feelings will demonstrate goodwill. For example, the union rep might demonstrate empathy by saying this:

> I can imagine what it will be like for some of you who, under this new plan, will go to the drug-store and find that there is now a high co-pay required for a drug you take that is no longer on the formulary. But I also guarantee that the plan formulary will have drugs that your doctor can prescribe that will be direct substitutes, or you will be able to appeal the co-pay.

Finally, to demonstrate goodwill, you will want to show your responsiveness to the audience. Being responsive is showing you care about the audience by acknowledging their feedback, especially subtle negative cues. The union rep can demonstrate responsiveness by referencing feedback that the membership had provided earlier:

> Before we started negotiations, we surveyed you, asking what changes you wanted to see in the health care program. Seventy-five percent of you said that your number one concern was keeping the office visit co-pay at $10, and in this contract we were able to do that.

Or, if she notices that some members of the audience are looking disgusted and shaking their heads, she might respond:

> I can see that some of you are disappointed with the increase in premiums. So am I. I wish we could have done better on this issue. But the fact is, health care costs have risen 15 percent nation-wide this year, and our usage has exceeded this average.

By establishing your goodwill, you enhance your credibility with the audience, which is especially important for audience members who are not personally involved with your topic.

In addition to demonstrating goodwill, several other techniques of good speaking can increase the audience's perception of your credibility. These include doing the following things you have learned about in previous chapters: (1) explain your qualifications; (2) establish common ground; (3) use and cite evidence from respected sources; (4) be vocally expressive; (5) dress appropriately; and (6) convey confidence with your posture, poise, and eye contact.

How to Increase Credibility

- establish goodwill
- explain your qualifications
- establish common ground
- use and cite evidence
- be vocally expressive
- dress appropriately
- convey confidence

© GAVIN DUNT/ISTOCKPHOTO.COM

LO⁶ Motivating Your Audience to Act through Incentives

When your speech proposition is aimed at influencing your audience members' attitudes or beliefs, you will use emotional appeals to encourage them to become involved with your topic. But when you want to influence your audience to act on what you have said, you will need to provide motivation by showing how what you are asking them to do will meet their needs. Motivation—"forces acting on or within an organism to initiate and direct behavior" (Petri, 1996, p. 3)—is often a result of incentives that meet needs.

An **incentive** is a reward promised if a particular action is taken or goal is reached (Petri, 1996, p. 3). Incentives can be physical (food, shelter, money, sex), psychological (self-esteem, peace of mind), or social (acceptance, popularity, status) rewards. Incentives are valuable only to the extent that they can satisfy a need felt by the audience members, and the value of the incentive for taking the action must not be outweighed by costs associated with the action.

Using Incentives to Satisfy Unmet Needs

motivation
forces acting on or within an organism to initiate and direct behavior

incentive
a reward promised if a particular action is taken or goal is reached

Incentives are more likely to motivate people when they satisfy an important unmet need. Various ways for categorizing needs have been developed. One of the most widely recognized is Maslow's hierarchy of needs. Abraham Maslow (1954) divided people's needs into five categories, illustrated in Figure 16.4: (1) physiological needs, including food, drink, and life-sustaining temperature; (2) safety and security needs, including long-term survival and stability; (3) belongingness and love needs, including the need to identify with friends, loved ones, and family; (4) esteem needs—ego gratification including material goods, recognition, and power or influence; (5) cognitive needs; (6) aesthetic needs; and (7) self-actualization needs, including the need to develop one's self to realize one's full potential and engage in creative acts (pp. 80–92). Maslow believed that these needs were hierarchical—that is, that "lower order" needs had to be met before we would be motivated by "higher order" needs. In theory, then, a person cannot be motivated to meet an esteem need of gaining recognition until basic physiological, safety, and belongingness and love needs have been met.

The hierarchical nature of needs is still debated because there is evidence that at times, some people will sacrifice lower order needs to satisfy higher order ones. Nevertheless, as a speaker, when you can tie the incentives that accompany your proposal with unmet audience needs, you increase the likelihood that the audience will take the action you are proposing. Let's see how this could work in the volunteering for literacy speech with a college student audience. Suppose that during the speech you point out that people who volunteer 30 hours or more a year receive a recognition certificate and are invited to attend a private dinner with the stars of the hot band that will be headlining the big spring campus concert. After announcing this, you add:

> I know that although most of you care about literacy, you're thinking about what else you could do with that hour. But the really cool part of spending your time as a literacy volunteer is that you will feel good about yourself because you have improved someone's life, and you also will be able to list this service and recognition on your résumé. As a bonus, you'll get to brag to your friends about having dinner with several celebrities.

Figure 16.4

Maslow's Hierarchy of Needs

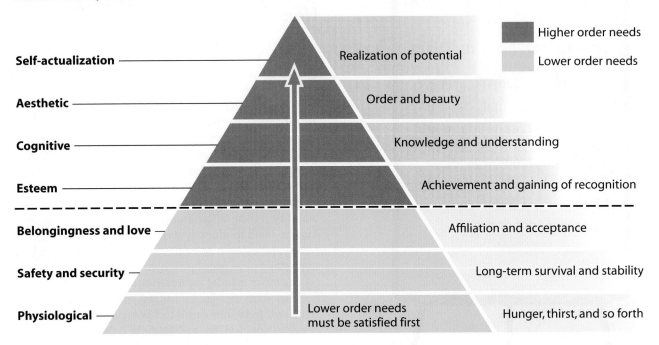

Self-actualization — Realization of potential

Aesthetic — Order and beauty

Cognitive — Knowledge and understanding

Esteem — Achievement and gaining of recognition

Belongingness and love — Affiliation and acceptance

Safety and security — Long-term survival and stability

Physiological — Hunger, thirst, and so forth

Higher order needs

Lower order needs

Lower order needs must be satisfied first

In the first part of this short statement, you have enumerated three incentives that are tied to volunteering: a physical incentive (a recognition certificate), a psychological incentive of enhanced self-concept (I feel good about myself because I have helped someone else), and a social incentive (having dinner with an elite group and meeting celebrities). In the second part, you have also tied each incentive to a need that it can satisfy. With enhanced résumés, people are more likely to get jobs that provide money for food and shelter. If by helping someone else we feel better about ourselves, then we have met a self-actualization need. And by attending the private dinner, we might satisfy both esteem needs and belongingness needs.

Creating Incentives That Outweigh Costs

As you prepare your speech, you must be concerned with presenting the incentives that meet the needs of your audience, and you also need to understand the potential costs for audience members who act in line with your proposal. For example, in the literacy speech, one obvious cost is the hour of free time each week that might subtract from time that audience members spend with their friends or family. This could create a potential deficit in their belonging-

ness need. To address this concern, you could point out, "Now, I know you might be concerned about the time this will take away from your friends or family, but relax. Your friends and family are likely to understand and admire you [*esteem need substitute for belongingness*]. Also, at the literacy center, you're going to have time before the tutoring starts to meet other volunteers [*belongingness*], and they are some really cool people [*esteem*]. I know a couple who just got engaged, and they met through their volunteering [*big-time belongingness*]."

© ISTOCKPHOTO.COM

When you can tie the incentives that accompany your proposal with unmet audience needs, you increase the likelihood that the audience will take the action you are proposing.

If, through your audience analysis, you discover that you cannot relate your proposition to meeting basic audience needs, or if the analysis reveals that the costs associated with your proposition would outweigh the incentives, then you probably need to reconsider what you are asking the audience to do. For example, if you discover that most of your audience members are overcommitted, then it is probably unrealistic to think you will be able to convince them to volunteer an hour a week. You may need to modify your proposition and persuade them to donate a book or money to buy a book for the literacy library.

Finally, if your incentives are going to motivate your audience members, they must be convinced that there is a high likelihood that if they act as you suggest, they will receive the incentives. It is important, therefore, that you discuss only incentives that are closely tied to the action you are requesting and are received by almost all people who act in the recommended way. Although there is an annual award for the literacy volunteer who has donated the most time that year, mentioning this in your speech is unlikely to motivate the audience, because only one person receives it and the cost is very high.

When you want to move audience members to action, you need to understand their needs and explain the incentives they can receive by taking the action you suggest. You also need to make sure that the incentives you mention fulfill unmet needs in the audience.

slightly different propositions that use the same or similar reasons.

Statement of Reasons

© MARIE-FRANCE BÉLANGER/ISTOCKPHOTO.COM

The statement of reasons pattern attempts to prove propositions of fact by presenting the best-supported reasons in a meaningful order. For a speech with three reasons or more, place the strongest reason last as this is the reason you believe the audience will find most persuasive. Place the second strongest reason first because you want to start with a significant point. Place the other reasons in between.

> *Proposition:* I want my audience to believe that passing the proposed school tax levy is necessary.

I.   The income will enable the schools to restore vital programs. [*second strongest*]
II. The income will enable the schools to give teachers the raises they need to keep up with the cost of living.
III. The income will allow the community to maintain local control and will save the district from state intervention. [*strongest*]

> **statement of reasons pattern**
> a straightforward organization in which you present the best-supported reasons you can find

LO⁷ Organizational Patterns for Persuasive Speeches

Having developed a proposition, selected evidence to support your reasons, identified ways to increase audience involvement through emotional appeals, determined how you will enhance your credibility by developing good-will, and identified the incentives you will use to motivate your audience, you are ready to choose a pattern to organize your speech. The most common patterns for organizing persuasive speeches include statement of reasons, comparative advantages, criteria satisfaction, refutation, problem-solution, problem-cause-solution, and motivated sequence. In this section, we describe and illustrate these persuasive organizational patterns and identify the type of proposition for which they are most commonly used. So that you can contrast the patterns and better understand their use, we will illustrate each pattern by examining the same topic with

Patterns for Organizing Persuasive Speeches

statement of reasons
comparative advantages
criteria satisfaction
refutation
problem solution
problem-cause-solution
motivated sequence

© KRISTOF DEGREEF/SHUTTERSTOCK

© ROBYN MACKENZIE/ISTOCKPHOTO.COM

comparative advantages pattern an organization that allows you to place all the emphasis on the superiority of the proposed course of action

criteria satisfaction pattern an indirect organization that first seeks audience agreement on criteria that should be considered when they evaluate a particular proposition and then shows how the proposition satisfies those criteria

refutation pattern an organization that challenges opposing arguments while bolstering your own

Comparative Advantages

The comparative advantages pattern attempts to prove that something has more value than something else. A comparative advantages approach to a school tax proposition would look like this:

Proposition: I want my audience to believe that passing the school tax levy is better than not passing it. *[compares the value of change to the status quo]*

I. Income from a tax levy will enable schools to reintroduce important programs that had to be cut. *[advantage 1]*
II. Income from a tax levy will enable schools to avoid a tentative strike by teachers who are underpaid. *[advantage 2]*
III. Income from a tax levy will enable us to retain local control of our schools, which will be lost to the state if additional local funding is not provided. *[advantage 3]*

Criteria Satisfaction

The criteria satisfaction pattern seeks audience agreement on criteria that should be considered when evaluating a particular idea and then shows how the proposition that the speaker is advocating satisfies the criteria. A criteria satisfaction pattern is especially useful when your audience is opposed to your proposition, because it approaches

the proposition indirectly by first focusing on the criteria that the audience may agree with before introducing the specific solution. A criteria satisfaction organization for the school levy would look like this:

Proposition: I want my audience to believe that passing a school levy is a good way to fund our schools.

I. We can all agree that a good school funding method must meet three criteria:
    A. A good funding method results in the reestablishment of programs that have been dropped due to budget constraints.
    B. A good funding method results in fair pay for teachers.
    C. A good funding method generates enough income to maintain local control, avoiding state intervention.
II. Passage of a local school tax levy is a good way to fund our schools.
    A. A local levy will allow us to re-fund important programs.
    B. A local levy will allow us to give teachers a raise.
    C. A local levy will generate enough income to maintain local control and avoid state intervention.

Refutation

The refutation pattern helps you organize your main points so that you persuade by both challenging opposing arguments and bolstering your own. This pattern is particularly useful when the target audience opposes your position. Begin by acknowledging the merit of opposing arguments and then provide evidence of their flaws. Once listeners understand the flaws, they will be more receptive to the arguments you present to support your proposition. A refutation pattern for the school tax proposition might look like this:

Proposition: I want my audience to agree that a school levy is the best way to fund our schools.

I. Opponents of the tax levy argue that the tax increase will fall only on property owners.
 A. Landlords will recoup property taxes in the form of higher rents.
 B. Thus, all people will be affected.
II. Opponents of the tax levy argue that there are fewer students in the school district, so schools should be able to function on the same amount of revenue.
 A. Although there are fewer pupils, costs continue to rise.
  1. Salary costs are increasing.
  2. Energy costs are increasing.
  3. Maintenance costs are increasing.
  4. Costs from unfunded federal and state government mandates are rising.
 B. Although there are fewer pupils, there are many aging school buildings that need replacing or retrofitting.
III. Opponents of the tax levy argue that parents should be responsible for the excessive cost of educating their children.
 A. A free public education is a hallmark of our democracy and ensures the future of our country.
 B. Parents today are already paying more than previous generations.
  1. Activity fees
  2. Lab fees
  3. Book fees
  4. Transportation fees
 C. Of school-age children today in this district, 42 percent live in families that are below the poverty line and have limited resources.

Problem-Solution

The problem-solution pattern attempts to argue that a particular problem can be solved by implementing the recommended solution. This organization works well when the audience is neutral or agrees only that there is a problem but has no opinion about a particular solution. In a problem-solution speech, the claim ("There is a problem that can be solved by X") is supported by three reasons that take the general form: (1) there is a problem that requires action, (2) Proposal X will solve the problem, and (3) Proposal X is the best solution to the problem because it will lead to positive consequences and minimize or avoid negative ones. A problem-

solution organization for the school tax proposition might look like this:

Proposition: The current fiscal crisis in the school district can be solved through a local tax levy.

> **problem-cause-solution pattern**
> an organization that provides a framework for clarifying the nature of the problem and for illustrating why a given proposal is the best one

I. The current funding is insufficient and has resulted in program cuts, labor problems resulting from stagnant wages, and a threatened state takeover of local schools. [*statement of problem*]
II. The proposed local tax levy is large enough to solve these problems. [*solution*]
III. The proposed local tax levy is the best means of solving the funding crisis.

Problem-Cause-Solution

The **problem-cause-solution pattern** is similar to the problem-solution pattern, but it has a main point about the causes of the problem and the solution is designed to alleviate those causes. This pattern is particularly useful for addressing seemingly intractable problems that have been dealt with unsuccessfully in the past as a result of treating symptoms rather than underlying causes. A problem-cause-solution organization for the school tax proposition might look like this:

Proposition: The current fiscal crisis in the school district can be solved through a local tax levy.

© VALENTYN VOLKOV/SHUTTERSTOCK

Figure 16.5

Persuasive Speech Evaluation Checklist

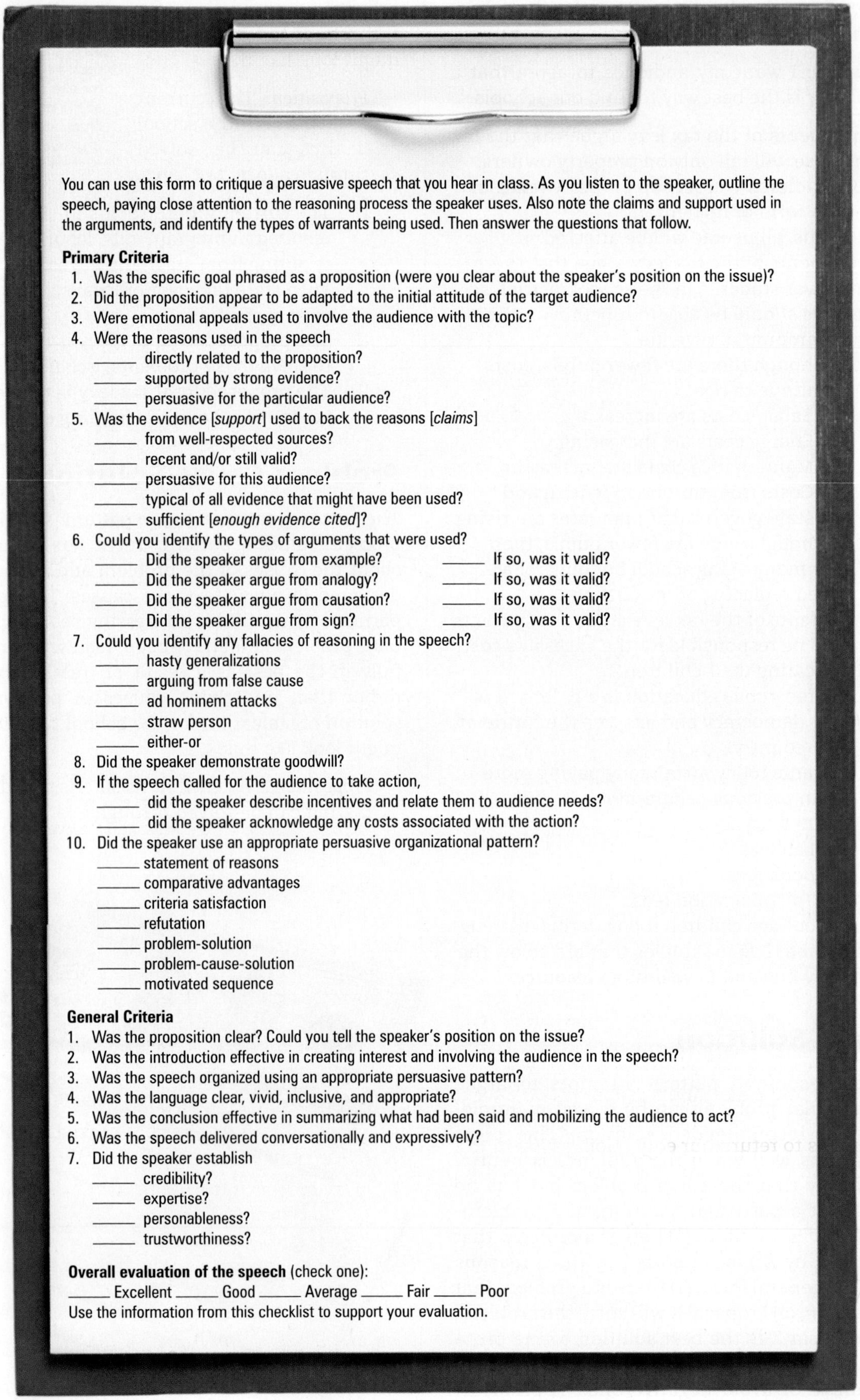

You can use this form to critique a persuasive speech that you hear in class. As you listen to the speaker, outline the speech, paying close attention to the reasoning process the speaker uses. Also note the claims and support used in the arguments, and identify the types of warrants being used. Then answer the questions that follow.

Primary Criteria

1. Was the specific goal phrased as a proposition (were you clear about the speaker's position on the issue)?
2. Did the proposition appear to be adapted to the initial attitude of the target audience?
3. Were emotional appeals used to involve the audience with the topic?
4. Were the reasons used in the speech
   _____ directly related to the proposition?
   _____ supported by strong evidence?
   _____ persuasive for the particular audience?
5. Was the evidence [*support*] used to back the reasons [*claims*]
   _____ from well-respected sources?
   _____ recent and/or still valid?
   _____ persuasive for this audience?
   _____ typical of all evidence that might have been used?
   _____ sufficient [*enough evidence cited*]?
6. Could you identify the types of arguments that were used?
   _____ Did the speaker argue from example?   _____ If so, was it valid?
   _____ Did the speaker argue from analogy?   _____ If so, was it valid?
   _____ Did the speaker argue from causation?   _____ If so, was it valid?
   _____ Did the speaker argue from sign?   _____ If so, was it valid?
7. Could you identify any fallacies of reasoning in the speech?
   _____ hasty generalizations
   _____ arguing from false cause
   _____ ad hominem attacks
   _____ straw person
   _____ either-or
8. Did the speaker demonstrate goodwill?
9. If the speech called for the audience to take action,
   _____ did the speaker describe incentives and relate them to audience needs?
   _____ did the speaker acknowledge any costs associated with the action?
10. Did the speaker use an appropriate persuasive organizational pattern?
   _____ statement of reasons
   _____ comparative advantages
   _____ criteria satisfaction
   _____ refutation
   _____ problem-solution
   _____ problem-cause-solution
   _____ motivated sequence

General Criteria

1. Was the proposition clear? Could you tell the speaker's position on the issue?
2. Was the introduction effective in creating interest and involving the audience in the speech?
3. Was the speech organized using an appropriate persuasive pattern?
4. Was the language clear, vivid, inclusive, and appropriate?
5. Was the conclusion effective in summarizing what had been said and mobilizing the audience to act?
6. Was the speech delivered conversationally and expressively?
7. Did the speaker establish
   _____ credibility?
   _____ expertise?
   _____ personableness?
   _____ trustworthiness?

Overall evaluation of the speech (check one):
_____ Excellent _____ Good _____ Average _____ Fair _____ Poor
Use the information from this checklist to support your evaluation.

© SERGHEI VELUSCEAC/ISTOCKPHOTO.COM

I. The current funding is insufficient and has resulted in program cuts, labor problems, and a threatened state takeover of local schools. [*statement of problem*]

II. These problems exist due to dwindling government support and increasing costs for operating expenses. [*causes*]

III. The proposed local tax levy will solve these problems by supplementing government support and enhancing operating budgets. [*solution*]

Motivated Sequence

The **motivated sequence pattern** combines a problem-solution pattern with explicit appeals designed to motivate the audience to act. The motivational sequence pattern is a unified five-point sequence that replaces the normal introduction-body-conclusion model with (1) an attention step, (2) a need step that fully explains the nature of the problem, (3) a satisfaction step that explains how the proposal solves the problem in a satisfactory manner, (4) a visualization step that provides a personal application of the proposal, and (5) an action appeal step that emphasizes the direction that audience action should take. A motivational pattern for the school tax levy proposition would look like this:

Proposition: I want my audience to vote in favor of the school tax levy on the November ballot.

I. Comparisons of worldwide test scores in math and science have refocused our attention on education. [*attention*]

II. The shortage of money is resulting in cost-cutting measures that compromise our ability to teach basic academic subjects well. [*need, statement of problem*]

III. The proposed increase is large enough to solve those problems in ways that allow for increased emphasis on academic need areas. [*satisfaction, how the proposal solves the problem*]

IV. Think of the contribution you will be making to the education of your children and also to efforts to return our educational system to the world-class level it once held. [*visualization of personal application*]

V. Here are "Vote Yes" buttons that you can wear to show you are willing to support this much-needed tax levy. [*action appeal showing specific direction*]

Because motivational patterns are variations of problem-solution patterns, the underlying assumption is similar: When the current means are not solving the problem, a new solution that does solve the problem should be adopted.

Sample Persuasive Speech: Sexual Assault Policy a Must

By Maria Lucia R. Anton[*]

motivated sequence pattern
an organization that combines the problem-solution pattern with explicit appeals designed to motivate the audience to act

This section presents the outline and transcript of a sample persuasive speech developed and presented by college student Maria Lucia R. Anton at the 1994 Interstate Oratorical Association competition. It is now published in an anthology of the winning speeches by college students that year. An adaptation plan was not required, so the one provided here has been created as an example for you to use as you develop your own persuasive speech.

1. Review the outline and adaptation plan for Maria's speech to petition her school's administration to create and implement a sexual assault prevention policy.

2. Read the transcript of Maria's speech.

3. Use the persuasive speech evaluation checklist from Figure 16.4 to help you evaluate this speech.

4. Write a paragraph of feedback to Maria describing the strengths of her speech and what you think she might do next time to be more effective.

Adaptation Plan

1. **Audience analysis:** My audience is composed of traditional-age college students with varying majors and classes. Most are European Americans from working- or middle-class backgrounds.

2. **Background knowledge:** My perception is that my audience knows about sexual assault on college campuses, but not about the nuances of it.

3. **Creating and maintaining interest:** I will involve my audience by appealing to several emotions including guilt, sadness, relief, hope, and most of all, compassion. I will use representative examples as short stories.

4. **Organization:** I have organized my speech using the motivated sequence.

[*]Used with permission of Maria Lucia R. Anton.

5. **Building credibility:** I will build credibility initially by pausing and looking listeners in the eye before beginning. Throughout the speech I will cite strong sources. I will dress professionally and sound emotionally convinced about the topic. I will provide credibility at the end by pausing and looking listeners in the eye for a moment after appealing to them with my call to action.

6. **Motivation:** The incentive that I will offer is that the audience members can act to create a sexual assault policy on their campuses. Doing so will appeal to hope and safety.

Outline

General purpose: To persuade
Speech goal: I want my audience to petition the administration on their campus to formulate and implement a sexual assault prevention policy.

Attention Catcher

I. "If you want to take her blouse off, you have to ask. If you want to touch her breast, you have to ask. If you want to move your hand down to her genitals, you have to ask. If you want to put your finger inside her, you have to ask." [*quotation from Antioch College's sexual offense policy*]

  A. The policy consists of three major points:
    1. If you have an STD, you must disclose it to a potential partner.
    2. It is not acceptable to knowingly take advantage of someone who is under the influence of alcohol or drugs.
    3. Obtaining consent is an ongoing process in any sexual interaction.
  B. The policy is designed to create a safe campus environment.

Need

II. Sexual assault on college campuses is a problem across the nation.

  A. Carlton College in Northfield, Minnesota, was sued for $800,000 in damages by four university women. [Time *magazine article*]
  B. Although college administration know of enrolled rapists, they need not say or do anything.
  C. One in every four college women have been assault victims. [Ms. Magazine *survey*]
  D. Between 30 and 40 percent of male students reported they might force someone to have sex if they knew they would escape punishment. [Ms. Magazine *survey*]
  E. The effects of sexual assault on victims is disturbing.

Transition: Many campuses are open invitations for sexual assault. The absence of a policy is a grand invitation.

Satisfaction

III. We need to push for sexual assault policies on our campuses.

  A. Antioch policy example.
  B. Fundamental points for any sexual assault policy.
    1. Input from students, faculty, staff, and administration is crucial when developing the policy.
    2. The policy must be publicized in many venues including the student handbook, newspaper, and radio station.
    3. Educational programs must be developed to educate the campus community about the sexual assault policy.
    4. Campuses should outline a step-by-step procedure for reporting and addressing sexual assault perpetrators.

Transition: It is pertinent that universities provide support to victims through such policies and procedures if college campuses are to be a safe environment for all students.

Visualization

IV. All students should feel safe leaving the classroom at night.

  A. The wheels of justice turn too slowly when sending victims to the local police.
  B. Without a policy, there are no specific penalties to prosecute offenders.
  C. With a policy, would-be offenders will think twice.
  D. With a policy, there is at least a chance that justice will be served.

Action

V. We students must voice our concerns.

  A. We must form petitions to demand that our universities create sexual assault policies.
  B. We must not stop until we've succeeded and our campuses have sexual assault policies.

Speech and Analysis

Speech

"If you want to take her blouse off, you have to ask. If you want to touch her breast, you have to ask. If you want to move your hand down to her genitals, you have to ask. If you want to put your finger inside her, you have to ask."

What I've just quoted is part of the freshman orientation at Antioch College in Ohio. In the sexual offense policy of this college, emphasis is given to three major points: (1) If you have a sexually transmitted disease, you must disclose it to a potential partner; (2) to knowingly take advantage of someone who is under the influence of alcohol, drugs, and/or prescribed medication is not acceptable behavior in the Antioch community; (3) obtaining consent is an ongoing process in any sexual interaction. The request for consent must be specific to each act.

The policy is designed to create a "safe" campus environment, according to Antioch President Alan Guskin. For those who engage in sex, the goal is 100 percent consensual sex. It isn't enough to ask someone if they would like to have sex; you have to get verbal consent every step of the way.

This policy has been highly publicized and you may have heard it before. The policy addresses sexual offenses such as rape, which involves penetration, and sexual assault, which does not. In both instances, the respondent coerced or forced the primary witness to engage in nonconsensual sexual conduct with the respondent or another.

Sexual assault has become a reality in many campuses across the nation. Carleton College in Northfield, Minnesota, was sued for $800,000 in damages by four university women. The women charged that Carleton was negligent in protecting them against a known rapist. From the June 1991 issue of *Time* magazine:

> Amy had been on campus for just five weeks when she joined some friends to watch a video in the room of a senior. One by one the other students went away, leaving her alone with a student whose name she didn't even know. "It ended up with his hands around my throat," she recalls. In a lawsuit she has filed against the college, she charges that he locked the door and raped her

Analysis

Attention catcher

This opening attracts our attention by personalizing the Antioch sexual offense prevention policy. Notice how the emotional impact of the policy changes as the acts described become more intimate.

Maria Lucia draws on language specific to the Antioch policy, referring to the "respondent" and the "primary witness." This language could be confusing to the audience. It would have been clearer to use the terms "aggressor" and "victim."

She could have helped the audience to better understand the purpose of the speech if she had previewed what was to come. The transition to the next step in the motivated sequence is very abrupt, which makes it difficult to follow.

Need

Maria Lucia's first subpoint in support of the need for campus sexual offense prevention policies is an excellent case example with first person narratives that dramatize the problem and pack a powerful emotional punch.

again and again for the next four hours. "I didn't want him to kill me, I just kept trying not to cry." Only afterwards did he tell her, almost defiantly, his name. It was on top of the "castration list" posted on women's bathroom walls around campus to warn other students about college rapists. Amy's attacker was found guilty of sexual assault but was only suspended.

Julie started dating a fellow cast member in a Carleton play. They had never slept together, she charges in a civil suit, until he came to her dorm room one night, uninvited, and raped her. She struggled to hold her life and education together, but finally could manage no longer and left school. Only later did Julie learn that her assailant was the same man who had attacked Amy.

Ladies and gentlemen, the court held that the college knew this man was a rapist. The administration may have been able to prevent this from happening if they had expelled the attacker, but they didn't. My campus has no reports of sexual assault. Is the administration waiting for someone to be assaulted before it formulates a sexual assault policy? This mistake has been made elsewhere; we don't have to prove it again.

Perhaps some statistics will help you understand the magnitude of the problem. According to *New Statesman and Society*, June 21, 1991, issue:

- A 1985 survey of sampled campuses by *Ms. Magazine* and the National Institute of Mental Health found that one in every four college women were victims of sexual assault, and 74 percent knew their attackers. Even worse, between 30 and 40 percent of male students indicated they might force a women to have sex if they knew they would escape punishment.
- In just one year, from 1988 to 1989, reports of student rape at the University of California increased from two to eighty.

These numbers are indeed disturbing. But more disturbing are the effects of sexual assault: a victim feeling the shock of why something this terrible was allowed to happen; having intense fears that behind every dark corner could be an attacker ready to grab her, push her to the ground, and sexually assault her; many waking moments of anxiety and impaired concentration as she remembers the attack; countless nights of reliving the traumatic incident in her sleep; mood swings and depression as she tries to deal internally with the physical hurt and the emotional turmoil that this attack has caused.

Many campuses are open invitations for sexual assault. The absence of a policy is a grand invitation. I have never been sexually assaulted so why do I care so much about a policy? You know why—because I

Here, the startling fact that administration knew the man was a rapist serves to heighten emotional appeal.

As the second subpoint supporting the need for these policies on campus, the speaker cites several startling statistics. Although the percentage of college women who were victims of an attack is surprising, and the fact that about three quarters of them knew their attacker is shocking, it is the third statistic that stuns.

These statistics from a sample of campuses across the nation demonstrate the breadth of the problem. The increase of rapes at the University of California, however, needs more explanation.

The third subpoint describes the effects of sexual assault on the victim. Maria Lucia uses vivid language to paint a picture of the aftermath of an attack on the life of the victim. She could have heightened the emotional impact by personalizing the information using personal pronouns as she described the effects.

could be assaulted. I won't sit and wait to be among one out of every four women on my campus to be assaulted. The first step to keep myself out of the statistics is to push for a sexual assault policy on my campus. One way to do this is through a petition to the university.

Although the Antioch policy sounds a little far-fetched and has been the target of criticism in comedy routines such as those on *Saturday Night Live,* and although students feel that formalizing such a policy is unnatural, many campuses are taking heed and revisiting their own policies. Campuses like mine don't have a sexual assault policy to revisit. Does yours?

By far the most controversial policy today is the one established at Antioch College. I'm not saying that we need one as specific as theirs, but every university has a responsibility to provide a safe environment for its students. Universities have an obligation to provide a sexual assault policy.

The following points are fundamental to the safety of the students and need to be addressed by universities:

1. Every campus should have a sexual assault policy that is developed with input from students, faculty, staff, and administration. The policy then needs to be publicized in the student handbook. The school newspaper should print and the campus radio broadcast the policy periodically to heighten awareness.

2. Campuses must institute programs to educate students and other campus personnel. Examples of these policies can include discussing the sexual assault policy during mandatory student orientation and conducting special workshops for faculty and other staff.

3. Campuses should outline a step-by-step written procedure to guarantee that sexual assault victims are assisted by the university. It is pertinent that they are not without support at this very critical time.

My vision is a campus where there is no place for any sexual assault. I want to leave the classroom at night knowing that my trip from the building to the car will not be one of fear for my personal safety.

You may be saying to yourself that there are laws to handle crimes like these. In the *Chronicle of Higher Education* May 15, 1991 issue, Jane McDonnell, a senior lecturer in women's studies at Carleton, says colleges cannot turn their back on women. "We'd be abandoning victims if we merely sent them to the police," she says. "The wheels of justice tend to grind slowly and rape has one of the lowest conviction rates of any crime."

Satisfaction
The ideal satisfaction step shows in a point-by-point fashion how the proposed solution, in this case a sexual assault prevention policy, would satisfy the needs presented earlier. We would expect the speaker to tell us how such a policy would (1) prevent scenarios like the one at Carleton College, (2) change the statistics on date rape, (3) change male students' perceptions about the likelihood of punishment, and (4) offer support for the victims.

Maria Lucia handles this step very well, although the organization of this section could be tighter. Specifically, she should have laid out four points, not three, as fundamental to an effective policy. Point 4 would have addressed disciplinary procedures and penalties specific to sexual assault. She implies that these are important but never makes the case.

Visualization
This section might have been more compelling had it been placed after the discussion of disciplinary procedures and victim support. The visualization also could have been developed a bit more. It would have been more effective had it been less "speaker specific" and instead invited the audience to visualize.

Without a policy, most institutions lack specific penalties for sexual assault and choose to prosecute offenders under the general student-conduct code. At Carleton College, for example, Amy's attacker was allowed back on campus after his suspension, and consequently he raped again.

Here she points to negative visualization—that is, what we can expect if action to create sexual assault policies is not taken.

Although the policy may not stop the actual assault, would-be offenders will think twice before committing sexual assault if they know they will be punished. In addition, it guarantees justice for victims of sexual assault. We need to make it loud and clear that sexual assault will not be tolerated.

Yes, universities have a big task in the struggle to prevent sexual assault.

This transition to the action step doesn't really follow from the previous discussion.

Action

You and I can actively assist in this task and can make a giant contribution to move it forward. On my campus, students have not only voiced their concerns, but we have also started a petition demanding that the university formulate a sexual assault policy.

Here Maria Lucia offers a specific action to be taken by the audience—that is, to petition for a sexual assault prevention policy on their campuses. The way she phrases it, however, is not as compelling as it could be. She could have been more effective by making her call to action more direct.

The bottom line is that we need to prevent sexual assault on campus. The key to prevention is a sexual assault policy. If your university does not have a policy, then you need to petition your administration to have one. I know I won't stop my advocacy until I see a policy on my campus.

She also fails to quickly review her main points and doesn't provide much direction to the audience about how to go about petitioning.

The speech ends abruptly with an indirect emotional appeal to the audience's sense of guilt. She doesn't really have a clincher. The speech seems to just end. Perhaps a tie back to the opening quotation and an appeal to compassion or hope would have served her purpose more effectively.

© NATALIA SIVERINA/SHUTTERSTOCK

There are even MORE Study Tools for Chapter 16 at www.cengagebrain.com

☑ Speech Builder Express
☑ Printable Flash Cards
☑ Interactive Games
☑ Interactive Video Activities
☑ Chapter Review Cards
☑ Online Quizzes with Feedback
☑ Audio Downloads

References

Ahladas, J. (1989, April 1). Global warming. *Vital Speeches of the Day*, 381–384.

Altman, I. (1993). Dialectics, physical environments, and personal relationships. *Communication Monographs, 60,* 26–34.

Andersen, P. A., Hecht, M. L., Hoobler, G. D., & Smallwood, M. (2003). Nonverbal communication across cultures. In W. B. Gudykunst (Ed.), *Cross-cultural and intercultural communication*. Thousand Oaks, CA: Sage.

Anderson, J. (1988). Communication competency in the small group. In R. Cathcart & L. Samovar (Eds.), *Small group communication: A reader*. Dubuque, IA: Brown.

Aron, A., Aron, E. N., Tudor, M., & Nelson, G. (2004). Close relationships as including other in the self. In H. T. Reis & C. E. Rusbult (Eds.), *Close relationships* (pp. 365–379). New York: Psychology Press.

Aronson, E. (1999). *The social animal*. New York: Worth.

Asch, S. E. (1946). Forming impressions of personality. *Journal of Abnormal and Social Psychology, 9,* 272–279.

Australian Museum. Shaping. *Body Art.* Retrieved n.d. from http://amonline.net.au/bodyart/shaping/

Ayres, J. (1991, June–December). Using visual aids to reduce speech anxiety. *Communication Research Reports,* 73–79.

Ayres, J., & Hopf, T. S. (1990, January). The long-term effect of visualization in the classroom: A brief research report. *Communication Education, 39,* 75–78.

Ayres, J., Hopf, T. S., & Ayres, D. M. (1994, July). An examination of whether imaging ability enhances the effectiveness of an intervention designed to reduce speech anxiety. *Communication Education, 43,* 252–258.

Baerwald, D. Narrative. *Northshore School District Web site.* Retrieved n.d. from http://ccweb.norshore.wednet.edu/writingcorner/narrative.html

Balgopal, P. R., Ephross, P. H., & Vassil, T. V. (1986). Self-help groups and professional helpers. *Small Group Research, 17,* 123–137.

Baron, R. A., Byrne, D., & Brascombe, N. R. (2006). *Social psychology* (11th ed.). Boston: Allyn & Bacon.

Bates, B. (1992). *Communication and the sexes.* Prospect Heights, IL: Waveland Press.

Baxter, L. (1982). Strategies for ending relationships: Two studies. *Western Journal of Speech Communication, 46,* 223–241.

Baxter, L. A., & Montgomery, B. M. (1996). *Relating: Dialogues and dialectics.* New York: Guilford.

Baxter, L. A., & West, I. (2003). Couple perceptions of their similarities and differences: A dialectical perspective. *Journal of Social and Personal Relationships, 20,* 491–514.

Becker, A. (2004). Television, disordered eating, and young women in Fiji: Negotiating body image and identity during rapid social change. *Culture, Medicine and Psychiatry, 28*(4), 533–559.

Beebe, S., & Masterson, J. (2006). *Communicating in groups: Principles and practices* (8th ed.). Boston: Pearson.

Behnke, R. R., & Carlile, L. W. (1971). Heart rate as an index of speech anxiety. *Speech Monographs, 38,* 66.

Berger, C. (1987). Communicating under uncertainty. In M. Roloff and G. Miller (Eds.), *Interpersonal processes: New directions in communication research* (pp. 39–62). Newbury Park, CA: Sage.

Berger, C., & Calabrese, R. J. (1975). Some exploration in initial interaction and beyond: Toward a developmental theory of interpersonal communication. *Human Communication Research, 1,* 99–112.

Beshara, T. (2006). *The job search solution: The ultimate system for finding a great job now!* New York: AMACOM Books.

Birdwhistell, R. (1970). *Kinesics and context.* Philadelphia: University of Pennsylvania Press.

Bommelje, R., Houston, J. M., & Smither, R. (2003). Personality characteristics of effective listeners: A five-factor perspective. *International Journal of Listening, 17,* 32–46.

Bonito, J. (2000). The effect of contributing substantively on perceptions of participation. *Small Group Research, 31,* 528–553.

Bonvillain, N. (2003). *Language, culture and communication: The meaning of messages* (4th ed.). Upper Saddle River, NJ: Prentice Hall.

Booher, D. D. (2003). *Speak with confidence: Powerful presentations that inform, inspire, and persuade* [Adobe Digital Editions version]. New York: McGraw-Hill. doi: 10.1036/0071420789

Boon, S. D. (1994). Dispelling doubt and uncertainty: Trust in romantic relationships. In S. Duck (Ed.), *Dynamics of relationships* (pp. 86–111). Thousand Oaks, CA: Sage.

Boyd, A. (1999). *How to handle media interviews*. London: Mercury.

Brownell, J. (2002). *Listening: Attitudes, principles, and skills* (2nd ed.). Boston: Allyn & Bacon.

Buber, M. (1970). *I and thou* (W. Kaufman, Trans.). New York: Scribner.

Burgoon, J. K., & Bacue, A. E. (2003). Nonverbal communication skills. In J. O. Greene & B. R. Burleson (Eds.), *Handbook of communication and social interaction skills* (pp. 179–220). Mahwah, NJ: Erlbaum.

Burgoon, J. K., Blair, J. P., & Strom, R. E. (2008). Cognitive biases and nonverbal cue availability in detecting deception. *Human Communication Research, 34,* 572–599.

Burgoon, J. K., Coker, D. A., & Coker, R. A. (1986). Communicative effects of gaze behavior: A test of two contrasting explanations. *Human Communication Research, 12,* 495–524.

Burgoon, J. K., & Hoobler, G. D. (2002). Nonverbal signals. In M. L. Knapp & J. A. Daly (Eds.), *Handbook of interpersonal communication* (3rd ed., pp. 240–299). Thousand Oaks, CA: Sage.

Burke, K. (1968). *Language as symbolic action.* Berkeley: University of California Press.

Burleson, B. R. (2003). Emotional support skills. In J. O. Green & B. R. Burleson (Eds.), *Handbook of communication and social interaction skills* (pp. 551–594). Mahwah, NJ: Erlbaum.

Burleson, B. R., & Goldsmith, D. J. (1998). How the comforting process works: Alleviating emotional distress through conversationally induced reappraisals. In P. A. Andersen & L. K. Guerrero (Eds.), *Handbook of communication and emotion: Research, theory, applications, and contexts* (pp. 248–280). San Diego, CA: Academic Press.

Callison, D. (2001). Concept mapping. *School Library Media Activities Monthly, 17*(10): 30–32.

Cegala, D. J., & Sillars, A. L. (1989). Further examination of nonverbal manifestations of interaction involvement. *Communication Reports, 2,* 45.

Chuang, R. (2004). An examination of Taoist and Buddhist perspectives on interpersonal conflict, emotions and adversities. In F. E. Jandt (Ed.), *Intercultural communication: A global reader* (pp. 38–50). Thousand Oaks, CA: Sage.

College learning for the new global century. (2008). *A Report from the National Leadership Council for Liberal Education and America's Promise.* Washington DC: Association of American Colleges and Universities.

Cupach, W. R., & Metts, S. (1986). Accounts of relational disclosure: A comparison of marital and non-marital relationships. *Communication Monographs, 53,* 319–321.

C. Vivian Stringer took the Imus firestorm instride. *New York Daily News.* Retrieved (2008, March 1) from http://www .nydailynews.com/entertainment /arts/2008/03/02/2008-03-02_c_vivian _stringer_took_the_imus_firestor.html

Dahl, S. (2004). *Intercultural research: The current state of knowledge* [Middlesex University Discussion Paper no. 26]. Available from SSRN Web site: http://SSRN.com/abstract=658202

Darling, A. L., & Dannels, D. P. (2003, January). Practicing engineers talk about the importance of talk: A report on the role of oral communication in the workplace. *Communication Education, 52,* 1–16.

Demo, D. H. (1987). Family relations and the self-esteem of adolescents and their parents. *Journal of Marriage and the Family, 49,* 705–715.

Dindia, K. (2000a). Relational maintenance. In C. Hendrick & S. S. Hendrick (Eds.), *Close relationships: A sourcebook* (pp. 287–300). Thousand Oaks, CA: Sage.

Dindia, K. (2000b). Sex differences in self-disclosure, reciprocity of self-disclosure, and self-disclosure and liking: Three metaanalyses reviewed. In S. Petronio (Ed.), *Balancing the secrets of private disclosures* (pp. 21–36). Mahwah, NJ: Erlbaum.

Dindia, K., Fitzpatrick, M. A., & Kenny, D. A. (1997). Self-disclosure in spouse and stranger interaction: A social relations analysis. *Human Communication Research, 23,* 388–412.

Dindia, K., & Timmerman, L. (2003). Accomplishing romantic relationships. In J. O. Greene & B. R. Burleson (Eds.), *Handbook of communication and social interaction* (pp. 685–722). Mahwah, NJ: Erlbaum.

Donoghue, P. J., & Siegel, M. E. (2005). *Are you really listening? Keys to successful communication.* Notre Dame, IN: Sorin Books.

Downey, G., Freitas, A. L., Michaelis, B., & Khouri, H. (2004). The self-fulfilling prophecy in close relationships: Rejection sensitivity and rejection by romantic partners. In H. T. Reis & C. E. Rusbult (Eds.), *Close relationships* (pp. 153–174). New York: Psychology Press.

Drummond, D. *Miracle meetings* [e-book]. Retrieved n.d. from http://www .superteams.com

Duch, B. J., Groh, S. E., & Allen, D. E. (Eds). (2001). *The power of problem-based learning.* Sterling, VA: Stylus.

Duck, S. (1987). How to lose friends without influencing people. In M. E. Roloff & G. R. Miller (Eds.), *Interpersonal processes: New directions in communication research.* Beverly Hills, CA: Sage.

Duck, S. (1999) *Relating to others.* Philadelphia, PA: Open University Press.

Duck, S. (2007). *Human relationships* (4th ed.). Thousand Oaks, CA: Sage.

DuFrene, D. D., & Lehman, C. M. (2002, March). Persuasive appeal for clean language. *Business Communication Quarterly, 65,* 48–56.

Dunkel, P., & Pialorsi, F. (2005). *Advanced listening comprehension: Developing aural and notetaking skills.* Boston: Thomson Heinle.

Durst, G. M. (1989, March 1). The manager as a developer. *Vital Speeches of the Day,* 309–314.

Dwyer, K. K. (2000, January). The multidimensional model: Teaching students to self-manage high communication apprehension by self-selecting treatments. *Communication Education, 49,* 79.

Edens, K. M. (2000). Preparing problem solvers for the 21st century through problem-based learning. *College Teaching, 48,* 55–60.

Eisenberg, J. (2007). Group cohesiveness. In R. F. Baumeister & K. D. Vohs (Eds.), *Encyclopaedia of Social Psychology* (pp. 386-388). Thousand Oaks, CA: Sage.

Estes, W. K. (1989). Learning theory. In A. Lesgold & R. Glaser (Eds.), *Foundations for a psychology of education* (pp. 1–49). Hillsdale, NJ: Erlbaum.

Evans, C., & Dion, K. (1991). Group cohesion and performance: A meta-analysis. *Small Group Research, 22,* 175–186.

Fairhurst, G. T. (2001). Dualism in leadership. In F. M. Jablin & L. M. Putnam (Eds.), *The new handbook of organizational communication* (pp. 379–439). Thousand Oaks, CA: Sage.

Forgas, J. P. (1991). Affect and person perception. In J. P. Forgas (Ed.), *Emotion and social judgments* (pp. 387–406). New York: Pergamon Press.

Forgas, J. P. (2000). Feelings and thinking: Summary and integration. In J. P. Forgas (Ed.), *Feeling and thinking: The role of affect in social cognition* (pp. 387–406). New York: Cambridge University Press.

Frances, P. (1994). Lies, damned lies . . . *American Demographics, 16,* 2.

Galvin, K. M., Byland, C. L., & Brommel, B. J. (2007). *Family communication: Cohesion and change* (7th ed.). Boston: Allyn & Bacon.

Gangestad, S. W., & Snyder, M. (2000). Self-monitoring: Appraisal and reappraisal. *Psychological Bulletin, 126,* 530–555.

Gibson, J. J. (1966). *The senses considered as perceptual systems.* Boston: Houghton Mifflin.

Gilbert, D., & Kahl, J. A. (1982). *The American class structure: A new synthesis.* Homewood, IL: Dorsey.

Graber, S. (2000). *The everything get-a-job book: From resume writing to interviewing to finding tons of job openings.* Avon, MA: Adams Media.

Hahner, J. C., Sokoloff, M. A., & Salisch, S. L. (2001). *Speaking clearly: Improving voice and diction* (6th ed.). New York: McGraw-Hill.

Hall, B. J. (2002). *Among cultures: The challenge of communication.* Belmont, CA: Wadsworth.

Hall, E. T. (1959). *The silent language.* Greenwich, CT: Fawcett.

Hall, E. T. (1968). Proxemics. *Current Anthropology, 9,* 83–108.

Hall, E. T. (1969). *The hidden dimension.* Garden City, NY: Doubleday.

Hanke, J. (1998). The psychology of presentation visuals. *Presentations, 12*(5), 42–47.

Hanks for the Oscars speech advice, Tom! *Mail Online.* Retrieved (2006 March 4) from http://www.dailymail.co.uk/tvshowbiz /article-378755/Hanks-Oscars-speech -advice-Tom.html

Hansen, R. S., & Hansen, K. n.d. What do employers really want? Top skills and values employers seek from job-seekers. *Quintessential Careers Web site.* Retrieved n.d. from http://www.quintcareers.com /job_skills_values.html

Hattie, J. (1992). *Self-concept.* Hillsdale, NJ: Erlbaum.

Haviland, W. A. (1993). *Cultural anthropology.* Fort Worth, TX: Harcourt, Brace, Jovanovich.

Head, S. W., Spann, T., & McGregor, M. A. (2001). *Broadcasting in America: A survey of electronic media* (9th ed.). Boston: Houghton Mifflin.

Heider, F. (1958). *The psychology of interpersonal relations.* New York: Wiley.

Hendrick, S. S. (1981). Self-disclosure and marital satisfaction. *Journal of Personality and Social Psychology, 40,* 1150–1159.

Henman, L. D. (2003). Groups as systems: A functional perspective. In R. Y. Hirokawa, R. S. Cathcart, L A. Samovar, & L. D. Henman (Eds.), *Small group communication theory and practice: An anthology* (8th ed., pp. 3–7). Los Angeles: Roxbury.

Hill, B., & Leeman, R. W. (1997). *The art and practice of argumentation and debate.* Mountain View, CA: Mayfield.

Hirokawa, R., Cathcart, R., Samovar, L., & Henman, L. (Eds.). (2003). *Small group communication theory and practice* (8th ed.). Los Angeles: Roxbury.

Hofstede, G. (1980). *Culture's consequences.* Beverly Hills, CA: Sage.

Hofstede, G. (Ed.). (1998). *Masculinity and femininity: The taboo dimension of national cultures.* Thousand Oaks, CA: Sage.

Hofstede, G. (2000). The cultural relativity of the quality of life concept. In G. R. Weaver (Ed.), *Cultural communication and conflict: Readings in intercultural relations.* Boston: Allyn & Bacon.

Holtgraves, T. (2002). *Language as social action: Social psychology and language use.* Mahwah, NJ: Erlbaum.

Honeycutt, J. M. (1993). Memory structures for the rise and fall of personal relationships. In S. Duck (Ed.), *Individuals in relationships* (pp. 60–86). Newbury Park, CA: Sage.

Hotz, R. L. (1995, April 15). Official racial definitions have shifted sharply and often. *The Los Angeles Times,* p. A14.

How to dress in women's professional attire. *eHow: How to do just about everything.* Retrieved n.d. from http://www.ehow .com/how_2064031_dress-womens -professional-attire.html

Humes, J. C. (1988). *Standing ovation: How to be an effective speaker and communicator.* New York: Harper & Row.

International Listening Association. Listening factoid. Retrieved n.d. from http://www .listen.org/pages/factoids.html

Jackson, R. L., II (Ed.). (2004). *African American communication and identities.* Thousand Oaks, CA: Sage.

Jandt, F. E. (2001). *Intercultural communication: An introduction* (3rd ed.). Thousand Oaks, CA: Sage.

Janis, I. L. (1982). *Groupthink: Psychological studies of policy decisions and fiascoes.* Boston: Houghton Mifflin.

Janusik, L. A., & Wolvin, A. D. (2006). *24 hours in a day: A listening update to the time studies.* Paper presented at the meeting of the International Listening Association, Salem, OR.

Jensen, A. D., & Chilberg, J. C. (1991). *Small group communication: Theory and application.* Belmont, CA: Wadsworth.

Johnson, D., & Johnson, F. (2003). *Joining together: Group theory and group skills* (8th ed.). Boston: Allyn & Bacon.

Jones, M. (2002). *Social psychology of prejudice.* Upper Saddle River, NJ: Prentice Hall.

Kaplan, R. M. (2002). *How to say it in your job search: Choice words, phrases, sentences and paragraphs for résumés, cover letters and interviews.* Paramus, NJ: Prentice Hall.

Kapoun, J. Teaching undergrads Web evaluation: A guide for library instruction. *College and Research Library News, 59*(7). Retrieved (2000, January 25) from http://www .ala.org/ala/mgrps/divs/acrl/publications /crlnews/1998/jul/teachingundergrads.cfm

Kellerman, K. (1992). Communication: Inherently strategic and primarily automatic. *Communication Monographs, 59,* 288–300.

Kelly, L., Phillips, G. M., & Keaten, J. A. (1995). *Teaching people to speak well: Training and remediation of communication reticence.* Cresskill, NJ: Hampton.

Kleinman, S. (2007). *Displacing place: Mobile communication in the twenty-first century.* New York: Peter Lang.

Klyukanov, I. E. (2005). *Principles of intercultural communication.* New York: Pearson.

Knapp, M., & Daly, J. (2002). *Handbook of interpersonal communication.* Thousand Oaks, CA: Sage.

Knapp, M. L., & Hall, J. A. (2006). *Nonverbal communication in human interaction* (5th ed.). Belmont, CA: Thomson Wadsworth.

Knapp, M. L., & Vangelisti, A. L. (2005). *Interpersonal communication and human relationships* (4th ed.). Boston: Allyn & Bacon.

Koerner, A. F., & Fitzpatrick, M. A. (2002). Understanding family communication patterns and family functioning: The roles of conversation orientation and conformity orientation. In W. B. Gudykunst (Ed.), *Communication yearbook 26* (pp. 36–68). Mahwah, NJ: Erlbaum.

Kolb, D. (1984). *Experiential learning: Experience as the source of learning and development.* Englewood Cliffs, NJ: Prentice Hall.

Koncz, A. (2008). *Job outlook 2009.* Bethlehem, PA: National Association of Colleges and Employers.

Krotz, J. *6 tips for taking control in media interviews. Microsoft Small Business Center.* Retrieved n.d.from http://www .microsoft.com/smallbusiness/resources /management/leadership-training/6-tips -for-taking-control-in-media-interviews.asp x#tipsfortakingcontrolinmediainterviews

Lawrence, S. G., & Watson, M. (1991). Getting others to help: The effectiveness of professional uniforms in charitable fund raising. *Journal of Applied Communication Research, 19,* 170–185.

Leary, M. R. (2002). When selves collide: The nature of the self and the dynamics of interpersonal relationships. In A. Tesser, D. A. Stapel, & J. V. Wood (Eds.), *Self and motivation: Emerging psychological perspectives* (pp. 119–145). Washington, DC: American Psychological Association.

Levin, B. B. (Ed.). (2001). *Energizing teacher education and professional development with problem-based learning.* Alexandria, MN: Association for Supervision and Curriculum Development.

Littlejohn, S. W., & Foss, K. A. (2008). *Theories of human communication* (9th ed.). Belmont, CA: Thomson Wadsworth.

Long, K. *Visual aids and learning*. Retrieved (1997 Aug 12) from University of Portsmouth, Audio Video Homepage: http://www.mech.port.ac.uk/av/AVALearn.htm

Luckmann, J. (1999). *Transcultural communication in nursing*. New York: Delmar.

Luft, J. (1970). *Group processes: An introduction to group dynamics*. Palo Alto, CA: Mayfield.

Lulofs, R. S., & Cahn, D. D. (2000). *Conflict: From theory to action* (2nd ed.). Boston: Allyn & Bacon.

Margulis, Stephen T. (1977). Concepts of privacy: Current status and next steps. *Journal of Social Issues, 33*(3), 5–21.

Martin, J. N., & Nakayama, T. K. (2000). *Intercultural communication in contexts* (2nd ed.). Mountain View, CA: Mayfield.

Martin, M. M., Anderson, C. M., & Horvath, C. L. (1996). Feelings about verbal aggression: Justifications for sending and hurt from receiving verbally aggressive messages. *Communication Research Reports, 13*(1), 19–26.

Maslow, A. H. (1954). *Motivation and personality*. New York: Harper & Row.

Mason, S. (2007, April). Equality will someday come. *Vital Speeches of the Day,* 159–163.

McCroskey, J. C. (1977). Oral communication apprehension: A review of recent theory and research. *Human Communication Research, 4,* 78–96.

Mead, G. H. (1934). *Mind, self, and society*. Chicago: University of Chicago Press.

Mehrabian, A. (1972). *Nonverbal communication*. Chicago: Aldine.

Menzel, K. E., & Carrell, L. J. (1994). The relationship between preparation and performance in public speaking. *Communication Education, 43,* 17–26.

Merton, R. K. (1968). *Social theory and social structure*. New York: Free Press.

Michener, H. A., & DeLamater, J. D. (1999). *Social psychology* (4th ed.). Orlando, FL: Harcourt Brace.

Midura, D. W., & Glover, D. R. (2005). *Essentials of teambuilding*. Champaign, IL: Human Kinetics.

Morris, T. L., Gorham, J., Cohen, S. H., & Huffman, D. (1996). Fashion in the classroom: Effects of attire on student perceptions of instructors in college classes. *Communication Education, 45,* 135–148.

Moser, K. New memorials: T-shirts, websites, autodecals. *Christian Science Monitor*. Retrieved (2006 May 25) from http://www.csmonitor.com/2006/0525/p15s01-lihc.html

Motley, M. (1997). COM therapy. In J. A. Daly, J. C. McCroskey, J. Ayres, T. Hopf, & D. M. Ayres (Eds.), *Avoiding communication: Shyness, reticence, and communication apprehension* (2nd ed., pp. 379–400). Cresskill, NJ: Hampton Press.

Mruk, C. (1999). *Self-esteem: Research, theory, and practice* (2nd ed.). New York: Springer.

Munger, D., Anderson, D., Benjamin, B., Busiel, C., & Pardes-Holt, B. (2000). *Researching online* (3rd ed.). New York: Longman.

Nabi, R. L. (2002). Discrete emotions and persuasion. In J. P. Dillard and M. Pfau (Eds.), *The persuasion handbook: Developments in theory and practice* (pp. 291–299). Thousand Oaks, CA: Sage.

Nelson, J. C. *Leadership*. Utah School Boards Association 83rd Annual Conference, Salt Lake City, Utah. Retrieved n.d. from http://www.ama-assn.org/ama/pub/category/15860.html

Neuliep, J. W. (2006). *Intercultural communication: A contextual approach* (3rd ed.). Thousand Oaks, CA: Sage.

O'Connor, J. V. FAQs #1. *Cuss Control Academy*. Retrieved n.d. from http://www.cusscontrol.com/faqs.html

Ogden, C. K., & Richards, I. A. (1923). *The meaning of meaning*. London: Kegan, Paul, Trench, Trubner.

O'Hair, D., O'Rourke, J., & O'Hair, M. (2001). *Business communication: A framework for success*. Cincinnati, OH: South-Western.

Olaniran, B. (2002–2003). Computer-mediated communication: A test of the impact of social cues on the choice of medium for resolving misunderstandings. *Journal of Educational Technology Systems, 31*(2), 205–222.

Omdahl, B. L. (1995). *Cognitive appraisal, emotion, and empathy*. Mahwah, NJ: Erlbaum.

Otzi, the ice man. *Dig: The archaeology magazine for kids*. Retrieved n.d. from http://www.digonsite.com/drdig/mummy/22.html

Parks, M. R. (2006). *Personal relationships and personal networks*. Mahwah, NJ: Erlbaum.

Patterson, B. R., Bettini, L., & Nussbaum, J. F. (1993). The meaning of friendship across the life-span: Two studies. *Communication Quarterly, 41,* 145.

Pearson, J. C., West, R. L., & Turner, L. H. (1995). *Gender & communication* (3rd ed.). Dubuque, IA: Brown & Benchmark.

Petri, H. L. (1996). *Motivation: Theory, research, and applications* (4th ed.). Belmont, CA: Wadsworth.

Petronio, S. (2002). *Boundaries of privacy: Dialectics of disclosure*. Albany: State University of New York Press.

Petty, R. E., & Cacioppo, J. T. (1996) *Attitudes and persuasion: Classic and contemporary approaches*. Boulder, CO: Westview Press.

Pew Research Center. *A portrait of "Generation Next": How young people view their lives, futures, and politics* (Survey Report). Retrieved n.d. from http://people-press.org/report/300/a-portrait-of-generation-next

Phillips, G. (1977). Rhetoritherapy versus the medical model: Dealing with reticence. *Communication Education, 26,* 34–43.

Phillips, P. A., & Smith, L. R. (1992). *The effects of teacher dress on student perceptions* (Report No. SP 033-944). Retrieved from ERIC Document Services. (ED347151)

Rabby, M., & Walther, J. B. (2003). Computer mediated communication effects in relationship formationand maintenance. In D. J. Canary & M. Dainton (Eds.), *Maintaining relationships through communication* (pp. 141–162). Mahwah, NJ: Erlbaum.

Rayner, S. G. (2001). Aspects of the self as learner: Perception, concept, and esteem. In R. J. Riding & S. G. Rayner (Eds.), *Self-perception: International perspectives on individual differences* (Vol. 2). Westport, CN: Ablex.

Renz, M. A., & Greg, J. B. (2000). *Effective small group communication in theory and practice*. Boston: Allyn & Bacon.

Richmond, V. P., & McCroskey, J. C. (1995). *Communication: Apprehension, avoidance, and effectiveness* (4th ed.). Scottsdale, AZ: Gorsuch Scarisbrick.

Richmond, V. P., & McCroskey, J. C. (2000). *Communication: Apprehension, avoidance, and effectiveness* (5th ed.). Scottsdale, AZ: Gorsuch Scarisbrick.

Roloff, M.E., & Ifert, D.E. (2000). Conflict management through avoidance: Withholding complaints, suppressing arguments, and declaring topics taboo. In S. Petronio (Ed.), *Balancing the Secrets of Private Disclosures* (pp. 151–163). Mahwah, NJ: LEA.

Rusbult, C. E., Olsen, N., Davis, J. L., & Hannon, P. A. (2004). Commitment and relationship maintenance mechanisms. In H. T. Reis &

C. E. Rusbult (Eds.), *Key readings on close relationships* (pp. 287–304). Washington, DC: Taylor & Francis.

Ryan, R. (2000). *60 seconds & you're hired*. New York: Penguin Books.

Salopek, J. J. (1999). Is anyone listening? *Training and Development, 531*(9), 58–60.

Samovar, L. A., & Porter, R. E. (2001). *Communication between cultures* (4th ed.). Belmont, CA: Wadsworth.

Samovar, L. A., Porter, R. E., & McDaniel, E. R. (2007). *Communication between cultures* (6th ed.). Belmont, CA: Thomson Wadsworth.

Samovar, L. A., Porter, R. E., & McDaniel, E. R. (Eds.). (2009). *Intercultural communication: A reader* (12th ed.). Belmont, CA: Cengage.

Samter, W. (2003). Friendship interaction skills across the lifespan. In J. O. Greene & B. R. Burleson (Eds.), *Handbook of communication and social interaction skills* (pp. 637–684). Mahwah, NJ: Erlbaum.

Scott, P. (1997, January–February). Mind of a champion. *Natural Health, 27,* 99.

Shaw, M. E. (1981). *Group dynamics: The psychology of small group behavior* (3rd ed.). New York: McGraw-Hill.

Shedletsky, L. J., & Aiken, J. E. (2004). *Human communication on the Internet*. Boston: Pearson.

Shihab Nye, N. (2000). Long overdue. In *Post Gibran: An anthology of new Arab American writing*. Syracuse, NY: Syracuse University Press.

Shimanoff, M. (1992). Group interaction and communication rules. In R. Cathcart & L. Samovar (Eds.), *Small group communication: A reader*. Dubuque, IA: William C. Brown.

Slayter, M. E. (2006, January 14). Rehearse, rehearse, repeat: Have a rock-solid plan when preparing for an interview. *The Forum,* p. E3.

Snell, W.E., Belk, S. S., & Hawkins, R. C., II (1986). The masculine and feminine self-disclosure scale: The politics of masculine and feminine self presentation. *Sex Roles, 15,* 249–267.

Snyder, B. Differing views cultivate better decisions. *Stanford Business*. Retrieved n.d. from http://www.gsb.stanford .edu/NEWS/bmag/sbsm0405/feature _workteams_gruenfeld.shtml

Spitzberg, B. H. (2000). A model of intercultural communication competence. In L. A. Samovar & R. E. Porter (Eds.), *Intercultural

communication: A reader* (9th ed., pp. 375–387). Belmont, CA: Wadsworth.

Stephens, M. (1999). The new TV: Stop making sense. In R. E. Hiebert (Ed.), *Impact of mass media: Current issues* (4th ed.; pp. 16–22). White Plains, NY: Longman.

Stereotype. *The American heritage new dictionary of cultural literacy* (3rd ed.). Boston: Houghton Mifflin. Retrieved n.d. from Dictionary.com Web site: http:// dictionary.reference.com/browse /stereotype

Stewart, C. J., & Cash, W. B. (2000). *Interviewing: Principles and practices* (9th ed.). Dubuque, IA: William C. Brown.

Stewart, L. P., Cooper, P. J., Stewart, A. D., & Friedley, S. A. (1998). *Communication and gender* (3rd ed.). Boston: Allyn & Bacon.

Stiff, J. B., Dillard, J. P., Somera, L., Kim, H., & Sleight, C. (1988). Empathy, communication and prosocial behavior. *Communication Monographs, 55,* 198–213.

Sultanoff, S. (1993). Tickling our funny bone: Humor matters in health. *International Journal of Humor Research, 6,* 89–104.

Sundstrom, E., DeMeuse, K. P., & Futrell, D. (1990, February). Work teams: Applications and effectiveness. *American Psychologist,* 120–133.

Taylor, D. A., & Altman, I. (1987). Communication in interpersonal relationships: Social penetration theory. In M. E. Roloff & G. R. Miller (Eds.), *Interpersonal processes: New directions in communication research* (pp. 257–277). Beverly Hills, CA: Sage.

Taylor, J., & Hardy D. (2004). *Monster careers: How to land the job of your life*. New York: Penguin Books.

Teams that succeed (2004). *Harvard Business Review*. Boston: Harvard Business School Press.

Tengler, C. D., & Jablin, F. M. (1983). Effects of question type, orientation, and sequencing in the employment screening interview. *Communication Monographs, 50,* 261.

Terkel, S. N., & Duval, R. S. (Eds.). (1999). *Encyclopedia of ethics*. New York: Facts on File.

Thompson, L. L. (2003). *The social psychology of organizational behavior: Key readings*. New York: Taylor & Francis.

Thorndike, E. L. (1920). A constant error on psychological rating. *Journal of Applied Psychology, 4,* 25–29.

Thurlow, C., Lengel, L., & Tomic, A. (2004). *Computer mediated communication: Social

interaction and the Internet*. Thousand Oaks, CA: Sage.

Ting-Toomey, S. (1999). *Communicating across cultures*. New York: Guilford Press.

Ting-Toomey, S. (2004). The matrix of face: An updated face-negotiation theory. In W. Gudykunst (Ed.), *Theorizing about intercultural communication* (pp. 71–92). Thousand Oaks, CA: Sage.

Ting-Toomey, S., Yee-Jung, K., Shapiro, R., Garcia, W., Wright, T., & Oetzel, J. G. (2000). Cultural/ethnic identity salience and conflict styles. *International Journal of Intercultural Relations, 23,* 47–81.

Tuckman, B. W. (1965). Developmental sequence in small groups. *Psychological Bulletin, 6393,* 384–399.

Tullar, W., & Kaiser, P. (2000). The effect of process training on process and outcomes in virtual groups. *Journal of Business Communication, 37,* 408–427.

Tversky, B. (1997). Memory for pictures, maps, environments, and graphs. In D. G. Payne & F. G. Conrad (Eds.), *Intersections in basic and applied memory research* (pp. 257–277). Mahwah, NJ: Erlbaum.

U.S. Census Bureau. Hispanic Americans by the numbers. Retrieved n.d. from http://www .infoplease.com/spot/hhmcensus1.html

Valacich, J. S., George, J. F., Nonamaker, J. F., Jr., & Vogel, D. R. (1994). Idea generation in computer based groups: A new ending to an old story. *Small Group Research, 25,* 83–104.

Walker, D. M. (2006, December). America at a crossroads. *Vital Speeches of the Day,* 752–762.

Walther, J. B. (1996). Computer-mediated communication: Impersonal, interpersonal and hyperpersonal interaction. *Western Journal of Communication, 57,* 381–398.

Walther, J. B., & Parks, M. R. (2002). Cues filtered out, cues filtered in: Computer-mediated communication and relationships. In M. C. Knapp & J. A. Daly (Eds.), *Handbook of interpersonal communication* (3rd ed., pp. 529–563). Thousand Oaks, CA: Sage.

Ward, C. C., & Tracy, T. J. G. (2004). Relation of shyness with aspects of online relationship involvement. *Journal of Social and Personal Relationships, 21,* 611–623.

Watzlawick, P., Bavelas, J. B., & Jackson, D. D. (1967). *Pragmatics of human communication*. New York: Norton.

Weaver, J. B., III, & Kirtley, M. B. (1995). Listening styles and empathy. *Southern Communication Journal, 60,* 131–140.

Weiten, W. (1998). *Psychology: Themes and variations* (4th ed.). Pacific Grove, CA: Brooks/Cole.

Widmer, W. N., & Williams, J. M. (1991). Predicting cohesion in a coacting sport. *Small Group Research, 22,* 548–570.

Wilson, G. L. (2005). *Groups in context: Leadership and participation in small groups* (7th ed.). New York: McGraw-Hill.

Wolvin, A., & Coakley, C. G. (1996). *Listening* (5th ed.). Dubuque, IA: Brown & Benchmark.

Wood, J. T. (2007). *Gendered lives: Communication, gender, and culture* (7th ed.). Belmont, CA: Wadsworth.

Wood, J. T., & Inman, C. (1993). In a different mode: Recognizing male modes of closeness. *Journal of Applied Communication Research, 21,* 279–295.

Wright, J. W. (2002). *New York Times Almanac.* New York: New York Times.

Young, K. S., Wood, J. T., Phillips, G. M., & Pedersen, D. J. (2007). *Group discussion: A practical guide to participation and leadership* (4th ed.). Long Grove, IL: Waveland Press.

Young, M. (2003). Integrating communication skills into the marketing curriculum: A case study. *Journal of Marketing Education, 25,* 57–70.

Zempke, R., Raines, C., & Filipczak (2000). *Generations at work.* New York: AMACOM Books.

Index

Chapter in Review

To help you succeed, we have designed a review card for each chapter.

LO1

communication
the process of creating or sharing meaning in informal conversation, group interaction, or public speaking

participants
individuals who [...] of senders and re[...] interaction

Here, you'll find the key terms and definitions in the order they appear in the chapter.

messages
verbal utterances, visual images, and non-verbal behaviors to which meaning is attributed during communication

meanings
thoughts in our minds and interpretations of others' messages

symbols
words, sounds, and actions that are generally understood to represent ideas and feelings

encoding
the process of putting our thoughts and feelings into words and non-verbal cues

decoding
the process of interpreting another's message

context
the settings in which communication occurs, including what precedes and follows what is said

physical context
the location, the environmental conditions (temperature, lighting, noise level), the distance between

How to Use This Card:

1. Look over the card to preview the new concepts you'll be introduced to in the chapter.

2. Read your chapter to fully understand the material.

3. Go to class (and pay attention).

4. Review the card one more time to make sure you've registered the key concepts. Take the chapter self quiz to test your comprehension.

5. Don't forget, this card is only one of many COMM learning tools available to help you succeed in your communication class.

in a society

channel
both the route traveled by the message and the means of transportation

interference (noise)
any stimulus that interferes with the process of sharing meaning

physical interference
sights, sounds, and other stimuli in the environment that draw people's attention away from intended meaning

LO1 Define the communication process and the settings in which communication takes place.

We have defined communication as the process of creating or sharing meaning, whether the context is informal conversation, group interaction, or public speaking. The elements of the communication [pro]cess are participants, messages, context, channels, noise, and feedback. Communication can take [plac]e in a wide range of settings. It can take the form of self-reflection or an informal interaction [bet]ween two people. Communication can occur within small groups or in larger public settings. These [diff]erent communication situations call for different skills.

LO2 Identify communication [...]

Our communication is guided [...] [com]munication has purpose. Second, communication is cont[...] [...]es vary in conscious thought. Messages may be spontaneous, [...] [...]munication is relational, defining the power and affection between people. Fifth, communication is guided by culture. Sixth, communication has ethical implications. Ethical standards that influence our communication include truthfulness, integrity, fairness, respect, and responsibility. And seventh, communication is learned.

In this column, you'll find summary points that give an overview of important concepts.

LO3 Discover how to increase communication competence.

A primary issue in this course is competence—we all strive to become better communicators. Competence is the perception by others that our communication behavior is appropriate as well as effective. We create the perception that we are competent at communicating through our verbal messages and non-verbal behaviors. It involves a desire to improve our communication by increasing our knowledge of communication, identifying and attaining goals, being able to use various skills, and presenting ourselves as credible and confident communicators.

Chapter 1 Quiz

True/False

A participant can either be the s[...]

Every chapter has a short self-assessment quiz for you to use while reviewing the chapter. You will find the answer key on the back page.

The context of a message is the [...]

Meaning shared in a communication can be affected by the physical context in which the message is delivered.

A primary issue in this course is competence, which is the perception by others that our communication behavior is appropriate as well as effective.

When you show regard or consideration for others and their ideas, even if you don't agree with them, you are demonstrating the ethical standard of fairness.

[Mul]tiple Choice

6. To understand how the process of communication works, we have to describe its essential elements, which are
   a. participants (who), messages (what), context (where), channels (how), interference (distractions), and feedback (reaction).
   b. [...]n (how), and the interference of white

   Prepare for Exams
   When it's time to prepare for exams, use the card and the technique to the left to ensure successful study sessions.

   c. [...], channels (how), and feedback

© 2012 Cengage Learning. All Rights Reserved. May not be scanned, copied or duplicated, or posted to a publicly accessible website, in whole or in part.

psychological interference
internal distractions based on thoughts, feelings, or emotional reactions to symbols

internal noise
thoughts and feelings that compete for attention and interfere with the communication process

semantic interference
distractions aroused by certain symbols that take our attention away from the main message

feedback
reactions and responses to messages

interpersonal communication
interactions among a small number of people who have relationships with each other

small group communication
participants who come together for the specific purpose of solving a problem or arriving at a decision

public communication
one participant, the speaker, delivers a prepared message to a group or audience that has assembled to hear the speaker

LO2 spontaneous expressions
spoken without much conscious thought

scripted messages
phrasings learned from past encounters that we judge to be appropriate to the present situation

constructed messages
messages put together with careful thought when we recognize that our known scripts are inadequate for the situation

immediacy
the degree of liking or attractiveness in a relationship

control
the degree to which one participant is perceived to be more dominant or powerful

culture
systems of knowledge shared by a relatively large group of people

ethics
a set of moral principles that may be held by a society, a group, or an individual

truthfulness and honesty
refraining from lying, cheating, stealing, or deception

moral dilemma
a choice involving an unsatisfactory alternative

integrity
maintaining a consistency of belief and action (keeping promises)

fairness
achieving the right balance of interests without regard to one's own feelings and without showing favor to any side in a conflict

respect
showing regard or consideration for others and their ideas even if we don't agree with them

responsibility
being accountable for one's actions and what one says

---

    d. recipients (who), messages (what), interaction (how), presence or absence of noise (distractions), and feedback (reaction).
    e. partners (who), channels (how), non-verbals (what), and feedback (reaction).

7. An example of intrapersonal communication is
    a. chatting around the dinner table with your family and friends.
    b. recounting a past experience during a speech to an audience.
    c. thinking to yourself about what you are going to make for dinner that evening.
    d. texting a message to a friend.
    e. entering into a discussion in a chatroom.

8. Why do we communicate?
    a. To meet our social needs
    b. To develop and maintain our sense of self
    c. To develop relationships
    d. To exchange information and influence others
    e. All of these answers are correct

9. In any communication setting, in addition to sharing content meaning, our messages also reflect which two important aspects of our relationship?
    a. morality and integrity
    b. truthfulness and honesty
    c. immediacy and control
    d. integrity and fairness
    e. respect and responsibility

10. If you feel anxious about speaking with a certain person or group of people, you are experiencing
    a. situational communication apprehension.
    b. audience-based communication apprehension.
    c. traitlike communication apprehension.
    d. general communication apprehension.
    e. context-based communication apprehension.

Chapter Quiz Answers:
1. T, 2. F, 3. T, 4. T, 5. F, 6. A, 7. C, 8. E, 9. C, 10. B

LO3 communication competence
the impression that communicative behavior is both appropriate and effective in a given situation

skills
goal-oriented actions or action sequences that we can master and repeat in appropriate situations

credibility
a perception of a speaker's knowledge, trustworthiness, and warmth

social ease
communicating without anxiety or nervousness

communication apprehension
the fear or anxiety associated with real or anticipated communication with others

COMMUNICATION PERSPECTIVES

Chapter in Review

LO¹ communication
the process of creating or sharing meaning in informal conversation, group interaction, or public speaking

participants
individuals who assume the roles of senders and receivers during an interaction

messages
verbal utterances, visual images, and non-verbal behaviors to which meaning is attributed during communication

meanings
thoughts in our minds and interpretations of others' messages

symbols
words, sounds, and actions that are generally understood to represent ideas and feelings

encoding
the process of putting our thoughts and feelings into words and non-verbal cues

decoding
the process of interpreting another's message

context
the settings in which communication occurs, including what precedes and follows what is said

physical context
the location, the environmental conditions (temperature, lighting, noise level), the distance between communicators, seating arrangements, and time of day

social context
the nature of the relationship that exists between the participants

historical context
the background provided by previous communication episodes between the participants that influence understandings in the current encounter

psychological context
the mood and feelings each person brings to the conversation

cultural context
the values, attitudes, beliefs, orientations, and underlying assumptions prevalent among people in a society

channel
both the route traveled by the message and the means of transportation

interference (noise)
any stimulus that interferes with the process of sharing meaning

physical interference
sights, sounds, and other stimuli in the environment that draw people's attention away from intended meaning

LO¹ Define the communication process and the settings in which communication takes place.
We have defined communication as the process of creating or sharing meaning, whether the context is informal conversation, group interaction, or public speaking. The elements of the communication process are participants, messages, context, channels, noise, and feedback. Communication can take place in a wide range of settings. It can take the form of self-reflection or an informal interaction between two people. Communication can occur within small groups or in larger public settings. These different communication situations call for different skills.

LO² Identify communication principles.
Our communication is guided by at least seven principles. First, communication has purpose. Second, communication is continuous. Third, communication messages vary in conscious thought. Messages may be spontaneous, scripted, or constructed. Fourth, communication is relational, defining the power and affection between people. Fifth, communication is guided by culture. Sixth, communication has ethical implications. Ethical standards that influence our communication include truthfulness, integrity, fairness, respect, and responsibility. And seventh, communication is learned.

LO³ Discover how to increase communication competence.
A primary issue in this course is competence—we all strive to become better communicators. Competence is the perception by others that our communication behavior is appropriate as well as effective. We create the perception that we are competent at communicating through our verbal messages and non-verbal behaviors. It involves a desire to improve our communication by increasing our knowledge of communication, identifying and attaining goals, being able to use various skills, and presenting ourselves as credible and confident communicators.

Chapter 1 Quiz

True/False

1. A participant can either be the sender or receiver of a message in an interaction.

2. The context of a message is the organizational aspect of the message.

3. Meaning shared in a communication can be affected by the physical context in which the message is delivered.

4. A primary issue in this course is competence, which is the perception by others that our communication behavior is appropriate as well as effective.

5. When you show regard or consideration for others and their ideas, even if you don't agree with them, you are demonstrating the ethical standard of fairness.

Multiple Choice

6. To understand how the process of communication works, we have to describe its essential elements, which are
   a. participants (who), messages (what), context (where), channels (how), interference (distractions), and feedback (reaction).
   b. participants (who), conversation (what), interaction (how), and the interference of white noise (distractions).
   c. public (who), conversation (what), context (where), channels (how), and feedback (distractions).

© 2012 Cengage Learning. All Rights Reserved. May not be scanned, copied or duplicated, or posted to a publicly accessible website, in whole or in part.

psychological interference
internal distractions based on thoughts, feelings, or emotional reactions to symbols

internal noise
thoughts and feelings that compete for attention and interfere with the communication process

semantic interference
distractions aroused by certain symbols that take our attention away from the main message

feedback
reactions and responses to messages

interpersonal communication
interactions among a small number of people who have relationships with each other

small group communication
participants who come together for the specific purpose of solving a problem or arriving at a decision

public communication
one participant, the speaker, delivers a prepared message to a group or audience that has assembled to hear the speaker

LO2 **spontaneous expressions**
spoken without much conscious thought

scripted messages
phrasings learned from past encounters that we judge to be appropriate to the present situation

constructed messages
messages put together with careful thought when we recognize that our known scripts are inadequate for the situation

immediacy
the degree of liking or attractiveness in a relationship

control
the degree to which one participant is perceived to be more dominant or powerful

culture
systems of knowledge shared by a relatively large group of people

ethics
a set of moral principles that may be held by a society, a group, or an individual

truthfulness and honesty
refraining from lying, cheating, stealing, or deception

moral dilemma
a choice involving an unsatisfactory alternative

integrity
maintaining a consistency of belief and action (keeping promises)

fairness
achieving the right balance of interests without regard to one's own feelings and without showing favor to any side in a conflict

respect
showing regard or consideration for others and their ideas even if we don't agree with them

responsibility
being accountable for one's actions and what one says

---

d. recipients (who), messages (what), interaction (how), presence or absence of noise (distractions), and feedback (reaction).
e. partners (who), channels (how), non-verbals (what), and feedback (reaction).

7. An example of intrapersonal communication is
a. chatting around the dinner table with your family and friends.
b. recounting a past experience during a speech to an audience.
c. thinking to yourself about what you are going to make for dinner that evening.
d. texting a message to a friend.
e. entering into a discussion in a chatroom.

8. Why do we communicate?
a. To meet our social needs
b. To develop and maintain our sense of self
c. To develop relationships
d. To exchange information and influence others
e. All of these answers are correct

9. In any communication setting, in addition to sharing content meaning, our messages also reflect which two important aspects of our relationship?
a. morality and integrity
b. truthfulness and honesty
c. immediacy and control
d. integrity and fairness
e. respect and responsibility

10. If you feel anxious about speaking with a certain person or group of people, you are experiencing
a. situational communication apprehension.
b. audience-based communication apprehension.
c. traitlike communication apprehension.
d. general communication apprehension.
e. context-based communication apprehension.

Chapter Quiz Answers:
1. T, 2. F, 3. T, 4. T, 5. F, 6. A, 7. C, 8. E, 9. C, 10. B

LO3 **communication competence**
the impression that communicative behavior is both appropriate and effective in a given situation

skills
goal-oriented actions or action sequences that we can master and repeat in appropriate situations

credibility
a perception of a speaker's knowledge, trustworthiness, and warmth

social ease
communicating without anxiety or nervousness

communication apprehension
the fear or anxiety associated with real or anticipated communication with others

2 Chapter in Review

LO1 perception
the process of selectively attending to information and assigning meaning to it

pattern
a set of characteristics used to differentiate some things from others

interpret
assigning meaning to information

LO2 self-concept
your self-identity

self-esteem
your overall evaluation of your competence and personal worthiness

LO3 incongruence
the gap between our inaccurate self-perceptions and reality

self-fulfilling prophecies
events that happen as a result of being foretold, expected, or talked about

self-talk
the internal conversations we have with ourselves

LO4 self-monitoring
the internal process of observing and regulating your own behavior based on your analysis of the situation and others' reponses to you

role
a pattern of learned behaviors that people use to meet the perceived demands of a particular context

LO5 uncertainty reduction
the process of monitoring the social environment to learn more about self and others

implicit personality theories
assumptions people have developed about which physical characteristics and personality traits or behaviors are associated with another

halo effect
to generalize and perceive that a person has a whole set of characteristics when you have actually observed only one characteristic, trait, or behavior

stereotypes
attributions that cover up individual differences and ascribe certain characteristics to an entire group of people

prejudice
a rigid attitude that is based on group membership and predisposes an individual to feel, think, or act in a negative way toward another person or group

LO1 Discuss the perception process.
Perception is the process of selectively attending to information and assigning meaning to it. Our perceptions are a result of our selection, organization, and interpretation of sensory information. Self-concept is our self-identity—the idea or mental image that we have about our skills, abilities, knowledge, competencies, and personality. Self-esteem is our overall evaluation of our competence and personal worthiness. Self-concepts come from interpretations of self based on our own experience and on the reactions and responses of others. The inaccuracy of a distorted picture of oneself becomes magnified through self-fulfilling prophecies and filtering messages.

Perception Process
- Attention and Selection
- Organization of Stimuli
- Interpretation of Stimuli

LO2 Examine self-perceptions and how they affect communication.
Our self-concept and self-esteem moderate competing internal messages in our self-talk, influence our perception of others, and influence our personal communication style. Our self-concept is socially constructed by us and by others, and the different roles we play in various situations create our multiple selves.

LO3 Describe how self-esteem is developed and maintained.
Self-esteem is the evaluation of our self-concept. It is based not only on how well we perform at something, but the importance we place on what we do well or poorly. There are a number of ways to change self-esteem, including comments that contradict current self-perception, therapy, and self-help. It is important to have an accurate and healthy self-perception, as it affects not only our self-talk but also how we talk to others and the level of apprehension we have at communicating with them.

LO4 Discuss how we present ourselves to others.
Though we have a certain self-perception, most of us mask our true selves when we communicate with others in order to meet their expectations or to avoid violating some norm. The process of self-monitoring allows us to become aware of how we come across to others.

LO5 Discuss how we perceive others.
We are faced with a number of questions. We can resolve these questions through uncertainty reduction, which involves monitoring the social environment to learn more about ourselves and the people we interact with. Our initial impressions of people are primarily based on how they look, their behavior, and their personality traits. It is important to remember also that our emotional state has a strong influence on how accurately we perceive other people.

© 2012 Cengage Learning. All Rights Reserved. May not be scanned, copied or duplicated, or posted to a publicly accessible website, in whole or in part.

discrimination
a negative action toward a social group or its members on account of group membership

attributions
reasons we give for others' behavior

perception check
a message that reflects your understanding of the meaning of another person's non-verbal behavior

Chapter 2 Quiz

True/False

1. The process of selectively attending to information and assigning meaning to it is called perception.

2. A person's culture has a strong influence on the self-perception process.

3. Self-created prophecies are predictions that you make about other people.

4. Implicit personality theories are assumptions about which physical characteristics and personality traits or behaviors are associated with each other.

5. A reality check is a message that reflects your understanding of the meaning of another person's non-verbal communication.

Multiple Choice

6. A pattern of learned behaviors that people use to meet the perceived demands of a particular context is called a
   a. role.
   b. self-concept.
   c. personality.
   d. temperament.
   e. persona.

7. Suppose you expect to be rejected when you ask someone out and then behave in ways that lead the person to reject you. This would be an example of
   a. poor self-esteem.
   b. incongruence.
   c. a self-fulfilling prophecy.
   d. filtering messages.
   e. a perception.

8. The process of monitoring the social environment to learn more about self and others is called
   a. observing others.
   b. uncertainty reduction.
   c. the halo effect.
   d. stereotyping.
   e. social construction.

9. If you grew up hearing that you were a "slow learner" and then a professor praised you for being a quick study, you might downplay the comment, not really hear it, or discount it entirely. This is an example of
   a. incongruence.
   b. filtering messages.
   c. poor self-perception.
   d. delayed reaction.
   e. a self-fulfilling prophecy.

10. Which of the following are performed during the process of a perception check?
    a. Watching the behavior of another person
    b. Describing the behavior
    c. Considering what the behavior means
    d. Putting your interpretation into words
    e. All of the above

Chapter Quiz Answers:
1. T, 2. T, 3. F, 4. T, 5. F, 6. A, 7. C, 8. B, 9. B, 10. E

3 Chapter in Review

LO¹ language

a body of symbols (most commonly words) and the systems for their use in messages that are common to the people of the same speech community

speech community
a group of people who speak the same language (also called a language community)

words
symbols used by a speech community to represent objects, ideas, and feelings

Sapir–Whorf hypothesis
a theory claiming that language influences perception

denotation
the direct, explicit meaning a speech community formally gives a word

connotation
the feelings or evaluations we associate with a word

syntactic context
the position of a word in a sentence and the other words around it

low-context cultures
cultures in which messages are direct, specific, and detailed

high-context cultures
cultures in which messages are indirect, general, and ambiguous

feminine styles of language
use words of empathy and support, emphasize concrete and personal language, and show politeness and tentativeness in speaking

masculine styles of language
use words of status and problem solving, emphasize abstract and general language, and show assertiveness and control in speaking

LO² specific words

words that clarify meaning by narrowing what is understood from a general category to a particular item or group within that category

concrete words
words that appeal to the senses and help us see, hear, smell, taste, or touch

precise words
words that narrow a larger category

dating information
specifying the time or time period that a fact was true or known to be true

indexing generalizations
the mental and verbal practice of acknowledging the presence of individual differences when voicing generalizations

LO¹ Discuss the nature and use of language.

Language is a body of symbols and the systems for their use in messages that are common to the people of the same language community. Language allows us to perceive the world around us. Through language we designate, label, and define; we evaluate, discuss things outside our immediate experience, and talk about language.

The relationship between language and meaning is complex because the meaning of words varies with people, people interpret words differently based on both denotative and connotative meanings, the context in which words are used affects meaning, and word meanings change over time.

Culture and gender influence how words are used and how we interpret others' words. In low-context cultures, messages are direct and language is specific. In high-context cultures, messages are indirect, general, and ambiguous. Societal expectations of masculinity and femininity influence language.

Purposes of Language

Although language communities vary in the words that they use and in their grammar and syntax systems, all languages serve the same purposes.

1. **We use language to designate, label, define, and limit.**

2. **We use language to evaluate.**

3. **We use language to discuss things outside our immediate experience.**

4. **We use language to talk about language.**

LO² Identify methods for improving language skills.

We can increase language skills by using specific, concrete, and precise language; by developing verbal vividness and emphasis; and by providing details and examples, dating information, and indexing generalizations.

Clarify with words that are:

✓ specific

✓ concrete

✓ precise

LO³ Develop linguistic sensitivity.

We can speak more appropriately by adapting our vocabulary to the level of the listener, using jargon sparingly, using slang that is appropriate to listeners and situations, using inclusive language, and using non-offensive language.

@#$%^&*

© 2012 Cengage Learning. All Rights Reserved. May not be scanned, copied or duplicated, or posted to a publicly accessible website, in whole or in part.

vivid wording
wording that is full of life, vigorous, bright, and intense

simile
a direct comparison of dissimilar things

metaphor
a comparison that establishes a figurative identity between objects being compared

emphasis
the weight or importance given to certain words or ideas

LO3 **jargon**
technical terms understood only by select groups

slang
informal vocabulary used by particular groups in society

generic language
using words that may apply only to one sex, race, or other group as though they represent everyone

Chapter 3 Quiz

True/False

1. A simile is a comparison that establishes a figurative identity between objects being compared.

2. Masculine styles of language typically use words of status and problem solving, emphasize abstract and general language, and show assertiveness and control in speaking.

3. We can improve our messages by choosing words that make our meaning clear and language that makes a message memorable and demonstrates sensitivity.

4. Inclusive sensitivity means choosing language and symbols that are adapted to the needs, interests, knowledge, and attitudes of the listeners and avoiding language that alienates them.

5. Generic language is not inclusive language.

Multiple Choice

6. What term or terms clarify meaning by narrowing what is understood from a general category to a particular item or group within that category?
   a. General responses
   b. Correct words
   c. Specific words
   d. Descriptive words
   e. Metaphors

7. The mental and verbal practice of acknowledging individual differences when voicing generalizations is called
   a. vivid wording.
   b. dating information.
   c. indexing.
   d. linguistic sensitivity.
   e. emphasis.

8. Which of the following sentences is an example of vivid wording?
   a. Jackson made a great catch.
   b. Emily tried hard to do well in school last year.
   c. Sam fell off his bike and hurt himself.
   d. Casey's bike smashed into the back of the red Mazda, and she went flying into the street, landing face-first on the asphalt.
   e. Haley baked a dessert for her friend's birthday.

9. The weight or importance given to certain words or ideas is called
   a. metaphor.
   b. simile.
   c. repetition.
   d. emphasis.
   e. communication.

10. Which of the following is NOT an example of linguistic sensitivity?
    a. If you are an industrial engineer and are talking to a neighbor you just met who is not, you use jargon to help him understand what it is that you do.
    b. If you are communicating with someone whose vocabulary is not as vast as yours and you adjust accordingly without talking down to the person.
    c. You're visiting with your grandmother and skip using slang because she won't understand what you are saying.
    d. You see a police car speed down your street and say, "Wow, I wonder where that police officer is heading in such a hurry!"
    e. During class, you refrain from using offensive language that you normally use when hanging out with friends.

Chapter Quiz Answers:
1. F, 2. T, 3. T, 4. F, 5. F, 6. C, 7. C, 8. D, 9. D, 10. A

4 Chapter in Review

LO¹ non-verbal communication behaviors
bodily actions and vocal qualities that typically accompany a verbal message

emoticons
symbolic pictures made with keyboard characters that represent the emotional tone that non-verbal behaviors add to face-to-face verbal messages

LO² kinesics
the interpretation of body motions used in communication

gestures
movements of our hands, arms, and fingers that we use to describe or to emphasize

illustrators
gestures that augment a verbal message

emblems
gestures that can substitute for words

adaptors
gestures that respond to a physical need

eye contact (or gaze)
how and how much we look at people with whom we are communicating

facial expression
the arrangement of facial muscles to communicate emotional states or reactions to messages

posture
the position and movement of the body

body orientation
posture in relation to another person

body movement
movement that helps clarify meaning (motivated) or movement that distracts listeners from the point being made (unmotivated)

haptics
the interpretation of touch

vocalics
the interpretation of a message based on the paralinguistic features

paralanguage
the voiced but not verbal part of a spoken message

pitch
the highness or lowness of vocal tone

volume
the loudness or softness of tone

rate
the speed at which a person speaks

LO¹ Identify characteristics of non-verbal communication.
Non-verbal communication refers to the interpretations that are made of bodily actions, vocal qualities, use of space, and self-presentation cues.

LO² Identify the different types of non-verbal communication.
Non-verbal communication is continuous, multichanneled, intentional or unintentional, possibly ambiguous, and the primary means by which we convey our emotions. The sources of non-verbal messages include use of the body (kinesics: gestures, eye contact, facial expression, posture, and touch); use of the voice (vocalics: pitch, volume, rate, quality, intonation, and vocalized pauses); and use of space (proxemics: personal space, physical space, and use of artifacts).

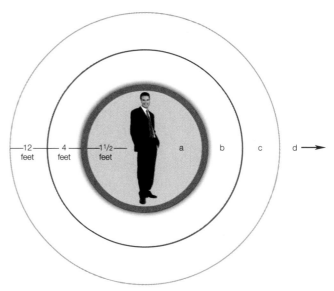

Zone a, **intimate space**: spouses, significant others, family members, and others with whom we have an intimate relationship
Zone b, **personal distance**: friends
Zone c, **social distance**: business associates and acquaintances
Zone d, **public distance**: strangers

LO³ Discuss how our self-presentation affects communication.
People gather information about us based on how they interpret our self-presentation cues. Self-presentation cues include physical appearance (for instance, body shape), clothing and grooming, and use of time (or our temporal orientation).

LO⁴ Understand guidelines for improving non-verbal communication.
We can improve our encoding of non-verbal communication by being conscious of the non-verbal behavior we are displaying, by being purposeful or strategic in its use, by making sure that our non-verbal cues do not distract from our message, by making our non-verbal communication match our verbal messages, and by adapting our non-verbal behavior to the situation.

© 2012 Cengage Learning. All Rights Reserved. May not be scanned, copied or duplicated, or posted to a publicly accessible website, in whole or in part.

quality
the sound of a person's voice

intonation
the variety, melody, or inflection in one's voice

vocalized pauses
extraneous sounds or words that interrupt fluent speech

proxemics
the interpretation of a person's use of space

personal space
the distance you try to maintain when you interact with other people

physical space
the physical environment over which you exert control

artifacts
objects and possessions we use to decorate the physical space we control

chronemics
the interpretation of a person's use of time

monochronic time orientation
a time orientation that emphasizes doing one thing at a time

polychronic time orientation
a time orientation that emphasizes doing multiple things at once

LO³ **endomorph**
round and heavy body type

mesomorph
muscular and athletic body type

ectomorph
lean and little muscle development

Chapter 4 Quiz

True/False

1. Studies show that talkers hold eye contact about 70 percent of the time and listeners only 40 percent of the time.

2. Individuals with a monochronic time orientation tend to concentrate efforts on finishing one task before they move on to another.

3. An ectomorphic shape is one that is round and heavy.

4. Some societies used body painting as a sign of slavery.

5. Fidgeting, tapping your fingers on a table, pacing, mumbling, and using vocal interferences and adaptors can hinder another person's interpretation of your message.

Multiple Choice

6. All of the following are characteristics of non-verbal communication EXCEPT
   a. continuous.
   b. multichanneled.
   c. intentional.
   d. unintentional.
   e. unambiguous.

7. Gestures that augment a verbal message are called
   a. emphasizers.
   b. illustrators.
   c. emblems.
   d. kinesics.
   e. adaptors.

8. Which of the following is an interrupter of fluent speech?
   a. the variety or melody, or inflections in one's voice
   b. pauses like "uh", "er", and "um"
   c. loudness or softness of a person's tone
   d. too much stridence in a person's voice
   e. the speed in which a person speaks

9. In a meeting of a well-established group, two people who share the same opinion might sit
   a. opposite each other.
   b. on a corner.
   c. side by side.
   d. separated by another person.
   e. as far away from each other as possible.

10. In interpreting non-verbal messages, you should
    a. consider the situation before making assumptions.
    b. not assume that another person will interpret a particular behavior the same way you do.
    c. pay attention to the relationship of the verbal message and the multiple non-verbal cues being sent.
    d. check in with someone else to see if your interpretation of what you think you are seeing is accurate or inaccurate.

Chapter Quiz Answers:
1. F, 2. T, 3. F, 4. F, 5. T, 6. E, 7. B, 8. B, 9. C, 10. D

Chapter in Review

LO1 listening
the process of receiving, constructing meaning from, and responding to spoken and/or non-verbal messages

LO2 appreciative listening
listening for enjoyment

discriminative listening
listening to understand the meaning of a message

comprehensive listening
listening to learn or remember

empathic listening
listening to understand the speaker's feeling about the message

critical listening
listening to evaluate the truthfulness or honesty of a message

LO3 attending
the perceptual process of selecting and focusing on specific stimuli from the countless stimuli reaching the senses

understanding
decoding a message accurately to reflect the meaning intended by the speaker

question
a statement designed to get further information or to clarify information already received

paraphrasing
putting into words the ideas or feelings you have perceived from the message

content paraphrase
one that focuses on the denotative meaning of the message

feelings paraphrase
a response that captures the emotions attached to the content of the message

empathy
intellectually identifying with or vicariously experiencing the feelings or attitudes of another

empathic responsiveness
experiencing an emotional response parallel to, and as a result observing, another person's actual or anticipated display of emotion

perspective taking
imagining yourself in the place of another; the most common form of empathizing

sympathetic responsiveness
feeling concern, compassion, or sorrow for another because of the other's situation or plight

remembering
being able to retain information and recall it when needed

LO1 Define "listening."
While people often think that hearing and listening are the same thing, they in fact are not. Hearing is a physiological process, while listening is a cognitive process. Listening only occurs when we choose to attach meaning to what we hear. Listening is important for effective communication because we spend 50 percent or more of our time in communication listening.

LO2 Identify the five types of listening.
The type of listening that is required of us depends on the situation. In order to be an effective listener in different situations, you must first consider the purpose for listening. There are five types of listening: appreciative, discriminative, comprehensive, empathic, and critical.

LO3 Identify the five steps of the listening process.
The five steps in the listening process are: attending, the process of focusing on what a speaker is saying; understanding, decoding a message to reflect the meaning intended by the speaker; remembering, retaining information; evaluating, critically analyzing what you have heard; and responding, supporting or critiquing someone's message.

A Summary of the Five Aspects of Listening

	Good Listeners	Bad Listeners
ATTENDING	Attend to important information	May not hear what a person is saying
	Ready themselves physically and mentally	Fidget in their chairs, look out the window, and let their minds wander
	Listen objectively regardless of emotional involvement	Visibly react to emotional language
	Listen differently depending on situations	Listen the same way regardless of the type of material
UNDERSTANDING	Assign appropriate meaning to what is said	Hear what is said but are either unable to understand or assign different meaning to the words
	Seek out apparent purpose, main points, and supporting information	Ignore the way information is organized
	Ask mental questions to anticipate information	Fail to anticipate coming information
	Silently paraphrase to solidify understanding	Seldom or never mentally review information
	Seek out subtle meanings based on non-verbal cues	Ignore non-verbal cues
REMEMBERING	Retain information	Interpret message accurately but forget it
	Repeat key information	Assume they will remember
	Mentally create mnemonics for lists of words and ideas	Seldom single out any information as especially important
	Take notes	Rely on memory alone
EVALUATING	Listen critically	Hear and understand but are unable to weigh and consider it
	Separate facts from inferences	Don't differentiate between facts and inferences
	Evaluate inferences	Accept information at face value
RESPONDING SUPPORTIVELY	Provide supportive comforting statements	Pass off joy or hurt; change the subject
	Give alternative interpretations	Pass off hurt; change the subject

© 2012 Cengage Learning. All Rights Reserved. May not be scanned, copied or duplicated, or posted to a publicly accessible website, in whole or in part.

mnemonic device
any artificial technique used as a memory aid

evaluation
the process of critically analyzing what you have heard to determine its truthfulness

factual statements
statements whose accuracy can be verified or proven

inferences
statements made by the speaker that are based on facts or observations

supportive messages
comforting statements that have a goal to reassure, bolster, encourage, soothe, console, or cheer up

Chapter 5 Quiz

True/False

1. Critical listening is the most demanding of the types of listening because it requires that you understand and remember both the verbal and non-verbal message, assess the speaker's credibility, and effectively analyze the truthfulness of the message.

2. The five steps in the listening process are: attending, understanding, remembering, evaluating, and responding.

3. Studies show that our brains can process between 400 and 800 words per minute, which gives us the ability to effectively listen, while at the same time rehearsing what we are going to say in response.

4. Empathy is putting into words the ideas or feelings you have perceived from the message.

5. A mnemonic device is any artificial technique used as a memory aid.

Multiple Choice

6. The process of receiving, constructing meaning from, and responding to spoken and/or non-verbal messages is:
   a. remembering.
   b. understanding.
   c. attending.
   d. evaluating.
   e. listening.

7. In the _____ listening situation, your goal is to accurately understand the speaker's meaning.
   a. discriminating
   b. critical
   c. comprehensive
   d. appreciative
   e. empathetic

8. Which listening method requires more psychological processing than other types?
   a. discriminative
   b. appreciative
   c. empathetic
   d. comprehensive
   e. critical

9. The process of selecting and focusing on specific stimuli from the countless ones that we receive is called
   a. listening.
   b. attending.
   c. understanding.
   d. remembering.
   e. evaluating.

10. _____ is the process of decoding a message so that the meaning accurately reflects that intended by the speaker.
    a. Listening
    b. Attending
    c. Understanding
    d. Empathizing
    e. Responding

Chapter Quiz Answers:
1.T, 2.T, 3.F, 4.F, 5.T, 6.E, 7.A, 8.E, 9.B, 10.C

6 Chapter in Review

LO1 culture
the values, attitudes, beliefs, orientations, and underlying assumptions prevalent among people in a society

culture shock
the psychological discomfort you may feel when you attempt to adjust to a new cultural situation

intercultural communication
refers to interactions that occur between people whose cultural assumptions are so different that the communication between them is altered

dominant culture
the attitudes, values, beliefs, and customs that the majority of people in a society hold in common

co-cultures
groups of people living within a dominant culture but exhibiting communication that is sufficiently different to distinguish them from the dominant culture

ethnicity
a classification of people based on combinations of shared characteristics such as nationality, geographic origin, language, religion, ancestral customs, and tradition

religion
a system of beliefs shared by a group with objects for devotion, rituals for worship, and a code of ethics

social class
an indicator of a person's position in a social hierarchy, as determined by income, education, occupation, and social habits

LO2 individualistic culture
emphasizes personal rights and responsibilities, privacy, voicing one's opinion, freedom, innovation, and self-expression

collectivist culture
emphasizes community, collaboration, shared interest, harmony, the public good, and avoiding embarrassment

low uncertainty-avoidance cultures
cultures characterized by greater acceptance of, and less need to control, unpredictable people, relationships, or events

high uncertainty-avoidance cultures
cultures characterized by a low tolerance for, and a high need to control, unpredictable people, relationships, or events

LO1 Examine how culture affects communication.
Culture encompasses the values, attitudes, beliefs, orientations, and underlying assumptions prevalent among people in a society. Culture shock refers to the psychological discomfort people have when they attempt to adjust to a new cultural situation. Intercultural communication takes place when people's distinct cultural assumptions alter the communication event. A shared system of meaning exists within the dominant culture, but meanings can vary within co-cultures based on gender, race, ethnicity, sexual orientation, religion, social class, and age.

LO2 Discuss how to identify cultural norms and values.
Cultural norms and values vary in systematic ways, and we can understand how similar or different one culture is from others by understanding where the culture is on the dimensions of individualism-collectivism, uncertainty avoidance, power distance, and masculinity-femininity.

Relative Comparison of Dimension Levels between Ten Countries

Individualism	High Uncertainty Avoidance	High Power Distance	Masculinity
USA	Japan	Russia	Japan
Netherlands	Russia	China	Germany
France	West Africa	Indonesia	USA
Germany	France	West Africa	Hong Kong
Russia	Germany	France	China
Japan	China	Hong Kong	Indonesia
Hong Kong	Netherlands	Japan	West Africa
China	Indonesia	USA	France
West Africa	USA	Netherlands	Russia
Indonesia	Hong Kong	Germany	Netherlands
Collectivism	**Low Uncertainty Avoidance**	**Low Power Distance**	**Femininity**

SOURCE: Hofstede, G. H. (1993). Cultural Constraints in Management Theories. *Academy of Management Executive*, 7 (1), 81–94.

LO3 Explain barriers to effective intercultural communication.
Barriers to intercultural communication include anxiety, assumptions about differences and similarities, ethnocentrism, stereotypes and prejudice, incompatible communication codes, and incompatible norms and values.

LO4 Analyze the development of intercultural communication competence.
To develop intercultural communication competence, we need to adopt correct attitudes about intercultural communication. We should learn to tolerate ambiguity, be open-minded, and be altruistic. We can acquire knowledge of other cultures by observing, through formal study, and through cultural immersion. Useful skills for intercultural communication competence are intercultural listening, empathy, and flexibility.

© 2012 Cengage Learning. All Rights Reserved. May not be scanned, copied or duplicated, or posted to a publicly accessible website, in whole or in part.

high power distance
the cultural belief that inequalities in power, status, and rank are "natural" and that these differences should be acknowledged and accentuated

low power distance
the cultural belief that inequalities in power, status, and rank should be underplayed and muted

masculine culture
a culture in which people are expected to adhere to traditional sex roles

feminine culture
a culture in which people, regardless of sex, are expected to assume a variety of roles based on the circumstances and their own choices

LO3 **ethnocentrism**
the belief that one's own culture is superior to others

stereotypes
attributions that cover up individual differences and ascribe certain characteristics to a group of people

prejudice
a rigid attitude based on group membership

LO4 **altruism**
a display of genuine and unselfish concern for the welfare of others

egocentricity
a selfish interest in one's own needs, to the exclusion of everything else

intercultural empathy
imaginatively placing yourself in the dissimilar other person's cultural world to attempt to experience what he or she is experiencing

flexibility
the ability to adjust your communication to fit the other person and the situation

Chapter 6 Quiz

True/False

1. Intercultural communication can be defined as the psychological discomfort of adjusting to a new cultural situation.

2. Once immigrants have learned the English language, they often speak it at home so they can learn to better fit in with their neighbors.

3. People who come from high uncertainty-avoidance cultures have a high tolerance for unpredictable people, relationships, and events.

4. Masculine cultures expect that people, regardless of sex, will assume a variety of roles depending on the circumstances and their own choices; they do not have any sex-role expectations.

5. An ethnocentric view of the world leads to attitudes of superiority and messages that are directly and subtly condescending in content and tone.

Multiple Choice

6. Which of the following is NOT one of the major contributors to co-cultures in U.S. society today?
   a. Gender
   b. Ethnicity
   c. Race
   d. Political beliefs
   e. Sexual orientation

7. According to the text, which of the following is the most obvious influence of ethnicity on communication?
   a. The foods you prefer
   b. Your religion
   c. The language of your original country
   d. Traditions handed down from your ancestors
   e. Distinguishable physical characteristics

8. When parents place emphasis on self-control, self-direction, and intellectual curiosity, they are likely to be associated with which social class?
   a. Upper class
   b. Lower class
   c. Elite
   d. Middle class
   e. Impoverished

9. Geert Hofstede identified four major dimensions of culture that affect communication. Which of the following is not one of them?
   a. Individualism-collectivism
   b. Religious beliefs
   c. Uncertainty avoidance
   d. Power distance
   e. Masculinity-femininity

10. In cultures characterized by _____, inequalities in power, status, and rank are underplayed and muted.
    a. high power distance
    b. low power distance
    c. masculinity
    d. femininity
    e. individualism

Chapter Quiz Answers:

1. F, 2. F, 3. F, 4. F, 5. T, 6. D, 7. C, 8. D, 9. B, 10. B

7 Chapter in Review

relationships
sets of expectations two people have for their behavior based on the pattern of interaction between them

good relationships
ones in which the interactions are satisfying to and healthy for those involved

LO1 acquaintances
people we know by name and talk with when the opportunity arises, but with whom our interactions are largely impersonal

impersonal communication
conversations that can be defined as essentially interchangeable chit-chat

saving face
the process of attempting to maintain a positive self-image in a relational situation

friends
people with whom we have negotiated more personal relationships that are voluntary

close friends or intimates
people with whom we share a high degree of commitment, trust, interdependence, disclosure, and enjoyment

platonic relationship
an intimate relationship in which the partners are not sexually attracted to each other or do not act on an attraction they feel

romantic relationship
an intimate relationship in which the partners act on their sexual attraction

trust
placing confidence in another in a way that almost always involves some risk

LO2 self-disclosure
sharing biographical data, personal ideas, and feelings that are unknown to the other person

feedback
verbal and physical responses to people (and/or their messages) within the relationship

Johari window
a tool for examining the relationship between disclosure and feedback in the relationship

LO3 relationship transformation
after an intimate relationship is over, continuing to interact and influence each other through a different type of relationship

LO1 Identify the major types of relationships.

Interpersonal communication helps develop and maintain relationships. A good relationship is any mutually satisfying interaction with another person. We have three types of relationships. Acquaintances are people we know by name and talk with, but with whom our interactions are limited in quality and quantity. Friendships are marked by degrees of warmth and affection, trust, self-disclosure, commitment, and expectation that the relationships will endure. Close or intimate friends are those with whom we share a high degree of commitment, trust, interdependence, disclosure, and enjoyment.

LO2 Explain how disclosure and feedback affect relationships.

A healthy relationship is marked by a balance of self-disclosure and feedback. The Johari window is a tool for analyzing this balance, categorizing information based on whether it is or is not known by the self and others.

The Johari Window

Sample Johari Windows

A low disclosure, low feedback B high disclosure, low feedback
C low disclosure, high feedback D high disclosure, high feedback

LO3 Examine levels of communication at various stages in relationships.

Relationships go through a life cycle that includes building and developing, maintaining, and perhaps de-escalating and ending. In the first stage of beginning and developing a relationship, we try to get to know each other to reduce uncertainty, we develop feelings of relaxation and confirmation, and we experience greater levels of disclosure and support. There are various ways to maintain a relationship, including spending time together; merging social networks; doing unselfish acts; and exchanging affection, self-disclosure, favors, and support. When relationships start to deteriorate, we tend to recognize feelings of dissatisfaction, notice each other's faults, experience more conflict, discuss only safe topics, and spend less time together. Effective communicators consciously end relationships with direct, open, and honest communication rather than manipulation, withdrawal, or avoidance.

LO4 Identify the sources of tension in relationships.

In any relationship, there exist competing psychological tensions that are known as relational dialectics. The three most common are autonomy-connection, openness-closedness, and novelty-predictability. The autonomy-connection dialectic refers to the competing desires to do things independent of your partner or to link your actions with your partner. The openness-closedness dialectic refers to the tensions between sharing intimate ideas and maintaining privacy. The novelty-predictability dialectic is the tension between originality and consistency. In managing dialectics in relationships, it is helpful to talk openly with your partner about tensions and reach an agreement about how to manage them going forward.

© 2012 Cengage Learning. All Rights Reserved. May not be scanned, copied or duplicated, or posted to a publicly accessible website, in whole or in part.

Chapter 7 Quiz

True/False

1. Sometimes a relationship may deteriorate simply because the partners are not vigilant in doing those things necessary to maintain the relationship at its current level.

2. Emphasizing each other's faults and downplaying virtues is an initial sign that a relationship is deteriorating.

3. Autonomy is the desire to link your actions and decisions with your partner.

4. Originality, freshness, and uniqueness in your own or your partner's behavior or in the relationship is referred to as novelty.

5. Topical segmentation is the strategy of compromising between the desires of one person and the desires of the other.

Multiple Choice

6. A relationship with people whom you share a high degree of commitment, trust, interdependence, and disclosure with is called
   a. platonic.
   b. intimate.
   c. romantic.
   d. impersonal.
   e. professional.

7. An intimate relationship in which the partners are not sexually attracted to each other or do not act on an attraction they feel is called
   a. platonic.
   b. intimate.
   c. romantic.
   d. impersonal.
   e. professional.

8. The Johari window is a tool for examining the
   a. relationship between disclosure and feedback in a relationship.
   b. level of trust in an intimate relationship.
   c. gender difference in communication styles.
   d. strength of a close friendship.
   e. life cycle of a relationship.

9. When romantic relationships turn into friendships, best friends become casual friends, and marriages continue on friendly or business-like terms because of shared values on child-rearing, this is an example of
   a. relationship maintenance.
   b. relationship connection.
   c. relational dialectics.
   d. relationship transformation.
   e. None of the above is correct.

10. Which of the following is a strategy in managing dialectical tensions in relationships?
    a. Choosing one desire and ignoring the other for the time being
    b. Compromising between the desires of one person and the desires of the other person
    c. Changing your perception about the level of tension in the relationship
    d. Choosing certain topics to satisfy one desire and other topics to satisfy the opposite desire
    e. All of the above are strategies in managing tensions in relationships.

Chapter Quiz Answers:

1. T, 2. T, 3. F, 4. T, 5. F, 6. B, 7. A, 8. A, 9. D, 10. E

8

Chapter in Review

LO1 comforting
helping people feel better about themselves, their behavior, or their situation by creating a safe conversational space where they can express their feelings and work out a plan for the future

buffering messages
comforting messages that are phrased very politely in ways that address another person's face needs

positive face needs
the desires to be appreciated and approved, liked, and honored

negative face needs
the desires to be free from imposition and intrusion

other-centered messages
comforting messages that encourage relational partners to talk about and elaborate on what happened and how they feel about it

reframing the situation
offerings ideas, observations, information, or alternative explanations that might help a relational partner understand a situation in a different light

giving advice
presenting the relevant suggestions and proposals that a person can use to resolve a situation

LO2 disclosure
revealing confidential or secret information about others as well as yourself

privacy management
exercising personal control over confidential information in order to enhance autonomy or minimize vulnerability

describing feelings
the skill of naming the emotions you are feeling without judging them

describing behavior
accurately recounting the specific behaviors of another without commenting on their appropriateness

praise
describing the specific positive behaviors or accomplishments of another and the effect that behavior has on others

constructive criticism
describing specific behaviors of another that hurt the person or that person's relationships with others

establishing a boundary
effectively respond to people who expect you to disclose information you prefer to keep private

LO1 Discuss how to comfort people.
Comforting is helping people feel better about themselves, their behavior, or their situation by creating a safe conversational space where they can express their feelings and work out a plan for the future. There are several skills that can help when providing comfort: clarifying supportive intentions, buffering face threats with politeness, encouraging understanding through other-centered messages, reframing the situation, and giving advice.

LO2 Examine the tension between openness and privacy.
In any relationship, people will experience a tension between openness and privacy. Though people often move toward deeper disclosure as their relationships develop this is not always the case. There are a number of strategies for managing privacy. Indirect strategies include changing the subject, masking feelings, or telling a white lie. Direct strategies include recognizing why you are choosing not to share the information, identifying your rule that guided the decision, and forming an "I"-centered message that briefly establishes a boundary.

LO3 Develop ways to negotiate in relationships.
A key communication need for people in relationships is to negotiate different needs, wants, and preferences in relationships. The dialectical tension between our need for autonomy and needs for connection can affect whether we choose to push to have a preference honored by our partner or whether we are willing to subordinate our wishes to maintain connectedness with our partner. We can communicate our needs, wants, and preferences by being passive, aggressive, or assertive.

Characteristics of Assertive Behavior

Own your feelings	Assertive individuals acknowledge that the thoughts and feelings expressed are theirs.
Avoid confrontational language	Assertive individuals do not use threats, evaluations, or dogmatic language.
Use specific statements directed to the behaviors at hand	Instead of focusing on extraneous issues, assertive individuals use descriptive statements that focus on the issue that is most relevant.
Maintain eye contact and firm body position	Assertive individuals look people in the eye rather than shifting gaze, looking at the floor, swaying back and forth, hunching over, or using other signs that may be perceived as indecisive or lacking conviction.
Maintain a firm but pleasant tone of voice	Assertive individuals speak firmly but at a normal pitch, volume, and rate.
Avoid hemming and hawing	Assertive individuals avoid vocalized pauses and other signs of indecisiveness.

LO4 Discuss conflict management styles.
Every relationship is marked by periods of interpersonal conflict, when the needs or ideas of one person are at odds with the needs or ideas of another. Conflicts can be resolved by withdrawing, or removing yourself from the conflict; accommodating, or satisfying others' needs while neglecting your own; and forcing, or satisfying your own needs with no consideration of others' needs.

© 2012 Cengage Learning. All Rights Reserved. May not be scanned, copied or duplicated, or posted to a publicly accessible website, in whole or in part.

Chapter 8 Quiz

True/False

1. Negative face needs are the desires to be free from imposition and intrusion.

2. The use of technology to develop and maintain relationships is impacting people's decisions about what to disclose and what to keep private.

3. Displaying our feelings can rise to the level of abuse, both verbal and physical. We can use the self-disclosure skill of describing feelings to share them with others in more appropriate ways.

4. When verbalizing specific feelings, it is most appropriate to begin with a "trigger" and follow with a "feeling."

5. Flattery is described as disclosing a specific positive behavior or accomplishment of another person and the effect that behavior has on others.

Multiple Choice

6. _____ means helping people feel better about themselves, their behavior, or their situation by creating a safe conversational space where they can express their feelings and work out a plan for the future.
   a. Encouraging
   b. Buffering
   c. Advising
   d. Welcoming
   e. Comforting

7. Which of the following is considered a direct communication strategy that you can use when being pressed to disclose something that you are not comfortable sharing?
   a. Giving a vague answer
   b. Changing the subject
   c. Masking your feelings
   d. Telling a white lie
   e. Setting a boundary

8. A straight-faced poker player whose expression is impossible to decipher has become a master of
   a. self-disclosure.
   b. rapport-talk.
   c. report-talk.
   d. masking feelings.
   e. managing privacy.

9. A(n) _____ person has the skill to stand up for him or herself in interpersonally effective ways.
   a. passive
   b. assertive
   c. aggressive
   d. accommodating
   e. collaborating

10. When people submit to others' demands even when it is inconvenient, against their best interests, or violates their rights, it is considered
    a. passive behavior.
    b. passive-aggressive behavior.
    c. assertive behavior.
    d. aggressive behavior.
    e assertive-aggressive behavior.

Chapter Quiz Answers:
1.T, 2.T, 3.T, 4.F, 5.F, 6.E, 7.E, 8.D, 9.B, 10.A

Chapter in Review

interview
a planned, structured conversation in which one person asks questions and another person answers them

LO1 interview protocol
an ordered list of questions that have been selected to meet the specific purpose of the interview

primary questions
lead-in questions that introduce one of the major topics of the interview conversation

secondary questions
questions designed to prove the answers given to primary questions

open questions
broad-based probes that call on the interviewee to provide perspective, ideas, information, feelings, or opinions as he or she answers the question

closed questions
narrowly focused questions that require the respondent to give very brief (one- or two-word) answers

neutral questions
questions that do not direct a person's answer

leading questions
questions that guide respondents toward providing certain types of information and imply that the interviewer prefers one answer over another

LO4 job seeker
anyone who is looking for a job or considering a job change

cover letter
a short, well-written letter expressing your interest in a particular job

résumé
a written summary of your skills and accomplishments

LO5 talking points
the three or four central ideas you will present as you answer the questions that are asked during a media interview

bridge
a transition you create in a media interview so that you can move from the interviewer's subject to the message you want to communicate

LO1 Discuss how to form and order a series of questions for an interview.
An effective interview protocol is marked by different types of questions. Primary questions are lead-in questions about one of the major topics of the interview. Secondary questions are follow-up questions designed to probe the answers given to primary questions. Open questions are broad-based probes that allow the interviewee to provide perspectives, ideas, information, feelings, or opinions as he or she wishes. Closed questions are narrowly focused and control what the interviewee can say, typically requiring short answers.

LO2 Discuss how to conduct information interviews.
When you are interviewing for information, you will want to define the purpose, select the best person to interview, develop a protocol, and conduct the interview according to the protocol.

LO3 Examine how to conduct employment interviews.
Employment interviews are a specific type of communication setting, with particular demands for both interviewer and interviewee. When you are interviewing prospective applicants for a job, structure your interview carefully to elicit maximal information about the candidate. Before the interview starts, become familiar with the data contained in the interviewee's application form, résumé, letters of recommendation, and test scores, if available. Be careful how you present yourself, do not waste time, do not ask questions that violate fair employment practice legislation, and give the applicant an opportunity to ask questions. At the end of the interview, explain to the applicant what will happen next in the process.

LO4 Discuss interview strategies for job seekers.
To get an interview, begin by taking the time to learn about the company and prepare an appropriate cover letter and résumé that are designed to motivate an employer to interview you. Electronic letters and résumés have become popular and need special preparation. For the interview itself, you should dress appropriately, be prompt, be alert, look directly at the interviewer, give yourself time to think before answering difficult questions, ask intelligent questions about the company and the job, and show enthusiasm for the position.

Before the Job Interview

1. Do your homework.
2. Based on your research, prepare a list of questions about the organization and the job.
3. Rehearse the interview.
4. Dress appropriately.
5. Plan to arrive on time.
6. Bring supplies.

During the Job Interview

1. Use active listening.
2. Think before answering.
3. Be enthusiastic.
4. Ask questions.
5. Avoid discussing salary and benefits.

After the Job Interview

1. Write a thank-you note.
2. Self-assess your performance.
3. Contact the interviewer for feedback.

© 2012 Cengage Learning. All Rights Reserved. May not be scanned, copied or duplicated, or posted to a publicly accessible website, in whole or in part.

Topics for an Interview with a Music Producer

- **Finding artists**
- **Decision process**
- **Criteria**
- **Stories of success and failure**

FAQs in Interviews

In what ways does your transcript reflect your ability?

Can you give an example of how you work under pressure?

What are your major strengths? Weaknesses?

Can you give an example of when you were a leader and what happened?

Tell me a time when you tried something at work that failed. How did you respond to the failure?

Tell me about a time you had a serious conflict with a coworker. How did you deal with the conflict?

What have you done that shows your creativity?

What kind of position are you looking for?

LO5 Identify strategies for dealing with news media.

To participate in media interviews, prepare by understanding the focus and format of the interview and considering the few main points you want to convey. During the media interview, you should present appropriate non-verbal cues, make clear and concise statements, realize that everything you say is on the record, and learn to use bridges as transitions to your message.

Appendix Quiz

True/False

1. Closed questions are broad-based probes, whereas open questions have a narrow focus and control what the interviewee can say.

2. Historically, a manager or human resource professional did most of the employment interviewing, but today organizations are placing coworkers in the role as interviewer.

3. A dedicated and effective job seeker will often land a job, even though she or he might not be the best qualified candidate for the job offering.

4. It's important to remember to discuss salary and benefits at the beginning of a job interview so you know whether or not to proceed with it.

5. Self-assessment of your performance in an interview is an important step in the follow-up process.

Multiple Choice

6. Which of the following is NOT a final step in creating an interview protocol?
   a. Ask short questions designed to get the interviewee involved in the conversation.
   b. Talk about topics of great importance in the beginning of the interview.
   c. Answer facts throughout the interview so as not to bore your interviewee.
   d. Inquire about past experiences first, the here and now second, and visions for the future last.
   e. Estimate the length of time it will take to ask and answer all the questions in an interview beforehand.

7. "Have you taken any courses in marketing?" is an example of a(n)
   a. open question.
   b. closed question.
   c. leading question.
   d. secondary question.
   e. inappropriate question.

8. Getting the interview begins with
   a. research.
   b. writing a cover letter.
   c. polishing your résumé.
   d. lining up references.
   e. networking.

9. In conducting an interview, it is always best to end with this step:
   a. Introduce yourself.
   b. Ask a series of prepared questions.
   c. Consider your verbal and non-verbal cues.
   d. Clarify the next steps.
   e. Use follow-up questions

10. According to Slayter, which is an example of specific information that you should look for when researching a position within an organization?
    a. Areas of operation
    b. Products and services
    c. Potential investors
    d. Ownership
    e. The organization's financial health

Chapter Quiz Answers:

1. F, 2. T, 3. T, 4. F, 5. T, 6. D, 7. B, 8. A, 9. D, 10. C

Chapter in Review

LO¹ group
a collection of three or more people who interact and attempt to influence each other in order to accomplish a common purpose

group communication
all the verbal and non-verbal messages shared with or among members of the group

healthy group
a group characterized by ethical goals, interdependence, cohesiveness, productive norms, accountability, and synergy

interdependent group
a group in which members rely on each other's skills and knowledge to accomplish the group goals

cohesiveness
the degree of attraction members have to each other and to the group's goal

team-building activities
activities designed to help the group work better together

norms
expectations for the way group members will behave while in the group

ground rules
prescribed behaviors designed to help the group meet its goals and conduct its conversations

accountability
group members being held responsible for adhering to the group norms and working toward the group's goal

synergy
a commonality of purpose and a complementariness of each other's efforts that produces a group outcome greater than an individual outcome

LO² forming
the initial stage of group development during which people come to feel valued and accepted so that they identify with the group

storming
the stage of group development during which the group clarifies its goals and determines the roles each member will have in the group power structure

groupthink
a deterioration of mental efficiency, reality testing, and moral judgment that results from in-group pressure

norming
the stage of group development during which the group solidifies its rules for behavior, especially those that relate to how conflict will be managed

LO¹ Analyze the characteristics of an effective work group.
Effective work groups meet several criteria: they develop clearly defined goals, have an optimum number of diverse members, work to develop cohesiveness, establish norms, create appropriate environments in face-to-face and virtual meetings, and achieve synergy.

LO² Explain various stages of group development.
Once groups have assembled, they tend to move through five stages of development: *forming,* getting people to feel valued and accepted so that they identify with the group; *storming,* clarifying goals while determining the role each member will have in the group power structure; *norming,* solidifying rules for behavior; *performing,* overcoming obstacles and meeting goals successfully; and *adjourning,* assigning meaning to what they have done and determining how to end or maintain interpersonal relations they have developed.

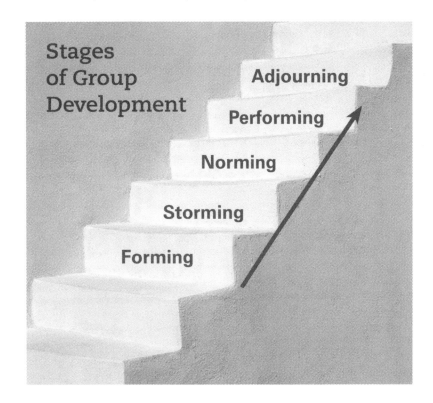

Stages of Group Development

Adjourning
Performing
Norming
Storming
Forming

LO³ Identify different types of groups.
The different types of groups include: families, social friendship groups, support groups, interest groups, service groups, and work groups.

LO⁴ Discuss how to evaluate a group's performance.
Effective groups periodically evaluate how their interactions affect what they do and how the members interact with each other. One way to evaluate group dynamics is to describe how each member performed his or her specific tasks and how well his or her communication contributed to the cohesiveness, problem solving, and conflict resolution processes in the group.

© 2012 Cengage Learning. All Rights Reserved. May not be scanned, copied or duplicated, or posted to a publicly accessible website, in whole or in part.

performing
the stage of group development when the skills, knowledge, and abilities of all members are combined to overcome obstacles and meet goals successfully

adjourning
the stage of group development in which members assign meaning to what they have done and determine how to end or maintain interpersonal relations they have developed

LO3 **family**
a group of intimates who through their communication generates a sense of home and group identity, complete with strong ties of loyalty and emotion, and experiences a history and a future

social friendship group
a group comprised of friends who have a genuine concern about each other's welfare and enjoy spending time together

support group
a group comprised of people who come together to bolster each other by providing encouragement, honest feedback, and a safe environment for expressing deeply personal feelings about a problem common to the members

interest group
a group comprised of individuals who come together because they share a common concern, hobby, or activity

service group
a group comprised of individuals who come together to perform hands-on charitable works or to raise money to help organizations that perform such work

work group
a collection of three or more people who must interact and influence each other to solve problems and to accomplish a common purpose

work group goal
a future state of affairs desired by enough members of the group to motivate the group to work toward its achievement

heterogeneous group
group in which various demographics, levels of knowledge, attitudes, and interests are represented

homogeneous group
groups in which members have a great deal of similarity

LO4 **group dynamics**
the way a group interacts to achieve its goal

Chapter 9 Quiz

True/False

1. In the norming stage, members may take sides and form coalitions.

2. According to your text, the use of active listening skills with an emphasis on paraphrasing and honest questioning helps a group avoid groupthink.

3. A nuclear family consists of two parents who live together with their biological or adoptive children.

4. Studies show that group meetings should be face-to-face, where all members come together in one physical location to make a decision or solve a problem, in order to be effective.

5. Habitat for Humanity is an example of an interest group.

Multiple Choice

6. A _____ group is one in which various demographics, levels of knowledge, attitudes, and interests are represented.
   a. homogeneous
   b. heterogeneous
   c. cohesive
   d. problem-solving
   e. synergistic

7. All of the following are factors leading to cohesiveness in groups EXCEPT
   a. attractiveness of the group's purpose.
   b. commitment to specific ground rules.
   c. voluntary membership.
   d. feeling free to share opinions.
   e. celebration of accomplishments.

8. The stage of group development during which the group clarifies its goals and determines the roles each member will have in the group power structure is called
   a. forming.
   b. storming.
   c. norming.
   d. performing.
   e. adjourning.

9. Which is the correct sequence in the stages of group development model?
   a. Forming, norming, storming, performing, adjourning
   b. Storming, forming, norming, performing, adjourning
   c. Forming, performing, norming, storming, adjourning
   d. Norming, forming, storming, performing, adjourning
   e. None of these is correct.

10. In _____ families, members may converse about an issue, but each member makes his or her own decision and is responsible for its consequences.
    a. Laissez-faire
    b. Consensual
    c. Protective
    d. Pluralistic
    e. Progressive

Chapter Quiz Answers:
1. F, 2. T, 3. T, 4. F, 5. F, 6. B, 7. B, 8. B, 9. E, 10. A

Chapter in Review

LO1 problem definition
a formal written statement describing a problem

question of fact
a question asked to determine what is true or to what extent something is true

question of value
a question asked to determine or judge whether something is right, moral, good, or just

question of policy
a question asked to determine what course of action should be taken or what rules should be adopted to solve a problem

criteria
standards or measures used for judging the merits of proposed solutions

brainstorming
an uncritical, non-evaluative process of generating possible solutions by being creative, suspending judgment, and combining or adapting ideas

decision making
the process of choosing among alternatives

LO2 informal or emergent leaders
members who gain power because they are liked and respected by the group

shared leadership functions
the sets of roles that group members perform to facilitate the work of the group and help maintain harmonious relationships between members

task roles
sets of behaviors that help a group acquire, process, or apply information that contributes directly to completing a task or goal

maintenance roles
sets of behaviors that help a group develop and maintain cohesion, commitment, and positive working relationships

procedural leadership roles
sets of behaviors that directly support a group process

LO3 agenda
an organized outline of the information and decision items that will be covered during a meeting

LO4 deliverables
tangible or intangible products of work that must be provided to someone else

LO1 Identify the steps in the problem-solving process.
A group that faces a problem can find a resolution either through a linear set of steps or a less-structured spiral pattern. In either case, the group must accomplish six tasks in order to find an optimal solution. First, it must identify and define the problem. Second, it must analyze the problem in order to find out as much about it as possible. Third, it must determine the criteria for judging the merits of proposed solutions. Fourth, it must identify alternative solutions. Fifth, it must evaluate the solutions and decide which solution should be used. Finally, the group will implement the agreed-upon solution.

LO2 Discuss shared leadership roles.
Leadership is often thought of as a role fulfilled by an individual. However, recent thinking holds that leadership tasks are performed by many members of the group. Leadership, in this view, is a set of functions that can be performed by one, more than one, or all group members at various times. The leadership roles within a group can be divided into task, maintenance, and procedural roles. Task roles help the group acquire, process, or apply information. Maintenance roles help the group develop and maintain cohesion, commitment, and positive working relationships. Procedural roles are sets of behaviors that directly support the group process.

LO3 Examine ways to make meetings effective.
Most managers and employees are required to attend meetings, and most of them feel that the majority of meetings are inefficient uses of time. To make group meetings effective and efficient, both the meeting leader and meeting participants should take certain actions before, during and after the meeting. By doing so, they can ensure that the meeting is an efficient and productive use of everyone's time.

Before the meeting . . .
- Leaders need to prepare and distribute an agenda; decide who should attend; manage logistics; speak with each participant.
- Participants need to study the agenda; study the minutes; do homework; list questions; plan to play a leadership role.

During the meeting . . .
- Leaders need to review and modify the agenda; monitor member interaction; monitor the time; praise in public and reprimand in private; check to see if the group is ready to make a decision; implement the group's decision rules; summarize decisions and assignments; set the next meeting.
- Participants need to listen attentively; stay focused; ask questions; take notes; play devil's advocate; monitor contributions.

After the meeting . . .
- Leaders need to review outcomes and process; prepare and distribute summary; repair damaged relationships; conduct informal progress reports.
- Participants need to review and summarize notes; evaluate effectiveness; review decisions; communicate progress; complete tasks; review minutes.

LO4 Identify ways that groups can communicate solutions.
A group can communicate its decisions in a number of ways. Written formats, including a written brief or comprehensive report, involve the production of a written document. Oral formats, such as oral briefs, oral reports, symposiums, or panel discussions, involve a spoken presentation by an individual or group. Groups can also use virtual reports, such as remote access reports and streaming video, which involve the use of technology and have the advantage of providing simultaneous communication to multiple locations.

© 2012 Cengage Learning. All Rights Reserved. May not be scanned, copied or duplicated, or posted to a publicly accessible website, in whole or in part.

written brief

a very short document that describes a problem, background, process, decision, and rationale so that a reader can quickly understand and evaluate a group's product

comprehensive report

a written document that provides a detailed review of the problem-solving process used to arrive at a recommendation

executive summary

a one-page synopsis of a comprehensive report

oral brief

a summary of a written brief delivered to an audience by a group member

oral report

a detailed review of a group's problem-solving process delivered to an audience by one or more group members

symposium

a set of prepared oral reports delivered sequentially by group members before a gathering of people who are interested in the work of the group

panel discussion

a structured problem-solving discussion held by a group in front of an audience

remote access report (RAR)

a computer-mediated audiovisual presentation of a group's process and outcome that others can receive electronically

streaming video

a pre-recording that is sent in compressed form over the Internet

Chapter 10 Quiz

True/False

1. Criteria are standards or measures that provide the blueprint for how a group will evaluate the virtues of each alternative solution.

2. A task-related role is a specific pattern of behavior that one group member performs based on the expectations of other members.

3. A tension reliever's main role is to momentarily distract the group from its task, which helps break monotony or tension within the group.

4. An oral brief is similar to a comprehensive report, whereas an oral report is a summary of a written brief delivered to an audience by a group member.

5. Panel discussions require careful planning and rehearsal to ensure that all relevant information is presented and that each speaker is afforded equal speaking time.

Multiple Choice

6. According to the problem-solving method, a process of identifying an alternative solution can be reached through
   a. performing.
   b. norming.
   c. storming.
   d. forming.
   e. brainstorming.

7. In reaching a group decision, five methods are commonly used. Which method has a group continuing deliberations until every member of the group believes that the same solution is best?
   a. The average group opinion method
   b. The unanimous decision method
   c. The majority rule method
   d. The expert opinion method
   e. None of these is correct.

8. _____ are neutral and impartial arbiters who guide discussions, whereas_____ intervene in the group's discussion when conflict is threatening group cohesiveness.
   a. Tension relievers; interpreters
   b. Interpreters; mediators
   c. Mediators; harmonizers
   d. Harmonizers; mediators
   e. Supporters; mediators

9. Which maintenance role do you play when you ensure that everyone has an opportunity to speak and be heard?
   a. Gatekeeper
   b. Encourager
   c. Harmonizer
   d. Peacekeeper
   e. Initiator

10. When running a meeting, be sure to complete each of the following tasks EXCEPT
    a. modifying the agenda based on members' suggestions.
    b. monitoring the roles that members assume.
    c. encouraging conflict and arguments among group members to elicit everyone's true feelings about the topic at hand, remembering that it's not necessary for the leader to play a harmonizing role.
    d. implementing the group's decision rules.
    e. periodically checking to see if the group is ready to make a decision.

Chapter Quiz Answers:

1. T, 2. F, 3. T, 4. F, 5. T, 6. E, 7. B, 8. C, 9. A, 10. C

11

Chapter in Review

LO1 subject
a broad area of knowledge

topic
some specific aspect of a subject

concept mapping
a visual means of exploring connections
between a subject and related ideas

LO2 audience analysis
the study of the intended
audience for your speech

audience adaptation
the active process of developing a
strategy for tailoring your information
to the specific speech audience

demographics
data to help you understand basic
audience characteristics

LO5 general speech goal
the intent of your speech

specific speech goal
a single statement of the exact
response the speaker wants from the
audience

LO6 credentials
experience or education
that qualifies a person to speak with
authority on a specific subject

secondary research
the process of locating information
about your topic that has been
discovered by other people

periodicals
magazines and journals that appear at
fixed intervals

primary research
the process of conducting your own
study to acquire information for your
speech

LO8 factual statements
statements that can be
verified

statistics
numerical facts

examples
specific instances that illustrate or
explain a general factual statement

expert opinions
interpretations and judgments made by
authorities in a particular subject area

expert
a person who has mastered a specific
subject, usually through long-term
study

anecdotes
brief, often amusing stories

LO1 Discuss how to identify topics for your speech.
Five simple action steps can help you to prepare effective speeches: (1) determine a specific speech goal that is adapted to the audience and occasion; (2) gather and evaluate material to use in the speech; (3) organize and develop the material in a way that is suited to the audience and occasion; (4) adapt the material to fit the needs of the specific audience; and (5) practice presenting the speech.

LO2 Understand how to analyze the audience.
To select an appropriate topic, you need to gather and analyze data about your audience members' information needs. Data should include demographic- and subject-related specifics. You can gather the data by conducting a survey, informally observing, questioning an audience representative, or by making educated guesses.

LO3 Understand how to analyze the setting.
When selecting a topic, you will also want to understand the setting in which you will be speaking and the occasion. You should consider specific expectations of your speech, an appropriate length, the size of the audience, the venue in which you will give the speech, and what equipment you will need in your presentation.

LO4 Discuss how to select a topic for your speech.
Based on your audience and setting analyses, you can eliminate topics that would be inappropriate, and then select your personal favorite from among the topics that remain.

LO5 Identify the general and specific goals of your speech.
Once you have a topic, you can move on to identify whether your general goal is to entertain, inform, or persuade. Finally, you can develop a specific goal—a single statement that identifies the exact response you want from your audience.

LO6 Develop strategies for locating and evaluating information sources and primary research.
The second action step of the speech preparation process is to gather and evaluate material to use in your speech. The three general sources for information include (1) your personal knowledge, experiences, and observations; (2) secondary source research; and (3) primary source research. If you are an expert on your topic, you may already have most of the information you will need to use in your speech. But most of the time you will also need to do secondary research and find resources like books, articles, newspaper accounts, statistics, biographical information, quotations, government documents, and Internet-based information on your topic.

LO7 Evaluate the accuracy, reliability, and validity of information.
Before using information from a source, you will need to evaluate it using four criteria: authority, objectivity, currency, and relevance.

LO8 Identify and select relevant information.
The information you find will include factual statements (statistics and examples), expert opinions, and elaborations (anecdotes and narratives, comparisons and contrasts, and quotations). As you look at information, you will want to draw from multiple cultural perspectives so that you accurately reflect what is known about your topic.

LO9 Discuss methods of drawing information from multiple cultural perspectives.
How we perceive facts and what opinions we hold are often influenced by our cultural background. It is therefore important to draw information from a variety of cultural perspectives by seeking sources with different cultural orientations.

© 2012 Cengage Learning. All Rights Reserved. May not be scanned, copied or duplicated, or posted to a publicly accessible website, in whole or in part.

narratives
accounts, personal experiences, tales, or lengthier stories

comparisons
illuminate a point by showing similarities

contrasts
highlight differences

plagiarism
the unethical act of representing a published author's work as your own

LO11 oral footnote
references to an original source, made at the point in the speech where information from that source is presented

LO10 Explain how to record information.
As you review your sources, you will want to record the information you find on note cards. Each note card should contain only one factual statement, opinion, or elaboration so that you can easily access, sort, and arrange the source material as you prepare the speech. Besides noting the information, you will want to identify it with a key word or category so you can group it with others that are similar. You will also want to note the appropriate bibliographic information so that you can relocate the source if you need to prepare your source list. Finally, on the back of each note card, you should write a short statement citing the source of this fact, opinion, or elaboration that you can use in your speech.

LO11 Explain how to cite sources in speeches.
Oral footnotes, references to original sources, are an effective way to cite sources in speeches. It is important to credit sources in order to avoid charges of plagirism, to provide the audience a background to evaluate the speech, and to add to your credibility.

Chapter 11 Quiz

True/False

1. A well-worded specific goal statement should always contain three central ideas.

2. Knowledge, experience, and education that qualify you to speak with authority on a subject are called credentials.

3. Encyclopedias are excellent sources of facts about and interpretations of both contemporary and historical issues.

4. Primary research is much more labor intensive and costly than secondary research.

5. Footnotes can be written or oral.

Multiple Choice

6. A _____ is a broad area of expertise about something such as movies, cognitive psychology, or computer technology.
   a. subject
   b. talking point
   c. topic
   d. main idea
   e. All of these answers are correct.

7. Demographic information of an audience member includes
   a. occupation, income, and education.
   b. gender and age.
   c. race and language.
   d. ethnicity and religion.
   e. All of these answers.

8. Each of the following questions should be asked about the speech setting to help with speech planning beforehand EXCEPT
   a. What are the special expectations for the speech?
   b. Will a meal be served before the speech?
   c. What is the appropriate length for the speech?
   d. How large will the audience be?
   e. Where will the speech be given?

9. Although _____ are excellent sources of in-depth material about a topic, most of the information is likely to be at least two years old at the time of publishing.
   a. statistical sources
   b. encyclopedias
   c. periodicals
   d. books
   e. government documents

10. When presenting information in a speech that you've learned from a secondary source, it is crucial to _____ or you could be accused of
    _____.
    a. tell the truth; unethical behavior
    b. cite sources; plagirism
    c. get your facts straight; lying
    d. use oral footnotes; being sloppy
    e. show confidence; having a lack of credibility

Chapter Quiz Answers:
1. F, 2. T, 3. F, 4. T, 5. T, 6. A, 7. E, 8. B, 9. D, 10. B

Chapter in Review

organizing
the process of selecting and arranging the main ideas and supporting material to be presented in the speech in a manner that makes it easy for the audience to understand

LO1 main points
complete sentence representations of the main ideas used in your thesis statement

thesis statement
a sentence that identifies the topic of your speech and the main ideas you will present

speech outline
a sentence representation of the hierarchical and sequential relationships between the ideas presented in a speech

parallel
wording in more than one sentence that follows the same structural pattern, often using the same introductory words

time (or sequential) order
organizing the main points by a chronological sequence, or by steps in a process

narrative order
dramatizes the thesis using a story or series of stories that includes characters, settings, and a plot

topic order
organizing the main points of the speech by categories or divisions of a subject

logical reasons order
emphasizes when the main points provide proof supporting the thesis statement

transitions
words, phrases, or sentences that show the relationship between or bridge ideas

section transition
a complete sentence that shows the relationship between or bridges major parts of the speech

signposts
short word or phrase transitions that connect pieces of supporting material to the main point or subpoint they address

LO2 rhetorical question
a question seeking a mental rather than a vocal response

direct question
a question that demands an overt response from the audience, usually by a show of hands

Action Step 3
Organize and Develop Speech Material to Meet the Needs of Your Particular Audience

LO1 Describe methods for developing the body of your speech.
Organizing is the process of selecting and structuring ideas that you will present in your speech; it is guided by your audience analysis. Once you have analyzed your audience, created a speech goal, and assembled a body of information on your topic, you are ready to identify the main ideas you wish to present in your speech and to craft them into a well-phrased thesis statement.

Once you have identified a thesis, you will prepare the body of the speech. The body of the speech is hierarchically ordered through the use of main points and subpoints. Once identified, main points and their related subpoints are written in complete sentences, which should be checked to make sure that they are clear, parallel in structure, meaningful, and limited in number to five or less. The sequential relationship between main point ideas and among subpoint ideas depends on the organizational pattern that is chosen. The three most basic organizational patterns are time, topic, and logical reasons order. You will want to choose an organizational pattern that best helps your audience understand and remember your main points. Main point sentences are written in outline form using the organizational pattern selected.

Subpoints support a main point with definitions, examples, statistics, personal experiences, stories, quotations, and so on. These subpoints also appear in the outline below the main point to which they belong. An organizational pattern will also be chosen for each set of subpoints.

Once the outline of the body is complete, transitions between the introduction and the body, between main points within the body, and between the body and the conclusion need to be devised so that the audience can easily follow the speech and identify each main point.

LO2 Explain how to create an introduction.
The first step in completing the organization process is creating an introduction. The introduction should get the audience's attention, introduce the thesis, establish credibility, set the tone for the speech, and create goodwill with the audience.

LO3 Explain how to prepare a conclusion.
The second step in completing the organization process is creating a conclusion to summarize the main points of the speech.

LO4 Examine guidelines for listing sources.
The third step in the organization process is compiling a list of sources from the bibliographic information you recorded on your research note cards.

LO5 Develop a method for reviewing the outline.
The complete draft outline should be reviewed as revised to make sure that you have used a standard set of symbols, used complete sentences for main points and major subdivisions, limited each point to a single idea, related minor points to major points, and made sure the outline length is no more than one-third the number of words of the final speech.

Chapter 12 Quiz

True/False

1. A speech should always be organized according to sequential order.

2. A direct question seeks a mental response from the audience, whereas a rhetorical question demands an overt response from the audience.

3. A clincher is a restatement of your speech's goal and summary of the main points.

© 2012 Cengage Learning. All Rights Reserved. May not be scanned, copied or duplicated, or posted to a publicly accessible website, in whole or in part.

joke
an anecdote or a piece of wordplay designed to be funny and make people laugh

personal reference
a brief account of something that happened to you or a hypothetical situation that listeners can imagine themselves in

quotation
a comment made by and attributed to someone other than the speaker

story
an account of something that has happened (actual) or could happen (hypothetical)

suspense
wording your attention getter so that it generates uncertainty and excites the audience

listener relevance link
a statement of how and why your speech relates to or might affect your audience

LO3 **clincher**
a one- or two-sentence statement that provides a sense of closure by driving home the importance of your speech in a memorable way

appeal
describes the behavior you want your listeners to follow after they have heard your arguments

4. If your speech is particularly short in length, it would be appropriate to list your sources alphabetically, by authors' last name.

Multiple Choice

5. A plot, characters, and settings to dramatize the thesis are used in which organizational pattern?
   a. topic order
   b. logical reasons order
   c. story order
   d. narrative order
   e. time order

6. Which of the following is NOT a technique used to get your audience's attention?
   a. personal references
   b. startling statements
   c. stories
   d. suspense
   e. signposts

7. _____ is used in a speech when the main points are the rationale or proof that support the thesis.
   a. A thesis statement
   b. Logical reasons order
   c. Time order
   d. Topic order
   e. Persuasive order

8. In the conclusion of a speech, you should
   a. summarize the main points.
   b. read the sources compiled from the bibliographic information recorded on research note cards for the audience.
   c. get the audience's attention.
   d. introduce the thesis.
   e. establish credibility.

9. In the final review of the outline before you move into adaptation and rehearsal, you should ask yourself all of these questions EXCEPT
   a. Have I used a standard set of symbols to indicate structure?
   b. Have I written main points and major subdivisions as complete sentences?
   c. Do main points and major subdivisions each contain multiple ideas to hold the audience's attention?
   d. Does the outline include no more than one-third the total number of words anticipated in the speech?
   e. Are potential subdivision elaborations indicated?

10. Startling statements, rhetorical questions, quotations, and personal references can all be used to
    a. state the thesis.
    b. gain your audience's attention in the introduction.
    c. conclude a speech.
    d. create a bond of goodwill with your audience.
    e. establish your credibility.

Chapter Quiz Answers:
1. T, 2. F, 3. F, 4. T, 5. D, 6. E, 7. B, 8. A, 9. C, 10. B

Five Action Steps Toward an Effective Speech Plan

Action Step 1

Determine a Specific Speech Goal
That Fits the Audience and Occasion.
(Chapter 11)

Action Step 1

1. Determine a Specific Speech Goal That Fits the Audience and Occasion

   a. Brainstorming and Concept Mapping for Topics
   In this activity, you will brainstorm topics based on your major or vocation, your hobbies and interests, and issues you are concerned about. Once you've completed your list, you will narrow down the topics you think you would most enjoy speaking about.

   b. Analyzing Your Audience
   Identify your audience characteristics, choose a method for gathering audience information, and collect the data.

   c. Understanding the Speech Setting
   Talk with the person who arranged your speaking opportunity to gather information about your speech setting.

   d. Selecting a Topic
   Use the information gathered in Action Steps 1.b and 1.c to narrow down the list you made in 1.a, and decide which of the remaining topics you would most enjoy presenting.

   e. Writing a Specific Goal
   In this activity, you will draft, revise, and write out your final speech goal.

Action Step 2

Gather and Evaluate Information to
Develop the Content of Your Speech.
(Chapter 11)

Action Step 2

2. Gather and Evaluate Information to Develop the Content of Your Speech

   a. Locating and Evaluating Information Sources
   Use this activity to identify, locate, and evaluate information sources for use in your speech.

   b. Preparing Research Cards: Recording Facts, Opinions, and Elaborations
   Using the source material you identified in Action Step 2.a, prepare note cards for each source with specific pieces of information you might wish to use in your speech.

   c. Citing Sources
   Write a brief source citation that you can use in your speech on the back of each note card.

Action Step 3

Organize and Develop Speech Material
to Meet the Needs of Your Particular
Audience. (Chapter 12)

Action Step 3

3. Organize and Develop Speech Material to Meet the Needs of Your Particular Audience

   a. Determining Main Points
   Use this activity to identify three to five main points that you will present in your speech.

© 2012 Cengage Learning. All Rights Reserved. May not be scanned, copied or duplicated, or posted to a publicly accessible website, in whole or in part.

b. Writing a Thesis Statement
Use your goal statement and main points from Action Steps 1.e and 3.a to develop a well-worded thesis statement for your speech.

c. Organizing and Outlining the Main Points of Your Speech
Summarize your main points and choose an organizational pattern to determine the order in which you will present them.

d. Selecting and Outlining Supporting Material
In this exercise, you will create a detailed outline for your supporting material.

e. Preparing Section Transitions
Prepare section transitions before or after each main point. Make sure you write them in complete sentences.

f. Writing Speech Introductions
Write three different introductions using the methods for gaining attention discussed in the chapter, then choose one. Include statements addressing the other goals of an effective introduction, and write your introduction in outline form.

g. Creating Speech Conclusions
Write three different conclusions for your speech that summarizes your important points and leaves your audience with a vivid impression or emotional appeal. Choose one of these conclusions, and write it in outline form.

h. Compiling a List of Sources
You will want to create a list of sources based on the note cards from Action Step 2.b that you actually used when you prepared your outline in 3.d. Each item should include all the necessary bibliographic information for each source.

Action Step 4

Adapt the Verbal and Visual Material to the Needs of the Specific Audience.
(Chapter 13)

Action Step 4

4. Adapt the Verbal and Visual Material to the Needs of the Specific Audience

a. Adapting to Your Audience Verbally
Using your audience analysis from Action Steps 1.b and 1.c and the outline from Action Steps 3.a through 3.h, create a plan to verbally adapt your material to your specific audience.

b. Adapting to Your Audience Visually
In this activity, you will decide which visual aids you will use in your speech.

Action Step 5

Practice Presenting the Speech.
(Chapter 14)

Action Step 5

5. Practice Presenting the Speech

a. Rehearsing Your Speech
Having finished writing your speech, you will want to rehearse. Follow the rehearsal procedure outlined in Chapter 14, analyze your presentation, and rehearse again. You may continue to rehearse and analyze as many times as you wish until you are satisfied with your presentation.

Chapter in Review

audience adaptation
the process of customizing your speech material to your specific audience

LO1 timely
showing how information is useful now or in the near future

proximity
a relationship to personal space

common ground
the background, knowledge, attitudes, experiences, and philosophies that are shared by audience members and the speaker

personal pronouns
we, us, and *our;* pronouns that refer directly to members of the audience

rhetorical questions
questions phrased to stimulate a mental response rather than an actual spoken response on the part of the audience

credibility
the level of trust that an audience has or will have in the speaker

knowledge and expertise
how well you convince your audience that you are qualified to speak on the topic

trustworthiness
both character and apparent motives for speaking

personableness
the extent to which you project an agreeable or pleasing personality

learning style
a person's preferred way of receiving information

jargon
the unique technical terminology of a trade or profession

slang
informal, non-standard vocabulary and definitions assigned to words by a social group or subculture

sensory language
language that appeals to the senses

LO2 presentational aid
any visual, audio, or audiovisual material used in a speech for the purpose of helping the audience understand some point the speaker is making

model
a three-dimensional scaled-down or scaled-up version of an actual object

diagram
a type of drawing that shows how the whole relates to its parts

LO1 Discuss the adaptation of your speech information to your audience.
Audience adaptation is the process of customizing your speech to your specific audience. You need to consider both how to adapt your supporting material as you present it and how to adapt it by using visual aids to help the audience understand and remember what you are saying.

You adapt to the audience verbally by: (1) demonstrating relevance through showing how the information you are presenting is timely, proximate, and has personal impact on the audience; (2) ensuring that your material is easily comprehended by the audience by orienting your audience, defining key terms, illustrating new concepts with vivid examples, personalizing the information to your audience, comparing unknown ideas with those your audience is familiar with, and using multiple methods for developing your point; (3) establishing common ground by using personal pronouns, asking rhetorical questions, and drawing from common experiences; (4) demonstrating credibility through showing your knowledge and expertise, establishing your trustworthiness, and displaying personableness; and (5) adapting to language and cultural differences through overcoming linguistic problems and choosing culturally sensitive material.

LO2 Discuss the adaptation of your visual material to your audience.
You also adapt to audiences by developing and using appropriate visual aids. The most common types of visual aids are objects, models, photographs, slides, film and video clips, simple drawings, maps, charts, and graphs. There are various methods that speakers can use to display visual aids, including computer-mediated presentation, overhead transparencies, flip charts, poster boards, chalkboards, and handouts. As you plan the visual aids you will use with a speech, consider the time and cost of preparation, the impact on the audience's understanding and memory, and the effect on speaker credibility.

Criteria for Choosing Visual Aids
1. What are the most important ideas the audience needs to understand and remember?
2. Are there ideas that are complex or difficult to explain verbally but would be easy for members to understand visually?
3. How many visual aids are appropriate?
4. How large is the audience?
5. Is the necessary equipment readily available?
6. Is the time involved in making or getting the visual aid and/or equipment cost effective?

Designing Effective Visual Aids
1. Use printing or type size that can be seen easily by your entire audience.
2. Use a typeface that is easy to read and pleasing to the eye.
3. Use upper- and lowercase type.
4. Limit the lines of type to six or less.
5. Include only items of information that you will emphasize in your speech.
6. Make sure information is laid out in a way that is aesthetically pleasing.
7. Add clip art where appropriate.
8. Use color strategically.

LO3 Identify different methods for displaying presentational aids.
There are a number of ways that presentational aids can be displayed. These include posters, whiteboards or chalkboards, flip charts, handouts, document cameras, LCD projectors, and computer-mediated slide shows.

Chapter 13 Quiz

True/False

1. The skill of adapting involves both verbally and visually adapting by preparing presentational aids that facilitate audience understanding.

© 2012 Cengage Learning. All Rights Reserved. May not be scanned, copied or duplicated, or posted to a publicly accessible website, in whole or in part.

charts
graphic representations that present information in easily interpreted formats

word charts
used to preview, review, or highlight important ideas covered in a speech

flow charts
charts that use symbols and connecting lines to diagram the progressions through a complicated process

graph
a chart that compares information

bar graphs
charts that present information using a series of vertical or horizontal bars

line graphs
charts that indicate changes in one or more variables over time

pie graphs
charts that help audiences visualize the relationships among parts of a single unit

presentation software
a type of computer program that enables you to electronically prepare and store your visual aids using a computer

LO³ flip chart
a large pad of paper mounted on an easel; it can be an effective method for presenting visual aids

2. In order to be timely, you must adapt the information in the speech so that the audience members view it as important to them.

3. People assess others' knowledge by judging their character and their motives.

4. Considering how to demonstrate your character is an important aspect to planning a speech.

5. When speaking in a second language, extra care must be taken in speech preparation because audience members are not likely to tolerate your mistakes.

Multiple Choice

6. When choosing the supporting material for your speech, it's important to select materials that demonstrate how the speech
   a. is relevant to the audience.
   b. helps the audience comprehend the information.
   c. establishes common ground between you and the audience.
   d. is appropriate for the audience's initial attitudes.
   e. accomplishes all of these things.

7. A speech that includes information about the audience's neighborhood or town is establishing
   a. relevance.
   b. timeliness.
   c. proximity.
   d. personal impact.
   e. credibility.

8. Which is NOT one of the five guidelines that can aid in adapting the information of your speech so that the audience can more easily understand it?
   a. Choosing clear language
   b. Orienting the audience with basic information
   c. Comparing unfamiliar ideas with those the audience would recognize
   d. Aappealing to your audience's diverse learning styles
   e. Using technical language where necessary

9. Kolb's Cycle of Learning conceptualizes learning style preferences along four dimensions. They are
   a. watching, learning, feeling, and thinking.
   b. feeling, watching, thinking, and doing.
   c. seeing, thinking, feeling, and doing.
   d. asking, watching, thinking, and feeling.
   e. thinking, seeking, learning, and adapting.

10. In a speech about a group of children who suffer from a rare congenital heart defect, which of the following presentational aids would be the most effective?
   a. A photograph
   b. An actual object
   c. A model
   d. A diagram
   e. A simple drawing

Chapter Quiz Answers:
1. T, 2. F, 3. F, 4. T, 5. F, 6. E, 7. C, 8. E, 9. B, 10. D

Chapter in Review

LO1 public speaking apprehension
a type of communication anxiety (or nervousness); the level of fear you experience when anticipating or actually speaking to an audience

performance orientation
seeing public speaking as a situation in which a speaker must impress an audience with knowledge and delivery, and seeing audience members as hypercritical judges

communication orientation
seeing a speech situation as an opportunity to talk with a number of people about a topic that is important to the speaker and to them

visualization
a method to reduce apprehension by developing a mental picture of yourself giving a masterful speech

systematic desensitization
a method to reduce apprehension by gradually visualizing increasingly more frightening speaking events

cognitive restructuring
a method to systematically rebuild thoughts about public speaking by replacing anxiety-arousing negative self-talk with anxiety-reducing positive self-talk

public speaking skills training
the systematic teaching of the skills associated with preparing and delivering an effective public speech, with the intention of improving speaking competence and thereby reducing public speaking apprehension

LO2 delivery
how a message is communicated orally and visually through the use of voice and body to be conversational and animated

conversational style
an informal style of presenting a speech so that your audience feels you are talking with them, not at them

spontaneity
a naturalness that seems unrehearsed or memorized

animated
lively and dynamic

LO3 pitch
the highness or lowness of the sounds produced by the vibration of your vocal cords

volume
the degree of loudness of the tone you make as you expel air through your vocal chords

rate
the speed at which you talk

LO1 Discuss public speaking apprehension.
Although speeches may be presented impromptu, by manuscript, or by memory, the material you have been reading is designed to help you present your speeches extemporaneously—that is, carefully prepared and practiced, but with the exact wording determined at the time of utterance.

Even though almost all of us experience public speaking apprehension, only 15 percent or less experience high levels of fear. The signs of speaking apprehension, or stage fright, vary from individual to individual. The causes of apprehension are still being studied—in fact, some speaking apprehension may be inborn. You can learn to manage it by recognizing that despite apprehension, you can make it through your speech by preparing carefully and rehearsing your speech.

LO2 Identify the characteristics of an effective delivery style.
An effective delivery style is marked by a conversational style and an animated speaker. Speakers who use a conversational style make the audience feel that they are being talked with, not talked at. An animated speaker is lively and dynamic, and able to convey passion for the subject through the speech.

LO3 Discuss what makes for effective use of your voice.
An effective use of voice depends, first of all, on the sound of the voice, which is controlled by pitch, volume, rate, and quality. The effectiveness of a voice also depends on how intelligible the speaker is, and his or her use of vocal expressiveness.

LO4 Discuss what makes for effective use of your body.
In addition to voice, a speaker can make a speech more effective through body movements. Facial expressions, gestures, movement, eye contact, posture, poise, and appearance all contribute to the impression that a speaker leaves on an audience.

LO5 Examine various methods for delivering a speech.
There are three common speech delivery methods: impromptu, scripted, and extemporaneuous. Impromptu speeches are those that are delivered with minimal preparation time. Scripted speeches are carefully prepared speeches, which in some cases might involve it being written word for word. Extemporaneous speeches are researched and planned ahead of time, but the exact wording is not scripted.

LO6 Discuss what makes for effective rehearsal.
Effective delivery also requires rehearsal. Experienced speakers schedule and conduct rehearsal sessions. Once outlines are complete, effective speakers usually rehearse at least twice, often using speech notes on cards that include key phrases and words. In many cases, speakers may use visual aids to help audiences understand and remember the material. To be effective, visual aids need to be carefully planned, shown only when being talked about, and displayed so that all can see. Moreover, effective speakers talk to the audience, not the visual aid.

A Sample Timetable for Preparing a Speech

© 2012 Cengage Learning. All Rights Reserved. May not be scanned, copied or duplicated, or posted to a publicly accessible website, in whole or in part.

quality
the tone, timbre, or sound of your voice

intelligible
understandable

articulation
using the tongue, palate, teeth, jaw movement, and lips to shape vocalized sounds that combine to produce a word

pronunciation
the form and accent of various syllables of a word

accent
the articulation, inflection, tone, and speech habits typical of the native speakers of a language

vocal expressiveness
the contrasts in pitch, volume, rate, and quality that affect the meaning an audience gets from the sentences you speak

monotone
a voice in which the pitch, volume, and rate remain constant, with no word, idea, or sentence differing significantly from any other

pauses
moments of silence strategically used to enhance meaning

LO4 facial expression
eye and mouth movements

gestures
movements of hands, arms, and fingers that illustrate and emphasize what is being said

movement
changing the position or location of the entire body

motivated movement
movement with a specific purpose, such as emphasizing an important idea, referencing a presentation aid, or clarifying macrostructure

eye contact
looking directly at the people to whom we are speaking

audience contact
when speaking to large audiences, creating a sense of looking listeners in the eye even though you actually cannot

posture
the position or bearing of the body

poise
graceful and controlled use of the body

appearance
the way we look to others

LO5 impromptu speech
a speech that is delivered with only seconds or minutes of advance notice for preparation and is usually presented without referring to notes

scripted speech
a speech that is prepared by creating a complete written manuscript and delivered by rote memory or by reading a written copy

extemporaneous speech
a speech that is researched and planned ahead of time, although the exact wording is not scripted and will vary from presentation to presentation

LO7 Identify criteria for evaluating speeches.
In addition to preparing and presenting, you are also learning to evaluate the speeches you hear, focusing on speech content, organization, presentation, and adaptation.

Chapter 14 Quiz

True/False

1. The symptoms of public speaking apprehension can be physical, emotional, or cognitive.

2. Years of study have shown that being nervous or in a state of tension can help you do your best.

3. Cognitive restructuring is transferring the calm feelings we attain while visualizing to the actual speaking event.

4. A pause is the total lack of vocal expressiveness.

5. You should show a visual aid only when talking about it.

Multiple Choice

6. How your voice sounds depends on its
   a. tone, pitch, quality, and rate.
   b. pitch, volume, rate, and quality.
   c. quality, volume, clarity, and tone.
   d. clarity, pitch, rate, and quality.
   e. volume, quality, clarity, and tone.

7. The position or bearing of your body while giving a speech is called
   a. articulation.
   b. gestures.
   c. posture.
   d. movement.
   e. poise.

8. The hallmark of a conversational style is
   a. poise.
   b. vocal expressiveness.
   c. spontaneity.
   d. fluency.
   e. eye contact.

9. Speeches that are researched and planned ahead of time, although the exact wording is not scripted and will vary from presentation to presentation, are called
   a. impromptu.
   b. scripted.
   c. extemporaneous.
   d. practiced.
   e. spontaneous.

10. When handling your presentational aids, what is the most important thing to consider?
    a. That you only share the aid when you are talking about it
    b. That you indicate on your outline exactly when you plan on revealing and concealing the presentational aid
    c. That you direct your attention to the audience, not the aid
    d. That you practice repeatedly the handling of your aid
    e. That you display your aid so everyone can see or hear it

Chapter Quiz Answers:
1. T, 2. T, 3. F, 4. F, 5. T, 6. B, 7. C, 8. C, 9. C, 10. D

LO6 rehearsing
practicing the presentation of your speech aloud

speaking notes
word or phrase outlines of your speech

15 Chapter in Review

© 2012 Cengage Learning. All Rights Reserved. May not be scanned, copied or duplicated, or posted to a publicly accessible website, in whole or in part.

LO1 Identify the characteristics of effective informative speaking.

An informative speech is one that has a goal to explain or describe facts, truths, and principles in a way that stimulates interest, facilitates understanding, and increases the likelihood that audiences will remember. In short, informative speeches are designed to educate an audience.

Effective informative speeches are intellectually stimulating, creative, and use emphasis to aid memory. Informative speeches will be perceived as intellectually stimulating when the information is new and when it is explained in a way that excites interest. Informative speeches are creative when they produce new or original ideas or insights. Informative speeches use emphasis to stimulate audience memory.

Figure 15.2

Techniques for Making Informative Speeches Memorable

TECHNIQUE	USE	EXAMPLE
Presentational aids	To provide audience members with a visual or auditory memory of important or difficult material	A diagram of the process of making ethanol
Repetition	To give the audience a second or third chance to retain important information by repeating or paraphrasing it	"The first dimension of romantic love is passion—that is, it can't really be romantic love if there is no sexual attraction."
Transitions	To help the audience understand the relationship between the ideas being presented, including primary and supporting information	"So the three characteristics of romantic love are passion, intimacy, and commitment. Now let's look at each of the five ways you can keep love alive. The first is through small talk."
Humor and other emotional anecdotes	To create an emotional memory link to important ideas	"True love is like a pair of socks, you have to have two, and they've got to match. So you and your partner need to be mutually committed and compatible."
Mnemonics and acronyms	To provide an easy memory prompt for a series or a list	"You can remember the four criteria for evaluating a diamond as the four Cs: carat, clarity, cut, and color."
		"As you can see, useful goals are SMART: S for specific, M for measurable, A for action oriented, R for reasonable, and T for time bound. That's SMART."

LO2 Describe methods for conveying information.

We can inform by describing something, defining it, comparing and contrasting it with other things, narrating stories about it, or demonstrating it.

Description is used to create verbal pictures of objects, settings, or images discussed in your speech. Definition offers an explanation of something by identifying its meaning through classifying and differentiating it, explaining its derivation, explaining use or function, or by using a synonym. Comparison and contrast demonstrates similarities and differences between your subject and other things. Narration explains something by recounting events. Narration can be presented in a first-, second-, or third-person voice. Demonstration shows how something is done, displays the stages of a process, or depicts how something works.

LO3 Discuss common frameworks for structuring informative speeches.

Two of the most common types of informative speeches are process speeches, which demonstrate how something is done or made, and expository speeches, which provide carefully researched information about a complex topic.

Chapter 15 Quiz

True/False

1. Creativity is the result of hard work, not a gift that some people have and some don't.

2. An acronym is a system of improving memory by using formulas.

3. Narrations are only presented in the first- or second person voice.

---

informative speech
a speech that has a goal to explain or describe facts, truths, and principles in a way that increases understanding

LO1 intellectually stimulating
information that is new to audience members

listener relevance links
statements that clarify how a particular point may be important to a listener

creative
using information in a way that yields different or original ideas and insights

LO2 description
the informative method used to create an accurate, vivid, verbal picture of an object, geographic feature, setting, or image

definition
a method of informing that explains something by identifying its meaning

synonym
a word that has the same or a similar meaning

antonym
a word that is a direct opposition

comparison and contrast
a method of informing that explains something by focusing on how it is similar to and different from other things

narration
a method of informing that explains something by recounting events

demonstration
a method of informing that explains something by showing how something is done, by displaying the stages of a process, or by depicting how something works

LO3 process speech
a speech that demonstrates how something is done or made, or how it works

expository speech
an informative presentation that provides carefully researched, in-depth knowledge about a complex topic

oral footnotes
oral references to the original source of particular information at the point of presenting it during a speech

© 2012 Cengage Learning. All Rights Reserved. May not be scanned, copied or duplicated, or posted to a publicly accessible website, in whole or in part.

4. The goal of an expository speech is to demonstrate how something is done or made, or how it works.

5. Lengthy expository speeches are better known as lectures.

Multiple Choice

6. The characteristics of effective informative speaking include all but the following:
   a. Relevant
   b. Sensitive
   c. Stimulating
   d. Creative
   e. Memorable

7. _____ thinking occurs when we contemplate something from many different perspectives.
   a. Creative
   b. Productive
   c. Informative
   d. Intellectually stimulating
   e. Outside-the-box

8. You can use visual aids, repetition, transitions, humor, and memory aids to
   a. highlight important information that you want your audience to remember.
   b. encourage productive thinking.
   c. create an informative speech.
   d. describe the specific goal of the speech.
   e. ensure that your main points are stated in parallel language.

9. Of the four ways to define a word or idea, which does your text quote as the quickest?
   a. Classifying it
   b. Explaining its history
   c. Using a synonym
   d. Using a comparison
   e. Explaining its use or function

10. All of the following should be considered frameworks of an expository speech EXCEPT
    a. acquiring information from reputable sources.
    b. using a variety of methods to keep the audience's attention.
    c. choosing an organizational pattern that is best suited to the material being presented.
    d. understanding what you are presenting.
    e. believing in what you are presenting.

Chapter Quiz Answers:
1. T, 2. F, 3. F, 4. F, 5. T, 6. B, 7. B, 8. A, 9. C, 10. E

PERSUASIVE SPEAKING
Chapter in Review

16

LO¹ persuasive speech
a speech that has a goal to influence the beliefs or behavior of audience members

LO² proposition
a declarative sentence that clearly indicates the speaker's position on the topic

proposition of fact
a speech goal designed to convince the audience that something is or is not true

proposition of value
a speech goal designed to convince the audience that something is good, fair, moral, sound, etc., or its opposite

proposition of policy
a speech goal designed to convince the audience that a specific course of action should be taken

target audience
the group of people a speaker most wants to persuade

uninformed
not knowing enough about a topic to have formed an opinion

impartial
knowing the basics about a topic but still having no opinion about it

apathetic
having no opinion because one is uninterested, unconcerned, or indifferent to a topic

LO³ argument
the process of proving conclusions you have drawn from reasons and evidence

logos
the logical reasoning a speaker uses to develop an argument

reasons
main point statements that summarize several related pieces of evidence and show why you should believe or do something

arguing from example
to support a claim by providing one or more individual examples

arguing from analogy
to support a claim with a single comparable example that is significantly similar to the subject of the claim

arguing from causation
to support a claim by citing events that have occurred to bring about the claim

arguing from sign
to support a claim by citing information that signals the claim

LO¹ Examine the Elaboration Likelihood Model.
Persuasive speeches are designed to influence the beliefs and/or the behavior of audience members. They present logical reasons but must also present those reasons in a way that motivates the audience to listen and think about what the speaker is saying. The Elaboration Likelihood Model (ELM) suggests that when people hear an argument, they can process it one of two ways. Either they can listen carefully, think about the information, and elaborate its implications for themselves, or they can make decisions about what they are hearing based on simple cues about the speaker's credibility. According to the model, people who feel personally involved with a proposition are more likely to process it carefully.

LO² Consider writing persuasive speech goals as propositions.
In preparing a persuasive speech, the speaker must choose a proposition (goal) that takes into account the audience's initial attitude. An audience may be opposed to the proposition, neutral (because they are uninformed, impartial, or apathetic), or in favor.

The speaker must choose good reasons and sound evidence. Reasons are main point statements that support the proposition. Evidence is information (facts, opinions, and so on) selected to support reasons. Then the speaker needs to identify and test the forms of argument that will be used in supporting the proposition and in supporting each reason. Four of the most common types of arguments are arguing by example, by analogy, from causation, and by sign. Speakers also need to check arguments so that they avoid three common fallacies that occur in reasoning: hasty generalizations, false cause, and ad hominem arguments.

LO³ Identify how to develop arguments to support a proposition.
The main points of a persuasive speech are the reasons that argue for the proposition. The reasons, and the evidence that supports them, are established from the information acquired during research. An argument is the logical relationship between the proposition and the reasons, or the reasons and the evidence. These can be arguments from example, from analogy, from causation, or from signs.

LO⁴ Discuss how to increase audience involvement.
Speakers can use emotional appeals to increase audience members' involvement with the proposition. Both appeals to negative and positive emotions can be effective. When speakers want their audience to act, they should also consider what incentives the audience has for acting in accord with the speakers' propositions and how these incentives meet the needs of the audience. Audience needs include physiological as well as safety, belongingness, esteem, and self-actualization. Speakers should also consider whether the costs that audience members may experience would outweigh the incentives attached to the proposition.

LO⁵ Examine how to cue your audience through credibility.
No matter how good your speech might be, there will be some in the audience who will only pay minimal attention. For these individuals, the most important cue of a speech is the speaker's credibility. This can be established by convincing audience members of your goodwill—that you understand, empathize with, and are responsive to them.

LO⁶ Discuss how to use incentives to motivate your audience.
When you want to influence your audience to act on what you have spoken about, you must find a way to motivate them to show how what you are asking them to do will meet their needs. Incentives can be physical, psychological, or social rewards.

LO⁷ Identify organizational patterns for persuasive speeches.
The reasons that support a proposition can be organized following one of five patterns: the statement of reasons pattern in which you present the best-supported reasons you can find; the comparative advantages pattern in which you show each of the advantages of your solution over others; the problem solution pattern in which you introduce the problem, offer a proposal to solve it, and show why it is the best solution; the criteria satisfaction pattern in which you present the

© 2012 Cengage Learning. All Rights Reserved. May not be scanned, copied or duplicated, or posted to a publicly accessible website, in whole or in part.

Glossary

hasty generalization
a fallacy that presents a generalization that is either not supported with evidence or is supported with only one weak example

false cause
a fallacy that occurs when the alleged cause fails to be related to or produce the effect

ad hominem
a fallacy that occurs when one attacks the person making the argument rather than the argument itself

either-or
a fallacy that occurs when a speaker supports a claim by suggesting there are only two alternatives when, in fact, others exist

straw person
a fallacy that occurs when a speaker weakens the opposing position by misrepresenting it in some way and then attacks that weaker (straw person) position

LO4 **pathos**
appeals to emotion

LO5 **ethos**
appeals to credibility

goodwill
the audience perception that the speaker understands, empathizes with, and is responsive to them

LO6 **motivation**
forces acting on or within an organism to initiate and direct behavior

incentive
a reward promised if a particular action is taken or goal is reached

LO7 **statement of reasons pattern**
a straightforward organization in which you present the best-supported reasons you can find

comparative advantages pattern
an organization that allows you to place all the emphasis on the superiority of the proposed course of action

criteria satisfaction pattern
an indirect organization that first seeks audience agreement on criteria that should be considered when they evaluate a particular proposition and then shows how the proposition satisfies those criteria

refutation pattern
an organization that challenges opposing arguments while bolstering your own

problem-cause-solution pattern
an organization that provides a framework for clarifying the nature of the problem and for illustrating why a given proposal is the best one

motivated sequence pattern
an organization that combines the problem-solution pattern with explicit appeals designed to motivate the audience to act

---

criteria that a proposition needs to meet to be acceptable and then show how the speaker's proposition meets all the criteria; and the motivational pattern (used for propositions that influence the audience to take action), which replaces the normal model by including an attention step, a need step, a satisfaction step, a visualization step, and an appeal step.

Chapter 16 Quiz

True/False

1. If your audience is very much opposed to your goal, you should aim to change their attitude from "opposed" to "in favor" by the end of your speech.

2. A proposition of value is a statement designed to convince your audience that they should take a specific course of action.

3. When dealing with a hostile audience, you should attempt to move them only a small degree in your direction.

4. An argument is the logical relationship between the proposition and the reasons or between the reasons and the evidence.

5. The statement of reasons pattern attempts to prove propositions of fact by presenting the best-supported reasons in a meaningful order, placing the strongest reason first because the audience will find it most persuasive.

Multiple Choice

6. You are arguing by _____ when you cite evidence that one or more events always or almost always brings about, leads to, creates, or prevents a predictable event or set of effects.
   a. examples
   b. analogy
   c. causation
   d. sign
   e. reasoning

7. Which of the following five common errors in reasoning occurs when the alleged cause fails to be related to or to produce the effect?
   a. Hasty generalization
   b. Ad hominem
   c. Either-or
   d. False cause
   e. Straw person

8. Speakers demonstrate _____ by showing the audience that they understand and emphasize with them.
   a. goodwill
   b. credibility
   c. positive emotions
   d. emotional appeals
   e. responsiveness

9. The _____ pattern is a form of persuasive organization used for arguing a proposition of value when the goal is to prove that something has more value than something else.
   a. statement of reasons
   b. problem solution
   c. comparative advantages
   d. criteria satisfaction
   e. motivated sequence

10. Which of the following patterns for organizing persuasive speeches helps you organize your main points so that you persuade by both challenging opposing arguments and bolstering your own?
    a. Statement of reasons
    b. Problem-cause-solution
    c. Criteria satisfaction
    d. Comparative advantages
    e. Refutation

Chapter Quiz Answers:
1. F, 2. F, 3. T, 4. T, 5. F, 6. C, 7. D, 8. D, 9. C, 10. E

Communicating Emotions Non-Verbally: Encoding and Decoding Skill and Practice

The Assignment

Your instructor will write a simple sentence on the board that you will recite to your classmates while attempting to convey a particular emotion non-verbally. First, you will use only your voice; then you will use your voice and face; and finally you will use your voice, face, and body. The sentence could be as simple as "I had bacon and eggs for breakfast this morning."

1. To find out the emotion you will convey, draw a card from a stack offered by your instructor. Without letting your classmates see, turn the card over to read what emotion is written on the front. Some possible emotions include *anger, excitement, fear, joy, worry,* and *sadness.* Consider how you will use vocalics and kinesics to convey that emotion.
2. When your instructor calls on you, go to the front of the classroom and face the wall (so your classmates cannot see your face). Try to convey that emotion with only your voice while saying the sentence with your back to the class.
3. The class might make some guesses about the emotion you are conveying and give some reasons for their guesses. You should not tell them whether they are correct at this point.
4. Turn around to face your classmates and say the sentence again, this time trying to reinforce the emotion with your face and eyes.
5. The class might again make some guesses.
6. Repeat the sentence once more, this time using your voice, face, and body to convey the emotion.
7. The class might again make some guesses.
8. Tell them the emotion that was on the card and what you did with your voice, face, and body to convey it.
9. Your instructor may lead a discussion about what worked and didn't as well as how you could have made the emotional message more clear.

Critical Listening

The Assignment

Find and attend a formal public presentation that is being given on campus or in your community. Your goal is to listen so that you remember and can critically evaluate what you have heard. Be sure to take notes and record the main ideas the speaker presents. After you have heard the speech, analyze what you heard. You can use the following questions to guide your initial thinking:

- What was the purpose of the speech? What was the speaker trying to explain to you or convince you about?
- Was it easy or difficult to identify the speaker's main ideas? What did you notice about how the speaker developed each point she or he made?
- Did the speaker use examples or tell stories to develop a point? If so, were these typical examples, or did the speaker choose examples that were unusual but seemed to prove the point?
- Did the speaker use statistics to back up what was said? If so, did the speaker tell you where the statistics came from? Did the statistics surprise you? If so, what would you have needed to hear that would have helped you accept them as accurate?
- Do you think the speaker did a good job? If so, why? If not, what should the speaker have done to be more effective?

When you have finished your analysis, follow your instructor's directions. You may be asked to write a short essay about the speech or to present what you learned to the class.

© 2012 Cengage Learning. All Rights Reserved. May not be scanned, copied or duplicated, or posted to a publicly accessible website, in whole or in part.

Panel Discussion

The Assignment

Form a small group with three to five classmates. As a group, decide on a social issue or problem you would like to study in depth. Then select one group member to serve as moderator and the others as expert panelists. Members should do research to find out all they can about the issue, why it is a problem, and how it affects people and to what degree as well as potential ideas for solving it. The moderator's role is to come up with four to six good questions to ask the panelists. The panelists should prepare notes about the research they discovered.

On the day determined by the instructor, you will engage in a 15- to 20-minute panel discussion in front of your classmates. The moderator will guide the discussion by asking questions of the panelists as well as asking for questions from the class.

Suggested Format

1. Moderator thanks audience for coming and introduces the panelists and the topic.
2. Moderator asks panelists a series of questions, letting a different panelist respond first each time.
3. Moderator asks follow-up questions when appropriate.
4. Moderator asks for questions from the audience.
5. Moderator thanks the panelists and the audience members for participating.

A Persuasive Speech

The Assignment

1. Follow the speech plan Action Steps to prepare a speech in which you change audience belief. Your instructor will announce the time limit and other parameters for this assignment.
2. Criteria for evaluation include all the general criteria of topic and purpose, content, organization, and presentation, but special emphasis will be placed on the primary persuasive criteria of how well the speech's specific goal was adapted to the audience's initial attitude toward the topic, the soundness of the reasons, the evidence cited in support of them, and the credibility of the arguments.
3. Use the Persuasive Speech Evaluation Checklist in Figure 16.4 to critique yourself as you practice your speech.
4. Prior to presenting your speech, prepare a complete sentence outline and source list (bibliography). If you have used Speech Builder Express to complete the Action Step activities online, you will be able to print out a copy of your completed outline and source list. Also prepare a written plan for adapting your speech to the audience. Your adaptation plan should address the following issues:
   - How does your goal adapt to whether your prevailing audience attitude is in favor, has no opinion, or is opposed?
   - What reasons will you use, and how will the organizational pattern you select fit your topic and audience?
   - How will you establish your credibility with this audience?
   - How will you motivate your audience?
   - How you will organize your reasons?